FUNDAMENTAL PROBLEMS IN PHONETICS

FUNDAMENTAL PROBLEMS IN PHONETICS

J.C.CATFORD

INDIANA
UNIVERSITY PRESS
BLOOMINGTON AND
LONDON

Published in Canada by Fitzhenry & Whiteside Limited, Don Mills, Ontario

Manufactured in Great Britain

Library of Congress Cataloging in Publication Data
Catford, John Cunnison, 1917–
Fundamental problems in phonetics.
Includes index.
1. Phonetics. 2. Speech. I. Title.
P221.C3 1977 414 76-47168
ISBN 0-253-32520-x
1 2 3 4 5 81 80 79 78 77

Preface

The present book is a survey of the sound-producing potential of Man and an outline of the parameters which appear to be needed for a systematic universal phonetic taxonomy. It can be used either as a textbook for a basic course in general phonetics that is more than a superficial practical introduction, or as an advanced text for students who have already acquired some basic phonetic knowledge and skills.

Although it is, I believe, comprehensive and systematic enough to serve as a course text, the book was in fact written chiefly because there were things I wanted to say. In particular, I have long felt that traditional works on phonetics pay insufficient attention to the important aerodynamic aspects of speech, and I have attempted here to show the relevance of 'aerodynamic phonetics' to many aspects of universal phonetic taxonomy. Secondly, I have attempted to show the necessity for general phonetics to make clear distinction between the three basic functional components of speech: initiation (air-stream mechanism), phonation and articulation. Finally, I attach a good deal of importance to the development of introspective insight into the motor aspects of one's own speech. I am convinced that it is impossible to become fully competent in phonetic 'theory', or, in many cases, to make adequate use of instrumental phonetic records, without this kind of intimate, personally experienced, kinaesthetic insight. Consequently, even in the course of quite sophisticated theoretical discussion, I suggest from time to time that the reader carry out introspective experiments in his own vocal tract. I hope that some readers will be linguists or linguistic phoneticians who are already skilled in the kinaesthetic introspection of the competent phonetician: obviously these readers can skip the experimental parts and concentrate on the more theoretical discussion. But since there will also be many readers who have not yet had the opportunity to develop the phonetic skills it seemed essential to show them how to do it.

In a book like this, one uses examples taken from the languages that one knows or is particularly interested in. In addition, then, to several of the better-known languages I have used a fair number of examples from the little-known, but phonetically fascinating, languages of the Caucasus. Most of the data on these languages was collected in a field trip to the USSR supported by a grant from the American Council of Learned Societies, with the generous assistance of many leading Soviet Caucasologists. In particular I would like to acknowledge the invaluable and cordial help of the late Professor E. A. Bokarëv, who was then head of the Caucasian 'sektor' of the Institute of Linguistics of the Soviet Academy of Sciences. A comprehensive account of the phonetics of all 37 Caucasian languages is the subject of another book now in preparation.

The present book, which has been in preparation since 1971, would never have been produced without the assistance of a number of people among whom I would like to give special thanks to my colleague Professor David Abercrombie and my student Dr Jared Bernstein, both of whom made valuable comments on the manuscript; to Dr Martha Krieg, who did a magnificent job of typing most of this typographically difficult book, and to Kathleen Wilson and Stanley Hansen for additional typing and editorial assistance.

Finally, my grateful thanks to my wife, Lotte, who not only typed a first draft of most of the book, but has been a constant source of patient encouragement during the long period of its gestation.

J.C. Catford
Ann Arbor, September 1976

Contents

ONE

Introduction

It was my original intention to entitle this book *Anthropophonics: the Phonetic Categorization of Human Sounds*. I was dissuaded from this course of action on the grounds that the use of this unusual term might be suggestive of an eccentricity that would discourage potential readers. The term *anthropophonics* has, however, a most respectable history of use in works on phonetics, going back to the great Polish-Russian linguist Jan Baudouin de Courtenay. Baudouin used the term in 1881 to refer to very much the kind of interest exemplified in this book.

By anthropophonics, Jan Baudouin de Courtenay meant the study of what is common to all mankind in the sphere of vocal sound production: the study of the total sound-producing potential of man. This, of course, is essentially the subject matter of *general phonetics*. But Baudouin's term is somewhat more evocative of the precise shade of interest that this book exemplifies: an interest in the study of a complex and universal human activity, the production of vocal sounds, whether these sounds are known to function as socially accepted norms in any particular language or not.

Phonetics is generally, and correctly, considered to be a *linguistic* discipline—the study of all aspects of the phonic material of *language*. But, in order to cope efficiently with the vocal sounds that constitute the sound-systems of particular languages, phonetics must proceed from the most general possible consideration of the human sound-producing potential. Only thus can it be prepared to categorize and, in some sense, to explain not only the sounds used as the manifestation of all known languages, but also those of languages yet unstudied, as well as the 'pre-language' sounds of infants and the whole range of deviant sounds encountered in pathological speech.

Speech is a complex process, and before we can proceed to a systematic survey of our subject we must look more closely at what is involved in it. The very first phoneticians known to us, the ancient Indian grammarians, saw this necessity two and a half millennia ago, and preceded their analysis of the sounds of Sanskrit by a quick survey of the stages involved in the generation of speech, in these words: 'The soul, apprehending things with the intellect, inspires the mind with a desire to speak; the mind then excites the bodily fire which in its turn impels the breath. The breath, circulating in the lungs, is forced upwards and, impinging upon the head, reaches the speech-organs and gives rise to speech-sounds.' (Pāṇiniya Sikṣa, translated in Allen 1953.)

Apart from modernisation of terminology, a not dissimilar survey is given by Laver (1968): 'There seem to be three stages, as a logical minimum, in the production of an utterance. These three stages are: (a) the selection of the appropriate semantic content of the message, or the *Ideation* stage; (b) the organization of the neural programme of the grammatical, lexical, phonological and phonetic characteristics of the selected message, or the *Neurolinguistic Programme* stage; (c) the temporally-ordered myodynamic performance of the neurolinguistic programme, or the *Myodynamic Performance* stage.'

Laver goes on to say that the ideation stage can be thought of as providing the semantic theme for the utterance, the neurolinguistic programme being a kind of central, cortical, 'script' for the resultant myodynamic performance, which is the actual dynamic muscular activity—that which 'impels the breath', to use the Indian phoneticians' term.

For the purposes of this book we must look at the stages, or *phases,* in the production of speech more closely. The very first of these stages, that of 'apprehending things with the intellect', or of ideation, is beyond the scope of phonetics. We start our account one step further on, at the stage of neurolinguistic programming, the central activity that organizes the selection, sequencing, and timing of the neurophysiological events that follow.

Thereafter, in a sequence and a rhythm no doubt determined during the stage of neurolinguistic programming, specific 'motor commands', as they are sometimes called, flow out through motor nerves to muscles in the chest, throat, mouth, and so forth. In other words, there is a simultaneous and successive 'firing of motor units', the motor unit being an efferent (motor) nerve cell, its 'outgoing end' (the axon process) and the particular small group of muscle fibres innervated by this one cell. This activity might be called the *neuro-motor* phase of the speech process. The direct result of this simultaneous and successive firing of great numbers of such motor units is the contraction of particular muscles and groups of muscles, in whole or in part, simultaneously or successively, more or less strongly. We might call this the *myo-motor* phase, or more simply, the *muscular* phase of the speech process.

The two phases we have just mentioned—*neuro-motor* (firing of motor units), and *muscular* (resultant contraction of muscles)—are indissolubly linked. Each motor unit terminates in some of the fibres of one particular muscle, and every muscular contraction involves the firing of at least one motor unit—the number and location of motor units that fire determining the location of the contraction (within a large muscle) and also its strength. By presently available techniques it is hardly possible to separately study the firing of motor units on the one hand, and the resultant muscle contractions on the other. We therefore lump the neuro-motor phase and the muscular phase together, calling them the *neuromuscular* phase.

As a result of the contraction of particular muscles and groups of muscles during the neuromuscular phase, the organs, to which these muscles are attached, adopt particular postures or make particular movements. At this point we have passed beyond the actions of individual muscles to the postures and movements of specific whole organs, such as the lungs, the larynx, the tongue and so on, and we therefore call this the *organic* phase. Some colleagues have objected to this use of the term 'organic'; there is, however, good precedent within phonetics. Henry Sweet, in his *Primer of Phonetics* (1902), refers to the 'organic' and 'acoustic' aspects of speech. Moreover, this usage is consistent with a major definition of 'organic' in any good dictionary, for example, 'of or pertaining to the bodily organs' (*Shorter Oxford Dictionary*)—this is precisely what is meant by organic phase.

The successive and overlapping organic postures and movements that occur during the organic phase shape the vocal tract into a series of canals, or pneumatic tubes, as it were, of rapidly varying size and shape. The immediate result of this is to compress and to dilate the air contained in the vocal tract, and to set it moving in constantly changing ways—in rapid puffs, in sudden bursts, in a smooth flow, in a rough, eddying, turbulent stream, and so on. All this constitutes the *aerodynamic* phase of speech.

As the air flows through the vocal tract during the aerodynamic phase, some of the things that happen to it set the air molecules oscillating in ways that can be perceived by our sense of hearing: in other words, some of the aerodynamic events generate sound waves, and these constitute the *acoustic* phase of speech. In the acoustic phase an air-borne sound wave radiates from the speaker's mouth, reaching the ear of any person within hearing distance, including the speaker himself. At the same time the sound wave travels still more rapidly, by bone conduction, through the speaker's skull to his own ear.

The sound wave, impinging on the eardrum of a hearer, is transmitted through the middle ear to the inner ear, or cochlea, where it stimulates sensory endings of the auditory nerve. Afferent neural impulses from the nerve-endings in the cochlea travel up the auditory nerve to the brain, where they presumably enter into communication with associational neural networks of various kinds. Since no phonetic purpose is served by subdividing it, we collapse this whole sequence consisting of peripheral stimulation and sensory neural transmission into a single phase—the *neuroreceptive* phase.

As a result of those associative neural events in which the neuroreceptive phase terminates, there is a further interpretative process, which gives rise, potentially or actually, to the conscious identification of the incoming neuroreceptive signals as this or that particular sound or sound sequence. We may call this the *neurolinguistic identification* phase, regarding it as more or less the obverse of the neurolinguistic programming phase with which we began. In this phase of the speech event, if we direct attention to the incoming signals, we are conscious of identifiable sensations of sound, specifically of speech sounds. In the actual exchange of conversation, however, attention is often directed much more to the *meaning* of what is said rather than to the sounds by which that meaning is manifested. In this case, the phase of neurolinguistic identification is below the threshold of consciousness, and we pass directly to the final *receptive ideational* phase, which is right outside the purview of phonetics, just as was the ideational phase that initiated the whole speech event. Assuming a speaker and a hearer both equally familiar with the language of the utterance, the terminal receptive ideation in the mind of the hearer will closely match the speaker's original ideation, and the hearer will be said to 'understand' the utterance.

Since it is most important to be clear about the sequence of events we have just described, we will number the phases and briefly recapitulate them. In this listing we omit, as outside of the scope of phonetics, the ideational event (conceptualisation for the purpose of linguistic encoding), which precedes and initiates the utterance, as well as the matching ideational event (decoding and conceptualisation of the linguistic message) with which it terminates. The sequence of events, then, is as follows:

1. *neurolinguistic programming:* selection, sequencing and timing of what follows.
2. *neuromuscular phase:* transmission of outbound (efferent) neural impulses, firing of motor units and contraction of individual muscles.
3. *organic phase:* postures and movements of whole organs.
4. *aerodynamic phase:* dilation, compression and flow of air in and through the vocal tract.

5. *acoustic phase:* propagation of sound waves from speaker's vocal tract.
6. *neuroreceptive phase:* peripheral auditory stimulation and transmission of inbound (afferent) neural impulses.
7. *neurolinguistic identification:* potential or actual identification of incoming signals as specific speech sounds.

In addition to all this, we must take note of at least two, and probably three other aspects or phases of the speech event. These are, first, two kinds of *feedback*. As the organs of speech posture and move about, sensory nerve-endings within the muscles and on the surface of the organs are stimulated both by muscle contraction itself, and by contact and pressure. As a result of these forms of stimulation, information is fed back into the central nervous system, where it may or may not give rise to conscious sensations of movement, touch, and pressure. As a general name for these proprioceptive and tactile sensations we have the term 'kinaesthesis', hence *kinaesthetic feedback*. The second type of feedback consists of the stimulation of the speaker's own peripheral hearing organs by the sound wave issuing from his own mouth and reaching his ears by both air conduction and bone conduction; this is *auditory feedback*.

These feedback systems make possible the monitoring and control of speech by the insertion into the motor system of information concerning ongoing muscular, organic, aerodynamic, and acoustic events. We know that they play an important rôle in the production of speech since their pathological or artificially induced abolition or distortion can drastically affect a person's speech performance. Most of the time, however, during actual spoken intercourse, they appear to go on below the threshold of consciousness. An important part of the task of the student of phonetics is to make these feedbacks conscious when desired, and much of practical phonetic training is directed to this end.

Finally, every competent phonetician is able to experience, when he is listening analytically to another speaker, a kind of 'empathic' immediate awareness of the organic movements going on in the speaker's vocal tract. As the speaker speaks, the analysing phonetician has an internalised kinaesthetic (and perhaps also visual) 'image' of what is going on in the speaker's vocal tract. For want of a better term I shall call this the *motor empathy* phase of speech. This motor empathy may be no more than a special aspect, or professional development, of phase 7, neurolinguistic identification. It is possible that something very like this kind of empathy is normally present, although usually unconscious, when any person listens to speech. The view that we normally recognize heard speech sounds by 'empathically' referring them to the organic mechanism of their production is known as 'the motor theory of speech perception', and has been chiefly promoted by workers at the Haskins Laboratories in New York (later Connecticut)—see Liberman (1957), Liberman et al. (1963), and thereafter the critical review in Lane (1965) and the further rejoinder in Liberman et al. (1967). For a somewhat relevant experiment on this subject, see Catford and Pisoni (1970); also compare Chapter 2 of Žinkin (1968).

In addition, then, to the phases that are listed above, we must add *kinaesthetic feedback, auditory feedback* and *motor empathy* as being related phenomena which play a rôle in the speech event.

The entire speech process, starting at phase 1 and ending at phase 7, naturally takes time. It is desirable to have some idea of the order of magnitude of the overall time, and also of the duration of each phase within the speech process. Any exact statement of this is impossible in view of such things as variability in the response times of muscles from one person to another, variability in the response times of different muscles within any one person, and variability in the measurement techniques of different researchers who provide us with data of this kind. However, by drawing on the disparate statements made by Draper, Ladefoged and Whitteridge (1960), van den Berg (1962), and Ohala (1970), we can see in table 1 a roughly estimated average time-scale for the speech process, assuming a speaker and hearer about six feet apart.

Table 1

time (*ms*)			
cumu-lative	*per phase*	*phases*	*feedbacks, etc.*
50	50	1. neurolinguistic programming	
60	10	2. neuromuscular	kinaesthetic
90	30	3. organic	kinaesthetic
110	20	4. aerodynamic	kinaesthetic
116	6	5. acoustic	auditory
126	10	6. neuroreceptive	
176	50	7. neurolinguistic identification	motor empathy

So far, we have followed the various phases of the speech process from its inception in the central nervous system of a speaker to its arrival and identification in a hearer, and we have seen that this whole sequence of events takes between a tenth and a fifth of a second. We must now turn our attention to another important aspect of speech, namely the fact that while this sequence of events (the sequence of phases) is unfolding, there is also another chain of events in progress. Within each and every phase of the speech process the state of affairs is constantly changing as time goes on. Whether we give attention, for instance, to the organic phase (a succession of continually changing postures and movements of organs) or to the neurolinguistic identification phase (a succession of continually changing identified sensations of sound) we perceive this as the *chain of speech*—that is, as a sequence of events of the kind we represent in writing as, for example, *How d'you do?*, or in phonetic transcription as [ˈhaɷ djɷ ˈdu:].[1] Here we have what is perceived as a sequence of separate sounds, following one another through time—an [h] followed by the diphthong [aɷ], followed by a [d], and so on. Each of these successive 'sounds' represents a different bit of neurolinguistic planning in phase 1, a different pattern of neuromuscular events in phase 2, a different sequence of organic movements in phase 3, a different aerodynamic event in phase 4 . . . and so on. In short, the successive phases of speech follow each other in time, a few milliseconds apart, as we saw above. But, in addition to this, *within each phase* there is a continual time-varying flux of changing states.

It is clear, then, that we have to think of speech as extending, or progressing, through time in *two dimensions:* a short-term (*microchronic*) dimension, which is the sequence of distinct phases of the speech process, and a much longer (*macrochronic*) dimension, which is the sequence of speech sounds that make up an utterance. The total duration of the microchronic dimension is, as we have seen, of the order of 170 milliseconds, or ·170 seconds. The macrochronic dimension, on the other hand, the sequence of sounds in an utterance, may have a much greater duration—up to an hour or so in a lecture, for example, and certainly up to five seconds or so between pauses in conversation. We can roughly represent the two time dimensions of speech as in figure 1.

As we have seen, speech is a complex dynamic phenomenon, extending macrochronically, that is, horizontally in figure 1, as a number of 'strands' of constantly varying activity at a number of different levels. We can characterise it as, on the one hand, a sequence of 'nodal points', or *segments* following one another macrochronically in the flow of speech; and on the other as a sequence of varying *phases* following one another along the microchronic time dimension.

The task of General Phonetics, is to supply classificatory (taxonomic) criteria for the description of those short stretches of sound—those 'nodal segments'—that we think we perceive in the flow of

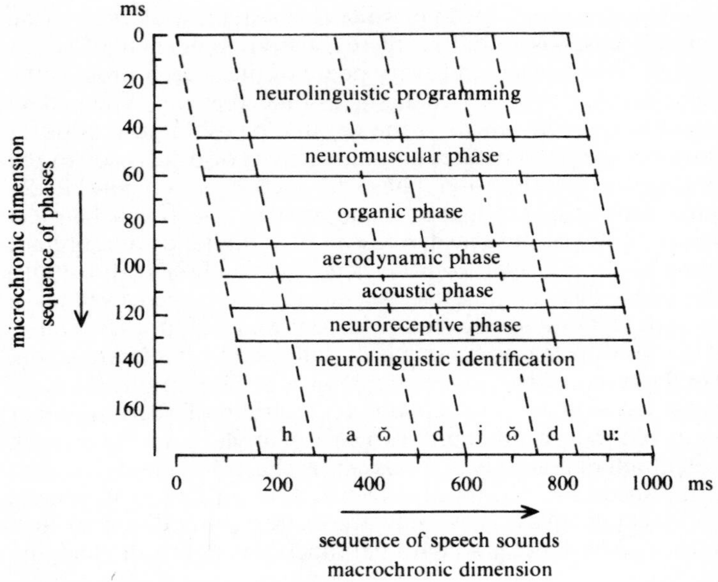

Figure 1. The time-dimensions of speech

speech along the macrochronic time dimension. Thus, we would like to have means of unambiguously characterising the [h], the [a], the [ʊ̆], the [d], the [j] . . . and so on, which we hear in sequence in [ˈhaʊ̆ djʊ̆ ˈduː]. Since what we perceive is but the end result, the final term, in the microchronic sequence of events which we have called phases, we could, in principle, describe each of the macrochronic perceptual segments in terms of events occurring in any one of the microchronic phases leading up to it, or, indeed, in all of them. It is, therefore, important to consider which particular phases of speech provide the best basis for the classification and description of segmental speech sounds.

The aspects of speech which are most obviously and immediately accessible to observation are, on the one hand, the *sensations of sound,* which constitute the conscious manifestation of the phase of neurolinguistic identification, and, on the other, the *organic movements,* either directly observed by sight, or apprehended through conscious kinaesthetic feedback. It is not surprising, therefore, that all early attempts to set up phonetic categories rely on those two phases: the ancient Greek and Roman grammarians, for instance, describe the sounds of Greek and Latin largely in terms of sound-sensations and organic positions.

Sound sensations do not lend themselves very readily to objective description, and hence can hardly be utilized as a general basis for classification of sounds, except in a somewhat crude and metaphorical way. For example, some persons perceive different qualities of vowel sound in terms of different colours, or in terms of oppositions such as 'hard–soft', 'pointed–blunt', and so on; on this see Fischer-Jørgensen (1967). Nevertheless, the system of Cardinal Vowels, which is described in Chapter 9, is a universal scale of reference vowels that is dependent at least partially on the subjective appreciation of relations between sensations of sound.

The *organic* phase is quite another matter. Not only is it partially accessible to the unaided eye (one can obviously see positions of the lips and jaw and sometimes of the tongue) but it is also immediately accessible to the subjective observation of posture and movement, of localisable places of organic contact, and so on, through kinaesthetic feedback. Various attempts, some of them remarkably sophisticated, at the description of speech sounds have been made since antiquity—by the ancient Indian grammarians (500–300 BC), the classical grammarians of Greece and Rome, medieval Arab scholars, and English phoneticians from Elizabethan times onwards. In all these early approaches attention was primarily given to the organic phase: it was the source of taxonomic and descriptive categories. In the second half of the nineteenth century, when instrumental methods of phonetic investigation became somewhat common, the organic phase was again the primary target of research. It is true that, very frequently, data were recorded from the aerodynamic rather than the organic phase: the kymograph, recording air-flow through the mouth and nose, was a popular instrument for phonetic research. But these aerodynamic data were chiefly regarded as symptomatic of events going on in the organic phase, rather than as data to be collected and generalised from in their own right. In Chapter 3 of this book we try to lay the foundations of a more sophisticated approach to a relatively independent study of the aerodynamic phase of speech—the foundations of what we may call *aerodynamic phonetics*.

The *acoustic* phase was far from being neglected, even in the nineteenth century, but it was not until the development of modern electronic devices for acoustic analysis—notably the cathode-ray oscilloscope in the 1930s and the sound spectrograph just after the second World War—that the acoustic phase became thoroughly accessible. Not that it is impossible to study this phase without instruments, as witness Sir Richard Paget's remarkable acoustic analysis by ear of the English vowels (Paget, 1922, 1930); but the advent of the oscilloscope and the spectrograph made acoustic analysis so easy that for a time the acoustic phase of speech tended to be studied to the exclusion of all else.

Indeed, arguments have been put forward, notably by Jakobson, Fant and Halle (1952) for the absolute primacy of the acoustic phase of speech over all others, and for the special utility of this phase as a basis for all description of speech. It is important, however, to remember that the acoustic phase is, of all phases, the least relevant to speech and language. Language is a human, social phenomenon; by means of speech a human being manifests utterances generated by his internalised grammatical rules. He does this for the purpose of communicating with a hearer, who perceives and interprets his speech. The acoustic phase—the physical sound wave—is not itself part of the human communicative process of language at all: it is merely the fortuitous medium that carries information about the speaker's utterance to the hearer. Its status within the speech process is analogous to that of light-waves in relation to writing and reading—the optical phase of the graphic process. No one has suggested that the best basis for the study of writing is the optical phase.

Although the acoustic phase is right outside of speech as the performance of the communicative process of language, the study of it is nevertheless of considerable interest and value. For one thing, the study of the acoustic phase sometimes casts light on the preceding organic and aerodynamic phases, and, more importantly, on the following perceptual phases, which are not otherwise easily accessible. Moreover, the study of acoustic phonetics has important engineering applications in relation to the development of equipment for the transmission, recognition and synthesis of speech.

In terms of accessibility and general taxonomic utility there are really only three phases of the speech process that can have any serious claims to attention: the organic phase, the aerodynamic phase, and the acoustic phase, the last named being important, but not nearly so basic as has sometimes been claimed. Indeed, of these three phases, the organic phase may more justly lay claim to a certain primacy. Speech is a human activity, and it consists quite specifically of movements and postures of certain organs. The investigation of these organic events is clearly the most direct way of studying speech as human behaviour. The aim of the organic movements is ultimately to convey information to a hearer. This process is mediated by the sound sensations the hearer experiences as a result of the speaker's organic movements. Since we cannot study these sensations directly it is, as we hinted above, often useful to look instead at the acoustic events that give rise to them; and this is a major justification of acoustic phonetics.

The aerodynamic phase is also an extremely important one. It is the link between the speaker's bodily activity (in the organic phase) and the resultant sound waves (in the acoustic phase). We must always remember that organic postures and movements *do not themselves generate sounds:* they merely create the necessary aerodynamic conditions, for the generation of speech sounds is in all cases an aerodynamic process. Some of the organic activities cause pressure changes in the vocal tract, which result in a flow of air; other organic activities regulate this flow in ways that create sounds, either by channelling the air-flow through narrow spaces, generating the audible hiss of turbulence, or by allowing it to burst forth in rapid periodic puffs, generating the sound of voice, and so on.

It has seemed to some that the neuromuscular phase might provide the simplest and most direct specification of the phonological units of languages, or, indeed, of speech sounds in general. Each motor unit either fires or does not fire, and if it fires it does so at a slower or faster rate; the strength of any muscular contraction depends, in fact, on (1) the number of motor units involved, and (2) the rate at which they are firing. The prospect of dealing with the simple 'off–on' and 'fast–slow' behaviour of individual motor units is certainly appealing. However, a little reflection shows that this phase would hardly be a useful one for a general phonetic taxonomy. There is, first, the practical difficulty that the firing of motor units can be detected only by somewhat difficult and delicate instrumental techniques. Moreover, specification in terms of motor units would not yield linguistically useful or relevant classifications. These classifications would be unmanageably complex because of the enormous number of motor units that one would have to keep track of and, moreover, they would lack the approach to invariance, which one would wish general phonetic categories to have, since the precise neuromuscular activity occurring at any one time depends on a number of variable factors. Thus, the muscles (and hence the motor units) involved in exhalation vary considerably according to how full the lungs are; again, the muscles used in articulating a particular sound vary according to what sounds precede or follow in the macrochronic flow of speech. As one of the leading investigators of the neuromuscular phase concludes: '. . . the essence of the speech production process is not an inefficient response to invariant central signals, but an elegantly controlled variability of response to the demand for a relatively constant end.' (MacNeilage 1970.)

All this is not to say that the electromyographic study of the neuromuscular phase of speech is unimportant or uninteresting. On the contrary, it is one aim of phonetic studies to push our understanding of the processes of speech as far back as possible, ideally right back to the phase of neurolinguistic programming. At present, the neuromuscular phase, which immediately follows the programming phase, is our best source of inferences about that earlier phase. Nevertheless, in a very real sense, these early stages—neurolinguistic programming and the entire neuromuscular phase—are 'merely the mechanics' underlying the 'genuine' activity of speech. It is not the innervation of this or that muscle that is the speaker's aim in speech, but rather the operation of this or that whole organ, with the purpose of (aerodynamically) generating audible sounds. This is what constitutes MacNeilage's 'relatively constant end'. As Abercrombie (1967) has pointed out, speech is 'audible gesture', and it behoves us to make the study of those gestures our central task. It is mainly in terms of the unifying general phonetic categories, based chiefly on the organic phase of speech, that we can ask useful and interesting questions about the neuromuscular phase: for example, 'What is the innervation pattern of "stress" in such and such a situation? What muscles are involved in the articulation of this or that vowel or consonant? How are the "motor commands" sequenced—what is the order of firing of motor units—when we have such and such overlapping articulations?', and so on. The converse is not possible: that is to say, we are not yet able to ask useful questions of the type 'What is the linguistically interesting result of the firing of motor units numbers 792, 4851, 31271?', and so on.

In this book we discuss the categories, or, better, the parameters of general phonetic classification chiefly in organic and aerodynamic terms, as is traditional in phonetics. At the same time, we do not hesitate to look 'backwards' to the neuromuscular phase, or 'forward' to the acoustic phase, whenever this appears to be particularly interesting or useful.

At the beginning of this chapter we indicated that anthropophonics must be able to capture taxonomically all the vocal sounds that human beings are capable of producing. Only in terms of such a stringent requirement can one develop a universal phonetics that is capable of unambiguously specifying the sounds of any utterance in any language. At the same time, phonetics is a *linguistic* discipline. The 'linguistic phonetician', to use Henry Sweet's term, must have an eye to the way in which the universal anthropophonic sound-producing potential is exploited in particular languages. This, the linguistic utilization of speech sounds is, essentially, the field of *phonology*. To clarify the relationship between phonetics and phonology we must consider the distinction between *phonic substance* and *phonological form*.

We may define phonic substance in the most general way as any physiologico-acoustic event (any specific sound or sounds) actually produced, or potentially produceable, by a human vocal tract. Phonic substance thus means either (a) the specific vocal sound(s) produced by a given person at a given time, or (b) the total range of all anthropophonically possible sounds, regarded purely as physiologico-acoustic events. By phonological form, however, we mean just those aspects of the phonic substance of particular utterances in a particular language that are linguistically relevant—which serve, in that particular language, to distinguish one linguistic form from another. For any specific utterance, the phonological form is a sequence of generalised, abstract, units called *phonemes,* or, alternatively, a matrix of successive groupings of distinctive features of sounds; these units or feature-combinations are, on any given occasion, manifested in a specific sequence of physiologico-acoustic events, which is the specific, objective phonic substance corresponding to the generalised, abstract, phonological form.

General phonetics supplies a set of universally valid parameters which may be drawn upon (1) for the description of any specific piece of actual phonic substance, and (2) for the description of those particular types or ranges of phonic substance that may be utilised as distinctive features in the phonology of a given language. We refer here quite deliberately to 'universally valid parameters' rather than to 'universal features'. In the last decade or two a number of scholars have posited specific limited sets of universal distinctive features (see Jakobson, Fant and Halle, 1952, Chomsky and Halle 1968, and Ladefoged 1971). Of these, Ladefoged's multivalued 'features' are more akin to our 'parameters' than are the more restrictedly, more positively, defined features of Jakobson, Chomsky, et al.

At this point it is worthwhile considering for a moment how far we may currently be justified in setting up any system of so-called 'universal' phonetic features. When we seriously assess how much empirical knowledge we possess concerning the phonetics of the languages of the world we find that it is astonishingly limited. There are something like 5000 languages; we possess full and reliable descriptions of the sounds of no more than a score or so of these languages, and we have moderately good phonetic information on, perhaps, a few hundred more. For the rest we either know nothing, or have merely inventories of phonemes, with the sketchiest of phonetic description. It thus appears that we can claim to have anything from 'full and accurate' down to 'moderately good' phonetic descriptions of not more than 10 per cent of the world's languages. This does not look like a very promising basis for a reliable listing of 'phonetic universals'. The situation is not quite so bad as it appears since the languages about which we have good to moderately good information are quite widely scattered. In other words, we have information about languages of many different kinds with the result that our phonetic knowledge covers a wider typological range than the figure of 10 per cent suggests. It is, indeed, noticeable that in descriptive linguistic phonetics we seem to have reached a point of diminished returns: it is only occasionally that some totally new and unknown phonetic phenomenon turns up. Nevertheless, we are obviously still some distance from being able to make empirically supported statements about 'phonetic universals' in the narrow sense of a highly restricted and positively defined specific inventory. It is not so many years, for instance, since the non-compatibility of *labialisation* and *pharyngealisation* (or velarisation) was enunciated as a 'universal'. We now know, however, that just this combination occurs in the pharyngealised and labialised uvular fricatives of the Bzyb dialect of Abkhaz in the North West Caucasus.

Apart from the problem of insufficient empirical phonetic knowledge, rigid and highly restrictive feature-systems tend to lead to the error of *procrusteanism*—the forcing of data into particular categories just because the categories exist, whether they are appropriate or not. There is no value in pretending that phenomena in different languages are 'the same' just because they have to be squeezed into the same predetermined feature categories.

Because of problems such as these—the gaps in our empirical knowledge and the danger of procrusteanism—we have resisted the temptation to present in this book yet another 'feature-system'. What we attempt to do in the following chapters is to explore in some detail the major parameters useful in the description of human sounds. There is, of course, an empirical basis to this, and at the same time there is a presumed deductive universality, in the sense that we may assume that any anthropophonically possible sound can be described in terms of values along some of these parameters. We simply refrain from positing a specific set of positive, fixed, parametric values that constitute 'the' universal set of distinctive phonetic features.

In later chapters we will present a detailed analysis and discussion of all the major parameters of phonetic classification. In order to do this effectively we have to make use of information about the taxonomically important organic, aerodynamic and acoustic phases of speech. To this end, in Chapters 2, 3 and 4 we survey the topography of the vocal tract, and some important features of aerodynamic and acoustic phonetics. But here we are faced with something of a dilemma, since we cannot deal effectively with these matters without already making use of some of the very taxonomic categories that are to be discussed later in the light of Chapters

2 to 4. To escape this dilemma, and to ensure that all readers are aware of the particular categories and terminology to be used in this book, we give here a brief sketch of the anthropophonic parameters.

From the organic-aerodynamic point of view the production of speech sounds involves (with trivial exceptions) two basic functional components: *initiation* (also called 'air-stream mechanism') and *articulation*.

Initiation is a bellows-like or piston-like movement of an organ (an *initiator*) that changes the volume of the vocal tract adjacent to it, thus compressing or dilating the air contained there and consequently *initiating* an actual or potential flow of air.

Articulation is a movement or posture of an organ (an *articulator*) that interrupts or modifies the air-flow in such a way as to give rise to a specific type of sound.

These two basic and essential functional components of speech production can easily be observed if one utters a prolonged 'f-sound' [fffff]. For this sound, the lungs operate as initiator, the act of initiation being their slow but continuous deflation: the lower lip and the upper teeth act as articulators, their conjunction creating an obstacle to air-flow, such that the flow past them becomes turbulent and generates a hiss-sound of the specific quality we identify as [f].

Both initiation and articulation can be of various types. In the example just given, [f], the initiator was the lungs, and the initiatory movement was one generating positive pressure in the vocal tract. We call this type *pulmonic pressure* initiation. It is, of course, possible to generate a sound of [f]-type with exactly the same articulation, but with the lungs dilating instead of deflating: in this case we have *pulmonic suction* initiation. Moreover, it is possible to initiate sounds at other locations than the lungs. If we form an articulatory stricture in the mouth, for example, [f] or [p], then close the glottis ('hold the breath') and slide the larynx upwards in the throat, air contained between the initiatory glottal closure and the articulatory oral closure is compressed. This is *glottalic pressure* initiation. In similar conditions a downward movement of the larynx will generate *glottalic suction* initiation. Initiation can also take place entirely in the mouth, for example in the 'clicking' sound [ʇ] represented in English orthography as *tut-tut*. Since this type of initiation involves a closure between the back of the tongue and the soft palate, or *velum*, it is called *velaric suction* initiation. Initiation types are dealt with in detail in Chapter 5.

Articulations, too, can be of many different types, particularly with respect to *stricture-type* (for example, complete closure, as in [p]; a narrow channel, giving rise to turbulent airflow, as in [f]; a wider channel, with non-turbulent airflow, as in [w]; . . . , and so on) and to *location* (for example, stricture at the lips, for [p]; between tongue-tip and upper teeth or gums, [t]; between back of tongue and soft palate, [k]; . . . , and so on). Articulation types are described in detail in Chapters 7 and 8.

The components named initiation and articulation are absolutely basic, since they occur in all speech sounds. It is impossible to give any truly systematic and exhaustive description of speech sounds without making reference to these basic components. There is, however, a third functional component of speech production which is almost, but not quite, as basic as the preceding two. This is *phonation*.

By *phonation* we mean any relevant activity in the larynx which is neither initiatory nor articulatory in function. Thus, the vocal-cord vibration that is characteristic of [v], as in *veer,* and that distinguishes *veer* from *fear* is a variety of phonation. Phonatory activities are described chiefly in terms of postures and movements of the vocal cords. These may be widely separated, as for *voiceless* phonation (such as [f], [s], [p]), or they may be brought together to form a narrow chink, without actually vibrating, as for *whisper* . . ., and so on. It is clear that phonation can occur only when we have a column of air passing through the larynx. This is potentially the case with all pulmonic sounds; it is absolutely excluded with velaric sounds, which make use of air trapped in the mouth, and are thus phonationless. With respect to glottalic sounds the situation is more complex and is discussed in Chapter 5. It is because phonation of some type or other definitely and always occurs only with pulmonic sounds that we must call phonation 'less basic' than the other components, initiation and articulation, which are absolutely essential to the production of all speech sounds. Phonation types are discussed in detail in Chapter 6.

TWO

The Vocal Organs

It has sometimes been pointed out that what we call the vocal organs are not, strictly speaking, vocal organs at all: that when we use our lungs, larynx, tongue, and so on, in speech we are merely making a secondary use of organs which have evolved for the purpose of breathing and eating: that it is just a matter of chance that these organs are usable for communication. This, however, as Lieberman has recently suggested, is probably not exact (Lieberman 1968). It seems reasonable to suppose that in the course of human evolution natural selection has tended to develop the larynx and other parts of the human vocal tract so as to make of them a rather more efficient instrument for communication than they would otherwise have been.

Be that as it may, since the organic phase of speech provides most of the data for universal anthropophonic categories it is necessary to have an outline knowledge of the structure and function of the major organs of the *vocal tract*. For the purpose of this book we take the vocal tract to consist of the following: the entire respiratory tract, from lungs to nose, plus the mouth and the oesophagus (since the latter is used in oesophagic initiation). It should be noted that this is a wider application of the term than is found in most other works. In these, 'vocal tract' means simply the tract from the larynx up through the mouth and nose. It is, however, more useful for phonetic purposes to use the term in the wider sense of all those tracts within the human body which can participate in the production of vocal sounds.

As we saw in Chapter 1, the function of the organic phase of speech is to generate certain aerodynamic conditions: to set the air in the vocal tract in motion, and to control this motion in ways which ultimately generate sounds. The vocal tract is thus best regarded as a pneumatic device whose ultimate function is the conversion of neural energy into acoustic energy. In our initial approach to the vocal tract we look at some of the aerodynamic functions of its parts before going on to consider the actual bodily structures. This account should be read in close conjunction with figure 2.

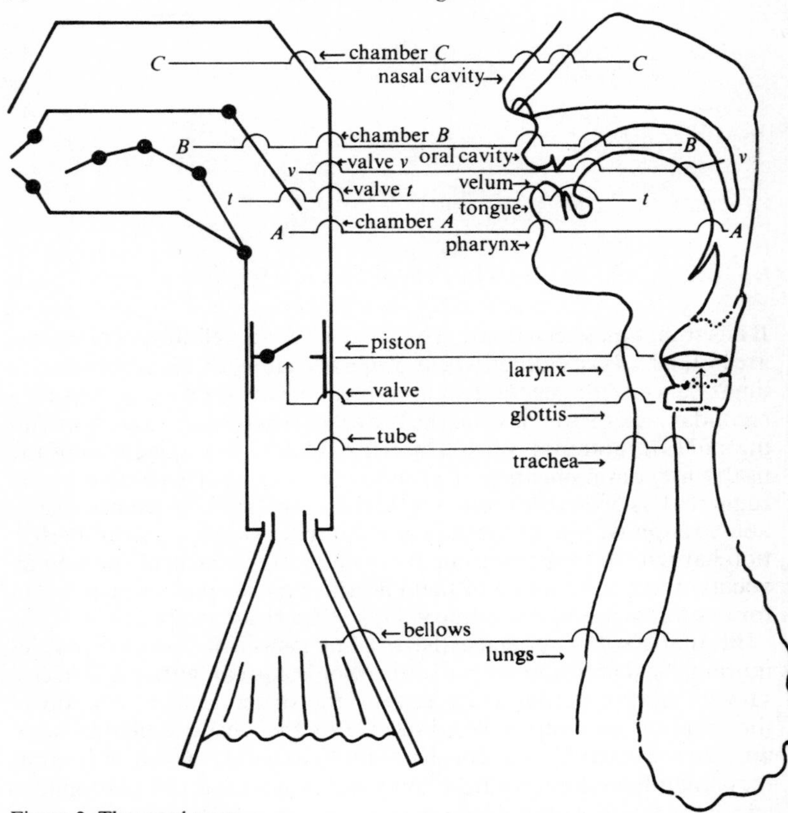

Figure 2. The vocal tract

The vocal tract is a pneumatic device consisting of a pair of bellows and various tubes and valves. The bellows (lungs) can expand to draw in half a gallon or so of air (2 or 3 litres—see Chapter 3), and contract to blow out a like quantity. In speech they do this usually quite slowly. There is a tube leading from each of the bellows (the bronchi), and these smaller tubes unite in a single large tube (trachea and larynx) roughly an inch in diameter and seven inches long. Towards the upper end of this tube there is a piston (larynx) which can slide up and down for an inch or so. This piston is somewhat complex since within it there is a valve (glottis) which can operate in a number of ways: when it is closed, upward or downward movements of the piston naturally tend to compress or dilate the air above or below it. The valve can also be opened to allow air to pass through the piston. This glottis valve can in fact operate in two main ways: either (a) as a *throttle valve*, which can vary from tightly closed, through different sizes of aperture to fully open, thus controlling the flow of air being pushed out or drawn in by the bellows; or (b) as a *metering valve* rhythmically opening and shutting and thus allowing the air to pass through in quasi-measured bursts, at varying rates, from about fifty bursts per second up to several hundred. Above the piston (larynx) with its valve (glottis) there are three chambers, *A* (pharynx), *B* (oral cavity), *C* (nasal cavity), which can be put into communication with each other, or separated off from each other by the valves *v* (velum or soft palate) and *t* (tongue). The valve *t* is highly mobile and can control air-flow through chamber *B* at a number of different places and in a number of different ways. Finally, the outer end of chamber *B* is provided with a double valve (lips).

Study of the 'pneumatic device' and the corresponding sketch of the vocal tract in figure 2 should make clear the main parts of the tract and their major phonetic functions. A more formal description of the vocal tract now follows. More detail on some parts of the tract will be provided, as needed, in later chapters.

The *lungs* are two large spongy elastic bodies consisting of numerous tiny tubes opening into larger and larger tubes, culminating in the two bronchi, or 'bronchial tubes', which unite at the base of the trachea. Each lung is suspended in an airtight chamber (the pleura) inside the thoracic cavity, which is bounded at the sides and above by the rib-cage, at the bottom by the diaphragm.

Expansion or *inflation* of the thoracic cavity, by muscles separating the ribs (external intercostals) and perhaps by others that lower the diaphragm, creates negative pressure in the pleura, and allows atmospheric pressure to force air into the lungs so that they expand. *Deflation* of the lungs is effected partly by collapse of the thoracic cage under its own weight and elasticity, partly by contraction of muscles that draw the ribs together (internal intercostals), and when the lungs are nearly reduced to their minimal volume, by the contraction of other (for example, abdominal) muscles that help to force the air out.

In general, during speech, when the lungs are full their deflation is at first due chiefly to the collapse of the rib-cage, with some braking effect by the external intercostals (the 'opening' muscles); as the lungs become more empty, the internal intercostals (the 'closing' muscles) come into play, and finally other (abdominal) muscles may assist in deflation. Pulmonic pressure initiation is thus mainly 'gravity operated' when the lungs are very full of air, but later becomes more and more 'muscle-power operated' as they become more nearly empty. They never empty completely.

The *trachea,* or windpipe, is a somewhat flexible and extensible tube about 11 cm (*c.* 4 in) long and with a cross-sectional area of about 300 to 490 mm^2 (*c.* .46 to .76 in^2). In structure it is a semi-flexible pipe composed of a series of incomplete cartilaginous rings, open at the back.

The *larynx* is a box of cartilage situated on top of the trachea to which it is somewhat distensibly attached. Indeed, the base of the larynx, the cricoid (ring-like) cartilage is, in fact, the topmost tracheal ring, closed and much enlarged at the rear. Poised upon the cricoid cartilage, and articulating with its sides, is the thyroid (shield-like) cartilage; this is a cartilage shaped like a shield, or, better, a snow-plough, open at the rear. The cricoid cartilage is often likened to a signet ring, the flat, swollen signet-part being to the rear. Poised on top of this swollen part of the cricoid cartilage are two small roughly pyramid-shaped cartilages, the arytenoid cartilages. Twin muscles, with their covering of tissue and ligament, run from the forward points ('vocal processes') of the twin arytenoid cartilages to the interior of the front of the thyroid cartilage, just behind where the latter can be felt projecting forward in the neck as the 'Adam's apple'. These are the 'vocal cords', 'vocal lips', or *vocal folds* as we shall call them. The vocal folds, then, are two shelves or projections of variable, but always somewhat wedge-shaped, section that run from back to front in the larynx. The space between the vocal folds is called the *glottis.* The glottis can assume a number of shapes: that is to say, the vocal folds can be put into a number of positions, largely by swivelling and sliding actions of the arytenoid cartilages. The tension of the vocal folds can be adjusted by the thyroid cartilage tilting forward so that its forward end comes closer to the front end of the cricoid cartilage—this movement is effected by the crico-thyroid muscle(s) whose action pulls the front of the thyroid and cricoid cartilages closer together. When opened as widely as possible, the cross-sectional area of the glottis is, according to Negus (1949), about 52 per cent of that of the trachea. The glottis thus permanently offers resistance to air-flow from below (and, incidentally, from above), and accelerates the flow of air through itself—velocity being inversely proportional to the cross-sectional area of the channel, for a given volume-velocity (see Chapter 3).

The *pharynx* is the chamber above the larynx, behind the mouth (oro-pharynx) and nose (naso-pharynx). The volume of the pharynx can be altered in various ways: by raising the larynx, by the backward movement of the tongue-root and epiglottis, by contraction or 'folding' of the back wall of the pharynx.

Above and in front of the pharynx are the two chambers of the *mouth* and *nasal cavities.* The floor of the mouth is largely taken up by the *tongue*, which is attached to the hyoid bone and the lower jaw, and has muscular attachments to structures above it—the soft palate, and certain bones of the head. At the front, the mouth is bounded by the teeth and the lips, and at the sides by the cheeks. The roof of the mouth which is part of the head (as distinct from the lower jaw), consists of the *upper teeth*, the *alveolar ridge* (immediately behind the teeth), the *hard palate*, and the soft palate or *velum*.

The velum terminates in a little hanging point, the *uvula*. The velum can be raised so as to close off the entrance from the oropharynx into the nasal cavity, or lowered, so that there is free communication between pharynx and nasal cavity. The nasal cavity is partitioned by a vertical median septum and more or less divided into channels by bony protrusions into it from the sides. The walls of the nasal cavity are covered by mucous membrane, which may be pathologically swollen, so blocking the passage way, but are not capable of independent muscular movement. Only the nostrils (or nares) at the point where the nasal cavity opens into the atmosphere, can be opened or closed to some extent.

We will go into more anatomical detail, particularly of the mouth, where this is necessary for the description of phonatory or articulatory processes. Meanwhile it is essential merely to bear in mind that the vocal tract consists of two bellows (the lungs), connected to a tube (the trachea), with, at its top, a piston (the larynx), which can slide up or down, and has within it a valve (the glottis), the space between the vocal folds, which are two shelving lips running from back to front. Above the larynx are three chambers (the pharynx, oral cavity and nasal cavity), and a number of valves, notably the velum (or soft palate), tongue, and lips. The tongue can also function as a kind of piston in generating pressure for velaric initiation.

All human vocal tracts are built on the same general plan. Consequently, to a very large extent all human beings have the same sound-producing potential. Nevertheless, there are small differences of detail from one person to another. We know, for instance, that vocal tracts vary in size, tongues vary in length and flexibility, and so on. Some variations appear to be associated with differences in genetic or ethnic grouping. Brosnahan (1961) summarizes some of the data available to him at that time.

With regard to the movements of the lips, for instance, it is interesting to note that the *risorius* muscle (which runs horizontally a short distance back from the corners of the lips and serves to retract them in a smile) is not present in all human beings. It has been found in only 20 per cent of Australians and Melanesians, in

60 per cent of Africans, in 75–80 per cent of Europeans, and in 80–100 per cent of Chinese and Malays. The implication of this from the anthropophonic point of view is that the ability to spread the lips widely (as for certain highly 'spread' types of [i]-vowel) is not universal.

Again, length of tongue differs from one ethnic group to another. Figures quoted by Brosnahan (for very small numbers of subjects) are shown in table 2. It is difficult to avoid the speculation that the shortness of Japanese tongues may have some relevance to the articulation of the sounds of the Japanese language.

Table 2

	no.	*lengths (mm)*	*mean (mm)*
Negroes	7	73–123	97
Melanesians	5	70–110	84
Japanese	127	55– 90	73

There are, of course, differences in the mere size of larynxes, and these differences have obvious effects on the voices of men, women, and children. More interesting, perhaps, are what appear to be ethnically specific differences in larynx musculature. For instance, the crico-thyroid muscle, the action of which is to tilt the thyroid cartilage forward and downwards towards the front of the cricoid cartilage, and hence to stretch the vocal folds, takes three main forms: (a) a single muscle running right across the cartilage; (b) two muscles meeting in the middle; and (c) two muscles completely separated. The frequency of occurence of these different types of muscle differs considerably from one ethnic group to another, as can be seen in table 3. Whatever the anthropophonic implication of this, the difference is quite striking.

Table 3

	no.	*type* (%)			*source*
		a	b	c	
Europeans	50	0	10	90	Graber (1913)
	?	0	16	84	Krause (1881)
Japanese	66	8	34	57	Loth (1931)
Hottentots and Hereros	45	82	0	18	Graber (1913)

Another laryngeal difference is in the presence or absence of what Brosnahan suggests is a 'phylogenetically decaying pair of muscles, *M. thyroepiglothicus inferior* and *M. thyreomembranosus*'. These have been found in the proportions shown in table 4. Presumably these muscles can participate in a general sphincteric closing of the pharynx or upper larynx. Unfortunately we have no data for other European peoples, so we cannot tell if the presence of the muscles has any relation to the occurrence of glottal constriction (the 'stød') in Danish, or the 'tight', squeezed-pharynx type of voice quality common amongst north Germans.

Table 4

	no.	*occurrences* (%)
Germans	140	85·7
Danes	80	83·7
Japanese	66	19·7

Although we do well to bear in mind that a few differences between the sound systems of different languages may be related to minor genetically determined differences in vocal tract anatomy, yet, for the most part, we can assume for general phonetic purposes that all vocal tracts are the same. If we go back up the evolutionary ladder we find greater anatomical differences. Lieberman (1971) has pointed out, for instance, that the form of the supra-laryngeal part of the vocal tract of Neanderthal Man is considerably different from that of modern man. From calculations of acoustic possibilities based on dimensions of the Neanderthal mouth and pharynx assumed from skeletal remains, he suggests that Neanderthal man could produce a very much narrower range of vowel sounds than can modern man. From this he concludes 'that "classic" Neanderthal man inherently could not have produced the range of sounds necessary for human speech'. This conclusion is not at all convincing, since it is certainly possible to speak with a very restricted range of vowels (to which Lieberman was primarily referring). The reader may experiment by speaking English with only one vowel, for example, [ə] or [i]: he will find that intelligibility is not much reduced. Moreover, Lieberman's 'normative data for modern man' are, in fact, derived only from a sampling of American English speakers. There are many modern languages with far fewer vocalic distinctions than English.

We can, then, regard the human vocal tract as, essentially, a universal. It is this that enables us to describe and classify all vocal sounds by means of a single limited set of parameters. In what follows, some more anatomical information is given where necessary, for instance in Chapters 6 and 8. A very detailed study of vocal anatomy and physiology is not necessary for general phonetic purposes, though it is highly desirable. For further details on the vocal tract the reader is referred to such works as Kaplan (1960), Zemlin (1964), Hill (1964) and Smith (1971).

THREE

The Aerodynamic Phase

In Chapter 1 we saw that an important stage in the speech process is what we termed the *aerodynamic* phase—the stage at which the air in the vocal tract is submitted to relatively large-scale and relatively slow pressure changes, which frequently result in a flow of air through the vocal tract. The aerodynamic phase is a particularly important one, since it is precisely at this stage that the sounds of speech are generated. Muscular contractions and the resultant postures and movements of vocal organs do not themselves generate sounds; they merely create suitable conditions for sound-generation, which is itself an aerodynamic process.

We must, therefore, turn our attention to the air contained in the vocal tract and to the various things that can be done to it by the vocal organs. For this purpose we review some basic physical concepts: these may be quite familiar to some readers (who may skim this chapter to pick out the specifically phonetic data that it contains), but to many others they will be useful.

The air in the vocal tract, like any gas, fills a certain space, or *volume;* it may be at any of a certain range of *pressures;* it may be static, or moving with a particular *velocity* and *volume-velocity,* and, if in motion, its flow may be of two main types. In this chapter we shall discuss these various characteristics of the air used in speech, and the relationships between them.

Volume

Volume is the three-dimensional space occupied by any solid, liquid, or gas. The standard unit of volume in the metric or c.g.s. (= centimeter-gram-second) system of measurement is the *litre,* which is equivalent to about ·220 gallons (1·76 pints) UK, ·264 gallons (2·1 pints) US. The litre is divided into *hundredths* (*centilitres* = cl) and *thousandths* (*millilitres* = ml). In phonetic literature, the millilitre is sometimes used as the unit of volume. More often, however, the *cubic centimetre* (cm^3 or cc) is used, since this has the advantage of underlining the relationship between *volume,* stated in cm^3, and *area,* stated in cm^2, and *length,* stated in cm. For all practical purposes the cm^3 is identical with the ml.[1]

For those not familiar with cubic centimetres we can give an idea of the actual volumes represented by mentioning that one UK pint = 568 cm^3, one US pint = 474 cm^3, and that a medium-sized thimble contains a volume of about 2 cm^3. As a further illustration, figure 3 is a representation of cubes with the volumes 1 cm^3, 10 cm^3 and 100 cm^3, respectively. For each cube, the face that is represented as being nearest to the onlooker is actual size—that is, has the actual area of one face of a cube of the given volume.

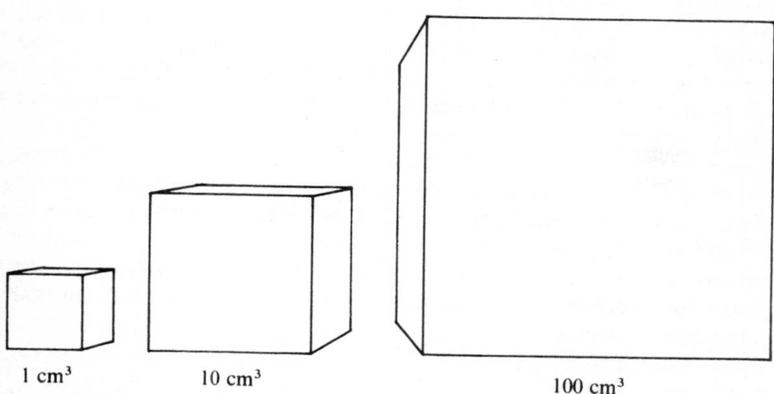

Figure 3. Visualizing cubic centimetres

Vocal Tract Volumes. The total volume of the vocal tract (in the sense used in this book, that is, from lungs to lips) varies within wide limits both from one person to another, and at different times within one and the same individual.

The absolute limits are of the order of 6500 cm^3, when a large person's lungs are fully inflated, down to about 1500 cm^3, which is approximately the volume of the residual air always left in the lungs when all the air that can be expelled has actually been forced out. Total vocal-tract volumes of about 2000 to 4500 cm^3 may be regarded as normal in speech, and we can take 3000 cm^3 as a good average value to use in aerodynamic phonetic calculations.

The total volume of the supraglottal part of the vocal tract—that part of the tract contained between the glottis and the lips—is also very variable, and it is not easy to find reliable estimates. We may, however, take it that with the larynx in a neutral position, the soft palate raised and the tongue relatively flat in the mouth, the total supraglottal volume (that is, the volume of the pharynx plus the oral cavity) is of the order of 120 to 160 cm^3. The volumes contained between the glottis and the oral closure for various *stop* consonants may then be estimated to be about as follows:

for p/b about 120–160 cm^3
for t/d about 70–100 cm^3
for k/g about 30–50 cm^3

In aerodynamic formulae dealing with the supraglottal cavities, the values 140 cm^3 (p/b), 85 cm^3 (t/d), 40 cm^3 (k/g) may be used as reasonable approximations.[2]

Volume Change. In the process of speaking, vocal-tract volumes are, of course, constantly changing. Between inhalations, in speech, volume changes of about 500 to 1000 cm^3 occur. As we shall see below, any change in the volume of the vocal tract, or of some part of it, must result in a change in the pressure of the contained air. If the vocal tract is completely closed at the time, this pressure change wili itself be the only result of such a volume change. If, however, the vocal tract is in free communication with the external air, the result of the volume change, or, more precisely, the result of the consequent pressure change, will be a movement—a flow—of air through the vocal tract. Vocal-tract volume change is thus related, although not in a completely simple way, to air-flow into or out of the vocal tract, and will be referred to again in that context below.

Pressure

Pressure is defined as *force per unit area.* In the c.g.s. system of units, the unit of force is the *dyne,* which is defined as the force that produces an acceleration of one cm per second per second (1 cm/s^2) when applied to a mass of one gram. Consequently, the basic c.g.s. unit of pressure, being 'force per unit area', is the *dyne per square centimetre* ($dyne/cm^2$).

The $dyne/cm^2$ is a very small pressure unit, appropriate for measuring some of the small pressures generated in the rapidly alternating compression and dilation of air that constitutes a sound-wave; a sound pressure, in this sense, of 1 $dyne/cm^2$ corresponds to a sound intensity of about 65 decibels, which, in turn, represents roughly the loudness of a fairly loud conversation.

The large-scale pressures that concern us in aerodynamic phonetics are more conveniently handled by other units, more akin to those used in measuring atmospheric pressure for meteorological purposes. The basic atmospheric pressure units are the *bar* (b), which equals one million (10^6) $dynes/cm^2$, and the *millibar* (mb), which is one thousandth of a bar. It is common practice, however, both in meteorology and in phonetics, to describe pressure not in terms of those units that are strictly measures of pressure, but rather in terms of the height of a column of liquid that could be supported by the given pressure. For atmospheric pressure a common unit is the millimetre of mercury (mm Hg); in phonetics we more commonly use *centimetres of water* (cm H_2O or cm aq). Since the density of mercury is 13·6 times that of water we can convert from pressure measured in mm Hg to cm H_2O by (1) dividing by 10 (to change from mm Hg to cm Hg), and (2) multiplying by 13·6 (to change from Hg to H_2O). More simply, we may combine these two operations by multiplying by 1·36.

In meteorology, standard atmospheric pressure, at sea-level and at a temperature of 0°C is stated to be 760 mm Hg. Multiplying by 1·36 we find the corresponding water pressure to be 1033·6 cm H_2O. Atmospheric pressure varies with height above sea-level, and also with temperature, as does the pressure of any gas. For phonetic experiments dealing with pressure, it is desirable to have in the laboratory a barometer, set to give readings of 'station pressure' —that is, of the actual ambient atmospheric pressure, not corrected to give an equivalent sea-level reading. Figure 4 is a curve showing values for atmospheric pressure at various heights above sea-level. Meanwhile, we may use 1030 cm H_2O as a convenient average pressure to use in aerodynamic formulae in places near sea-level. From figure 4 one may select an average atmospheric pressure for the particular altitude at which one is working.

In phonetics, of course, we are chiefly concerned with *differences* between atmospheric pressure and pressures in the vocal tract, and these, indeed, are what we measure. It is, however, sometimes important to remember that when we record, for instance, an intra-oral pressure of 10 cm H_2O, this is, in fact, 10 cm H_2O *in excess* of atmospheric, or base-line pressure, and represents, in absolute terms, about 1040 cm H_2O, or whatever pressure is appropriate for the altitude.

Vocal Tract Pressures. The pressures which can be generated in the vocal tract vary considerably, just as volumes do. Maximum pulmonary pressures generated by normal males, as given in Rahn et al. (1946), who quote their own data and also those of five other authorities, range from 130 to 180·88 cm H_2O for maximum expiratory pressure. The mean is 155, so we may reasonably quote 'about 160 cm H_2O' as being normal maximum vocal-tract expiratory pressure. Rahn et al. give only two values for maximum inspiratory pressure, namely 88·8 cm H_2O and 108·8 cm H_2O. Experiments conducted by the author at Edinburgh University in 1960, consisting of blowing through tubes of varying diameter with maximum force, give further indirect information on maximum vocal tract

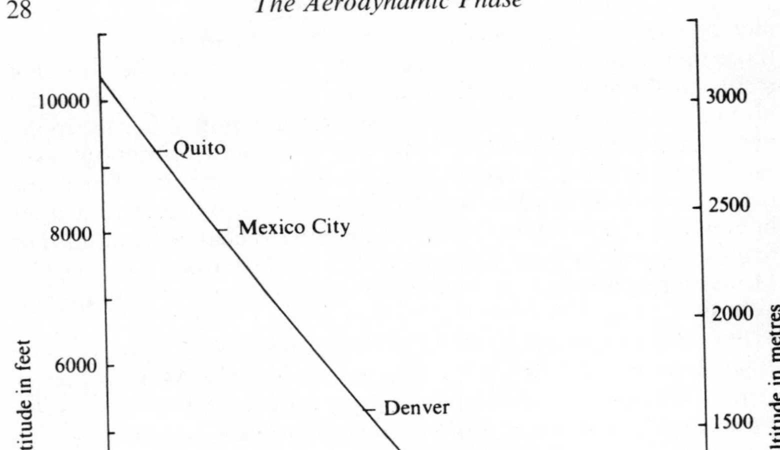

Figure 4. Atmospheric pressure and altitude

pressures. In this experiment, what was measured directly was, in fact, the volume-velocity of air-flow through tubes of varied diameter. The pressure was estimated by means of formulae (3a) and (2b). Maximum vocal-tract pressure can be generated only when expiration is being attempted against resistance. As shown below, blowing with maximum force through a tube of 1 mm diameter generated estimated pressure around 150 cm H_2O, which is quite close to the absolute maximum pressure of Rahn et al. Beyond that, the greater the diameter of the tube, the lower the pressure.

On the basis of the data given in Rahn et al. we can state that the possible range of pressures generated in the human vocal tract runs from about -100 to $+160$ cm H_2O. Only a very small part of this potential range occurs, however, in speech. Pressures within the mouth (intra-oral pressures) of, roughly, 3 to 15 cm H_2O are quite common, and for the production of voice a minimum pressure difference across the glottis of about 2 cm H_2O is necessary—that is, the sub-glottal pressure must be at least 2 cm H_2O higher than the supra-glottal pressure in order to keep the vocal folds in vibration. In shouting, considerably higher sub-glottal pressures, up to about 40 cm H_2O are generated. Using a glottalic, rather than a pulmonic initiatory mechanism (see Chapter 5) intra-oral pressures of 40 to 50 cm H_2O can easily be generated, but in languages that normally use glottalic egressive sounds (ejectives) it is improbable that such high pressures are commonly utilized.

Pressure and Volume. Pressure and volume are in inverse proportion. This is easily understood in the light of what is known as the 'kinetic theory of gases'. According to this theory, the molecules that constitute a gas are constantly flying about in a random way at a mean velocity that depends upon temperature—the higher the temperature the higher the mean velocity. At any given temperature the gas molecules hit the sides of the container with a certain constant average frequency. It is just this frequency of molecular impact that determines the pressure: the more frequent the impacts, the higher the pressure, and vice versa. Assuming, then, that the temperature does not change, if the volume of the container is reduced, the trajectories of the molecules must be shortened, and the frequency of their impacts upon the container's surface will necessarily be increased; in other words, the pressure will rise.

This is what is known as Boyle's Law, which is often stated thus: 'The pressure of a given quantity of gas whose temperature remains unaltered varies inversely as its volume.' This can be expressed symbolically in several ways: for example, $P \propto 1/V$ (pressure is directly proportional to reciprocal of volume), or $P \times V = K$ (constant). For various phonetic purposes, however, the formulae 1a–1d are particularly useful.

$$p_2 = \frac{V_1 \times p_1}{v_2} \tag{1a}$$

$$p_1 = \frac{p_2 \times V_2}{v_1} \tag{1b}$$

$$V_1 = \frac{p_2 \times V_2}{p_1} \tag{1c}$$

$$V_2 = \frac{p_1 \times V_1}{p_2} \tag{1d}$$

In all of these V_1 = *initial volume* (of container), V_2 = *new volume*, p_1 = *initial pressure* and p_2 = *new pressure*. We normally express V_1 or V_2 in cm^3, and p_1 and p_2 in cm H_2O. It must be remembered that here we are dealing with *absolute* pressure: p_1, in fact, is normally *atmospheric* pressure, which, for most purposes, we can take to be 1030 cm H_2O.

Using formula 1a we can answer such questions as: 'assuming an initial vocal tract volume of 3030 cm^3, which is reduced to 3000 cm^3 by the compression of the lungs, what air pressure will be generated behind the closure of a stop consonant such as [p] or [t]?'

$$V_1 = 3030, \quad V_2 = 3000, \quad p_1 = 1030$$

therefore

$$p_2 = \frac{3030 \times 1030}{3000} = 1040{\cdot}3 \text{ cm } H_2O$$

Or, since we normally state phonetic pressures in terms of the excess over atmospheric pressure, the pressure behind our stop consonant is 10·3 cm H_2O.

On the other hand, using formula 1d, we can answer the question 'in a glottalic pressure [p'] (see Chapter 5), the air in the pharynx and mouth is compressed by an upward movement of the larynx. Assuming a supra-glottal volume of 140 cm^3 and an intra-oral pressure of 40 cm H_2O, what is the volume displaced by the upward movement of the larynx?' The answer will be $V_1 - V_2$, so we have to find V_2. By formula 1d

$$V_2 = \frac{p_1 \times V_1}{p_2} = \frac{1030 \times 140}{1070} = 134{\cdot}8 \text{ cm}^3$$

Therefore the volume displaced by the upward larynx movement is 140 – 134·8 cm^3 = 5·2 cm^3.

Velocity of Flow

There are two kinds of velocity to be considered, each in its way important for phonetics. These are *velocity* proper, or 'particle-velocity', and *volume-velocity*.

Particle-velocity. Velocity proper, or particle-velocity, is rate of change of position. It is measured as distance per unit time, for example, miles per hour, or, for our purposes, centimetres per second (cm/s). Velocity is a 'vectorial quantity', that is to say, it implies change of position *in a specified direction* indicated by the use of positive numbers for velocities in that specified direction, velocities in the opposite direction being indicated by negative numbers.

It is possible to generate very high velocities of air-flow in the vocal tract, up to nearly half the velocity of sound (Mach ·5). However, the normal velocities of flow are much lower, being, for instance, of the order of 1000 to 4000 cm/s through the articulatory channels for fricatives. Velocity proper is not without its importance, but it is difficult to measure directly, and consequently often has to be calculated from other data, notably from pressure and volume-velocity (see below).

One relevant relationship between pressure and velocity is as follows: when a gas with a given pressure (p_1) flows through a narrow opening into another space with a lower pressure (p_2), the velocity of this 'pressure-flow', as it is called, may be calculated from a formula that takes account of the pressure difference, gravitational acceleration, density, and so on. Simplified versions of this, particularly applicable to phonetic purposes, are given by Roos (1936) and Meyer-Eppler (1953). The formula of Roos for air at a temperature of 35°C and saturated with water vapour (as is the air in the vocal tract) is

$$u = 4{\cdot}12\sqrt{p} \qquad (2)$$

Where u = velocity in metres per second, $p = p_1 - p_2$, that is, the excess 'upstream' pressure in mm H_2O (N.B. *millimetres,* not centimetres). To give a result directly in cm/s rather than m/s we insert 412 in place of 4·12 in the formula, thus

$$\text{Velocity } (u) \text{ (in cm/s)} = 412\sqrt{p} \text{ (in mm } H_2O) \qquad (2a)$$

To calculate pressure from a known velocity we use the formula

$$p \text{ (in mm } H_2O) = \left(\frac{u \text{ (in cm/s)}}{412}\right)^2 \qquad (2b)$$

As we have seen; the maximum expiratory pressure that can be generated in the vocal tract is of the order of 160 cm H_2O. Using formula (2a) we have

$$u = 412\sqrt{1600} = 412 \times 40$$
$$= 16480$$

Thus, the theoretical maximum velocity of air flowing out of the vocal tract is 16480 cm/s, which is very nearly Mach ·5, that is, half the velocity of sound—which, in air at 35°C, is 35285 cm/s. As mentioned earlier, maximum expiratory pressure can only be generated by blowing—that is, applying pulmonic pressure—against an obstacle, such as the closed mouth. Near maximum pressure may be generated by blowing through a very narrow channel, which offers strong resistance to flow. In the experiments referred to on page 27, volume-velocities of 125 and 500 cm^3/s were recorded through tubes of 1 mm and 2 mm diameter. By formula (3a) these work out at velocities of 15923 cm/s and 13158 cm/s respectively; and by formula (2b) we find the pressures to be 149 cm H_2O and 102 cm H_2O. The first of these velocities is, as we see, quite close to Mach ·5 and the corresponding pressure is not far below the maximum of Rahn et al. As the diameter of tubes increases, the velocity decreases (implying a corresponding decrease in pressure) till with a tube of 1 cm diameter the calculated maximum pressure is 52 cm H_2O, and in blowing with maximum force through the wide open glottis and open mouth the calculated maximum pressure is only 11·9 cm H_2O. The major resistance to flow in this case is provided by the glottis itself, which, even when wide open, has little more than half the cross-sectional area of the trachea, which is immediately below it. Figure 5 is a graph showing the relationship between excess upstream pressure, and velocity, in pressure-flow.

While discussing relationships between velocity and pressure we should take note of the theorem associated with the name of the eighteenth-century Swiss physicist Daniel Bernoulli. Bernoulli's theorem states that along any particular line of fluid flow—along any *streamline,* to use the technical term—the sum of the 'pressure head' and the 'velocity head' is constant. The 'pressure head' of the stream is the height of a column of fluid that, at rest, would exert the pressure actually measured in the stream, and the 'velocity head' is the height of a column of fluid that would generate the observed stream velocity if it flowed through a hole at the bottom of the column. In simpler terms, Bernoulli's theorem tells us that, along a streamline, velocity and pressure are inversely proportional: increase the velocity and you lower the pressure, and vice versa.

Bernoulli's theorem explains a number of everyday phenomena. For example, the shape of an aircraft wing is such that flow over its upper surface is accelerated, thus lowering the pressure there and generating 'lift' by, in effect, causing the wing (and the aircraft) to be 'sucked' upwards. Again, the flow of water in a shower entrains air with it, generating a certain velocity of air-flow inside the shower that is higher than the velocity of the (relatively) still air outside the shower. The consequent drop in air pressure inside the shower causes the shower curtains to billow inwards and wrap themselves clammily round the person taking the shower. Finally, the 'spin' of a cricket ball, or baseball, creates a circulatory motion of the air in the direction of rotation. This motion, superimposed on the flow of air

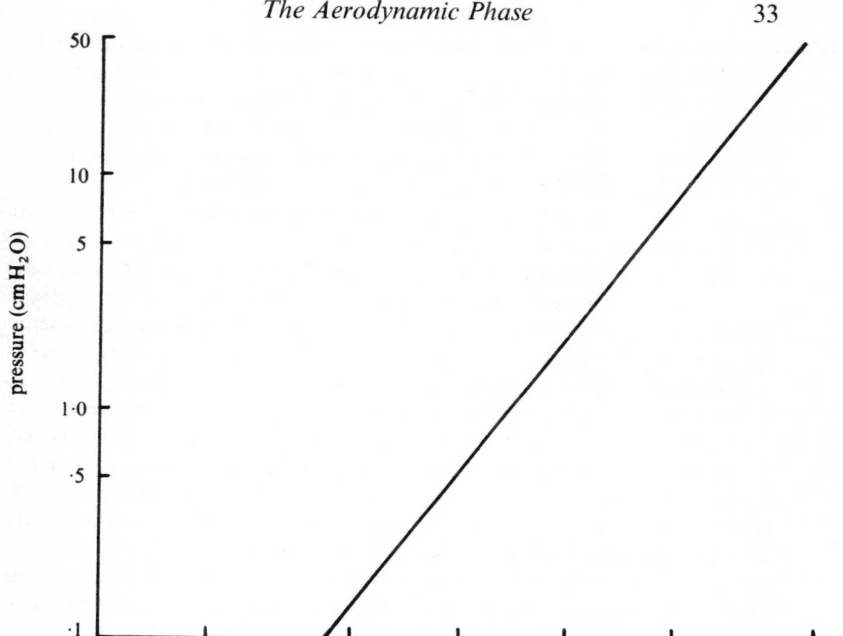

Figure 5. Pressure flow : the relation of pressure to velocity

relative to the ball, generates an acceleration on one side of the ball and a deceleration on the other, and, consequently (by Bernoulli's theorem) a pressure difference which causes the ball to veer to one side.

In phonetics, the Bernoulli effect is chiefly important in relation to the generation of *voice* and no doubt other periodic 'trill'-type sounds that involve oscillatory opening and closing of a channel in the vocal tract. In the production of voice, the flow of air is much accelerated by the narrow glottal opening, and the pressure in the glottis is consequently lowered—down to as much as -3 cm H_2O with a fairly high intensity of voice production. This Bernoulli-type pressure drop is partly responsible for the snapping together of the vocal folds in the closing phase of the glottal vibratory cycle in voice production.

Volume-velocity. Volume-velocity, sometimes also known as *volume-flow* or *discharge-rate,* is simply the volume of fluid passing through a system in unit time. For phonetic purposes, this is the volume of air passing through the vocal tract, or any part of it, in unit time. It is stated in millilitres per second (ml/s), or, more commonly, in cubic centimetres per second (cm^3/s). In quiet speech, volume-velocity averages from about 100 to 250 cm^3/s, with peaks of 1000 cm^3/s or more during [h] sounds, and the release of aspirated voiceless stops, such as English stressed [p, t, k].

For any given volume-velocity the particle-velocity depends on the cross-sectional area of the channel through which the flow is taking place. Obviously, the smaller the channel, the higher must be the velocity if the same total volume is to pass through in a given time. For those who find it difficult to visualize the relationship between particle-velocity and volume-velocity an analogy from traffic-flow may be helpful. The speed at which any particular car is travelling corresponds to particle-velocity: thus a car travelling at 30 mph in a given direction may be said to have a velocity of 30 mph. The analog of volume-velocity is the *volume of traffic*, measured as the number of cars per unit time flowing along a given road, or past a given point. Imagine cars travelling two abreast, along a two-lane highway, at a speed (particle-velocity) of 30 miles per hour and at a traffic volume (volume-velocity) of 20 cars per minute. Now, if the highway suddenly narrows to one lane, then it is clear that in order to keep the traffic flowing at the same volume-velocity as before, assuming the cars retain the same spacing between them, they must all double their speed. One can imagine the anti-traffic-safety road sign: *Road narrows—Double your speed.*

The relationship between mean (particle) *velocity* ($\bar{u}$), *volume-velocity* (Vv), and cross-sectional *area* of channel (a), are expressed by formulae (3a–3c).

$$\frac{Vv}{a} = \bar{u} \tag{3a}$$

$$\frac{Vv}{\bar{u}} = a \tag{3b}$$

$$a \times \bar{u} = Vv \tag{3c}$$

In these formulae, Vv is expressed in cm^3/s, u in cm/s and a in cm^2. Thus, for a typical [s]-sound, given a volume-velocity of 200 cm^3/s through a channel of cross-sectional area 10 mm^2 ($= \cdot 10$ cm^2), the velocity, by formula 3a, is

$$\frac{200}{\cdot 10} = 2000 \text{ cm/s}$$

Formula 3b, together with formula 2b, enables us to calculate the cross-sectional areas of articulatory channels in speech. For example, let us assume that from a simultaneous recording of the two quantities we know that during an [s]-sound the volume-velocity is 220 cm^3/s and the intra-oral pressure is 7 cm H_2O. We can first calculate the mean velocity ($\bar{u}$) by formula (2b), as

$$\begin{aligned}\bar{u} &= 412\sqrt{70}\\ &= 412 \times 8{\cdot}36\\ &= 3444 \text{ cm/s}\end{aligned}$$

We can then use this result as the value for $\bar{u}$ in formula (3b) and calculate the articulatory channel area as follows:

$$\frac{220}{3444} = {\cdot}064 \text{ cm}^2$$

$$= 6{\cdot}4 \text{ mm}^2$$

Results obtained by this means give a *precise* indication of relative channel areas, and a close *approximation* to the absolute area. On the reasons for this see, for example, Hixon (1966).

Knowledge of the cross-sectional area of articulatory channels is important in providing criteria for distinctions between certain types of sounds, for example, fricatives and approximants (see Chapter 7 below).

Initiator-velocity. We have been discussing the velocity of air-flow through the vocal tract in terms of both particle-velocity (the mean velocity of flow at any particular place or time) and volume-velocity (the volume of air discharged per unit time). The latter measure is closely related to the rate at which the volume of the vocal tract itself changes as a result of the movement of an initiator (see p. 15). For example, during a sustained vowel sound the volume of the lungs may be steadily decreasing at, say, the rate of 150 cm^3/s; since the function of the lungs here is to *initiate* the air-flow for sound production, we can say that we have here an *initiation-velocity* (or, referring to the rate of movement of the actual organs an *initiator-velocity*) of 150 cm^3/s.

In a case like the one just given, where we have a maintained, steady-state vowel, initiator-velocity is identical to the volume-velocity of air-flow, since the rate at which the volume of the lungs is decreasing is exactly the same as the rate at which the air is flowing out through the vocal tract. There are, however, many circumstances in which volume-velocity and initiator-velocity are not the same. An obvious case is during the pressure build-up of a stop consonant, particularly one at the start of a syllable.

For example, before the release of a voiceless stop consonant a pressure of, perhaps, 7·5 cm H_2O is generated. This pressure is built up during a period of, let us say, eleven hundredths of a second (eleven centiseconds, 11 cs). During those 11 cs the vocal tract is completely closed and there is no flow of air. Nevertheless, in order to generate that pressure, the vocal-tract volume must have decreased by about 21 cm^3—and to do this in 11 cs implies an average rate of initiatory volume change of 190 cm^3/s. Here, then, there is no flow at all, and, consequently, volume-velocity is zero. The initiator is, however, in quite rapid motion. In other cases, rapid articulatory movements, such as sudden openings and closings of the mouth, superimpose velocities on the basic volume-velocity set up by initiator movement. For example, while a steady rate of lung-volume decrease (a steady initiator-velocity) is generating a steady flow of air up the trachea through the glottis and into the mouth, a rapid opening of the mouth may so much increase the volume of the oral cavity that the pressure there is momentarily lowered, and the volume-velocity of the air-flow through the mouth correspondingly reduced. In rare cases, the rate at which the mouth volume increases may exceed the rate at which the lung volume decreases, with the result that there is a momentary reversal of the direction of flow out of the mouth. There is an example of this on page 494 in the great work, *Principes de phonétique expérimentale* (1901), of the Abbé Rousselot. Air-flow (volume-velocity) tracings are shown of the syllables [na] and [la] pronounced by a Russian. It is clear that the flow momentarily becomes negative (ingressive) on the release of the consonant in each case. Rousselot wrongly places these examples in a section devoted to 'articulations inspiratoires', when clearly this flow-reversal is not 'inspiratoire' but is simply due to the sudden great increase of oral volume from a strongly velarised [n] or [l]. One can easily replicate these recordings of Rousselot's by recording air-flow of these syllables, deliberately pronounced with strong velarisation and a sudden sharp opening to [a].

It must, then, be borne in mind, particularly in instrumental work, that measured rates of flow of air out of the mouth do not correspond in a simple way with rates of initiatory volume change, or initiator-velocity. The final volume-velocity of flow out of (or into) the mouth is the sum of the rate of initiatory volume change plus the rate of articulatory volume change—that is, the sum of initiator-velocity and articulator-velocity.

Types of Flow

There are two principal types of fluid flow. In one of these, the fluid (for example, water in a river, air in the vocal tract) flows in a smooth steady way. If we were to follow the flow of any one particle of fluid along a streamline in this type of flow we should find that it exhibits no sudden changes of direction or velocity: the streamlines keep moving steadily along in a path determined by the form of the channel through which the fluid is flowing. This type of flow, in which the fluid moves in stratified layers, without mixing or sudden velocity fluctuations, is called *laminar* flow.

In the other major type of flow the movements of the fluid are irregular. The streamlines no longer follow a path determined by the form of the channel, but intercross and mix: small irregular motions are superimposed upon the main motion of the fluid, in the form of sudden small velocity changes both in the direction of the main flow itself, and also in the two directions that lie at right angles to it, namely 'up and down' and 'side to side'. This type of flow is called *turbulent*.

When fluid flow, whether laminar or turbulent, takes place past an obstacle placed in the stream a highly disturbed region of flow, called a *wake*, is created downstream from the obstacle. The precise characteristics of the wake vary according to the shape of the obstacle; if it is a bluff shape or projects at a sharp angle into the flow the wake will be composed of turbulence and large eddies or 'whirlpools' known as *vortices*. The eddying wake resulting from a jet of air impinging on a sharp edge gives rise to a regular ('periodic'—see Chapter 4) series of vortices on alternating sides of the obstacle, and these generate a sound of definite frequency. This is the principle of an organ pipe or a wood-wind instrument. The frequency of the resultant note depends on the velocity of the jet: the higher the velocity the higher the frequency. If the sharp edge is not facing the jet but is more nearly at right angles to it the wake is highly turbulent, but still contains some periodically eddying components that tend to generate a sound of definite frequency, the frequency varying with the jet velocity and also with the size of the obstacle.

We shall call the two types of turbulent flow referred to here *channel turbulence* (the turbulence generated simply by flow through a channel) and *wake turbulence* (the turbulence, including more or less regularly spaced, that is, periodic vortices, generated downstream from an obstacle).

The presence or absence of turbulence in vocal-tract air-flow is of great importance to phonetics, since it is turbulent airflow which generates the 'hiss' noise of fricative consonants. In the case of some fricative sounds we have to do simply with channel turbulence—the turbulence resulting from flow at certain velocities through the articulatory channel. In other cases, however, we have wake turbulence as well as channel turbulence. The most clear-cut cases of this kind are in the production of sounds of the types [s] as in *sip,* and [ʃ] as in *ship*. In sounds of these types (discussed more fully in Chapter 8) an articulatory channel is formed between the tongue and the alveolar ridge, just behind the upper teeth. Air-flow through the channel thus formed is normally turbulent—this is channel turbulence; but since the channel is very narrow (of the order of 5 to 12 mm^2 cross-sectional area) the flow of air through it is much accelerated, and a high-velocity jet is thus projected against the edges of the upper and lower teeth. Consequently, a turbulent wake is generated downstream from the teeth, and this wake turbulence contributes to the production of the sound. The articulatory channel for [s] is formed far forward, very close to the teeth; that for [ʃ] some distance (5 to 10 mm) further back. Since the jet for [ʃ] has further to travel than that for [s], by the time it strikes the teeth it has both lost some velocity and fanned out somewhat. Consequently, [ʃ] has a jet of lower velocity flowing past a wider stretch of teeth-edge (a larger obstacle) than [s] and, as a result, that part of the hiss-sound which is created by wake turbulence is of lower frequency in [ʃ] than in [s]. We probably also have a wake-turbulence effect in lateral fricative sounds, [ɬ] and [ɮ] (see p. 132), in which the hiss is generated by air-flow past the molar teeth, which serve as obstacles creating a downstream wake. Again, in voiceless falsetto, or 'glottal whistle', it is probable that the effect is partly due to a kind of wake turbulence—in this case, periodic vortex-formation in the turbulent wake of air-flow past the thinned edges of the vocal folds.

In channel turbulence, the acoustic *intensity,* and consequent loudness, of the hiss is related to the velocity of flow through the channel; we shall look at this in more detail below. In wake turbulence this is no doubt still true; but, in this case, in addition, not only intensity, but also frequency (perceived as 'pitch') is proportional to velocity.

If we start off with laminar flow through a channel or past an obstacle, and gradually increase the velocity of the flow, a particular velocity will eventually be reached—what is called a 'critical' velocity—at which the flow begins to be turbulent. Likewise, if we start with a high velocity, and consequently turbulent flow, and then gradually decrease the velocity, once again a critical velocity will be reached at which the flow now ceases to be turbulent. The first of these two critical velocities is higher than the second: we thus have a *higher critical velocity* at which the change-over from laminar to turbulent flow occurs, and a *lower critical velocity* at which the change-over from turbulent to laminar flow occurs. The lower critical velocity is the more stable of the two, and for this reason it is the lower critical velocity which is normally cited, in fluid dynamics, as 'the' critical velocity.

Critical velocity depends on a number of factors—in particular the density and viscosity of the fluid, and some characteristic dimension of the system where the flow occurs, for example, the width, or diameter, of the channel. The relationship between these factors is summed up in a dimensionless number called the *Reynolds Number* (R or Re), after the nineteenth-century English engineer, Osborne Reynolds, who first drew attention to this relationship.

The Reynolds Number is, in fact, a measure of the ratio of the *inertial* forces (related to the density of the fluid, the size of the channel or obstacle, and the velocity of flow) to the *viscous* forces (the viscosity of the fluid):

$$\mathrm{Re} = \frac{\text{length} \times \text{velocity} \times \text{density}}{\text{viscosity}}$$

or, since

$$\frac{\text{density}}{\text{viscosity}} = \text{kinematic viscosity},$$

then

$$\mathrm{Re} = \frac{\text{length} \times \text{velocity}}{\text{kinematic viscosity}}.$$

For flow through tubes or enclosed channels (such as the vocal tract) we take *diameter* (d) as our relevant 'length'—meaning for irregularly shaped channels, as in the vocal tract, estimated or assumed diameter expressed in cm, derived from cross-sectional area. The *kinematic viscosity* of air (v), derived from a viscosity of about ·0188 poises and a density of ·0013 gm/cm^3 is about ·14. With ($\bar{u}$) standing for (mean) velocity of flow in cm/s, the relevant formula for Reynolds Number is:

$$\mathrm{Re} = \frac{d \times \bar{u}}{\cdot 14} \tag{4a}$$

and the following additional formulae are also useful:

$$d = \frac{\mathrm{Re} \times \cdot 14}{\bar{u}} \tag{4b}$$

$$\bar{u} = \frac{\mathrm{Re} \times \cdot 14}{d} \tag{4c}$$

For example, supposing we have a flow at a volume velocity of 200 cm^3/s through an articulatory channel of 10 mm^2 (as in a typical fricative), then, by formula (3a) we have a mean velocity ($\bar{u}$) of 2000 cm/s. A channel area of 10 mm^2 has an equivalent diameter of about 3·5 mm, that is ·35 cm. Using formula (4a) we find that

$$\begin{aligned} \text{Re} &= \frac{\cdot 35 \times 2000}{\cdot 14} \\ &= 5000 \end{aligned}$$

The Reynolds Number enables us to make generalizations that are true over a very wide range of conditions. For example, for flow through circular pipes a (lower) critical Reynolds Number of 2300 is often quoted. This means that in flow through such pipes, irrespective of what fluid is involved (for example, air, water, lubricating oil), or of the actual dimensions of the pipe, or of the velocity of flow, or even of the internal roughness of the pipe (which makes little difference), the change-over from turbulent to laminar flow occurs when the combination of variables expressed in

$$\frac{\text{diameter} \times \text{velocity}}{\text{kinematic viscosity}}$$

works out at 2300. The critical Reynolds Number (Re(crit)) for pipes of rectangular section has been found to be about 1440. Meyer-Eppler (1953) found an Re(crit) of 1800 for tubes of elliptical section, this being roughly the shape of articulatory and phonatory orifices and channels in the vocal tract. The experiments on air-flow through tubes referred to on pp. 27 and 32, which we carried out in Edinburgh in 1960, supplemented by further studies of volume-velocity of air-flow in various types of speech sounds, indicate that Re(crit) = 1700 is a fairly good average for speech. However, the varying shapes of articulatory and phonatory channels introduce a good deal of uncertainty and variability into the relevant measures, and it is preferable to regard Re(crit) = 1700 ± 200 as the critical Reynolds Number for speech.

We mentioned above that the velocity of turbulent flow in fricatives is related to the intensity of the hiss-sound thus produced. Some crude, but interesting, data on this were obtained in the Edinburgh experiments, which we present here since they also provide a good example of the generalizing power of the Reynolds Number.

Recordings were made of the volume-velocity of flow through short tubes of diameters ·6, ·4, and ·22 cm—the last was intended to be ·2 cm, but various data suggested that it was about 10 per cent too big. At the same time the acoustic signal level of the resultant hiss-sounds was observed on the VU meter of a Ferrograph tape-recorder. Since the diameters and cross-sectional areas of the tubes were known it was possible to calculate the velocities of air-flow. Table 5 gives the velocities, in cm/s, recorded for four different signal levels (SL). If we plot these results on a graph of velocity versus signal level we get three quite separate curves, as shown in figure 6. From these curves we see that signal level is roughly proportional to the square of the velocity of air-flow through a tube or channel of a specific diameter (or a specific cross-sectional area).

Table 5

S/Ls	*tube diameters (cms)*		
	·22	·4	·6
1	5763	3040	2260
2	8158	4300	2800
3	10000	5000	3360
4	11579	6000	3900

Table 6

S/Ls	*tube diameters*		
	·22	·4	·6
1	9056	8685	8971
2	12820	12285	12000
3	15714	14285	14400
4	18195	17143	18857

Instead of having three separate curves referring to tubes of different diameters, as here, we would like to collapse our data into a single curve—that is to say, to generalize it. This is where the Reynolds Number is useful, as we see when we calculate the Reynolds Numbers for our data, as in table 6. From this we see that for each SL the Reynolds Number is virtually the same for all diameters, having an average maximum deviation of only 5·9 per

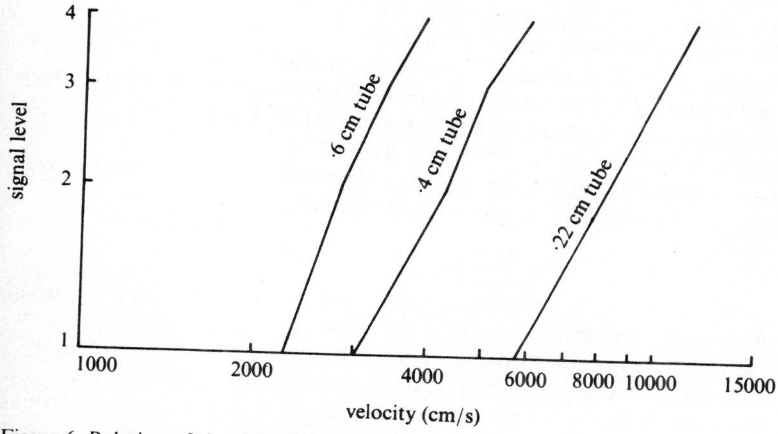

Figure 6. Relation of signal level to velocity

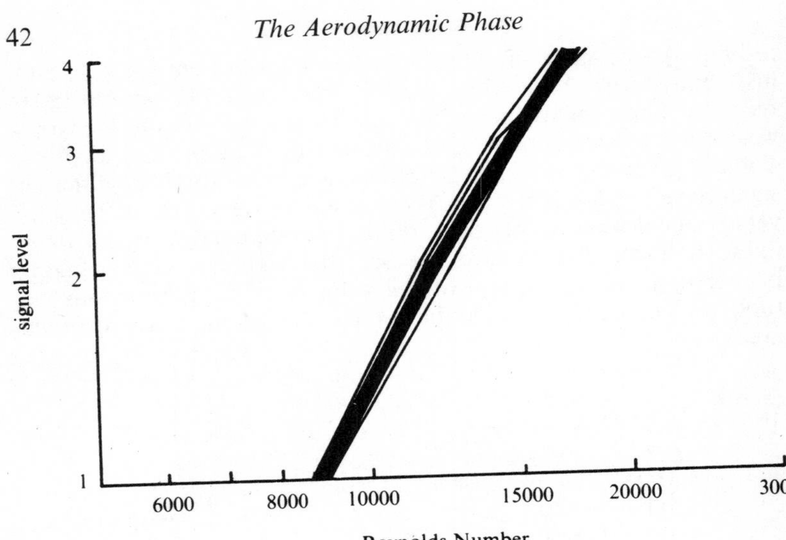

Figure 7. Relation of signal level to Reynolds Number

cent, which is well within the range of observational error in a rather crude experiment of this type. Plotting the average values for Reynolds Numbers we get the consolidated curve shown in figure 7.

From this we see that the Reynolds Number, like the velocity, is related to signal level, only in a more general way, independent of the specific diameter of the tube. SL is roughly proportional to the square of the Reynolds Number: in other words, if you increase

Re by 1·4 you increase SL by 2
Re by 2 you increase SL by 4
Re by 3 you increase SL by 9, and so on.

We can now sum up our information about flow-types, Reynolds Number, and noise generation in speech as follows:

$Re < 1700 \pm 200 =$ laminar flow
$Re = 1700 \pm 200 = Re(crit)$—transition to turbulent flow
$Re > 1700 \pm 200 =$ turbulent flow

and

$$Re > 1700 \pm 200 \propto \sqrt{SL}$$

So far we have referred only to critical velocity and to critical Reynolds Number in relation to velocity. In phonetics, however, we very often deal with the velocity of flow through channels of definite diameter, or, better, a definite cross-sectional area; we can therefore, often refer to *critical volume-velocity* rather than critical velocity—for the relationship between velocity, channel area, and

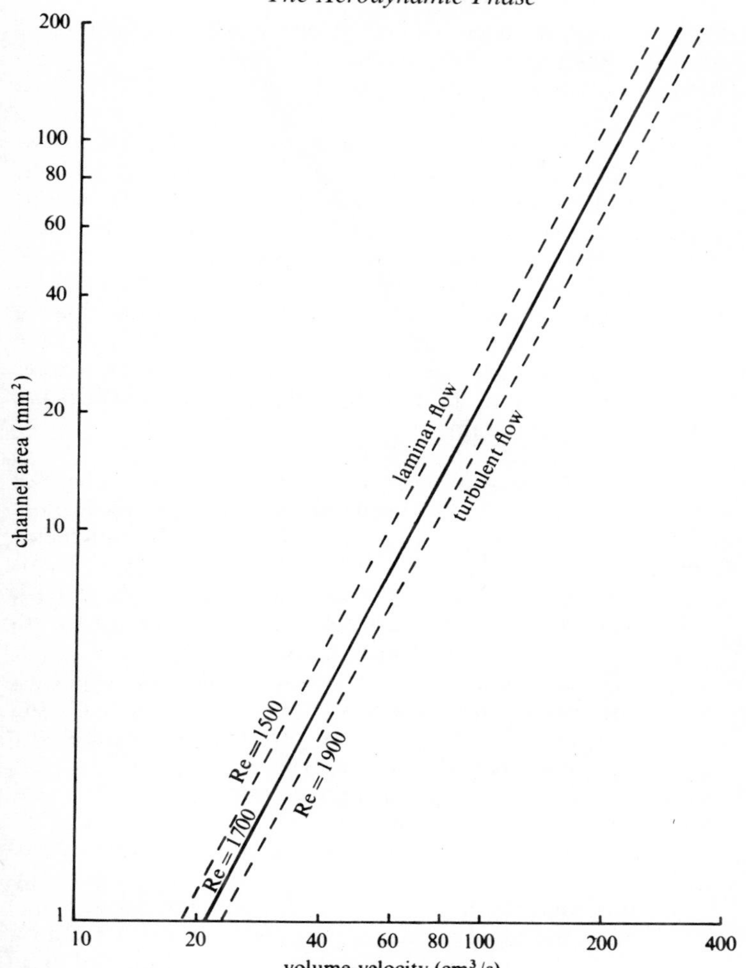

Figure 8. Laminar and turbulent flow, channel area and volume velocity

volume-velocity, see formulae (3a–3c) above. This is the more useful since it is, in fact, volume-velocity that we normally measure.

Figure 8 is a graph showing the relationship between the cross-sectional area of articulatory (or other) channels and volume-velocity for a critical Reynolds Number of 1700.

The following is a list of critical volume-velocities for various categories of sound generated by turbulent air-flow through the vocal tract. These are approximate figures based on averages of from 2 to 10 utterances of each sound.

f 47 cm^3/s θ 90 cm^3/s s 50 cm^3/s

ʃ 46 cm^3/s ʂ 55 cm^3/s ɹ̥ 120 cm^3/s χ 73 cm^3/s

Reference to figure 6 gives a rough indication of what the cross-sectional channel area would be for these critical volume-velocities. The value for the approximant [ɹ̥] is about 34 mm^2 (which accords well with a measured value of 36); the wider channel (*c.* 17 mm^2) for [θ] as opposed to the narrower fricatives [s] (*c.* 5·5 mm^2), [ʃ] (*c.* 4·6 mm^2) and [ʂ] (*c.* 6·5 mm^2), is also as expected. In the artificial situation of trying to produce narrow fricatives with air-flow at critical velocity it is probable that the [s]-type channels have been narrowed more than usual. There are indications that channel areas for [s]- and [ʃ]-type sounds at more normal operating velocities are often in the region of 10 mm^2.

The precise and quantitative analysis of the aerodynamic phase of speech requires instrumental techniques, such as those described in Chapter 12. It is, however, possible to verify some of the statements made in this chapter in a rough and ready way by experiments performed in one's own vocal tract. Indeed, here, as elsewhere in the study of phonetics, it is highly desirable for the student to be not merely a passive reader, but an active performer.

One can 'feel' various degrees of air pressure inside the vocal tract if one closes the mouth and then makes varying degrees of exhalatory effort—that is, tries to breathe out, at first pressing quite weakly with the lungs, then moderately, then more strongly.

If, in the course of this experiment, one replaces the absolutely closed mouth by a very small opening, a tiny chink between the lips, one can get the feel of the relationship between pressure and velocity.

Holding the back of one's hand in front of the mouth, and blowing through the small labial aperture, one can easily feel how the velocity of the jet striking one's hand increases as the feeling of effort and internal pressure increases.

Some idea of the nature of volume-velocity, and its relationship to both velocity and channel area can be gained by inhaling until the lungs are comfortably full (not straining) and then exhaling under *relaxation pressure*—that is, by merely allowing the lungs to collapse by their own elasticity, stopping the exhalation at the point where its continuation would involve muscular effort. Every time one follows this procedure one exhales very roughly the same volume of air, which we can thus use as a more or less 'standard quantity' for comparative purposes. If then, one exhales this standard quantity first through a very narrow opening at the lips, and then through a wider opening, one can observe two things:

(1) The discharge of the standard quantity of air through the narrow opening takes measurably longer than it does through a wider opening. In other words, the volume discharged per unit time (the volume-velocity) of the flow is higher through the wider channel. (2) By simultaneously feeling the flow on the back of the hand one can perceive that the velocity of the flow is the same, or, more probably, lower through the wider channel.

Exhaling in this way under relaxation pressure one can observe that some speech sounds require more time—that is, have a *lower* volume-velocity—than others, and this implies that the cross-sectional area of their articulatory channels is smaller. Compare, for example, the English fricative sounds [s] (as in *sin*) and [θ] (as in *thin*). It will probably be found that the exhalation time for [s] is longer than that for [θ], demonstrating that the articulatory channel area of [θ] is greater than that of [s]. It is also instructive to compare the exhalation times of various vowel sounds, preferably whispered rather than voiced. It will readily be seen that the 'closer' vowels such as [i] (as in English *see*), or [u] (as in English *two*) have longer exhalation times (that is, lower volume-velocities) than more 'open' vowels such as [ɛ] (as in English *bed*), or [æ] (as in English *bad*). The inference again is that [i] or [u] have narrower articulatory channels than [ɛ] and [æ].

By blowing with carefully modulated force, and hence varied velocity, through articulatory channels one can experience the concept of critical velocity.

For example, form a small channel between the lips and then start blowing very gently, so that flow through the channel is absolutely silent. Gradually increase the effort, that is, the internal pressure and consequently the velocity, and a time will come when a faint hiss is heard. This is the *higher critical velocity*. Continue increasing the velocity, and the intensity of the hiss will increase.

The experiment can be repeated in reverse, starting with a high velocity of flow, and loud hiss, then gradually decreasing the velocity till the hiss vanishes—usually quite suddenly. This happens at the *lower critical velocity*.

This experiment can be repeated with labial articulation channels of various sizes, and with articulations at other parts of the vocal tract.

We saw above that there are two kinds of turbulence, which we called channel turbulence and wake turbulence. We can get a practical demonstration of the first type by simply blowing through the lips, at a rate somewhat above critical volume-velocity, or by producing such fricative sounds as [x] or [ç]. To demonstrate wake turbulence one can blow through the lips, and, while doing so, hold a piece of card in front of the face at right angles to the stream of air issuing from the lips. If one holds the card first touching the nose with its lower edge just below the tip of the nose, then slides it slowly downwards till it cuts into the stream of air from the lips, one can easily hear the audible effect of the turbulent wake created downstream from the card. If one now slowly moves the card further away from the lips one can hear how not only the intensity but also the frequency (perceived as 'pitch') of the hiss-sound decreases. This is because as the jet issuing from the mouth gets further away from its source at the lips it fans out (so covers a larger area) and also loses some of its velocity. These two factors—large area of impact with the obstructing card, and lower velocity—generate a lower frequency of vortices. In this experiment we are, in effect, simulating the aerodynamic conditions which give rise to [s]-type and [ʃ]-type sounds: namely, channel turbulence plus high-velocity jet striking an obstruction (the teeth edges) very close to the source of the jet, for [s], or somewhat further away, for [ʃ]. A further experiment will help to demonstrate the contribution made by teeth-edge wake turbulence to the sounds [s] and [ʃ]. Pronounce each of these sounds normally, then, taking care to maintain exactly the same articulatory posture, reverse the air-flow, pronouncing each of them on inhalation rather than exhalation. In the ingressive [s] and [ʃ] there is turbulent flow through the articulatory channel, and this generates a noticeable hissing sound. However, the high-velocity jet generated in the articulatory channel shoots out into the empty space of the mouth without meeting any obstruction. Consequently, the relatively high-frequency wake turbulence present in normal, egressive [s] and [ʃ] is absent.

For the student of phonetics who wants to pursue the study of aerodynamic phonetics further there are no really suitable books available. However, the following are readable introductions to some of the relevant aspects of aerodynamics that do not demand much background in physics or mathematics: Theodore von Karman (1954); John E. Allen (1963); Ascher H. Shapiro (1961).

FOUR

The Acoustic Phase

Having surveyed the topography of the organic phase of speech in Chapter 3, and some aspects of the aerodynamic phase in Chapter 4 we continue the logical progression to those phenomena that are the immediate consequence of the aerodynamic phase, namely, the *acoustic* phase. Having been generated by the basic component of speech production known as *initiation,* the aerodynamic events are modified by the second basic component *articulation,* and by *phonation* (when present) in such a way as to generate *sounds.* And these sounds, generated chiefly by turbulent flow through narrow channels, or else by the release of intermittent high-velocity bursts of air, constitute the acoustic phase of speech.

As mentioned in Chapter 1, within the whole process of speech the acoustic phase is the most remote from language and speech as a human activity, for it is merely the physical medium that transmits information about the speaker's speech performance to a hearer—it is not itself part of the human communicative event, which is the linguistic phonetician's central interest. Nevertheless, it is essential for the student of phonetics to give attention to the acoustic phase, partly because technical developments in the last thirty or forty years have made the acoustic phase one of the most accessible to (instrumental) observation, and partly because each phase in the speech process helps to throw light on the preceding and succeeding one. Acoustic data often assist us in estimating what is going on in the aerodynamic phase, and, more importantly, are one of our chief sources of information or inference about the succeeding receptive and perceptual phases.

There are several excellent books and a multitude of articles dealing with the acoustic phase of speech. For this reason we attempt here no more than a brief survey of some of the principal concepts of acoustics and of 'acoustic phonetics' as the study of the acoustic phase is sometimes called.

We give the name 'sound' to any physical phenomenon that can stimulate the auditory nerve through the mechanism of the ear.

Physically, sound is an oscillatory movement of air molecules. This movement may be somewhat irregular and chaotic, resulting from the random multi-directional small velocity changes that constitute turbulent air-flow; or, on the other hand, it may be quite rhythmic and regular, resulting from regular vibrations, as of the vocal folds, or from the resultant regular, intermittent, pulsating release of high-velocity bursts of air. It is customary in approaching acoustics to deal first with this more regular type of oscillation, which is called *periodic*.

A vibrating or pulsating *source* displaces adjacent air molecules, which move back and forth, becoming alternately more densely packed together (compression) and then more widely dispersed (dilation or rarefaction). Each individual molecule thus swings to and fro—oscillates—without being permanently displaced from its original average location; but as each molecule swings one way in the compression phase of its oscillation it, so-to-speak, jostles neighbouring molecules, and passes on the energy of its oscillation to the next molecule, which now swings into oscillation and passes energy on to the next molecule, which in turn passes energy on to yet another, and so on. In other words, although each individual molecule merely oscillates in its own place, energy is passed on and on from one molecule to the next, and consequently a *wave* of alternate compression and dilation spreads steadily outward from the source. The rate of progress of this wave, which we call a sound-wave, is about 343 metres per second (1126 feet per second or 768 mph) through air at a temperature of 65°F (18°C). A sound-wave can thus be pictured as a series of rapidly expanding concentric spheres of alternate compression and dilation, radiating from the source.

Figure 9 is a diagrammatic representation of part of a sound-wave travelling outward from its source in the direction of the horizontal arrow. The alternate spheres of compression and rarefaction are suggested by dots packed close together (representing compression), thinning out to nothing (representing dilation). Since each area of closely packed dots represents an area of compression (positive pressure), and each blank or sparsely dotted area represents an area of rarefaction (negative pressure), we can superimpose a curve on this diagram representing the rise and fall of pressure above and below zero, corresponding to the swinging together and apart again of the oscillating molecules, as in figure 10. A single complete oscillation—say from zero to maximum pressure, back across the zero line to minimum pressure, then back to zero again (or from any other starting point back to the same point)—is called a *cycle*.

Frequency is the number of cycles completed in one second,

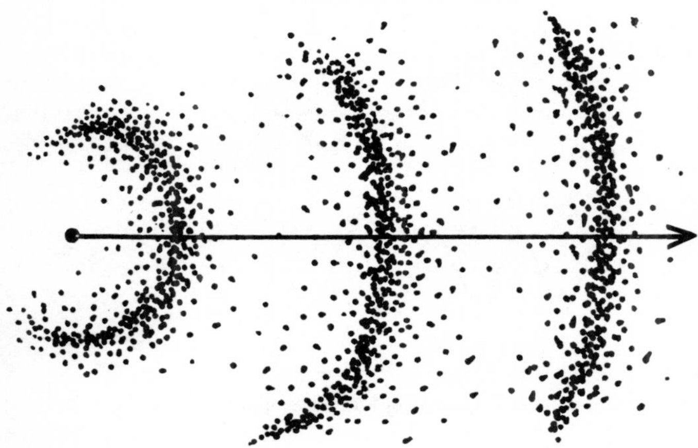

Figure 9. The propagation of a sound wave

formerly quoted in English-language publications as cps, that is, 'cycles per second', but now normally given in the international notation as Hz (Hertz): note that cps and Hz mean exactly the same.

Figure 11 represents two waves with *different frequencies* (although the same amplitude, see below). The time scale shows that one cycle of the wave labelled (a) lasts ·01 seconds: the frequency of (a) is thus 100 cycles per second, or 100 Hz. One cycle of (b) lasts a third of this time—there are three cycles in one hundredth of a second—consequently the frequency of (b) is 300 Hz.

The range of frequencies that can be perceived (by young people) is about 20 to 20,000 Hz. Most of the frequencies which are important in speech lie between 50 Hz and 8000 Hz.

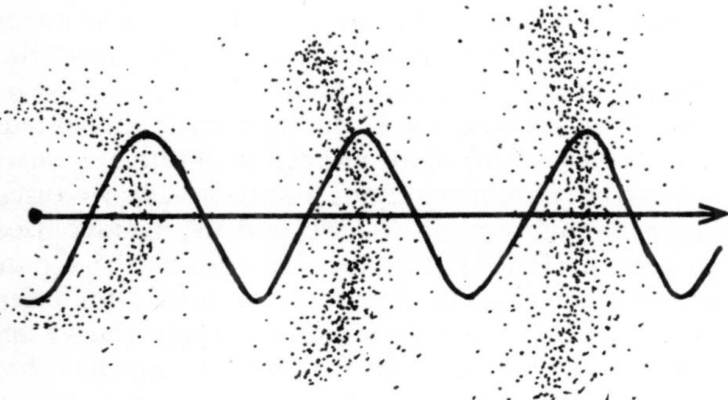

Figure 10. Curve of pressure variation in a sound wave

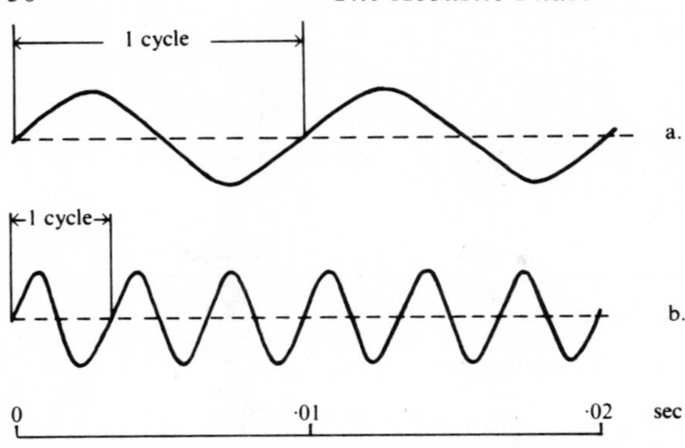

Figure 11. Waves with different frequencies but same amplitude

It is, of course, variations of frequency that correspond to variation in perceived pitch. The smaller the frequency, the lower the pitch; the greater the frequency the higher the pitch. Thus, the average conversational pitch of a moderately deep-voiced (baritone) man is around 100 Hz, that of a contralto woman, around 200 Hz, while the high singing notes of a soprano are around 1300 Hz. However, the relation between frequency differences and perceived pitch differences is not quite simple. The ear, in fact, is more sensitive to frequency differences at frequencies below 1000 Hz than at frequencies above this value. Consequently two pairs of notes separated by the same frequency difference will appear more different in pitch if they are below 1000 Hz, less different in pitch if they are above 1000 Hz. Roughly speaking, below 1000 Hz the relation between pitch and frequency is linear; above 1000 Hz it is logarithmic.

Amplitude is the amount of deviation of the oscillating molecules from the rest position: in other words, it is the positive or negative pressure attained by a sound-wave. Figure 12 represents two waves of the same frequency but different amplitudes. The lines $a-a^1$ and $b-b^1$ represent the amplitude of the waves a and b.

By the very nature of a sound-wave, the amplitude, or sound-pressure, is constantly varying from one moment to another. Consequently, to make useful statements about a sound-wave we often have to calculate an average sound-pressure, and the average used is the 'root-mean-square' (RMS) pressure. This means 'the square root of the mean of the squares of the pressures' attained at different points in the cycle. RMS pressure is found by noting the values (on a pressure scale) of all the points through which a line like that in figure 12 a or b passes, squaring them (simply in order to convert negative values to positive ones), summing the squares,

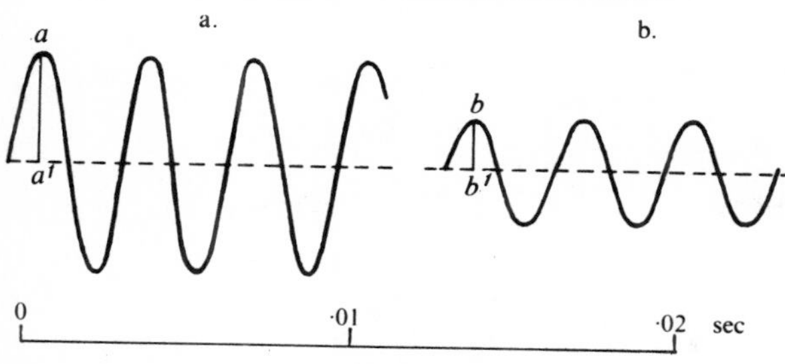

Figure 12. Waves with different amplitudes but same frequency

dividing by the number of points (which give the mean square), then taking the square root of that. This sounds complicated but is really quite simple, and indeed, this kind of average, the RMS sound-pressure, is the only feasible value to use when one is dealing with complex wave-forms. The average amplitude, or RMS sound-pressure, is related to the power, or intensity, of a sound, which is the energy per second transmitted along the direction of the sound-wave. The intensity, in fact, depends on the square of the sound-pressure: double the sound-pressure and you multiply the intensity by 2^2, that is, by 4, treble the sound-pressure and you multiply the intensity by 3^2, that is, 9.

It will be remembered that we found a roughly similar relation to exist between turbulence and sound intensity in fricatives: double the degree of turbulence (as measured by the Reynolds Number) and you approximately multiply the sound-intensity by 4.

We are often less concerned about the actual intensity of a sound than about its relative intensity with respect to another sound, and the sound-intensity scale of *decibels* is a relative scale of this type. Taking the quietest possible sound—a sound which would just be barely audible very close to the ear—as our basic reference point, we measure the intensity of all other sounds in relation to this, in terms of the ratio of the intensity of other sounds to that of the reference sound.

This minimal barely audible reference sound has a sound-pressure of ·0002 dynes/cm^2, and a power, or intensity, of 10^{-16} Watts. In view of the relation between sound-pressure and intensity mentioned above, if we double the sound-pressure we quadruple the intensity; if we multiply the sound-pressure by 10 we multiply the intensity by 100, and so on.

The scale of decibels (db) is logarithmic: that is to say, the decibel scale progresses in steps that are proportional to the powers (in the mathematical sense of, for example, '10 to the 3rd power') of

Table 7

Reference-level: sound pressure ·0002 dynes/cm^2
intensity 10^{-16} watts

ratios

sound-pressure	*intensity*	*decibels*	*examples*
1 : 1	1 : 1	0	threshold of hearing
	10^1 : 1	10	virtual silence
10^1 : 1	10^2 : 1	20	whisper four feet away
	10^3 : 1	30	watch ticking at three feet
10^2 : 1	10^4 : 1	40	quiet street
	10^5 : 1	50	quiet conversation
10^3 : 1	10^6 : 1	60	normal conversation at three feet
	10^7 : 1	70	loud conversation
10^4 : 1	10^8 : 1	80	door slamming
	10^9 : 1	90	busy typing room
10^5 : 1	10^{10} : 1	100	near loud motor horn
	10^{11} : 1	110	pneumatic drill
10^6 : 1	10^{12} : 1	120	near aeroplane engine
	10^{13} : 1	130	threshold of pain

the intensity ratios. Thus an intensity ratio of $10:1 = 10^1$ to $1 = 10$ db, $100:1 = 10^2$ to $1 = 20$ db, $10{,}000:1 = 10^4$ to $1 = 40$ db, and so on.

Table 7 shows a scale of sound-pressure ratios, intensity ratios and decibels, all in relation to the just audible reference sound with a sound-pressure of ·0002 dynes/cm^2, together with a rough indication of the loudness of sound at each step in pressure and intensity. The decibel scale is a scale of physical sound-intensities, not of perceptual loudness. The relation between physical intensity and loudness is not quite simple: the ear, in fact, is a more efficient instrument in the middle frequency range than it is for low (below about 300 Hz) or very high (above about 8000 Hz) frequencies. Moreover, a further complicating factor enters in when judgments of loudness are made not about sounds in general, but specifically about speech sounds. It seems that here, the listener judges what he calls 'loudness' in part, at least, in terms of the physiological effort *he* would have had to make to produce a sound of that perceived 'loudness' (see Ladefoged and McKinney 1963). We can, however, say in a general way that *amplitude* (sound-pressure) and *intensity* (power) are the physical correlates of loudness.

Acoustic Spectrum

So far we have seen only simple sounds such as can be represented by a simple regular wave of the type known as a *sinusoid,* as in

Figure 13. A typical complex wave-form

figures 10, 11, and 12 above. A tuning fork generates a sound-wave of this simple sinusoidal type. The vast majority of sounds, however, are far from simple and their wave-forms must therefore be represented by a complex wavy line, such as is shown in figure 13. A complex wave of this type can be analysed into a number of superimposed simple waves, as in figure 14. Here, the complex wave-form d is the result of superimposing the three simple wave-forms a, b and c. It will be seen that the frequency of the three waves is a 300 Hz, b 200 Hz and c 100 Hz, and their amplitudes are a 15, b 20, c 30.

We can draw lines representing these three component waves on a graph whose horizontal axis represents frequency and whose vertical axis represents amplitude, as in figure 15. Such a graph represents the acoustic spectrum of a sound. It indicates the number and nature of the various partial vibrations that combine to form the total complex oscillation of a complex sound-wave. The spectra of real sounds are generally much more complex than this: for example, figure 16 shows spectra of the vowels [i] and [a]. The distinctive *quality* of a perceived sound, which differentiates it from all other sounds, depends upon its acoustic spectrum. The difference in sound between [i] and [a], for instance, depends on the different ways in which the total acoustic energy is distributed over the frequency scale, as indicated by their different acoustic spectra.

The lowest frequency component in a complex sound-wave—the component with a frequency of 100 Hz in figure 15 for instance—is known as the *fundamental*. Each of the other components in figures 15 and 16 is a *harmonic*, that is, a whole-number multiple of the fundamental. Harmonics are numbered as if the fundamental were in fact harmonic No. 1: thus, the harmonic immediately above the fundamental is the 'second harmonic'. The second harmonic has twice the frequency of the fundamental, the third harmonic has three times the frequency of the fundamental, and so on. For example, for

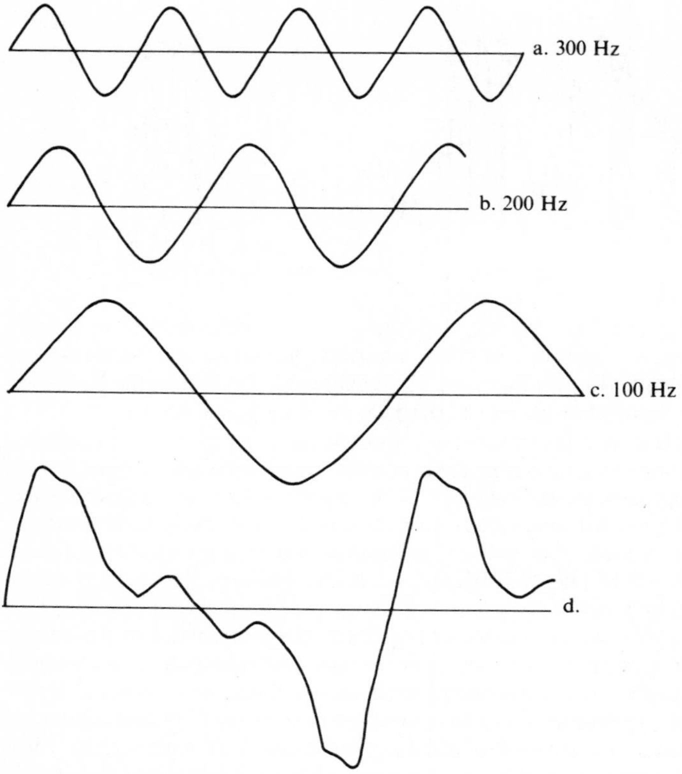

a. 300 Hz

b. 200 Hz

c. 100 Hz

d.

Figure 14. The composition of a complex wave-form

complex waves of fundamental frequencies 120 Hz and 160 Hz, some of the harmonics would be:

fundamental:	120 Hz	160 Hz
2nd harmonic:	240 Hz	320 Hz
3rd harmonic:	360 Hz	480 Hz
4th harmonic:	480 Hz	640 Hz
10th harmonic:	1200 Hz	1600 Hz

Resonance

Many kinds of object, including any enclosed body of air, have a tendency to vibrate at a frequency dependent on various factors, such as the size of the object, or the size and shape of the container of the body of air. We know that if we give a sharp tap to a glass it will give out a 'ping' of a particular pitch, and that the pitch of

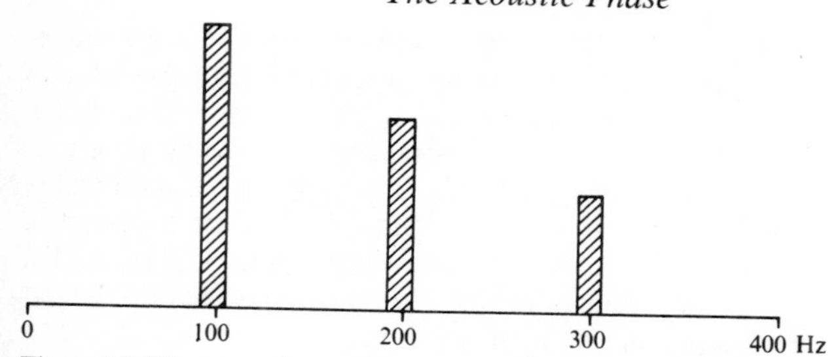

Figure 15. The acoustic spectrum of the complex wave-form of figure 14

this 'ping' will get higher and higher as we pour more and more water into the glass. It is, of course, the vibration of the air in the glass which generates the 'ping', and the frequency of the air vibration gets higher as the volume of air gets smaller.

If we sing or play a note of the same frequency near the glass it will not merely 'ping' as when tapped, but will begin to 'ring' with increasing loudness. What is happening is this: the note we are sounding alongside the glass is sending out a sound-wave, consisting, of course, of alternate pulses, or moments of compression, followed by moments of dilation of air. If the frequency of the note is the same as the natural frequency of the air in the glass, then every new moment of compression will correspond to a moment of compression of the air in the glass, and every new moment of dilation to a moment of dilation. Provided the pushes of the sound-wave arrive at just the right moments they will set the air in the glass vibrating more and more strongly, just as small pushes applied at the right moment to a swing will set it swinging higher and higher.

This is the phenomenon of *resonance,* whereby any body having a natural tendency to vibrate at a certain frequency can be set in

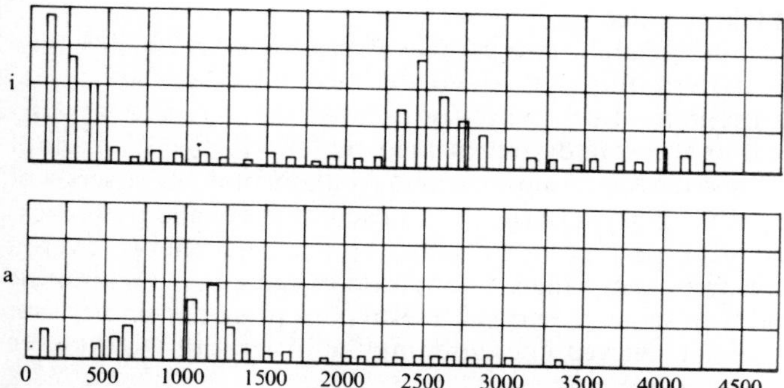

Figure 16. Acoustic spectra of two vowel sounds; after Malmberg *Phonetics* p. 12

vibration by another body vibrating at that frequency; and, moreover, if the actively vibrating source continues, the vibrations induced by resonance will build up in amplitude. It should be noted that a resonator will respond not only to a simple sound-wave (such as that produced by a tuning fork) or to the fundamental of a complex wave, but also to harmonics above the fundamental of a complex wave. Thus, a glass which may resonate to a note sung by a powerful singer may 'ring' to any component of the complex wave produced by the singer provided it is powerful enough.

The part of the vocal tract above the glottis acts as a resonator: it is an air-filled tube about 17 cm long, and, when the glottis is closed, or vibrating as in the production of vowel sounds, it may be regarded as closed at one end and open at the other. In a uniform tube, the lowest resonant frequency equals the frequency of a sound wave four times the length of the tube. The frequency of a sound wave 17×4 ($= 68$) cm in length is about 500 Hz. The tube would have other resonant frequencies which are odd-number multiples of this (1500 Hz, 2500 Hz, 3500 Hz, etc.). In fact, of course, the vocal tract is far from being a uniform tube, and it is constantly changing its shape in speech. It thus acts as a resonator of very variable frequency, and this is important in speech.

The resonating cavities of the vocal tract may also be regarded as acoustic *filters,* which pass, or facilitate the passage of, the particular frequencies to which they are tuned.

Non-repetitive Sound-waves

So far we have dealt with sounds for which the wave-form repeats itself in, for practical purposes, an identical pattern at each cycle. But in speech, waves that do not exactly repeat themselves from cycle to cycle are not uncommon. Such non-repetitive wave-forms occur, for example, when a rapid transition from one sound to another is taking place.

An important class of non-repetitive waves are those which follow no regular pattern at all, in which the molecular oscillations are extremely irregular. Such wave-forms are characteristic of *hiss*-noises, such as the sounds represented by [s] and [ʃ]. We cannot describe such sounds as composed of a fundamental and a series of harmonics of various amplitudes and each of a specific frequency, but rather as a general distribution of acoustic energy over a considerable frequency range. The spectra of these hisses cannot be represented by a series of vertical lines representing harmonics, but rather by a single curved line outlining the general distribution of maxima of acoustic energy.

Figure 17 shows the spectra of [ʃ] and [s]. It will be seen that for

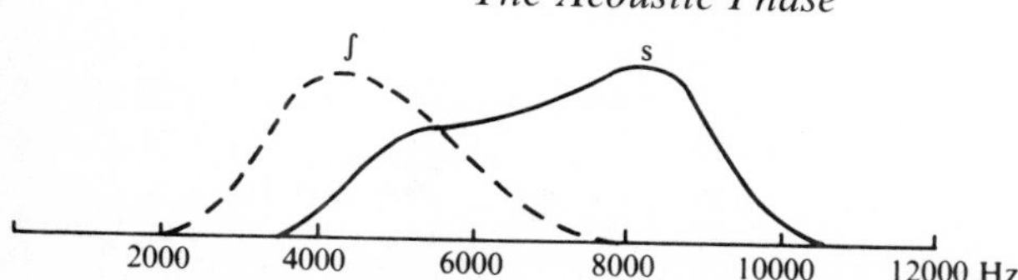

Figure 17. Acoustic spectra of the fricatives [ʃ] and [s]; from Ladefoged *Elements of Acoustic Phonetics*

[s] most of the energy is in the range of about 6000 to 9000 Hz, while for [ʃ] it is concentrated rather in the range of 3000 to 5000 Hz. Consequently [s] is heard as a higher pitched hiss than [ʃ].

Acoustics of Speech

From the acoustic point of view, the vocal tract functions as both a *generator* of sounds and a system of variable *resonators* that respond to frequencies in the generated sounds.

As a generator, the vocal tract operates in two ways: on the one hand, by setting up small articulatory channels for fricatives, hiss-noises are generated by turbulent air-flow through these channels; on the other hand, by releasing the air in high-velocity bursts through the vibrating vocal folds, the complex sound of *voice* is generated. In *voiced fricatives*, both types of sound co-exist.

The resonators respond to both types of excitation, hiss and voice, but generally with more sharply-tuned resonances—a greater concentration of acoustic energy into particular frequency bands—in voiced sounds, particularly vowels, which we will discuss first.

There are two ways of viewing the production of vowel-sounds in the vocal tract. One is to regard the powerful high-velocity bursts of air which shoot upwards into the pharynx at every opening of the vibrating vocal folds as a rapid series of 'taps' given to the vocal tract resonators: the resonator thus 'rings' at its natural frequency, which is determined by its size and shape. On this view, the rapid air-jets that constitute voice would themselves provide only the fundamental frequency, and set the resonators 'ringing' at *their* frequencies.

The other view is that the vocal-tract resonator acts as an acoustic filter, selectively reinforcing certain frequencies present in the complex wave-form of voice. The net result of the superposition of the vocal tract resonator upon the sound of voice is that each specific vowel-sound (and some other sounds) is characterized by an acoustic spectrum with peaks at a number of points on the frequency scale. The location of the peaks varies from one vowel to another. The spectral peaks, or frequency bands, where the acoustic energy is concentrated, are known as *formants*. Each vowel is characterized

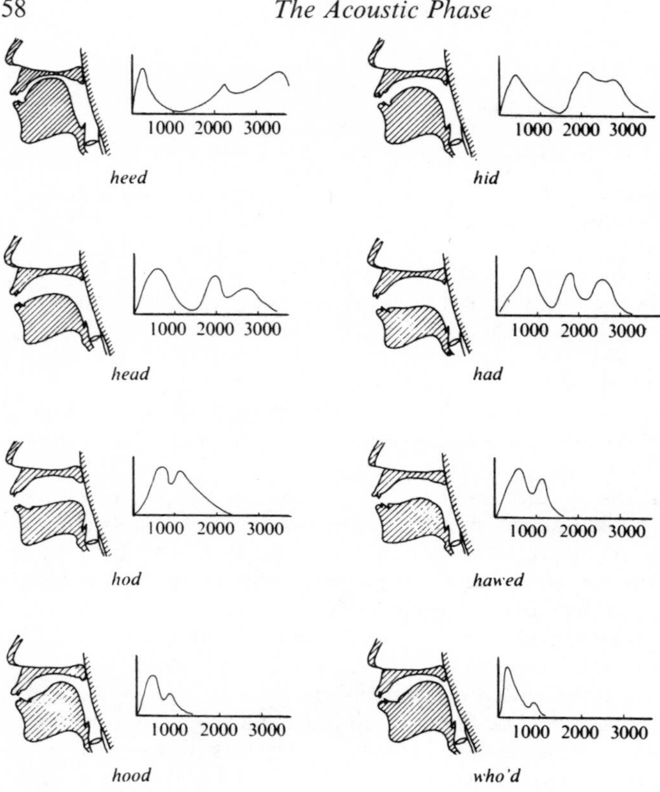

Figure 18. The position of the vocal organs and the spectra of the vowel sounds in the words *heed, hid, head, had, hod, hawed, hood, who'd*; from Ladefoged *Elements of Acoustic Phonetics* pp. 96–7

by a series of such formants, of which the lowest three are most important for the identification of specific vowels. This second view is the more generally accepted one.

Figure 18, from Ladefoged 1962 (pp. 96–7), shows spectra for a number of English vowels, the horizontal axis being calibrated in Hz, the vertical, uncalibrated axis representing amplitude. Accompanying the spectra are drawings (based on X-rays) of the position of the vocal organs for the various vowels. Table 8, which shows the average frequencies of the first three formants (F1, F2, F3) of English vowels, is taken from Denes and Pinson 1963. (Denes and Pinson's table 7.1).[2]

Figure 19 shows another way of displaying vowel formants. These are means of the men's and women's first and second formants from

Table 8

	ee	I	e	ae	ah	aw	U	oo	A	er
	First formant frequency									
male	270	390	530	660	730	570	440	300	640	490
female	310	430	610	860	850	590	470	370	760	500
	Second formant frequency									
male	2290	1990	1840	1720	1090	840	1020	870	1190	1350
female	2790	2480	2330	2050	1220	920	1160	950	1400	1640
	Third formant frequency									
male	3010	2550	2480	2410	2440	2410	2240	2240	2390	1690
female	3310	3070	2990	2850	2810	2710	2610	2670	2780	1960

the above table. The vertical axis represents frequencies from 0 to 3000 Hz, and the horizontal axis represents time; the diagram may thus be thought of as showing the first and second formants of a series of vowels spoken one after the other. This manner of representing vowel formants resembles the display of a *sound spectrograph,* an instrument that marks a sheet of special paper in such a way that the horizontal scale represents time, and the vertical scale frequency, the lightness or darkness of the trace indicating amplitude.

As figure 19 shows, different vowel-sounds are clearly distinguished from each other by the location, on the frequency scale, of the first and second bands of concentration of acoustic energy—the first and second formants. Other formants, particularly the third, also play a part in determining vowel quality. However, the first and second formants are such obviously important characteristics that it is useful to plot vowels on a two-dimensional chart in which the vertical and horizontal axes represent the first and second formants

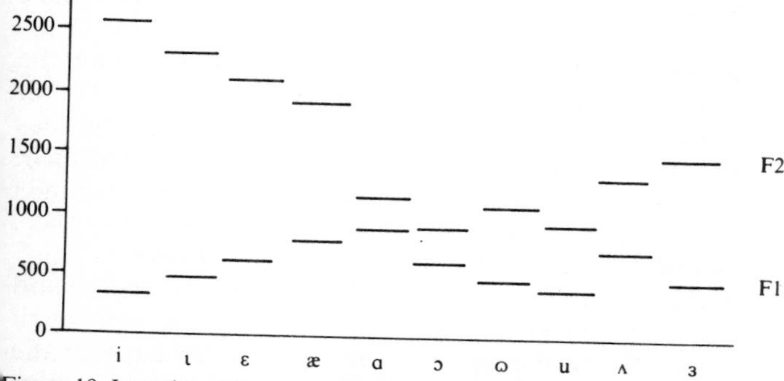

Figure 19. Location of formants for some English vowel-sounds

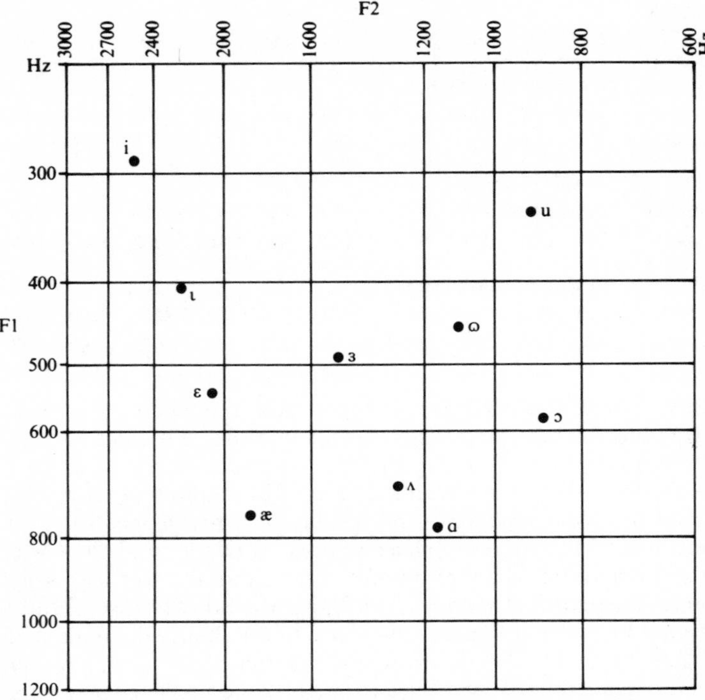

Figure 20. The English vowels of figure 19 on a two-dimensional formant chart

respectively, as in figure 20. Here, the frequencies of the first and second formant are represented on logarithmic scales, and these are disposed the way they are because in this arrangement the relative positions of the plotted vowels correspond rather well with traditional vowel-charts based on auditory or articulatory characteristics. On this compare Chapter 9.

Vowels are most commonly voiced, that is, produced with the vocal folds vibrating. They can, however, be voiceless or whispered. In whisper the turbulent flow of air through the glottis generates a hiss—a non-repetitive sound-wave of the type already described. The air in the resonating chambers of the throat and mouth responds selectively to whisper in much the same way as it does to voice, so that the qualities of vowels are still apparent in whisper.

Hiss noises (for example, *fricative* consonants, like [s] and [ʃ] and the hiss of whisper) are generated by turbulent air-flow through various channels. When the source of the hiss is far back in the vocal tract, as in whisper or in a velar fricative [x], the non-repetitive sound-wave passing through the filter system has some of its frequencies emphasized. Consequently such hiss-sounds show a good deal of formant shaping. Hisses produced in the front of the mouth, such as [s] or [f] generally show less concentration of acoustic energy into formant bands. However, if the overall intensity of the hiss-noise is weak, some formant shaping may be seen even with those articulated in the front of the mouth. Thus sounds like [f], and [θ] (as in *thin*), are often of rather low intensity and show some formant bands.

Many consonants are characterised acoustically to a great extent by noise of various kinds, for example, as we have just seen, the fricatives, and also the release sound of stops, which consists of a very brief burst of noise. Consonants are characterised, however, in another way as well: the transitions to and from the articulatory position of a consonant entail rapid changes in the mouth shape, and consequently in the resonant frequency of the mouth cavity. As a result, consonants are also characterised by the bending or 'warping' of vowel formants in their neighbourhood. Thus, though the vowel [ɩ] has characteristic values for F1 and F2, such words as *bib, did* and *gig* exhibit warpings of the formants at the beginning and end of the vowel that are characteristic of the particular consonants, and serve to distinguish these words from each other acoustically and auditorily.

It is possible to hear some of the resonant frequencies of the vocal tract in a number of ways.

First, produce a prolonged [ŋ] sound—that is, the sound of the *dorso-velar nasal* which occurs at the end of such a word as *long*—with the back of the tongue up against the soft palate, which is lowered to let the (voiced) air-stream pass out through the nose. Produce a very prolonged [ŋ], and while doing so change the shape of the lips. For example, start with the lips very closely rounded, forming a very small round hole. Slowly widen the lip aperture till it is fully open. If you keep the [ŋ] sounding loudly during all this time you will hear a little, clear, bell-like *arpeggio* as different resonant frequencies become audible.

Secondly, you can hear the first formant of a number of vowel-sounds in the following way. Close the glottis and, while holding the glottis closed, put the mouth into position for a vowel, say [æ] as in *had*. Now, flick a finger against the throat, preferably at the level of the thyroid cartilage, just to the side of the Adam's apple. You should hear a clear, sharp tone ring out. If you don't, it may mean that your glottis is not closed, so try again making sure that the glottis is tightly closed and that there is a clear passageway from the glottis through the mouth, that is, that the tongue is genuinely in position for a vowel, and not making contact with the roof of the mouth, as for [ŋ]. Now go through the series of vowels shown in figure 20, shaping the mouth for each, but keeping the glottis closed. You should hear the pitch of the 'glottal percussion' note rising as you pass from [i] to [a], falling from [ɔ] to [u], going up again for [ʌ] and then down again for [ɜ]. In fact, what you should hear is the first formant of all these vowels, in the relative positions on the frequency scale as shown in figure 20.

Finally, in order to hear the second formant, try whispering the same set of vowels. As you whisper [i, ɩ, ɛ, æ] the descending pitch of the note should be clearly audible, following the descending frequency of the second formant of these vowels. The whisper-pitch of the second formant of the other vowels is somewhat less clear; but with a little perseverance and practice it can be heard.

It is interesting to note that in 1921 Sir Richard Paget determined the frequencies of the first and second formants of the vowels of English (and later of other languages) by these techniques (Paget 1922 and 1930). Not only did Paget *hear* the formants by these non-instrumental means, which any one can do, but he also established their frequencies in a non-instrumental manner, which he later described thus: 'The work required no appliances but pencil and paper, for though I have not got the faculty of recognizing instinctively the "absolute pitch" of any musical sound, I can always identify any note—within less than a semitone—by mentally comparing it with a fixed note which I literally carry in my head. This head-note is a ♯g″ of about 812 vibrations per second . . . which I hear on tapping my skull just above either ear. Another independent head-note ♭″966～—three semi-tones higher than the first—is heard when I tap the centre of my forehead. These head-notes, which apparently are due to vibrations of portions of the skull, constitute two natural tuning forks, of seemingly invariable pitch, which I have used as my standard throughout these investigations' (Paget 1930, pp. 40–1).

The formant frequencies established by Paget are precisely (well within the limits of personal variation) those established twenty to thirty years later by instrumental means. Others have done excellent work on vowel formants in this and similar ways, as indicated in Svend Smith (1947). However, it is more usual nowadays to make use of the considerable amount of instrumentation that is available for acoustic analysis.

Here we have presented only the barest outline of Acoustic Phonetics. For more detailed information the reader is referred to specialized books such as Joos (1948), Ladefoged (1962), Chapter 2 of Ladefoged (1967), and Lehiste (1967).

FIVE

Initiation

Sounds can be generated in the vocal tract in a number of different ways. For example, one can clash the teeth together, or, pressing the upper and lower teeth together, and moving the jaw from side to side, one can scrape the teeth together making the unpleasant sound known as 'grinding the teeth'. Another type of sound is generated by suddenly slapping two organs together, or snapping them apart. For instance, by rapidly opening and shutting the mouth in such a way as to slap the lips together and then snap them apart, one can produce quite loud sounds. Similarly, if one raises the tip of the tongue and curls it backwards, then lets it slap down suddenly on the floor of the mouth, quite a loud 'plop' is produced. Such sounds as these have been termed 'percussives', and for some discussion of them see Pike (1943, pp. 103–5).

Apart from some trivial cases such as those just mentioned, all humanly produced vocal sounds involve two basic components: *initiation* and *articulation,* and many involve a third component, *phonation.* In this chapter we examine initiation in some detail.

By *initiation* we mean a bellows-like or piston-like movement of an organ or organ-group (an initiator), which generates positive or negative pressure in the part of the vocal tract adjacent to it, that is, between the initiator and the place of articulation. The term 'initiation' is used for this component of speech production since it is the activity that 'initiates' the flow of air essential for the production of almost all sounds.

The immediate result of the movement of an initiator is to change the volume of part of the vocal tract adjacent to it, and it is this volume change which causes the change of air pressure there (cf. Boyle's law in Chapter 3). One parameter of initiation is thus *direction*. The initiatory movement may be such as to *decrease* the adjacent vocal-tract volume and thus generate *positive* pressure—this is compressive, or more simply, *pressure* initiation. Or the initiatory movement may be such as to *increase* the tract volume and thus generate *negative* pressure—that is, rarefactive, or more simply, *suction* initiation.

The result of pressure initiation is normally to set air flowing upwards and outwards in the vocal tract, and pressure initiation has thus been called 'egressive'. Suction initiation, on the other hand, normally sets air flowing inwards and downwards in the vocal tract, and has thus been called 'ingressive' (Pike 1943). The terms 'egressive' and 'ingressive', however, as names for the basic initiatory types themselves have proved to be misleading, as will become apparent in our discussion of *voiced glottalic suction* sounds below. In this book, therefore, I use the terms 'egressive' and 'ingressive' only to refer to actual directions of air-flow outwards or inwards in the vocal tract. For the basic initiation types themselves I use the older terms (Catford 1939) 'pressure' and 'suction'.[1]

Pressure and suction types of initiation refer in fact to opposite ends of a continuous parameter, or scale, of *initiator velocity* on which pressure implies positive rates of volume *decrease* (generating positive pressure) and suction implies negative rates of volume decrease (generating negative pressure), that is, rates of volume *increase*. The phonetically important concepts of initiator velocity and initiator power are discussed below.

The second major parameter of initiation is *location:* the initiatory activity may be carried out by various organs, notably the lungs (*pulmonic*), the larynx (*glottalic*), by a variety of organs in the mouth (*oralic*), but most importantly by the tongue, forming an airtight closure with the soft palate or velum (*velaric*), and finally, the oesophagus (*oesophagic*). Oesophagic initiation is used involuntarily in belching, and as a substitute for pulmonic initiation by persons whose larynx has been surgically removed or sealed, and will not be further dealt with here. The only initiatory locations of serious anthropophonic importance are *pulmonic, glottalic, velaric.*

In table 9 we may thus sum up the major types of initiation. Those initiation types which are known to be regularly utilized in languages for the initiation of linguistically relevant sound types, or phonemes, are italicised. Of these, *pulmonic pressure*

Table 9

location	direction	
	compressive	rarefactive
lungs	*pulmonic pressure*	pulmonic suction
larynx	*glottalic pressure*	*glottalic suction*
mouth	velaric pressre	*velaric suction*

initiation occurs in all languages, *glottalic pressure* initiation is widespread, *glottalic suction* somewhat rarer, and *velaric suction* is used for regular linguistically relevant sounds in a few languages of Africa.

Pulmonic suction and velaric pressure, with one exception, are not known to be linguistically utilized in the languages of the world.

The greatest variety of initiation types in any one language is apparently to be found in Damin, ritual language of the Lardil, a people of Mornington Island, N. Queensland, Australia. I am informed by Professor Kenneth Hale of MIT that in addition to pulmonic pressure initiation, which is normally the only initiation type in Australian languages, Damin has glottalic pressure and velaric suction sounds, as do some other, non-Australian, languages. In addition to this, Damin has a pulmonic suction [l] and a velaric pressure type of [p]: these are unique in the world, so far as we know. So unusual does this ritual language appear that we may perhaps hypothesize that its sound system is a deliberately invented one.

It is clear that *pulmonic* initiation types involve, with only one exception, an air column between the initiator and the articulator, which passes through the larynx, and they can consequently be combined with phonation. The exception is glottal stop, in which the glottis is tightly closed to form the articulation, and cannot simultaneously have a phonatory function. *Velaric* initiation types, on the other hand, utilize only air within the mouth: they are completely cut off from the larynx and are thus always phonationless, although, of course, they may be performed simultaneously with a pulmonic sound which *is* phonated. Thus, when one performs a series of *tut-tut* [ʇʇ] sounds while humming through the nose, one is simultaneously producing unphonated velaric suction [ʇ] and phonated pulmonic pressure [ŋ].

The status of *glottalic* initiation with respect to phonation is more complex, since the initiatory movement here is performed by the larynx itself, with the glottis closed. But the glottis may either be tightly closed, or more loosely closed—disposed, in other words, for the production of voice. In the first case, we have unphonated glottalic sounds, such as the glottalic pressure stops [p', t', k']; in the second case we have voiced glottalic sounds, such as the voiced glottalic suction stops [ɓ, ɗ, ɠ]. The question of voicing in relation to both glottalic and pulmonic sounds, particularly stops, is discussed below.

Meanwhile, we survey more generally the various types of initiation.

Pulmonic Initiation

Pulmonic Pressure. The initiator is the lungs, which decrease in volume, generating positive pressure in the whole subglottal vocal tract, and, if the glottis is open so that there is no obstruction in the larynx, throughout the whole vocal tract. The positive pressure in the lungs tends to initiate an egressive air-flow up the trachea, through the larynx and out of the mouth and/or nose.

The volume of air upon which the pulmonic initiator operates is, of course, the full capacity of the vocal tract, varying from, say 2000 to 5000 cm^3. This means that, with an average initiator velocity (rate of lung-volume decrease) of, say, 200 cm^3/s, generating an egressive volume-flow of the same long-time average value, the pulmonic initiator can in theory keep speech going for about ten to twenty-five seconds, although in fact it is seldom in actual conversation, or even lecturing, that anyone talks as long as this without taking breath. Normally, speakers utilize between 500 and 1000 cm^3 between breaths, and this means, at normal initiator velocities of 100 cm^3 to 300 cm^3, duration of 'breath-groups' of the order of two to ten seconds.

The pulmonic initiator can develop very high positive pressures, up to 180 cmH_2O, as we saw in Chapter 3. However, the pulmonic pressures generated in normal speech generally range between about 1 and 12 cmH_2O, going up to 40 cmH_2O only in 'parade-ground shouting'.

It should be noted that although the flow generated in the lower vocal tract by pulmonic pressure initiation is necessarily egressive, nevertheless, the final flow of the air-stream at the exit from the mouth is also affected by articulatory movements. These articulatory movements superimpose velocities upon the basic initiator velocity, some of which may be negative. Thus, let us suppose the pulmonic initiator is steadily pushing air up the trachea and through the mouth at 200 cm^3/s. A sudden opening up of the mouth cavity, say from a strongly 'velarized' [ɫ] (with the tongue bunched up to fill a good deal of the mouth space) to an 'open' *a*-type vowel, may occur at a rate of, say, 300 cm^3/s. Since this is a volume increase it will tend to generate an ingressive flow of -300 cm^3/s, and this negative flow of -300 cm^3/s superimposed on the basic positive initiatory flow of 200 cm^3/s will naturally lead to a momentary actual, measured, ingressive flow of -100 cm^3/s. In instrumental phonetic work one must always be alert to the important distinction between the component of flow-velocity that is derived from the basic initiatory movement, and the component of the velocity that is superimposed upon it by articulatory movements.

The actual range of pulmonic pressure initiator-velocities in speech is quite large, ranging from occasional zeros (during voiceless stop consonants; of course, *some* compressive initiator movement normally occurs here, although the initiator may come to rest before the release of the stop) through a value of about 50 cm^3/s, which generates the minimal flow for the production of chest voice, to norms of 150–350 cm^3/s during speech with peaks at 1000 cm^3/s or more during [h] sounds, and the release of voiceless 'aspirated' stops, such as the [p^h] [t^h] [k^h] before stressed vowels of many types of English.

Pulmonic pressure initiation is controlled by the muscles involved in breathing. As Draper et al. (1960) have shown, the particular muscles involved vary according to the fullness of the lungs. Just after an inspiration, when they are relatively full, the lungs collapse under the weight of the rib-cage and the elasticity of the dilated tissues. At this stage, in speech, the external intercostal muscles—normally regarded as muscles of inspiration—may act to retard the rate of lung-volume decrease. Later, the internal intercostals come into play, to actively compress the lungs by squeezing the ribs together. Finally, when the lungs are more nearly empty, other muscles, notably the diaphragm and abdominal muscles may come into action to force the remaining air out of the lungs. Thus in pulmonic pressure initiation, the initiator operates by 'gravity drive' when the lungs are nearly full, muscle power being used only for 'braking'; when the lungs are more nearly empty, positive 'muscle drive' takes over.

The articulation occurring with pulmonic pressure initiation may be at the glottis, for glottal stop [ʔ] or for [h] sounds regarded as *glottal fricatives*, or at any point above this. Glottal stop is naturally phonationless, since here the (closed) glottis is functioning as articulator, not as phonator. (On the question of 'voiced h' see next chapter.) All other pulmonic pressure sounds involve a column of air passing through the glottis, and are therefore subject to phonatory modifications of any type. (On the special problems of pulmonic and glottalic *voiced stops* see pp. 73–77.)

The anthropophonic distribution of pulmonic pressure sounds is universal. Most sounds in all languages have this type of initiation. This is not surprising since, as we have seen, pulmonic initiation makes use of a large volume of air, which allows one to talk for relatively long periods without having to stop and 'recharge' the initiator with air. And the vocal folds, by their shape, present converging, nozzle-like, surfaces to air-flow from below, but present flat surfaces, at right angles to the flow, to airflow from above. They are, consequently, better adapted to the egressive flow of pulmonic pressure than the ingressive flow of pulmonic suction.

Pulmonic Suction. The initiator is, again, the lungs, which have to be emptied, or partially emptied, before the inhalatory pulmonic suction initiation begins. The volumes, pressures, initiator-velocities and volume-flows involved are much the same as for pulmonic pressure, except that now we have negative pressure and velocities (and note that the absolute maximum inspiratory pressure that can be generated in the vocal tract is somewhat lower than maximum expiratory pressure, being about 100 cm H_2O—see Rahn et al. 1946).

In practice, pulmonic suction is rarely used in speech. Occasionally, in rapid *sotto voce* counting, we may alternate between pulmonic pressure and pulmonic suction initiation, following the regular egressive–ingressive rhythm of breathing; and pulmonic suction initiation is also used occasionally in saying the words *yes* and *no*. In the first, the [ɟɛ-] is ingressive (suction), the [s] egressive (pressure); *no*, however, may be entirely ingressive. Dieth (1950) describes the Swiss-German custom of 'Fensterle', whereby a village boy speaks to his sweetheart through her window, disguising his voice from her parents by using pulmonic suction initiation.

Pulmonic suction initiation, as indicated above, does not accord well with the shape of the vocal folds. Consequently, it is impossible to produce good pulmonic suction voiced sounds; a 'croaking' type of inverse voice can, however, be produced with pulmonic suction.

The reader should now experiment with the production of a wide range of voiceless, voiced and whispered pulmonic pressure and suction sounds.

Glottalic Initiation

Glottalic Pressure. For glottalic initiation the initiator is the larynx. In the simplest case, that of unphonated glottalic pressure initiation, the glottis is tightly closed, and the larynx is jerked upwards by action of the extrinsic laryngeal muscles, which attach the larynx to the hyoid bone and other structures above it. There may, in addition, be some secondary sphincteric compression of the pharynx.

The volume of air upon which the glottalic initiator operates is the relatively small quantity contained between the glottis and some stricture in the mouth. As we saw in Chapter 3, this volume is of the order of 100 cm^3. Since upward or downward movements of the larynx can easily change the volume of the supralaryngeal cavities by 5 to 7 cm^3 it is clear that quite high pressures can be generated by glottalic initiation. For instance, given a volume of, say, 140 cm^3 contained between the glottis and the lips, it is easy to calculate (by formula 1a given in Chapter 3) that a reduction of 6 cm^3 will generate an intra-oral pressure of 48 cm H_2O. Pressures of precisely this order of magnitude have been recorded in the production of energetic glottalic pressure stops, in the laboratory. It is probable, however, that in languages where glottalic pressure sounds regularly occur, the upward larynx movement is quite small, and much lower pressures are generated, not far in excess of those generated in pulmonic pressure initiation.

A number of different types of articulation can be combined with glottalic pressure initiation, and the reader should now practise making various stop and fricative articulations with glottalic pressure initiation. Then say the glottalic pressure stops [k', t', p'], and after that, forming very narrow fricative articulation channels so that the small quantity of available air is not immediately exhausted, say the glottalic pressure fricatives [f', s', ʃ']. Now try to say [k'] followed immediately by a vowel, thus [k'a]. At first, you will probably have to release the articulatory closure [k'] some considerable time before you release the glottal closure [ʔ], so that you are saying [k' . . . ʔa]. Take care to hold the breath (maintain the glottal closure) throughout the formation and release of the [k'] closure, only releasing the glottal closure later into the vowel [a]. Try to shorten the time-interval between release of the articulatory [k']-closure and the initiatory [ʔ]-closure, until they are almost, but not quite, simultaneous. Repeat this same exercise with [t', p'] and [f', s', ʃ'].

When a glottalic pressure sound occurs in the stream of speech it is, of course, accompanied by a glottal closure; this glottal closure is released only after the release of the articulatory oral closure. Thus, in a sequence such as [p'a], the rather 'hollow' sounding 'pop' on release of the glottalic pressure stop [p'] is heard a moment before the glottal closure is released, in the form of an abrupt start of voicing. The interval between the articulatory release and the following release of the glottal closure in 'real languages' is quite variable, and appears to be language-specific. Halle and Stevens (1971) in a paper on laryngeal features (referred to again in Chapter 6) state that 'there is a delay of 50-odd ms before the adducting glottal musculature can be relaxed and the glottis can assume a configuration appropriate for the onset of vocal-cord vibration'. This suggests that a delay of 50 ms is an anthropophonic universal, based on a physiological constraint. The empirical facts, however, do not support this view. Gaprindashvili (1966), for instance, reports variations from 16 to 60 ms for this interval in dialects of Dargi, a Caucasian language of Dagestan. My own data on a dozen or so Caucasian languages show even greater variation for the average duration of the interval between the glottal and oral release in glottalic pressure sounds, ranging from only 12 ms in Abkhaz, through 28 ms in Kabardian, and 70 ms in Chechen, to about 100 ms in Avar and in the Bzhedukh dialect of Adyghe.

Glottalic pressure sounds have been known by a number of names. British phoneticians commonly call them 'ejectives', and the term 'recursive' has also been used in English, French and German. In Russian they are often termed *abruptivnye,* 'abruptives', or else, sounds *s nadgortannym pridyxatel'nom,* 'with supraglottal aspiration'. American writers most commonly use the term 'glottalized'. This last is an unfortunate term since in phonetic terminology adjectives ending in *-ized* normally refer to secondary articulation. It is misleading to use such a term to describe instead an initiation type, which is one of the basic components of speech production. Such inconsistency in scientific terminology is not to be recommended. Moreover, having pre-empted the term 'glottalized' for a basic initiation type, it is no longer available for possible use in the sense of 'with some kind of glottal modification'.[2] On this see further under 'Multiple and Modified Articulation', Chapter 10. Jacobson, Fant and Halle (1952) used the term 'checked' for glottalic pressure sounds, but are apparently under a misapprehension about the nature of these.[3]

Glottalic pressure sounds are quite common in the languages of the world. In English they occasionally occur as the realization of final [p, t, k] in pathological speech, and in some northern English dialects. They are also an occasional realization of final [p, t, k] in French. Other Indo-European languages in which they occur regularly are Ossetic (an Iranian language spoken in the Caucasus) and some dialects of eastern Armenian (although in educated Erevan speech they seem to be simply 'unaspirated' voiceless [p, t, k]). They also occur in Gujerati and some other Indian languages. They are characteristic of all thirty-seven Caucasian languages (for example, Georgian, Circassian, Chechen, Awar) and are found sporadically in numerous languages of East Asia. In Africa they occur in Amharic and other Ethiopic languages, and also in many other languages throughout the continent. Finally, they are to be found in many languages in all parts of the American continent.

Glottalic pressure initiation can be applied effectively to all the narrower types of articulation. Although only stops, affricates, and fricatives initiated by glottalic pressure seem to occur as regular phonemic norms in languages, glottalic pressure trills occasionally occur as variants of normal pulmonic trills in a glottalic environment, at least in Caucasian languages.

Glottalic Suction. Unphonated glottalic suction initiation is simply the converse of glottalic pressure. There is an articulatory stricture in the mouth, and the larynx, with glottis tightly closed, is jerked downwards, rarefying the air contained between the initiator and the articulatory stricture.

The reader, having mastered glottalic pressure stops and fricatives, should now produce glottalic suction stops. Probably the easiest way to do this is to alternate *pressure–suction–pressure–suction:* having, for instance, raised the closed glottis and released the [k']-closure for glottalic pressure [k'] one should immediately re-form the [k']-closure, taking care to keep the glottis closed, and jerk the larynx down again, releasing the [k]-closure as it nears the end of its descent, producing glottalic suction [k̂'].

Alternate in this way:

[k'–k̂'–k'–k̂']
[t'–t̂'–t'–t̂']
[p'–p̂'–p'–p̂']

Now try to pronounce glottalic suction [p̂', t̂'] and [k̂'] in isolation, and finally, followed by a vowel : [p̂'ɑ, t̂'ɑ, k̂'ɑ]. Note, here, that the vowel is a normal pulmonic pressure sound: beginners sometimes get confused, and having produced a glottalic suction stop try to carry on with some kind of ingressive vowel.

Unphonated glottalic suction sounds have been reported as occurring in Tojolabal, a language of Guatemala (Pike 1967), but are clearly very rare—much rarer than the voiced glottalic suction sounds dealt with below.

Oralic Initiation

Within the mouth, pressure and suction can be generated in a number of ways: for example, if the lower lip is inclined somewhat inwards over the lower teeth, and if the tip and rim of the tongue are placed low down against the inner side of the lower lip, and then slid upwards, negative pressure is generated between the underside of the tongue and the inner part of the lower lip, and when the tongue finally breaks away from the lower lip a 'labio-sublingualic-suction stop' is heard. Again, holding the teeth about 1 cm apart, one can expand the tongue so that it squeezes out sideways between the teeth and makes contact with the inner cheeks roughly from near the canine to the molar teeth. If the tongue is then suddenly laterally contracted, it breaks away from the cheek with a 'tongue-cheek' or 'linguo-genalic' suction stop. These, and other minor initiatory mechanisms, which the reader can probably find by experiment, are anthropophonically trivial. The only oralic initiation types of any significance are *velaric,* and of these, departing from our practice in this chapter, we will discuss velaric *suction* initiation first.

Velaric Suction. The reader should experiment by saying the *tut-tut* sound [ʇʇ] a number of times, slowly, deliberately, and introspectively, and preferably while watching his mouth in a mirror. He should try to feel for himself where the tip of the tongue is, and where the back of the tongue is, and in general what is happening in [ʇ]. It should not be difficult to discover that [ʇ] starts with the tip of the tongue making airtight contact with the gums behind the upper teeth, and with the back of the tongue making airtight contact with the soft palate. There is thus a small airtight chamber between the surface of the tongue and the vault of the palate. Next, the central part of the tongue is drawn downwards a little, and this is marked kinaesthetically by a slight feeling of strain and suction. The little chamber has, in fact, been enlarged, generating a considerable negative pressure. Finally, the tip of the tongue is pulled downwards off the gums, and there is the implosive sound of the release of a suction stop.

Another experiment can be carried out with a bilabial velaric suction stop, a kind of perfunctory kiss. The lips are closed—they may be pouted as for a kiss, but this is not essential—the back of the tongue makes airtight contact with the soft palate. The tongue, maintaining this contact, moves back a little, enlarging the cavity between tongue and lips, and generating negative pressure there. When the lip contact is broken, there is the implosive sound of the release of a velaric suction stop.

In general, then, a velaric suction sound involves an *initiatory closure* between the back of the tongue and the soft palate, or velum, and an *articulatory closure* further forward in the mouth. A downward and/or backward movement of the centre of the tongue generates negative pressure, and an ingressive air-flow when the articulatory closure is released. Various types of stop and affricate articulation are possible with velaric suction initiation.

A velaric suction type of initiation is used by pipe-smokers drawing smoke into their mouths. Velaric suction is also used in kissing, not only the perfunctory 'smacking' type of kiss described above, but also in prolonged, silent, kissing. It is also used as indicated in the *tut-tut* [ʇʇ] that signifies concern, or regret in Western Europe, and the similar, single [ʇ] which is part of a gesture of negation in the Eastern Mediterranean region and the Near East. Another well-known velaric suction sound is the 'lateral click'—the velaric suction [tl]-like sound, phonetic symbol [ʖ], sometimes used in Western Europe to urge on horses.

The only languages in which velaric suction sounds, known as 'clicks', occur as regular elements in the structure of words in everyday speech are Sandawe and Hadzapi of Tanzania, and Bushman, Hottentot, Xosa and Zulu of southern Africa. Indeed the name of one of these languages, Xosa, begins with a lateral click [ʖoːsa]; but note the special case of Damin mentioned above.

When velaric suction stops are integrated into the normal pulmonic pressure stream of speech, as in the African 'click'-using languages, they necessarily involve a kind of hiatus in the pulmonic pressure initiatory mechanism, and a secondary release of the velaric closure before the main-stream pulmonic initiation can resume (just as unphonated glottalic sounds involve a subsequent glottal release). As a matter of fact, velaric suction 'clicks' are often accompanied by some kind of pulmonic or glottalic sound: that is, the dorso-velar closure which has an initiatory function with respect to the velaric suction 'click', may have an articulatory function with respect to the simultaneous pulmonic or glottalic sound. Thus, a velaric suction [ʇ] for instance, may be accompanied by a pulmonic pressure [k, g, ŋ] or even [ʔ], or a glottalic pressure [k'], and this *inner* articulation will be released almost simultaneously with, but slightly subsequent to, the release of the *outer* articulation (of the velaric sound). Thus Beach (1938) describes for Hottentot (Nama dialect) twenty click phonemes, which involve only four different velaric suction sounds ('influxes' in Beach's terms), but five different pulmonic or glottalic pressure inner sounds ('effluxes' in Beach's terms).

Velaric Pressure. Clearly, if the organic position for one of the sounds mentioned above is assumed, and the tongue is moved in such a way as to decrease rather than increase the volume of the space between the initiatory and articulatory closures, then a velaric pressure sound is generated. Such sounds are rare, and are not known to occur as regular sounds in any ordinary language. A bilabial velaric pressure stop (lips closed, slightly pursed; tongue back against velum; forward tongue-movement, air compression, and slight explosive release of articulatory labial closure) sometimes accompanies a raising of the eyebrows, a shrug of the shoulders, and an outward turning of the palms of the hands as part of a western European (sp. French) gesture of dismissal, or self-exculpation.

Voiced Glottalic and Pulmonic Stops

So far we have considered only unphonated glottalic sounds—those glottalic sounds from which phonation is excluded because they are produced with the glottis tightly closed. It is, however, possible to produce glottalic suction sounds, particularly stops, which are voiced. Such sounds are commonly called *voiced implosives,* and are represented by the phonetic symbols [ɓ, ɗ, ɠ], and so on. There are important similarities and differences between the mechanism of *voiced implosives* and *voiced plosives* (that is, voiced pulmonic pressure stops), and for that reason we will discuss both here, beginning with the pulmonic sounds.

In order to produce normal *voice* it is necessary to have a pressure difference of about 2 cm H_2O or more across the glottis, the subglottal pressure being higher. This ensures an upward, egressive, air-flow through the vibrating vocal folds. If the pressure difference is less than 2 cmH_2O the glottal vibrations, and the flow, will cease. Now, if there is a complete closure in the mouth, say at the lips, as for [b], then as the air flows up through the glottis into the pharynx and mouth, the pressure in the mouth will rapidly rise, so that the transglottal pressure difference of 2 cmH_2O or more will be abolished. It is easy to show that, unless something is done about it, the flow will cease very quickly. For instance, let us assume a supraglottal volume behind the lips of 140 cm^3/s at the moment when the labial closure is formed. Since the air cannot escape from the mouth, the flow will rapidly drop to zero. We can posit an average flow, then, of somewhat less than half-way between 150 cm^3/s and zero—say 50 cm^3/s. Now let us further assume that the intra-oral pressure is atmospheric (0) at the moment when the [b]-closure is made, and that the subglottal pressure is quite high, say 10 cmH_2O. It is clear that the transglottal flow will cease when the supraglottal pressure reaches 8 cmH_2O. By formula 1d (Chapter 3) we find that this will occur when 1·1 cm^3 of air have flowed up into the supraglottal cavity, and, at 50 cm^3/s this will take about 20 ms, or only two cycles of vocal fold vibration at 100 Hz. This, in fact, is a conservative estimate: with lower subglottal pressure or faster flow the critical pressure will be reached even sooner.

It is clear that, in order to produce a fully voiced stop, something must be done to prevent the supraglottal pressure rising to the critical point too soon, and what, in fact, happens is that the supraglottal cavities are enlarged by lowering of the larynx and other forms of pharyngeal expansion.[4] At this point the reader should experiment with the production of fully voiced stops: [b, d, g]. It should be possible by lowering the larynx (and also increasing the subglottal pressure) to produce fully voiced stops, that is, stops which are accompanied by the muffled sound of vocal-fold vibration during the whole of their closure period. By starting with the larynx raised and the supraglottal cavity generally tightened up as much as possible, controlling the transglottal air-flow, and lowering the larynx, expanding the pharynx and finally blowing out the cheeks to the maximum, one can prolong a fully voiced [b] for about four seconds, a [d] for about three seconds and a [g] for one and a half to two seconds. To begin with, however, the production of a fully voiced [b] lasting, say, one tenth of a second is a good enough target. In a short pulmonic pressure voiced stop, the pharynx expansion is, of course, very slight and can easily pass unnoticed.

A voiced glottalic suction stop, or voiced implosive, uses a similar mechanism, but with two differences, one of them vital. The vital difference is that in a voiced implosive, the *pulmonic initiator is static:* the lungs are fixated, contributing nothing to the initiation of the sound except possibly the static maintenance of pressure; the sound is initiated solely by a pharynx expansion largely caused by a downward movement of the larynx, and this is why we call these sounds *glottalic* rather than pulmonic, and *suction* rather than pressure sounds. The initiatory activity is purely one of supraglottal expansion, generating negative pressure there. The somewhat less vital difference is that the degree, and speed, of larynx-expansion is greater in voiced glottalic suction stops than in voiced pulmonic pressure stops. Measurements made on cine-X-ray films[5] of long [bb, dd, gg], and short [ɓ, ɗ, ɠ], indicate differences in speed of pharynx expansion. The measurements were made of the back–front width of the pharynx just above the larynx (about 48 mm below the tip of the epiglottis). This back–front pharynx expansion is perhaps due in part simply to the downward movement of the larynx: as the hyoid bone, to which the larynx is attached, is pulled downwards it tends to swing forward, as a result of the way it is suspended from structures above and in front. The forward movement (and horizontal pharynx expansion) may also be partly due to active contraction of that part of the digastric muscle which attaches the hyoid bone to the chin. In any case, there is no doubt that this measurement of the front–back pharynx width is an indicator of larynx-lowering as well as of pharynx expansion. The figures for the average rate of pharynx expansion are shown in table 10. The actual duration of gg was about 27 centiseconds; the pattern of pharynx expansion was anomalous—most of it took place at a rate of about 128 mm/s during the first 3 cs—but the average rate for the entire duration was about 52 mm/s.

Table 10

pulmonic (mm/s)		*glottalic (mm/s)*	
bb	61	ɓ	85
dd	84	ɗ	128
gg	128 (52)	ɠ	228

It can be seen from these figures that the rate of front–back pharynx expansion for a voiced glottalic suction stop is higher (by a factor of 1·4 to 1·8) than that of the corresponding long voiced pulmonic pressure stop, and, incidentally, that the rate of expansion increases as one goes from bb and ɓ to gg and ɠ pretty much in the proportion that one might predict from the estimated volumes of the supraglottal cavity given in Chapter 4 (that is, behind bb/ɓ 120–160 cm^3, behind dd/ɗ 70–100 cm^3, behind gg/ɠ 30–40 cm^3).

Although both types of stop involve larynx-lowering it is clear that this is greater and faster for (short) voiced glottalic suction stops [ɓ, ɗ, ɠ] than for long voiced pulmonic pressure stops [bb, dd, gg]. In the case of quite short [b, d, g] there can be no doubt that the difference is even greater, the larynx-lowering then being quite minimal. Consequently, although not absolutely accurately, the best way of understanding the essential difference between the two types of sound is to think of them as follows: in *pulmonic pressure voiced plosives a moving column of air flows upward through a (nearly) static glottis;* in *glottalic suction voiced implosives a moving glottis slides downward over a static column of air.*

We can now see how misunderstandings about the nature of these two types of sound have been engendered by the use of the terms 'egressive' and 'ingressive' with reference to initiation types rather than merely to air-flow. It is clear that the initiation of such sounds as [ɓ, ɗ] is of suction type; it is the sudden expansion of the supraglottal cavity, generating negative pressure there, that initiates the sound. The fact that there is an upward, or quasi-egressive air-flow through the glottis is totally irrelevant to the initiation type. One might more accurately say there is an ingressive 'flow' of the glottis down over a static aircolumn! Irrelevant, too, is the fact that, quite often, by the time the articulatory closure of a glottalic suction stop, such as [ɓ, ɗ], is released, the intra-oral pressure has reached atmospheric level or even higher, in which case there may be a slight egressive flow out of the mouth (Pike 1943, and Ladefoged 1964 and 1971). It is not the direction of the airflow that is the crucial characteristic of 'implosives', or, indeed, of *any* initiation type; it is the location of the initiator and the direction (*compressive* or *rarefactive*) of its initiatory movement that is crucial. It is thus a little misleading to say, as Ladefoged (1971) does, that 'The difference between implosives and plosives is one of degree rather than of kind' and that, since the larynx tends to jerk downwards in voiced plosives as well as implosives, 'An implosive is simply a sound in which this downward movement is comparatively large and rapid'. We have seen that this latter statement is quite true; but far more crucial to the difference between the two sound-types is the relative (or, more probably, absolute) absence of pulmonic initiator activity in implosives. This fixation of the thoracic cage—implying suppression of pulmonic initiatory activity—can easily be observed introspectively. In those languages with clear contrasts between (ex)plosive voiced pulmonic pressure stops such as [b] and implosive voiced glottalic suction stops such as [ɓ] (Igbo or Kalabari (Ladefoged 1964) or Sindhi and Multani), the very fact that there is often little or no difference in their 'egressive-ingressiveness' shows that direction of air-flow cannot be a distinctive feature of either [b] or [ɓ], and strongly suggests that the crucial contrasting feature is, as I have said, not the flow, but rather the different location and direction of movement of the initiator. The raising of the back of the tongue (velarization) in Igbo [ɓ] shown in figure 3 of Ladefoged (1964) is no doubt an accessory movement: it may have the function of 'filling up' the oral cavity somewhat for the production of [ɓ], since, of course, the smaller the chamber at the start, the smaller the expansion required to generate a given negative pressure; oral volume-reduction by velarization could thus be an aid to glottalic suction initiation.

Other Phonated Glottalic Sounds

The anthropophonically most important phonated glottalic sounds are the *voiced implosives* just described. Incidentally, it is perfectly possible to produce voiced glottalic ingressive *fricatives* and *flaps* as well, but these are not known to be utilized by any language. The reader, exploring anthropophonic possibilities, should nevertheless experiment with them.

Having understood the mechanism of [ɓ, ɗ, ɠ]—glottalic suction initiation engendering a 'leak' of air upwards through the glottis producing normal 'egressive voice'—it is easy to understand the mechanism of *voiced glottalic pressure* stops. In these, there is an oral closure (as, for instance, in [p', t', k']), and the larynx is not tightly closed but disposed for *voice* (or perhaps *creak*—see next chapter). The larynx is jerked upwards (as for ejective [p', t', k']). This generates a quite high positive pressure in the pharynx and mouth—and, incidentally, a very slight negative pressure below the glottis;[6] consequently, there is a *downwards*, ingressive leaking of air through the glottis, activating the vocal cords for croaky 'inverse voice' or possibly 'inverse creak'. Thus, during the closure of glottalic pressure ingressive-voiced stops, which we may write as [ɓ', ɗ', ɠ'], a muffled somewhat frog-like croak is heard. In figure 21, the mechanism of a glottalic pressure inverse-voiced (croaked) stop is shown at *e*.

Another possibility is to combine pulmonic pressure and glottalic pressure as follows—particularly with creak, since this requires tighter glottal closure than voice, and so makes possible the generation of glottalic pressure: there is an oral closure; the glottis is then closed, but disposed for creak or for a rather 'tight' or tense voice; the pulmonic initiator starts up compressively, generating phonation; while this is in progress the glottalic initiator also starts up, compressively, that is, the larynx rises, compressing the air in the mouth, but not enough to stop the pulmonically driven flow of air for phonation. In figure 21 the mechanism of a combined glottalic pressure plus pulmonic pressure voiced stop is shown at f.

Neither of these last two types of sound are as yet known to occur in any language.

Illustrations. To clarify much of the foregoing rather complicated discussion, figure 21 a–f illustrates diagrammatically the mechanism of six of the initiation types, and their combination with phonation, discussed in this chapter. Each section shows three stages of a stop consonant of the type indicated, within a stylized 'vocal tract'. = open glottis; = closed glottis; = glottis disposed for voice; = glottis disposed for creak or tight, tense, voice; O = atmospheric pressure; + = slight and + + considerable positive pressure; – = slight and – – = considerable negative pressure.

Initiator-velocity

As we have seen 'pressure' and 'suction' refer to the direction in which an initiator moves. If it moves towards its associated articulator (or phonator) it reduces the volume of the intervening space and consequently generates positive pressure. If it moves away from its associated articulator (or phonator) it increases the volume and consequently generates negative pressure. Now, in the course of its initiatory movement the initiator may travel at a range of speeds from a fast pressure-generating movement at one end of the scale through zero (no movement at all) to a fast suction-generating movement at the other end of the scale. The terms 'pressure initiation' and 'suction initiation' are thus seen to refer to opposite ends of a continuous scale, or parameter, of rate of initiator movement, or, to adopt the vectorial term (with direction of movemen built into it), *initiator-velocity*.

Although the assignment of polarity (positive or negative values to a scale is arbitrary, it seems reasonable to assign positive value to velocities that generate positive pressures, negative values t velocities that generate negative pressures. Velocity in the most usua sense of distance moved per unit time can be most easily envisage in relation to glottalic initiation: in this, the glottis slides up or dow in the throat at linear velocities that are, in theory at least, measurabl in terms of cm/s. Other initiator movements, however, such as th compression or dilation of the lungs in pulmonic initiation, tak place in three dimensions, and cannot be simply stated in linea cm/s. Moreover, the effective result of any initiator movement change of volume of an adjacent part of the vocal tract. Cons quently, what we call 'initiator-velocity' is, more properly, *rate initiatory volume change* (with the direction specified). *Positi initiator velocity* is thus rate of initiatory volume decrease, (positive) cm^3/s, which generates *positive* pressure. Thus, during

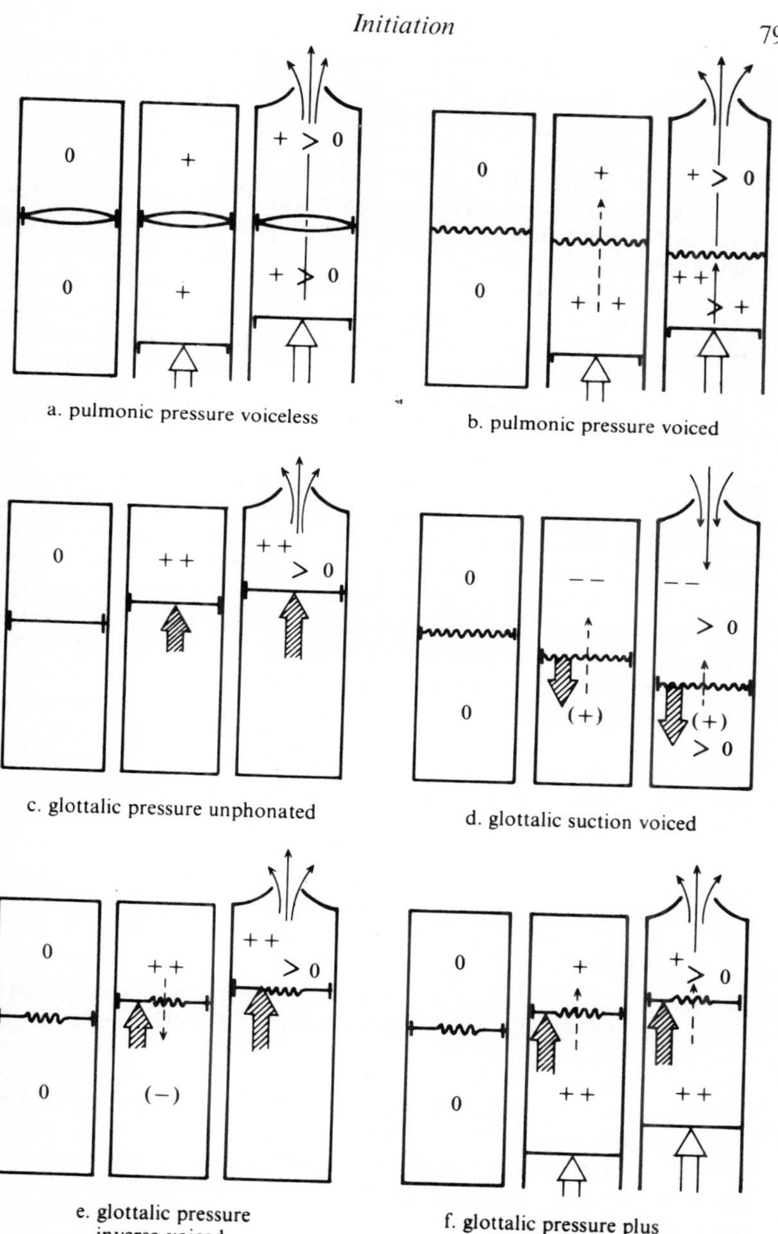

a. pulmonic pressure voiceless

b. pulmonic pressure voiced

c. glottalic pressure unphonated

d. glottalic suction voiced

e. glottalic pressure inverse-voiced

f. glottalic pressure plus pulmonic pressure voiced

Figure 21. The mechanism of some initiation types

sustained vowel with air flowing up and out of the vocal tract at $150\ cm^3/s$ we have a positive initiator-velocity of $150\ cm^3/s$. *Negative initiator-velocity* is rate of initiatory volume increase, in (negative) cm^3/s, which generates *negative* pressure.

It is not easy to measure initiator-velocity directly, although, for the pulmonic initiator, a moderately accurate indication can be obtained by measuring rate of chest contraction or expansion (by placing the subject in a body plethysmograph—see Chapter 12 on Instrumental Phonetics). Generally we can only derive initiator-velocity inferentially from measurements of volume-velocity of air-flow. Such measurements must, however, be treated with caution. As mentioned in Chapter 3, air-flow out of or into the mouth is a reliable indication of initiator-velocity only during relatively long periods of steady-state articulation. Most of the time, oral articulatory volume changes are adding positive or negative velocities to the basic, initiator-generated air-flow, occasionally down to complete arrest during stop consonants. During the closed phase of stop consonants mean initiator-velocity can sometimes be approximately assessed from measurable information on time and pressure. Thus, we may discover that during a pulmonic pressure voiceless stop consonant, pressure builds up to 10 $cm\,H_2O$ in, say, 10 cs. Now, assuming an open glottis (so that the volume of air behind the stop is the entire vocal-tract volume), a starting vocal tract volume of 300(cm^3, and a starting absolute pressure of 1030 $cm\,H_2O$, we can calculate the amount of vocal-tract volume decrease by the formula (see Chapter 4)

$$v_2 = \frac{p_1 \times v_1}{p_2}, \qquad \text{(1d}$$

where $p_1 = 1030\ cm\,H_2O$, $v_1 = 3000\ cm^3$, $p_2 = 1040\ cm\,H_2O$, an $v_2 =$ the new volume in cm^3.

The answer is $v_2 = 2971\ cm^3$.

Therefore, the tract volume decrease is 29 cm^3, and since this tak place in 10 cs, the mean initiator-velocity is 290 cm^3/s.

Initiator Power

Perhaps more important than initiator-velocity is the concept initiator power.

When an initiator is in operation, it moves at a particular veloci against a certain resistance, or 'load', imposed upon it by the a pressure against which it is moving. Thus, during a stretch pulmonic pressure initiation (that is, all of the time in most languag and most of the time in all other languages), varying phonatory a articulatory strictures in the throat and mouth impose constantly varying degrees of impedance on the egressive flow of air up and out of the vocal tract. The 'back-pressures' caused by these impediments to flow, react on the initiator, which is either slowed down by them, or else has to work harder to overcome the resistance.

In more basic physical terms, the initiator is constantly exerting *force* against the air it is driving before it. We normally quantify the initiator-driven body of air in terms of *volume*, that is, in cubic centimetres (cm^3). But we can also think of the operation of the initiator in another way. Every *volume* of one cubic centimetre of air displaced by the initiator may be regarded as an *area* of one square centimetre pushed forwards a *linear* distance of one centimetre. Measurements of air-pressure in the part of the vocal tract adjacent to the initiator enable us to calculate the force exerted by the initiator upon each square centimetre of displaced air. We measure phonetic pressure in centimetres of water (cm H_2O): but every cm H_2O is equal to a pressure of 980·4 dynes per square centimetre (dynes/cm^2). From pressure in cm H_2O we can thus discover, by simple multiplication, the initiatory force applied to each square centimetre. Thus if, during the closure of a stop consonant, we record a pressure of 5 cm H_2O we know that this corresponds to a force of $5 \times 980{\cdot}4$ dynes applied to every square centimetre, that is, 4902 dynes/cm^2.

Now, suppose that while exerting this force the initiator displaces 10 cm^3 of air. As we saw above, we can regard this as 1 cm^2 pushed forward 10 cm; in other words we can regard this as a movement of the initiator over a linear distance of 10 cm. In our present example, then, we may say that the initiator exerts a force of 4902 dynes over a distance of 10 cm. To do this, it has to expend some energy, to do some work; and the mechanical concept of work is precisely defined as *force* times *distance moved by the point of application of the force*—in our case, 4902 dynes $\times$ 10 (cm) = 49020 ergs, the *erg* (the mechanical unit of work) being defined as 1 dyne/cm, that is, the work done when a force of one dyne is applied over a distance of one centimetre.

Work can, however, be done at various *rates:* a given force can be applied over a given distance for a longer or shorter period of time. Clearly, to generate exactly the same force over a shorter period of time requires more energy, or *power*. This is precisely the mechanical concept of power—the rate of doing work, measured in ergs per second (erg/s).

In our example, we saw that when an initiator displaces 10 cm^3 of air, at a pressure of 5 cm H_2O it is doing an amount of work, quantified as 49020 ergs. Now, suppose that the initiator displaces these

10 cm^3 of air in one tenth of a second, which corresponds to a volume-velocity, or rate of initiatory volume change, of 100 cm^3/s. This means that the initiator is applying a force of 49020 ergs for a period of one tenth of a second: this corresponds to a rate of application of force (that is, a *power*) of $49020 \times 10 = 490200$ ergs per second. The erg/s is a very small unit of power, and it is usually desirable to express initiator power in the next larger unit, namely the watt. One watt $= 10^7$ erg/s, that is, 10,000,000 erg/s. To convert from erg/s to watts we must therefore divide by 10,000,000 (or multiply by ·0000001). In our present example, then, we have a power of 490200 erg/s × ·0000001 = ·04902 watts.

In the preceding discussion we have shown how the mechanical factors of force, distance and time are related in the concept of initiator power. In the actual quantities measured in phonetics, force is involved in pressure, and the factors of distance and time are combined in volume-velocity (or initiator rate). We can, therefore, calculate initiator power (*IP*) in watts, by using the formula:

$$IP = \frac{p \times 980{\cdot}4 \times Vv}{10^7} \qquad (5a)$$

where $p =$ pressure in cm H_2O, converted by the factor 980·4 to dynes/cm^2, Vv is volume-velocity (initiatory volume change rate) in cm^3/s. Since $980{\cdot}4/10^7$ is the same as ·00009804/1 we can simplify the formula to:

$$IP = p \times {\cdot}000098 \times Vv \qquad (5b$$

Suppose, for example, that during the production of a particula sound (for example, the vowel of the stressed syllable of the wor *phonetic*) the mean initiator-velocity is 195 cm^3/s and the mea pressure is 3·9 cm H_2O. Then the initiator power in watts will b given by the formula:

$$IP = 3{\cdot}9 \times {\cdot}000098 \times 195$$
$$= {\cdot}074 \text{ watts}$$

It is possible to make a further simplification for the purpose c making quick, rough, calculations of *IP* by taking the dynes/cm equivalent of 1 cm H_2O to be 1000 rather than 980·4. The relativ crudity of most phonetic measures of pressure and volume-velocit is such that to introduce an error of 2 per cent is not going to have very significant effect upon our results. With this further simplific tion our formula becomes:

$$IP = p \times {\cdot}0001 \times Vv$$

The example just given would thus take the form:

$$IP = 3{\cdot}9 \times {\cdot}0001 \times 195$$
$$= {\cdot}076 \text{ watts.}$$

In cases where the IP is known, we can find either the pressure or the volume-velocity by use of the formulae:

$$p = \frac{IP}{Vv \times {\cdot}000098} \text{ or (say) } \frac{IP}{Vv \times {\cdot}0001} \qquad (5c)$$

$$Vv = \frac{IP}{p \times {\cdot}000098} \text{ or (say) } \frac{IP}{p \times {\cdot}0001} \qquad (5d)$$

Figure 22 is a graph showing the relationship between volume-velocity and initiator power for a number of different cross-sectional areas of channels.

Various writers have used the concept of 'subglottic power' (for example, van den Berg 1956, Isshiki 1964)—the product of subglottal pressure and egressive air-flow through the glottis; but for general anthropophonic purposes we need the more general concept of initiator power which has been presented here. We have to be able to talk about initiator power, irrespective of whether we are dealing with the pulmonic initiator, or one of the other initiators, and

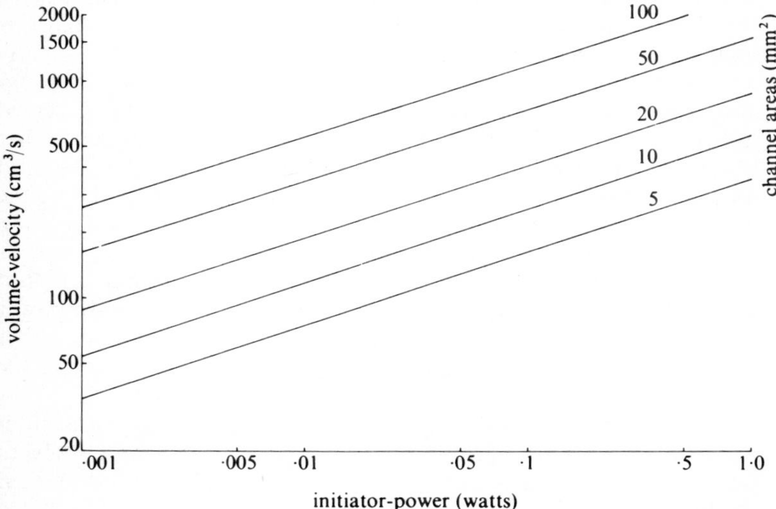

Figure 22. Initiator power and volume velocity (power required to drive air at given volume-velocities through channels of the given cross-sectional areas)

certainly irrespective of whether the sounds we are dealing with are voiced or not. 'Subglottic power' is too restricted a concept for general phonetic purposes.

Stress

There seems to be little doubt now that initiator power is the organic-aerodynamic phonetic correlate of what is often called 'stress'. Unfortunately, the concept of stress with respect to English has been very considerably confused and obfuscated by certain phoneticians (particularly in England in the 1930s) who lumped together both initiator-power phenomena, and intonational (frequency) phenomena under the general heading of 'stress'. The question whether stress is really tone, and so on, has been raised with respect to such pairs as *ímport* (noun) and *impórt* (verb). Of course, when such pairs of words are pronounced in isolation, they exhibit a tonal difference. Any investigation of stress or presumed stress must, therefore, begin by manoeuvring the items to be studied into a position where there can be no possible tonal difference: for example, the words *ímport* and *impórt* in a frame such as '*I* said ímport!' and, '*I* said impórt!', with a strong, contrastive, emphatic tone on *I*, so that the rest of the utterance is pronounced more or less on a monotone. Only after such precautions as these can questions relating to stress be studied in isolation from obfuscating questions of tone.

In a series of experiments carried out at the University of Edinburgh with R. Beresford in 1964, we found that in such pairs as *ímport impórt, pérvert pervért, ábstract abstráct,* placed in a tonally neutral frame as above, the perceived 'stressed' syllable was, in every case, pronounced with higher initiatory power than the perceived 'unstressed' syllable; that is to say, irrespective of whether either the subglottal pressure by itself, or the initiator velocity by itself, in any particular case was higher or lower in the 'stressed' syllable, the *product* of the two was always higher in the 'stressed' syllable. In other experiments, with simple pulmonic pressure fricatives, such as ['ff, f'f, 'ss, s's] and ['vv, v'v], the same results were obtained: in that part of the fricative which is perceived as 'stressed' the initiator power is higher than in the other part, even though in some cases either vocal-tract pressure or volume-velocity was actually higher in the 'unstressed' syllable.[7]

A further piece of evidence is the following. If we compare either the peak, or the mean, volume-velocity (corresponding closely to initiator-velocity) and pressure in initial [h] or [s] as in *hat* and *sat* we find considerable differences. The volume-velocity of [h] is often 1000 cm^3/s or more, while that of [s] is often of the order of 200 to 300 cm^3/s. On the other hand, the intra-vocal-tract pressure of [s] is likely to be 5 or 6 times that of [h]. In a given, imaginary, but plausible case, we might have the following figures:

volume-velocity	[h] 1200,	[s] 220 cm^3/s
pressure	[h] ·4,	[s] 2·3 cm H_2O.

Now if initiator-velocity by itself were the chief physiological correlate of stress we should expect to feel that the [h] of *hat* is stronger or more stressed than the [s] of *sat:* but this is not the case. On the other hand, if pressure by itself were (as some people believe) the chief physiological correlate of stress, we should expect to feel that the [s] of *sat* is 'stronger' or more stressed than the [h] of *hat:* but this is not the case.

What, in fact, we feel is that both [h] and [s] are about equally stressed, and the reason for this becomes clear when we calculate their respective approximate initiator powers, using formula 5b given above. For the plausible pressure and volume-velocity values just given the *IP*s are approximately [s] = ·050 watts, [h] = ·048 watts. We feel them to be about equally stressed because they both require about the same initiator power for their production. A glance at figure 22 will show how volume-velocity and initiator power are related for sounds with articulatory channels of 10 or so mm^2 (as for [s]) and 100 or more mm^2 (as for [h]). In general, then, where the picture is not obscured by an overlay of pitch, the more strongly stressed a sound is, the greater the initiator power.

Isochronism

In all languages the principal 'carrier wave' of speech is a pulmonically initiated egressive air-stream. In many, if not in all languages, this main stream of pulmonic egressive air appears to be delivered in more or less rhythmic bursts, or 'quanta'. For instance, in English, it seems clear that the pulmonic initiator operates in a series of pressure pulses each consisting of a single sharp rise in initiator power followed by a slower decline, then a new sharp rise at the beginning of the next pulse, and so on. Within any short stretch of speech of even tempo (particularly within any one intonation unit or 'tone-group') each of these pulses of initiator power has about the same duration, and presumably involves about the same power output. These pulses have been termed 'feet' (Abercrombie 1964, Catford 1966), and it has often been pointed out that English has more or less *isochronous* feet—that is, feet of more or less equal duration; or, what comes to the same thing, that the intervals between the stressed syllables (the peaks of the initiator-power curves) are approximately equal—within the units indicated, although not, of course, throughout long stretches of speech, where changes of tempo will change the duration of the isochronous feet in different tone-groups. Not surprisingly, attempts to discover a kind of unrestricted, overall, isochronism in English have produced negative results (cf. Shen & Peterson 1962, Ohala 1972).

The reader can experience this kind of isochronism for himself by, for example, saying the alphabet with various kinds of groupings of letters, but at an even rhythm. In the following example each vertical line indicates the start of a new 'foot': the wavy line at the top represents the pulmonic pressure initiator-power curve, and the letters of the alphabet indicate different groupings of these letters. The acute accent indicates what would generally be called 'the stressed syllable' (but is, of course, simply the peak of the initiator-power curve).

Á	B́	Ć	D́
Á B	Ć D	É F	Ǵ
Á B	Ć	D́ E	F́
Á B	Ć	D́ E F	Ǵ

To bring out the isochronism of the feet more clearly, one can 'beat time' in such a way that the 'down beat' corresponds to the peak of each power curve, or foot. This imparts an only slightly artificial regularity to the utterance: in completely natural reading the rhythm is pretty much of the same type. Further experiments can be made with such sentences as the following:

Jóhn bought	twó new	bóoks there	yésterday
Jóhn	bóught two	néw books	thére
Jóhn	bóught two new	bóoks there	yésterday
Jóhn	sáw a black	bírd there	yésterday
Jóhn saw a	bláck bird	yésterday	

This example, incidentally, indicates how English exploits the moveable location of the division between feet to give surface expression to differences in emphasis, or in the grouping of syntactical units. That, however, is not our present concern. Measurements show that although feet are approximately isochronous they are not absolutely so. In addition to variations in foot duration due to variations in tempo, already mentioned, Halliday (1967) refers to a sample of loud reading of English in which 'the ratio of the average durations of one-, two- and three-syllable feet was shown instrumentally to be about 5 : 6 : 7'. Although this shows that isochronism is not absolute, it is powerful evidence for a tendency in that direction. If foot duration depended merely on the number of syllables within the foot we should expect the average duration to be in the ratio 5 : 10 : 15. The very striking deviation from these predicted ratios can hardly be explained otherwise than as indicating an attempt to maintain isochronism. It may be more exact to say that feet are *isodynamic*, each foot involving about the same initiator-power output. This would undoubtedly lead to feet being approximately, but not exactly, isochronous.

Returning to our more general anthropophonic concerns from this illustrative digression into English, we can say that many, perhaps all, languages have some form of built-in isochronism or isodynamism, initiator power being parcelled out into roughly equal 'quanta'. In some languages, however, the initiator-power quanta seem to coincide with another unit, called the 'syllable'. French is usually regarded as a language of this type: thus the distribution of initiator-power pulses in a French sentence such as *Voici le garçon que j'ai rencontré hier matin* is more like the following:

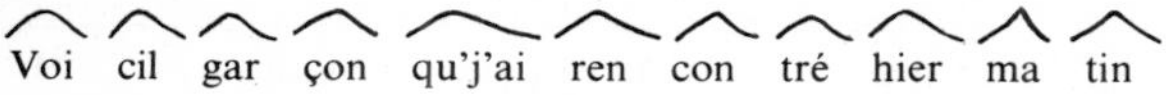

Voi cil gar çon qu'j'ai ren con tré hier ma tin

A French speaker tends to carry over this kind of distribution of initiator-power pulses into other languages, so that his pronunciation of the English translation of the sentence might be something like:

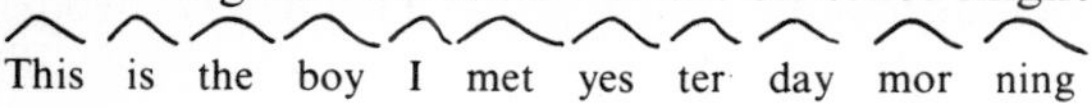

This is the boy I met yes ter day mor ning

instead of:

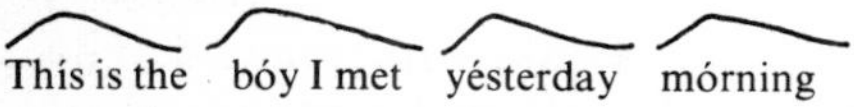

Thís is the bóy I met yésterday mórning

On the other hand, an English speaker tends to carry over his distribution of initiator power into French, saying something like:

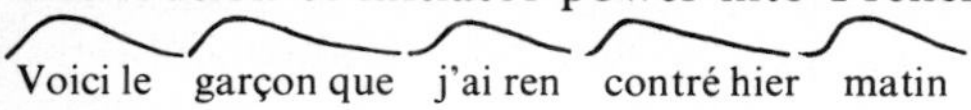

Voici le garçon que j'ai ren contré hier matin

In real life, none of these French, Anglo-French or Franco-English utterances would be carried out with the metronome-like precision which seems to be implied by these notations, but the tendencies are definitely there. These two different trends of initiator-power distribution are often called, following Pike (1943), 'stress-timed rhythm' (the English type) and 'syllable-timed rhythm' (the French type).

Not a great deal is known in detail about the different types of initiator-power distribution in the languages of the world, and no doubt numerous variations are possible. Thus, for example, it seems as if Russian, like English, distributes its initiator power in quanta of more than syllable length—that is, has 'feet' or 'stress-timed rhythm'. Nevertheless, one gets the impression that within each quantum, the ‘slope’ of the Russian power curve is the opposite to that of English. Thus a Russian sentence like *Ja ne xoču govorit´ ob etom* (‘I don’t want to talk about this’) appears to have initiator-power curves somewhat as follows (here the transliteration is followed by a phonetic transcription):

Já nexočú govorít′ ob é tom
ˈja ɲĭxaˈtʃu gǝ̆vaˈɽiţ abˈɛ tǝ̆m

An English speaker may subtly mispronounce this sentence by applying to it an English division into feet, with the English type of falling initiator-power curve within each foot, thus:

já ne xo čú go vo rít′ ob étom
ˈjɑnjɩhǝ ˈtʃugʌvǝ ˈri · tjǝb ˈɛtǝm

The distribution of initiator power throughout utterances undoubtedly permits of a good deal of anthropophonic variation, but it is an area of phonetics that has not been adequately studied. The remarks given above about English, French and Russian are tentative, and (except for the English ‘foot’) they are based on empathic direct observation, unconfirmed by instrumental means.

The Syllable

In the above we have referred several times to the syllable as though this were an entity that could be taken for granted. This, however, is not the case. Probably all Western Europeans would agree that such a word as *democratic* has four syllables. A Japanese, however, might say that *democratic* has six syllables, not four. This would tend to suggest that there is no universal anthropophonic entity to which we can apply the term syllable. The American psychologist R. H. Stetson (1928, new edition 1951), investigating expiratory muscle activity in speech, suggested that each syllable involved a ballistic burst of activity of intercostal muscles. This would seem to correspond more closely to our concept of the foot or initiator-power pulse. But as Ladefoged (1967) points out there is no simple, regular, relationship between bursts of muscle activity and syllables, or even feet.

In English, the division between feet may also be a division between what all English speakers would agree are syllables, for example, in the slow, deliberate, enunciation of the alphabet in which each letter is assigned its own foot, or burst of initiator power:

A B C D E etc.

However, it is equally clear that any one foot may contain several syllables, as in:

Á B   Ć D   É F G etc.

For English, then, it seems that we can define the foot as being a single initiator-power pulse (what has sometimes been called a 'stress group' or 'rhythmic group'). The syllable is therefore either co-extensive with the foot or is, as it were, a 'ripple' on the surface of the initiator-power curve, as, for instance, in:

Á B   Ć D   É F G

Syllable divisions consist of momentary slight retardations of the initiator movement, imposed either by articulatory closures (as in Á B, Ć D) or by a slight self-imposed retardation and re-acceleration of the initiator, as in E F = [iːɛf]—although it may be that here we perceive a pseudo 'syllable division' simply because of the sudden switch of vowel quality from [iː] to [ɛ]. It is certainly the case that perceived syllable divisions correspond to momentary initiator retardations in cases where the vowel quality remains essentially the same throughout, for example in such English sentences as 'They *saw all* these people', or 'That's a *bee-eater*'. If any syllable division at all is produced in the sequences [sɔːɔːl] and [biːitə] it is marked either by very slight self-imposed initiator retardation, or, by the insertion of a glottal stop [sɔːʔɔːl], [biːʔiːtə] producing a momentary articulatorily imposed initiator retardation. In some other languages, for example, German, a glottal stop would here be obligatory as syllable divider. In French self-imposed initiator retardation may, according to Paul Passy (1907), function as syllable divider as in *Papa a à aller à Paris* [papa a a ale a paʁi]. This still leaves the case of Japanese unexplained. The reason a Japanese might claim six syllables for *democratic* is that if this occurred as a Japanese word, it would have to be merely a contracted version of a longer form such as [dɛmɔkɯratʃikɯ] in which a vowel occurs after each consonant, because that is how Japanese words are structured. In its full form, the Japanese utterance would indeed be divided up into six minor bursts of initiator activity separated from each other by momentary, articulatorily imposed, retardations.

It seems possible, then, to sum up the discussion so far by saying that in all languages initiator power is delivered in quantum-like bursts, containing a single power peak. These correspond to English feet. If the initiator-power curve within each burst is not subject to any slight momentary diminution, or retardation, then the power curve itself (the foot) is co-extensive with what is called a syllable. If, on the contrary, there are articulatorily imposed (or, much more rarely, self-imposed) momentary retardations of the initiator-power movement, within the foot, then these are divisions between syllables within the foot. A syllable then, is a minimal 'chunk', or stretch, of initiator activity, bounded by either minor, intra-foot, retardations, or by the foot divisions themselves. The additional syllables in the above Japanese assessment of *democratic* must then be called pseudo-syllables or merely potential syllables, in the sense that they could be there if the word were pronounced slowly and carefully in its Japanese form.

I must at this point return to the remark made above by Ladefoged that there is 'no simple correlation between intercostal [muscle] activity and syllables'. It is worth quoting further from Ladefoged (1967 pp. 20–1, or 1958 pp. 6–7): 'Sometimes a single increase in tension spans a group of articulations including two vowels separated by a consonant closure (our records show that words such as *pity* and *around* may be spoken in this way); and sometimes there are two separate bursts of activity in what is normally regarded as a single syllable (for example, in *sport, stay,* and other words beginning with a fricative followed by a plosive)'. Referring to the intercostal muscle activity in a sentence containing the word *agreed* he remarks that the second syllable here is not only preceded by a burst of muscle activity, but that there is a second burst of activity in the middle of the long [iː] vowel 'a pattern of activity which we often observed during long vowels'.

These remarks are consistent with, and, indeed, may be taken as striking confirmation of the view expressed in Chapter 1, that the speaker's 'target' in speech is certainly not the firing of this or that motor unit, or the contraction of this or that muscle, but the production of a particular organic-aerodynamic effect. Thus, if the 'target' in a word such as *pity* or *stay* is in each case, a single foot, a single initiator-power quantum, the speaker may achieve this by firing only one burst of muscle-drive for *pity,* but two for *stay.* In *pity,* for instance, when the initiator-power curve has passed its peak in the first syllable and is on the decline, the momentary, syllable-forming retardation of the short intervocalic [t] may have a negligible effect on the course of the curve, and may thus not require the firing of a second, corrective burst of muscle drive. On the other hand, in a word like *stay* the target is a smooth initiation curve, building up to full power at or about the release of the [t]. We may assume that a first burst of muscle-drive sets the initiator in motion and that velocity and power steadily increase, until closure for [t] suddenly clamps down, imposing an infinite resistance to flow; at this point the pressure load on the initiator suddenly increases and the initiator is about to come to a halt. Obviously, the speaker may have to fire a second, or booster, burst of muscle-drive, to keep the initiator on its course in a smooth build-up of power.

Before concluding these observations on initiator power (or stress), initiator-power quanta (or feet), and minimal stretches of initiator activity bounded by 'lows' (syllables), we must remark that for universal, or anthropophonic, purposes we have to make sure that these concepts are generally applicable, no matter which particular initiator is functioning at any one time. So far we have spoken as if only the pulmonic initiator were involved in these activities. This, of course, is not necessarily so, and this is why we refer to 'initiator power' and not to the more restrictive 'subglottic power' of van den Berg and others. Initiator power is $Vv \times p \times \cdot 0001$, no matter which initiator is operating. In actual practice, so far as we know, 'stress', 'feet', and 'syllables' are normally functions of pulmonic initiation (normally pulmonic pressure, but of course, pulmonic suction in the rare cases mentioned above). However, it is perfectly possible to produce sequences of feet or syllables purely by glottalic pressure, with varied stress: for example ['ts̓'t's'] or [ts̓''t's'], each being a sequence of purely glottalic pressure sounds—in ['ts̓'t's'] presumably a single glottalic pressure foot, with an initiator-power curve of the type ⁄⋀⋀⟍, divided into two syllables by the retardation effect of the medial [t'] articulation, the first syllable being stressed since it contains the initiator-power peak. One can, for instance, pronounce whole English words (in outline as it were) with purely glottalic pressure initiation.

The reader should try such words as *potato* [p'-t'-t'-], the vowels being suggested by the formation of appropriate oral resonance cavities during the 'hollow' popping release of each stop—or *participated* [p'-t'-s'-p'-t'-t']. Such utterances are occasionally heard in pathological speech. Somewhat less unusual is the utterance of whole syllables on glottalic pressure initiation, surrounded by normal pulmonic pressure initiation. I believe I have heard the first syllable in a Kabardian word such as /pɕɨˈkʷ't'/, 'twelve', uttered as a purely glottalic sequence in [p'ɕ'kʷ'ut'].

Conclusion

In this chapter we have examined in some detail the various types of initiation: *pulmonic, glottalic, velaric,* both *pressure* and *suction*. In addition we have considered some of the additional operations or functions of initiators. Among these we have noted the following:

Initiator-velocity: the rate of initiatory volume change, pressure-generating volume decrease being regarded as positive, and suction-generating volume increase as negative.

Initiator power: the product of initiator-velocity and the pressure-load against which the initiator is acting. This, we suggest, is the organic-aerodynamic correlate of what is most commonly called *stress*.

Initiator-power quanta: the more or less rhythmical bursts of initiator power, each rising to a single peak value, in which initiator activity is delivered in speech. This is what is called the *foot* or 'stress-group' in English and in other languages with 'stress-timed rhythm'; perhaps always conterminous with the syllable in languages like French, with 'syllable-timed rhythm'.

Minimal intra-foot smooth stretches of initiator power bounded either by major foot boundaries or by minor intra-foot retardations of initiator activity. These are what are most commonly called *syllables*.

SIX

Phonation

Logically, the next step after a chapter on initiation would be one about the other basic and obligatory component of all sounds of speech, namely articulation; however, we will find it extremely useful to have information on phonation to refer back to when we come to examine articulation.

By *phonation* we mean any laryngeal activity of speech that has neither initiatory nor articulatory function. It is clear, for instance, that the glottal closure and upward thrust of the larynx in a glottalic pressure stop such as [t'] is a 'laryngeal activity'; its function, however, is initiatory, not phonatory. Similarly, the glottal closure of a [ʔ] is a laryngeal activity; its function, however, is articulatory (forming the articulation of a glottal stop) not phonatory. On the other hand, the vibration of the vocal folds producing the *voice* of vowel-sounds, or voiced fricatives such as [v, z], is a laryngeal activity that has a phonatory function.

In this chapter we shall have occasion to look a little more closely at some aspects of laryngeal anatomy and function than we did in Chapter 3.

Figures 23a, b, c, and d represent the larynx as seen from the left side, from the back, from above, and in a transverse section. *hb* represents the hyoid bone in the neck from which the larynx is suspended; *tc* is the thyroid cartilage, which is suspended from the hyoid bone by *thm*, the thyro-hyoid muscle; and *sht* the superior horns of the thyroid cartilage. The thyroid cartilage articulates by means of its inferior horns, *iht,* with the sides of the cricoid cartilage, *cc*. Poised on top of the swollen back part of the cricoid cartilage are the twin arytenoid cartilages, *ac*. Running forward from the vocal processes, *vp,* of the arytenoid cartilages to the inside of the front wall of the thyroid cartilage are the vocal folds, *vf*. Just above and parallel with the vocal folds is an additional pair of folds running from back to front, the 'false vocal cords' or ventricular bands, *vb*. The thyroid cartilage is attached to the cricoid cartilage at the front by the crico-thyroid muscle, *ctm*, which can

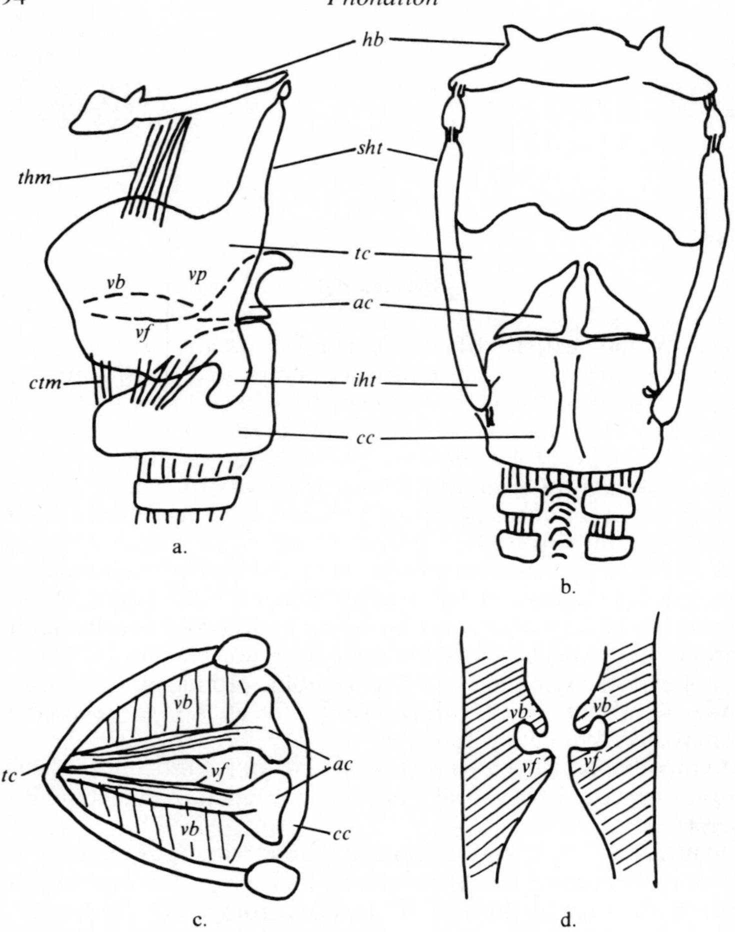

Figure 23. The larynx viewed from (a) the left-side, (b) behind, (c) above, (d) in transverse section

act to tilt the thyroid cartilage forward and thus stretch the vocal folds.

The above is sufficient preliminary anatomical background for discussion of phonation.

It is traditional for works on phonetics to describe at the very least the two phonation types, *voiceless* and *voiced,* which we have already referred to. However, it is clear that many more varieties of phonatory activity are possible. Catford (1964) surveyed the possibilities in terms of (a) *stricture-type* (degree and type of approximation of vocal folds) and (b) *location* (which particular parts of the larynx were involved). On the basis of these two parameters alone some twenty-three types of phonation were enumerated, not to mention additional parameters of vocal-fold length and thickness, vertical displacement of larynx, and so on. To a small extent, the data on which those descriptions were based were speculative, and may have been somewhat over-confident with respect to some locational labels. In particular, the locational opposition 'arytenoidal/ligamental' may be too specific, the vaguer 'posterior' and 'anterior' being, perhaps, more desirable labels.

Since 1964 there have been one or two other attempts to characterize phonation types, notably in Lindqvist (1969), Ladefoged (1971), and Halle and Stevens (1971); these are discussed below. They do not, however, indicate the need for any radical change in the 1964 classification, which we therefore present here with little modification. We begin in a practical, experimental way by asking the reader to carry out various operations in his own vocal tract.

Phonatory Stricture-types

First, breathe fairly deeply in and out through the mouth once or twice. Pay particular attention to the egressive (pulmonic pressure) breathing, and note that it is somewhat noisy. The glottis is quite wide open, but at the volume-velocities normal in deep breathing the flow through the glottis is turbulent, and hence generates a kind of hiss-noise. Controlling the outflow by means of the respiratory muscles one can slow the flow down to the point where turbulence ceases, and we have merely silent breath. This should occur, in fact, when the volume-velocity is reduced to somewhere about 200 cm^3/s to 300 cm^3/s, which is the order of magnitude of the critical velocity for flow through the wide-open glottis, although of course a good deal of variation is possible according to just how big, and how wide open, the individual glottis is.

Breathing through the open glottis like this is the phonation type known as *voiceless*—the phonation of sounds like [p, t, k, f, s, ʃ, h], and so on. But we have seen that two varieties of voiceless phonation are possible: one with turbulent flow and resultant noise, and the other with laminar, noiseless, flow. It is convenient to have special names for them: *breath* for noisy voiceless flow at volume-velocities above about 200–300 cm^3/s, and *nil*-phonation for silent voiceless flow at volume-velocities below about 200–300 cm^3/s. The high-velocity flow at rates around 1000 cm^3/s, common in English initial [h-], or in the 'aspirated' h-like release of stressed initial voiceless [p^h-, t^h-, k^h-], is normally breath phonation, while the lower velocity flow in voiceless fricatives, such as [f, s, ʃ], is often nil-phonation. The distinction is important chiefly in relation to the discussion of 'voiceless vowels'. In order to be audible at all, a voiceless vowel must have turbulent flow through *one* of its orifices: the oral orifice for close (approximant) vowels like [i, u], the glottal orifice for open (resonant) vowels like [ɛ, a].

Continue the experiments now by deliberately switching from *breath* to *whisper*. Switch back and forth, comparing them: thus, *breath–whisper–breath–whisper,* and so on. Note how, in whisper you can feel a tenseness in the larynx that is not present in breath. Try switching over, within the same exhalation, from whisper to breath : breathe in, start up *whisper,* then, keeping the pulmonic egressive air-stream going, switch to *breath*. You should feel a kind of relaxation in the larynx as you pass from whisper to breath, and you cannot fail to notice the sudden greatly increased volume-velocity of the air-flow. Try silently switching between whisper and breath, that is, don't breathe, or at least let the air-flow out so slowly that no sound is produced, and *imagine* yourself alternately whispering and breathing, introspecting all the time about the kinaesthetic sensations. From this, and the previous experiments, it will be clear that whisper involves a narrowing of the glottis. A number of different types of whisper can be produced, but at this stage, all one need note is that whisper is a strong, 'rich' hushing sound, generated by turbulent air-flow through a considerably narrowed glottis. In whispered speech, normally voiced sounds are whispered, while normally voiceless sounds remain voiceless. For example, if you whisper such words as *fish,* or *six,* you will see that, in fact, only the vowel in each case is whispered : the voiceless consonants [f-ʃ] or [s-ks] remain voiceless. On the other hand, whisper the word *vision* ['vɩʒᵊn] and notice how whisper is substituted for voice throughout: you can prove this by comparing the word *fission* ['fɩʃᵊn]. When these two words are whispered one after the other the difference between voiceless [f, ʃ] and whispered [v, ʒ] is quite clear.

We saw that with voiceless fricatives like [f, ʃ] phonation is most commonly *nil* (noiseless), because the velocity of flow through the glottis is below the critical value of about 200–300 cm^3/s. The critical velocity for whisper is naturally very much lower, since the glottal orifice for whisper is very much smaller than that for voiceless phonation. One can easily feel this by producing noisy breath, and slowing down the air-flow till turbulence ceases, then saying whisper and slowing down the air-flow till turbulence ceases. It is easy to feel that the sub-critical flow velocity for whisper is much lower than that for voicelessness. In fact, the critical volume-velocity for whisper is about 25–30 cm^3/s as opposed to 300 cm^3/s or so for voicelessness. In theory, one can have a continuum of degrees of glottal opening going from 'widest possible' in breathing, or voiceless phonation, down to a very small glottal chink, for strong whisper. In practice, however, it seems that we make two quite distinct glottal adjustments for the two phonation types: a wide one, probably of about 60 to 95 per cent of the maximal glottal area for voiceless, and a distinctly narrow one, probably of less than 25 per cent of the maximal glottal area, for whisper.

The next phonation type to be experimented with is *voice*. First, alternate voiceless and voiced fricatives, such as [fvfvfv] [s zs zs z]. Now carry out the same operation with the mouth fairly wide open, without any narrow fricative-type articulation, that is, [əhəh], with an 'indeterminate' central vowel, somewhat like that of the (British) English word *bird*. Now say a long [əːː], then suddenly cease voicing and open up the glottis for [h], thus, [əːːh]. Do this several times aloud, and silently; note the feeling of closed glottis for voice and open glottis for voiceless phonation. In the production of voice the vocal folds are adducted and subjected to a certain degree of tension. The process of vocal fold vibration may start with the folds in a suitable state of tension, but slightly open. As the pulmonic egressive air-stream goes through the very narrow glottal chink it is accelerated, and consequently the pressure in the glottis falls (the Bernoulli effect, see p. 32). As a result, the vocal folds snap together, to be forced open again a moment later by the subglottal pressure, to close again a moment later by their own elasticity and the Bernoulli effect; and so the cycle repeats itself again and again.

The description of vocal-fold activity that we have just given is often called the 'myoelastic' theory of voice production, since it assumes that the vocal folds are set in vibration solely by the combined effects of subglottal pressure, the elastic properties of the vocal folds, and the Bernoulli effect. In the 1950s a different theory was put forward by the French scientist Raoul Husson. Husson's theory is known as the 'neurochronaxic' theory, and holds that vocal-fold vibrations are not aerodynamically or 'myoelastically' produced, but are, rather, the result of periodic neural stimulation and contraction of muscles in the vocal folds. Up to about 200 Hz (200 muscular contractions per second) nerve fibres of the recurrent laryngeal nerve operate *in phase*. Above that frequency, the fibres go out of phase, so that their combined firing will set the glottis opening and closing rhythmically at frequencies higher than the maximum frequency of in-phase innervations. So long as there is some subglottal pressure, these neurally induced rhythmic openings of the glottis will release periodic air-jets into the pharynx, thus generating the sound of voice (on this see Husson 1960, 1962). The neurochronaxic theory is of dubious validity and not generally accepted. For criticism of it, see van den Berg (1954 and 1958).

In order to generate voice (low-pitched chest voice) a subglottal pressure of at least 2 to 3 cm H_2O is needed, and the liminal volume-velocity is about 50 cm^3/s. In speech, mean volume-velocities of 100–350 cm^3/s are normal. Assuming that the glottis is, on the average, open for about half of each cycle of glottal vibration (as it normally is at fairly low pitches) this represents a true mean volume-velocity through the glottis, during each open phase, of 200–700 cm^3/s. For a maximum glottal opening of about 20 mm^2, and a mean of about 10 mm^2, a mean volume-velocity of 250 cm^3/s would indicate a mean velocity of 2500 cm/s (and mean subglottal pressure of 3·7 cm H_2O). At each opening of the glottis, then, a fairly high velocity air-jet, averaging about 2000 to 5000 cm/s, shoots up into the pharynx. It is this periodic series of high-velocity jets which set the resonating chambers of the supraglottal cavities 'ringing' in the production of vowels.

Voice starts with the vocal folds forming a narrow glottal chink. There is, however, still one more degree of closure before the complete, tight, closure of glottal stop is reached; this is the closure for *creak*. The precise mechanism of creak is unclear, but one way of producing it is to sing down the scale to the lowest note you can reach, then go still further down. With a little trial and error, adjusting vocal fold tensions, one can, in this way, achieve a clear, low frequency (about 40 to 60 Hz) rapid series of taps, rather like the sound of a stick being run along a railing, or of one of those noise-making devices in which a wooden toothed wheel in turning round repeatedly engages and 'tweaks' a wooden clapper. In creak the vocal folds are in close contact, but not much tensed, and air escapes in small periodic bursts through a very small aperture near the forward end of the vocal folds. The subglottal pressure is very low, and so too is the volume-velocity, being of the order of 12 cm^3/s up to a maximum of about 20 cm^3/s. A further stage of contraction will, of course, create glottal stop, but this, we have seen, never has a phonatory function. A glottal stop is either an *articulation* (the final shaping of a sound) superimposed on a pulmonically initiated air-stream, or else it is itself a concomitant of *initiation*.

Combinations of Stricture-types

We have now demonstrated, experimentally, that it is possible to segment the continuum of degrees of openness of stricture in a natural, non-arbitrary way. Having thus discovered *voiceless* (breath and nil), *whisper, voice* and *creak* as phonatory stricture-types we can proceed to see how these basic types can be combined.

We start with the combination of breath and voice. Take in a deep breath, then let it out rapidly and noisily trying to get the sound of voice mixed in with breath. The effect is somewhat like that of sighing. This is *breathy voice:* the glottis is narrowed from its most open position, but not narrowed enough to generate whisper, that is, it is still at considerably more than 25 per cent of its maximal opening, probably, in fact, around 30 to 40 per cent. The vocal folds are vibrating, but without ever closing or, indeed, coming anywhere near closing. They simply 'flap in the breeze' of the high-velocity air-flow. The liminal volume-velocity for the production of breathy voice is of the order of 90 to 100 cm^3/s: more commonly, however, it is much faster, around 900 to 1000 cm^3/s. Try filling the lungs to capacity and then generating breathy voice for as long as you can. Owing to the high volume-velocity of breathy voice, this probably will not be more than four or five seconds. Breathy voice often occurs when one tries to blurt out a message when extremely out of breath. It is also the phonation type of 'voiced h'.

Experiment next with the combination of whisper and voice. Take in a deep breath and start to produce pulmonic egressive whisper. While producing whisper, and taking care to keep it going, 'switch on' voice, and keep that going as well. You ought now to be producing a mixed sound, in which the periodic vibrations of voice are audible at the same time as the continuous 'hushing' sound of whisper. This is *whispery voice.* A second approach to whispery voice may be made by starting with normal, relaxed, low frequency voice, and then, while it is going on, relaxing the vocal folds further till continuous whisper is heard mixed in with voice. Whispery voice is produced by normal, though relaxed, production of voice, with a concomitant chink constantly open. In one type of whispery voice, perhaps the most common kind, the arytenoid cartilages are somewhat separated, so that there is a whisper-generating chink at the posterior end of the glottis, while the vocal folds, forward from the vocal processes are vibrating normally—that is, with a normal cycle of closed and open phases. In another type of whispery voice there is probably no localised arytenoidal chink: the vocal folds are simply somewhat relaxed and vibrate without ever closing completely, so that there is a constant whisper-generating escape of air. The airflow of whispery voice is naturally somewhat lower than in breathy voice, since in whispery voice there must always be a glottal chink small enough to generate whisper rather than breath: the liminal volume-velocity is about 60 to 70 cm^3/s and the normal flow is of the order of 300–400 cm^3/s, rather than the 900 to 1000 or so of breathy voice. Consequently, if you fill the lungs to capacity and then generate whispery voice for as long as you can the duration of the utterance will be about three times that of breathy voice. Whispery voice is an anthropophonically important phonation type since it is not uncommon in the languages of the world. In English, and possibly other languages, it is associated with tenderness or mild sexual excitement. In other languages it is a regularly utilized type of phonation, often referred to in the literature as 'murmur' or (incorrectly) as 'breathy voice'.

Whisper may be combined with creak, to produce *whispery creak*. Once you can produce creak, it is not very difficult to keep creak going and then open a chink (between the arytenoid cartilages), and let a whisper-generating air-stream escape simultaneously with creak. It is doubtful if whispery creak is ever used in any language, but its production is a means of 'getting the feel' of a posterior (arytenoidal) glottal opening, since we know that creak demands complete closure of the front part of the glottis, with a periodic very small opening there.

Finally, voice may be combined with creak, to produce *voiced creak*, or, as it is more commonly called, *creaky voice*. The precise mechanism of this is unknown, but it is an empirical fact that a combination of voice and creak can occur, with very relaxed vocal folds. Both creak and creaky voice seem to be quite common in final very low-pitched stretches of utterances in British English, particularly in varieties of RP (Received Pronunciation), which are regarded by non-RP speakers as particularly 'drawling' and 'affected'.

We may now briefly summarize the various types of phonatory stricture-types studied so far.

Voiceless: glottis wide open (about 60 to 95 per cent of maximal opening); at volume-velocities below about 200 to 350 cm^3/s flow is non-turbulent ('nil-phonation'); above this rate flow is turbulent, generating the sound of audible breathing ('breath phonation').

Whisper: glottis considerably narrowed (less than 25 per cent of maximal opening); volume-velocity, from about 25 cm^3/s upwards, strongly turbulent, generating the relatively, 'rich', 'hushing' sound of whisper, clearly modulated to produce 'vowel-like' sounds, by the oral resonator.

Voice: glottis closed, and vocal folds subjected to varying degrees of tension, such that they vibrate (at volume-velocities from about 50 cm^3/s upwards and from about 2 to 3 $cm\,H_2O$ up to about 30 $cm\,H_2O$ subglottal pressure), emitting periodic high-velocity puffs of air, generating the periodic sound known as 'voice'. Strictly speaking, this description refers only to that rather basic form of voice known as 'chest voice', characteristically occurring with low frequencies from about 60 to 150 or so Hz. In other types of (higher pitched) voice, such as mid-voice and falsetto, minimal volume-velocities and pressures are higher: according to Van den Berg and Tan (1962) the minimal volume-velocities and the range of subglottal pressures are mid-voice (lowest pitch 130 Hz) above 60 cm^3/s and pressures 10–30 cm H_2O, falsetto (lowest pitch 200 Hz) above 70 cm^3/s and pressure less than 15 cm H_2O. Moreover, the full closure and opening of the glottis described above may be characteristic only of chest voice; in other 'registers', as they are often called, there may be no absolute closure of the glottis. This is particularly true of falsetto, where the vocal folds are tensed and their edges vibrate in the passing air-stream.

Creak: glottis closed, very low subglottal pressure, very low mean volume-velocity (about 12 to 20 cm^3/s), and low-frequency (about 40 to 50 Hz) periodic bursts of air through a very small chink near the front end of the vocal folds. This generates a 'tapping' sound.

Breathy Voice: glottis considerably less open than for voiceless phonation, but not narrowed enough to produce whisper. Vocal folds 'flapping in the breeze' to produce a sigh-like mixture of breath and voice which, because of its high volume-velocity (around 900 to 1000 cm^3/s) cannot be long maintained.

Whispery Voice: somewhat relaxed vocal cords vibrating to generate voice, with continuous, simultaneous, richly turbulent escape of air through a chink, generating whisper. Two types are possible: (a) normal (fully closing) voice-vibrations 'up front' with a space for escape of whisper-air between the arytenoid cartilages, and (b) relaxed vocal folds never closing completely so that there is always a chink for escape of whisper-air somewhere along their length. Airflow much slower than for breathy voice—about 60 to 300/400 cm^3/s. Often wrongly called 'breathy voice'. Sometimes known (for example, in Gray 1939, Pandit 1957, Ladefoged 1971) by the uninformative label 'murmur'. The term 'murmur' was perhaps first used by Bell (1867, p. 46) for a sound which he describes as 'whisper and voice heard simultaneously'. Bell's further elucidation of this sound suggests, however, that he believed the whisper component to be produced in the pharynx. For general phonetic purposes it is best designated by the unambiguous analytic term 'whispery voice'.

Whispery Creak: continuous whisper-generating air-escape combined with creak.

Creaky Voice: creak combined with voice. Both creak and creaky voice occur with low pitch in certain types of British English.

The eight types of phonation listed here do not exhaust the possibilities. They represent simply four 'stricture-types' (four degrees of narrowing of the glottis) and four combinations of these. We must now consider differences in the *location* of these strictures.

Location

One can probably distinguish four different locations for phonation within the larynx: they are represented in figure 24 as follows: a. full glottal. b. anterior. c. posterior. d. ventricular.

Full Glottal may be regarded as 'normal' articulation, and therefore does not usually have to be specified. In this type of phonation the entire length of the glottis—both the anterior (ligamental) and the posterior (arytenoidal) parts—can be regarded as (potentially) functioning as a single unit. There is no active restriction of activity to one particular part. It is true that both creak and falsetto (voice and whisper) appear to involve only the front part of the glottis. Nevertheless, when the active compression of the rear end of the glottis characteristic of anterior phonation is absent they may be regarded as 'normal' or 'full glottal'.

Anterior. In anterior phonation the arytenoid cartilages are apparently clamped tightly together and only the front, ligamental part of the glottis actively participates in phonation. At the same time, the whole upper part of the larynx may be constricted to some extent: it appears as if the arytenoidal constriction essential for anterior phonation is part of a general sphincteric construction of

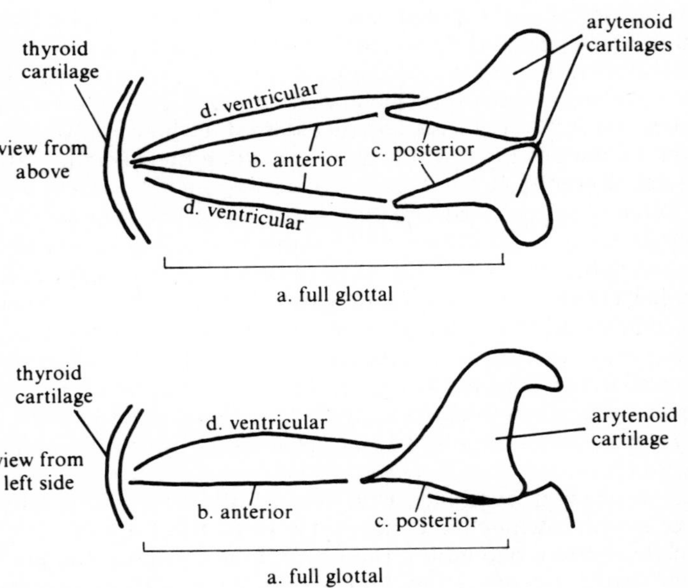

Figure 24. Phonatory locations within the larynx

the (upper) larynx. Voice produced at the anterior location has a somewhat 'tight', 'hard' quality and appears to be what Chiba and Kajiyama (1958) call 'sharp', and Lindqvist (1969) calls 'tense' voice. The best way to learn anterior voice is to contrive to get a general feeling of tenseness into the larynx, and it may help to follow the directions for 'sharp' voice given by Chiba and Kajiyama (p. 19), who say, 'We can easily produce this voice with our head drawn back while keeping it bent forward'. Anterior, hard, voice is characteristic of many North German speakers. In Britain some degree of 'anteriorness' is very common in the dialects of North East Scotland, especially Aberdeenshire and Banff, as opposed to the very lax, full-glottal, voice commonly heard in Central Scotland.

Having acquired *anterior voice* it is not difficult to acquire *anterior creak* and *anterior whisper*. The technique is to produce anterior voice: stop the air-flow but hold the phonatory posture, then, while being careful to hold that position, start up creak or whisper. If you can produce falsetto it is worth experimenting with 'anterior falsetto'. As we have already pointed out, both creak and falsetto (that is, 'normal' or 'full glottal' varieties) are in fact produced towards the front end of the glottis. Nevertheless, deliberate production of anterior creak and falsetto shows that, even in these cases, active restriction to anterior phonation produces a different effect: the anterior creak is 'sharper' more 'staccato', and the anterior falsetto is 'thinner' more 'reedy'.

Posterior phonation implies complete static closure of the forward, ligamental, part of the glottis, phonation occurring only at the arytenoidal end. It is known with certainty that one type of whisper can be produced here: a strong 'goose-hiss' type.

Ventricular phonation is produced between the ventricular bands or 'false vocal cords'. These can be approximated to generate turbulent *ventricular whisper;* they can be set in vibration to produce *ventricular voice;* and they can be completely closed to produce *ventricular stop.* Ventricular phonation can be learned by exaggerating the upper larynx constriction occurring with anterior phonation. When ventricular voice is combined, as it can be, with glottal voice, the combination is sometimes called 'double voice'. People can learn to control both types of voice so as to sing two notes at once. Paget (1930, p. 34) describes such a case: 'In September 1928, Sir James Dundas-Grant and I examined Mr Strath Mackay, who has the peculiar accomplishment of being able to sing two notes at once. The higher notes (tenor register) are produced by the vocal cords; the lower notes, which normally vary with the upper notes so as to maintain a constant musical interval of 17 semitones (an octave and a fifth), appeared, from Sir James Dundas-Grant's observations, to be made by the bringing together of the false vocal cords, so that they vibrated like true vocal cords.

The observations were confirmed by a similar examination of my own throat while imitating (so far as possible) Mr Mackay's double notes. Sir James was able to see the ventricular bands definitely in vibration while a very low note was being produced. It seems clear that in certain types of shouting—so as to produce a raucous sound —the false vocal cords are brought together so as to vibrate on their own account.'

Double voice (ventricular plus glottal voice) appears to be used by certain Tibetan monks who, with long training, learn to intone melodiously and impressively on two notes simultaneously. Much less melodious was the harsh ventricular plus glottal vibration often used in the 1930s in a type of jazz singing known as 'scat singing' and particularly associated with the name of Cab Calloway. Elsewhere, 'ventricular voice' and 'diplophonia' are referred to as 'speech defects' (van Riper and Irwin 1958, pp. 220, 221, Kaplan 1960, p. 168). Turbulent flow through the ventricular bands, with occasional ventricular vibration (ventricular fricative and trill), occurs as a regular sound in several Caucasian languages, as also does complete closure, or 'ventricular stop'. These activities are more properly to be regarded as articulatory rather than phonatory, since they generate single sounds patterning with consonants in the structure of these languages rather than as phonatory modifications of sounds articulated elsewhere.

Glottal Stops. As we mentioned earlier, complete closure of the glottis has either an initiatory or an articulatory function: the former in phonationless glottalic initiation and the latter in glottal stop as an articulatory type functionally parallel in languages to other kinds of stop articulation. Nevertheless, it will be well to say something about glottal stops here while we are discussing laryngeal functions in speech.

Stops can be produced at full, anterior, and ventricular locations in the larynx. Experiment with full glottal stops: make a series of gentle, minimal, glottal stops, that is, with very little subglottal pressure and no exaggerated constriction of the larynx. Let them explode mildly into a very brief h-like sound: [ʔhʔhʔh]. Now, constrict the larynx as for anterior voice and make a series of anterior glottal stops [ʔhʔhʔh]. Note that these have a slightly sharper, slightly more high-pitched release sound. Glottal stops can, of course, be released into voicelessness, into whisper, or into voice. A mild glottal stop released into voice is the 'hard onset' or 'hard attack' or 'fester Einsatz' of singers: in this case there is a build-up of positive pressure below the glottis and the vocal fold vibration starts with the folds bursting open, then swinging shut again, as opposed to the open starting position and closure by Bernoulli suction characteristic of the 'soft' or 'smooth' attack.

An intense constriction of the upper larynx will bring together the ventricular bands. Whether they can be closed without simultaneous closure of the glottis proper is doubtful: 'ventricular stop' is probably always 'ventricular plus glottal' stop. In any case, it is easy to feel and hear the difference between simple glottal stop, and ventricular (plus glottal) stop. The latter involves a considerable feeling of upper-larynx constriction, which is quite absent from the former. Moreover, simple glottal stop has no influence on the quality of neighbouring vowels: thus, apart from the abrupt cessation and recommencement, [aʔa] or [ɛʔɛ] sounds no different from prolonged [aː] or [ɛː]. On the other hand, ventricular stop imparts a noticeable 'strangulated' nuance of pharyngealization to preceding and following vowels. Thus, using [ʕʔ] to represent ventricular stop, compare [aː] [aʔa] [aʕʔa], [ɛː] [ɛʔɛ] [ɛʕʔɛ]. Glottal stop [ʔ] is a common sound in the languages of the world, either as a syllable separator, or as a consonantal articulation in a series of stop consonants, as in Arabic, the Adyghe languages, and elsewhere. Ventricular plus glottal stop [ʕʔ] occurs as a regular sound in several north Caucasian languages, particularly the Nakh languages Chechen, Ingush and Batsbiy, where it contrasts with ordinary glottal stop, as in Chechen [daʔa] *to eat* [daʕʔa] *to castrate*. A similar distinction occurs in the Tigrinya language of north Ethiopia.

Lindqvist (1969) describes and exemplifies as 'glottal stop' what appears in reality to be ventricular plus glottal stop, or at least glottal stop with strong upper larynx constriction. This is a quite unusual type of glottal stop. Normal glottal stop does not involve the intense upper larynx constriction seen in Lindqvist's laryngoscopic photographs. Note the phonological opposition of this 'intense', ventricular plus glottal stop to normal glottal stop referred to in the preceding paragraph.

Summary of Phonation Types

We summarize the main phonation types (including, for the moment, the stops which are more properly articulations) in table 11. Ladefoged (1971) lists phonation types in the form of a single continuum. This listing leaves out ventricular phonation (or ventricular articulation), but otherwise may be quite a useful listing for phonological purposes. It fails, however, to take explicit account of locational differences, and this makes it less useful for anthropophonic purposes—for the unambiguous categorization of the phonatory possibilities of man. A distinction is made between 'murmur' and 'lax

Table 11

stricture type	location		
	glottal	*anterior*	*ventricular + glottal*
1. wide open	voiceless		
2. narrowed	whisper	anterior whisper	ventricular whisper
3. vibrating freely	voice	anterior voice 'tense', 'sharp' voice	ventricular voice double voice
4. low frequency taps	creak	anterior creak 'tense' creak	ventricular creak
1 + 3 open, vibrating	breathy voice		
2 + 3 narrowed vibrating	whispery voice, murmur	anterior whispery voice	

voice'. Now the former is clearly one form of whispery voice: that which occurs with and following 'voiced aspirated stops', [bh, dh, etc.] in a number of Indian languages. The latter is said to occur in Indonesian. If this is similar to the 'lax voice' occurring in Javanese, then it is also somewhat 'whispery'. In Javanese the so-called voiced stops, usually transliterated [b, d, ɖ, ɟ, g], are, in fact, totally voiceless (except when a nasal precedes), as are [p, t, ʈ, c, k]. However, the phonation type of vowels following [p, t, ʈ, etc.] is anterior or 'tense'; that of vowels following [b, d, ɖ, etc.] has the larynx lowered and a distinctly lax, slightly whispery quality. The larynx-lowering of [b, d, ɖ, etc.] is easily observed, and air-flow records show very clearly that the volume-velocity of air in vowels after [b, d, g] is very much faster than after [p, t, k]. This implies some form of leakage of air in Javanese lax voice. It seems possible that Ladefoged's 'murmur' (the 'whispery voice' of Indian languages) is anterior voice plus posterior (arytenoidal) whisper, while 'lax voice' is simply pure, full glottal, whispery voice.

Lindqvist (1969) has a two-dimensional approach to phonation. Taking *voice* as the basic phonation type, he describes two kinds of departure from that basis: these are the 'glottal abduction gesture', and the 'glottal stop gesture', which produces what he calls 'laryngealization'.

This simple two-dimensional array takes us quite a long way: by larynx abduction we proceed from 'voice' through 'lax voice' and 'breathy voice' to 'unvoiced'; by laryngealization we proceed from voice through 'tense voice' and 'creak' to 'glottal stop'.

Unfortunately, however, the whole system is invalidated by the fact that it is founded upon what appears to be a misconception concerning the nature of glottal stop. Lindqvist takes as 'normal' the ventricular plus glottal stop discussed above. Since this already involves ventricular approximation it makes it impossible, in Lindqvist's system, to deal separately with phonatory activities at glottal and ventricular locations. It is interesting to note that Lindqvist takes the 'voicing position' as basic, describing all other phonatory states as departures from that norm. A somewhat similar view is adopted by Chomsky and Halle (1968), who regard the voicing position of the glottis as part of the 'neutral' state of the vocal tract. There may be some reason for adopting voice as the 'norm' since in many languages, perhaps in most, voicing occurs more of the time during speech, than voicelessness. This at least is true of the better-known Western European languages, though it is not necessarily the case in other languages. In table 12 the percentages are based on a count of the numbers of voiced and voiceless phonemes in short *texts* in various languages; if we simply counted the number of voiced and voiceless sounds in the phoneme *inventories* of languages we should find a great many languages in which voiceless phonemes far outnumber voiced ones.

Table 12

	voiced	*voiceless*
French	78%	22%
Swedish	75	25
Italian	71	29
English	72	28
Finnish	63	37
Russian	61	39
Chinese (Pekin)	57	43
Abkhaz (Caucasus)	56	44
Chinese (Canton)	41	59

Be that as it may, from the general phonetic point of view, voice is only one condition on a quasi-continuum which has fully open glottis at one end and completely closed glottis at the other.

The paper by Halle and Stevens (1971) makes an interesting contribution to the study of phonation. On the basis of a theoretical model of larynx operation, they postulate two independently controlled parameters: vocal cord stiffness and degree of glottal opening. Since two anthropophonically utilized values are assumed for each parameter, they have four *features*, as follows: (1) spread glottis, (2) constricted glottis, (3) stiff vocal cords, (4) slack vocal cords. Since the glottis cannot be simultaneously spread and constricted and the vocal cords cannot be simultaneously stiff and slack, the four features yield nine distinct phonetic categories, which Halle and Stevens then enumerate and discuss.

In spite of its ingenuity, this system has shortcomings. In the first place it suffers from what is almost an inevitable defect of all purely theoretical and highly restricted systems of features, namely, a tendency to the procrustean forcing of items into particular categories, whether this categorization corresponds to reality or not. Secondly, it fails to take account of the different functions—initiatory, phonatory, and articulatory—of the larynx; true, no such distinctions are implied by the very general title of the paper, 'A note on laryngeal features', but it should be clear by now that it is essential for any truly systematic phonetic taxonomy to distinguish between the basic componential functions.

Both shortcomings are exemplified in the feature assignments for the sounds represented by [b] and [ɓ], which are distinguished as respectively [+ slack vocal cords] and [+ constricted glottis], all other features having minus values in each case. It seems, however, that the only reason for assigning the features [+ constricted glottis] and [− slack vocal cords] to [ɓ] is the procrustean one that this particular feature-combination is otherwise unused: there is no empirical justification for thinking that [ɓ] necessarily has either less slack vocal cords or a more constricted glottis than [b], in spite of the authors' statement that 'the true implosive [ɓ] apparently does not cause a lowering of the tone of an adjacent vowel, as would normally be expected from a voiced ([+ slack]) consonant like [b] . . . since the vocal cords are not slack'. The truly relevant distinction between [b] and [ɓ] is that [b] has pulmonic pressure initiation while [ɓ] has glottalic suction initiation. The 'lowering of the tone of an adjacent vowel' next to voiced obstruent, especially stop, consonants, is a well-known phenomenon, which will be referred to again later. It results from reduction of the transglottal pressure difference due to the impedance imposed by a close oral stricture; it has nothing to do with vocal cord tension *per se*. In a voiced glottalic suction stop, such as [ɓ], the sudden downward larynx movement may enlarge the supraglottal cavity so much that the transglottal pressure difference is actually *increased,* leading to a *higher* frequency (a 'raised tone') in the adjacent vowel.

Another failure to differentiate between initiatory and articulatory functions occurs in the category characterized by [+ constricted glottis] and [+ stiff vocal cords] which includes what they transcribe as [pʔ], [ʔ, ʔw] and [ʔy (= IPA ʔj)] and 'glottalized vowels'. The classification fails to make clear the difference between glottalic pressure [p'] and pulmonic pressure [pʔ] (that is, co-articulated glottal + labial stop). It is clear from the discussion that the transcription [pʔ] refers to the glottalic pressure stop, but [ʔ, ʔw] and [ʔy], which are put in the same feature category, are, of course, *pulmonic* pressure sounds.

We find another problematic sound listed for the feature-combination ([+ constricted glottis] [+ slack vocal cords]): this is described as 'voiced glottal stop' and represented by [ʔ̬]. Whatever it actually is, this sound, said to occur in Jingpho, a language of northern Burma, cannot possibly be a voiced glottal stop. Glottal stop requires total, tight, closure of the glottis, maintained for an appreciable time. Voicing requires periodic opening and closing (vibration) of the glottis, maintained for an appreciable time. A voiced glottal stop would require these mutually incompatible events to occur simultaneously. We cannot even evade this impossibility by postulating that Jingpho [ʔ̬] is in reality a *ventricular* stop (formed at the 'false vocal cords') with simultaneous voicing. A moment's calculation shows that this, too, is quite impossible. With the ventricular bands tightly closed for a ventricular stop the only place for the air flowing up through the glottis to go would be the space between the 'true' and 'false' vocal cords—the ventricles of Morgagni. The volume of this space, however, is very small—perhaps only 1 cm^3—and certainly not more than 2 cm^3. A further calculation shows that for plausible subglottal pressure (say 8 cmH_2O), and a mean volume-velocity even as low as 100 cm^3/s, flow would cease after only ·00012 seconds; in other words, for practical purposes there would be no flow, and certainly no voice.

Apart from the points mentioned here, Halle and Stevens' contribution is an interesting one, which directs attention to several important laryngeal features, even though it must be read with caution.

Vocal-fold Modifications

We have enumerated the major phonation types in terms of phonatory stricture and location. Now we must consider some modifications. These are principally variations in the *thickness, length,* and *tension* of the vocal folds. Variations in the thickness of the vocal folds correlate with variations in their length, and also with the frequency of glottal vibration in voice. On this see Hollien (1960), Hollien and Moore (1960) and Hollien and Curtis (1960). In general, the vocal folds are thicker and shorter in 'chest register' than in 'mid-register'. In falsetto, the vocal folds are tautened and their edges are narrowed. These effects can be heard, and felt, if one produces glottal stops with the vocal folds arranged as for chest voice and as for falsetto. In falsetto glottal stop (released into voicelessness—[ʔh]) one can hear the sharp, delicate contact and release of the very narrow edges of the folds. In chest voice glottal stop, the release sound is 'heavier' and 'sloppier': one can hear and feel that the contacting edges of the vocal folds are deeper, and the movement is less delicate than in falsetto glottal stop. Analogous differences can be heard and felt between whisper in falsetto and chest voice.

When the vocal folds are in vibration in voice, breathy voice, whispery voice or creaky voice (but probably not in creak), the frequency of their vibrations can be varied quite considerably, the actual frequency ranges for singers of different types being (on the average) as in table 13. In speech, of course, variation is considerably smaller and confined to the lower end of the range.

Table 13

bass	76 to 256 Hz
baritone	96 to 384
tenor	140 to 512
contralto	217 to 665
mezzo	256 to 768
soprano	384 to 1024 (or, exceptionally, 2048 Hz) (Curry 1940)

The precise mechanism of frequency variation in voice is still a matter for discussion, but one thing is certain, namely, that frequency changes may be brought about (a) by changes in muscle activity, resulting in tensing and thinning, or relaxing and fattening the vocal folds, and (b) by changes in the pressure-differences above and below the vocal folds. We pointed out earlier that with an egressive air-stream passing up through the glottis, a pressure-difference of 2 to 3 cm H_2O is necessary for the production of voice. If the pressure-difference drops below this, voicing will cease. At pressures somewhat above this liminal value any sudden change of pressure will change the frequency of vibration of the vocal folds, irrespective of the muscular tension. In an experiment in which a subject had his chest unexpectedly pressed, a subglottal pressure change of about 7.5 cm H_2O produced a pitch change of about half an octave (Ladefoged 1963). On this see also Ohala (1970).

There has been some recent controversy as to whether laryngeal muscle action directly on the vocal folds or subglottal pressure changes are responsible for certain linguistically relevant pitch changes in English (Lieberman 1967, Ohala and Ladefoged 1969, Vanderslice 1967). It seems to have been established that laryngeal muscle action is normally responsible. Nevertheless, frequency changes in response to pressure-difference across the glottis are important in another context. We have already discussed in Chapter 5 the fact that in voiced stop consonants the air cannot escape from the mouth, which raises the intra-oral pressure and so tends to abolish the transglottal pressure difference, and we saw that supraglottal expansion may occur to obviate this danger. It is, of course, true also of any sounds involving oral constriction, for example, fricatives, that this will tend to cause a rise in intra-oral pressure to a greater or lesser degree. Consequently not only in stops, but in fricatives, the transglottal pressure-difference is lowered, and hence there is a tendency for the frequency of voice to *drop* during these sounds. This phenomenon of lowered frequency during voiced consonants has often been observed, and is a well-known factor in the genesis of tones in the history of various languages.

Variations of frequency of voice occur during speech in all languages. Nobody speaks all the time in a monotone. Languages differ, however, in the way in which frequency variations are utilized linguistically. On the one hand, frequency variations may be systematically related to long stretches of utterance, which may be many syllables in length, and which correspond to relatively 'large' grammatical units such as clause or sentence. Frequency patterns (pitch patterns) utilized in this way are called *intonations,* and languages utilizing pitch in this way are 'intonation languages'. Many of the best known languages of the world are intonation languages, for example, English, French, Spanish, Russian, Arabic, Hindi, and Indonesian.

On the other hand, systematic pitch variations and pitch patterns may be related to short stretches of utterance of about syllable length, and to 'short' grammatical units such as word or morpheme. Pitch patterns used in this way are called *tones* and languages utilizing pitch in this way are 'tone languages'. Typical tone languages are Chinese, Vietnamese, Thai, many African languages, such as Igbo and Zulu, and many Amerindian languages.

Voicing and Aspiration

We have already referred to differences between 'voiced' and 'voiceless' sounds. Here we must look at this distinction more closely, with special reference to English. Although the English consonants [b] as in *be,* [d] as in *do,* [g] as in *go,* [v] *vie,* [ð] *thy,* [z] *zoo,* [ʒ] *leisure* are traditionally described as *voiced,* in contradistinction to [p] as in *pie,* [s] as in *sigh,* and so on, some misgivings have been felt by many writers in using this description, since in certain circumstances the former group seems to involve little or no vibration of the vocal folds. In particular the initial and final 'voiced' stops, as in *babe* or *dead,* and the initial and final 'voiced' fricatives, as in *verve* and *zoos* sometimes seem to be almost completely voiceless. For this reason, some scholars have preferred to describe the two series as *lax* or *lenis* [b, d, g, v, z, ð, ʒ] and *tense* or *fortis* [p, t, k, f, θ, s, ʃ]—on which see Chapter 10.

The relative voicelessness of initial [b, d, g] in English, and of initial and final [v, z], and so on, was pointed out by Henry Sweet nearly a century ago (Sweet 1877, pp. 75–80). Moreover, Sweet anticipated recent instrumental findings that show that even though the so called 'voiced' stops and fricatives of English may, on occasion, completely lack vocal fold vibrations, nevertheless they do have a narrowed glottal opening. In Sweet's words 'Final [z] may . . . be . . . fully vocalized throughout, or else, gradually devocalized, passing from voice to whisper while the consonant position is still being maintained. Both may be heard (but generally the latter) in the E[nglish] "is", etc. In final buzzes after other voice consonants the gradual devocalization is very clearly marked in E. Thus in the final buzz in "bills", "thieves", "adze", etc., the vocality is of so short a duration that the final [z] is almost a purely whispered consonant. In this last case the glottis is not fully opened till the consonant is finished, which therefore consists of voice passing into whisper, followed by a breath-glide. If the transition from voice to breath is completed during the beginning of the consonant itself, we have the Icelandic final [s] "ís", "las", etc., which sounds like (zs)'.

Recent glottographic and laryngoscopic studies show that the English 'voiced' stops and fricatives, even when not actually voiced, exhibit considerable whisper-like narrowing of the glottis. As we point out in Chapter 10, it is thus unnecessary to postulate a lenis/fortis distinction. Even when the vocal cords are not actually vibrating, English [b, d, v, z] are distinguished phonationally from [p, t, f, s] by the fact that the former are accompanied by a narrowing of the glottis. They are thus potentially, if not actually, voiced, and there is no need to invoke a dubious and ill-defined concept of 'tenseness'.

A further distinction with regard to phonation types has to do, in its most immediately observable aspect, with time-relations between voicing and oral strictures referred to by the terms 'unaspirated' and 'aspirated'. If the reader is a native speaker of English the chances are that he will be able to hear a good example of an aspirated stop in a fairly forcible pronunciation of the word *car*. He will observe that the voicing for the vowel [aː] does not begin until a noticeable time (about 50 to 80 milliseconds) after the release of the dorso-velar closure of [k]. The word may thus be transcribed phonetically as [k^haː], in which [^{h}] represents the period of voicelessness that precedes the voicing of the vowel. This retardation in the onset of voicing, or 'voicing-lag' as it is called is characteristic of aspirated consonants. Lisker and Abramson (1964) studied this phenomenon in a number of languages. These included (1) a group of languages which are generally said to possess unaspirated voiceless stops

(Dutch, Spanish, Hungarian, Tamil), (2) a language which possesses aspirated voiceless stops (English) and (3) several languages in which there is a phonological opposition between unaspirated and aspirated voiceless stops (Cantonese, east Armenian, Thai, Hindi).

The mean voicing lag times in ms for all stops of the [p, t, k] and [pʰ, tʰ, kʰ] types in these languages are shown in table 14. The voicing lag in all cases was longest for [k] or [kʰ]. The actual mean figures in ms are shown in table 15.

Table 14

	unaspirated [p, t, k]	*aspirated* [pʰ, tʰ, kʰ]
Group 1	15	
Group 2 (English)		70
Group 3	16	78

Table 15

	unaspirated			*aspirated*		
	[p]	[ʇ]	[ʞ]	[b$_{\mu}$]	[ʇ$_{\mu}$]	[ʞ$_{\mu}$]
Group 1	7	12	27			
Group 2 (English)				58	70	80
Group 3	7·7	13·2	27	72	67	94

Not only stops can be aspirated, but several other types of sound as well, notably affricates (see Chapter 11) and fricatives. Moreover, something analogous to the 'voicing-lag' of voiceless aspirated stops can be observed with the so-called 'voiced aspirated stops' of Hindi and other north Indian languages, usually represented in phonetic transcription by [bh, dh, gh], and so on. The use of the term 'voiced aspirated stop' for these sounds has been criticized by Ladefoged (1971) on the grounds that in this usage 'one is using neither the term voiced nor the term aspirated in the same way' as in the description of voiceless aspirated stops such as [pʰ, tʰ, kʰ]. Ladefoged's objection, however, loses much of its validity when one thinks of both voiceless and voiced aspirated sounds as involving delayed onset of *normal* voicing: the fact is that in such sounds as [bh] there is *whispery voice* rather than voice during the stop and for a certain period after its release.[1] Just as with voiceless aspirated stops, there is thus a delay in the onset of normal voice. Moreover, instrumental recordings of intra-oral air-pressure in voiced aspirated stops show that the pattern of air-pressure in these stops differs from that of the corresponding voiced *unaspirated* stops in precisely the same way as does the intra-oral pressure in aspirated and unaspirated *voiceless* stops. It is characteristic of (initial) aspirated stops, both voiceless and voiced, that the intra-oral pressure goes on rising right to the end of the period of closure. At the moment of release the pressure is still rising, often at an increasing rate. In unaspirated stops, both voiceless and voiced, the pressure increase tends to flatten off, and may even be falling slightly by the time the release occurs. This difference in pressure pattern is undoubtedly related to the glottal-stricture difference mentioned below.

Just as there may be a time-lag between the release of a stop or fricative stricture and the *onset* of voicing (*aspiration*), so there may equally well be a time-lag between the *offset,* or cessation, of voicing and the formation of the stop (or fricative) stricture. In this latter case we have *pre-aspiration*. Pre-aspiration, represented by, for example, [^{h}p, ^{h}t, ^{h}k], is a well-known phenomenon in Icelandic, Scots Gaelic, and the English spoken by Scots Gaelic speakers. It also occurs in the north Caucasian languages, Chechen and Ingush.

Aspirated consonants can, no doubt, be most easily detected by means of the voicing-lag which we have been discussing. Nevertheless, this is only a symptom of what we may regard as a more fundamental characteristic of these sounds, namely, the state of the glottis. It was already suggested by Sweet (1877) that in aspirated [k^{h}a] 'the glottis is left open while the stop is being formed and the chords are not brought into the voice position till the moment of loosening the stop, so that before the glottis has time to form voice there is a slight escape of breath between the stop and the vowel—the glide from the stop to the vowel is breathed'. On the other hand, in unaspirated [ka] 'the glottis is in the position for voice during the stop, but without any air being forced through it, and consequently the stop is as inaudible as in the case of [k^h], but voice begins the moment the stop is loosened, and the glide is therefore voiced'. Later writers, tended to exaggerate the glottal closure of unaspirated stops. Grammont (1933) for instance, appeared to claim that the unaspirated [p, t, k] of French and some other languages involved *complete* glottal closure. But this was clearly wrong, as it would mean that normal French, Italian and other [p, t, k] were either glottalic pressure stops [p, t, k,] or pulmonic glottal and oral stops, like the [ʔp, ʔt, ʔk] sounds of many (British) English dialects, a point which was made in Catford (1947). Recent investigations, however, have shown that Sweet was essentially right, and Grammont was wrong only in attributing *complete* glottal closure to [p, t, k]. Modern techniques of glottography and laryngoscopy show that unaspirated voiceless sounds have a narrowed (though not completely closed) glottis while aspirated sounds have a more or less widely open glottis Indeed, a study of Korean stops (Kim 1970) shows an almost linear relation between the area of glottal opening during the stops and the duration of the voicing-lag following release of the stop. Kim's data

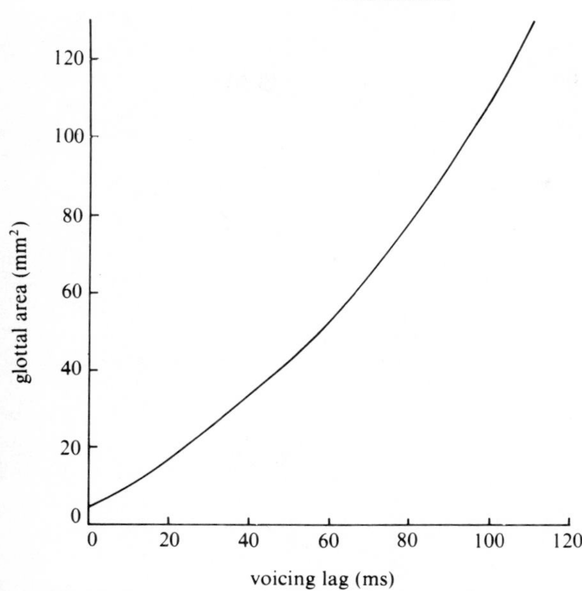

Figure 25. Relation of voicing-lag to glottal area

may be summed up in figure 25 (where the maximum glottal *areas* have been estimated from Kim's actual figures for maximum *width* of the glottal opening).

These figures, of course, are precisely valid only for the specific Korean stops investigated by Kim. Nevertheless, they undoubtedly express a relationship which is generally true. Aspirated, or pre-aspirated, sounds are produced with a relatively large glottal opening during the stricture ; unaspirated sounds with the glottis restricted as to cross-sectional area. This distinction applies also to voiced sounds. Voiced unaspirated sounds involve relatively tight glottal closure alternating periodically with the relatively minimal openings through which high velocity jets burst upwards into the pharynx. Aspirated voiced sounds involve a wider glottal opening, in the sense that the vocal cord vibrations are accompanied by a continuing escape of air through a moderately large chink.

The relation between area of glottal opening and duration of voicing-lag also helps to explain why stressed initial voiceless stops in English, as in *par, tar, car,* are strongly aspirated, while stops preceded by /s/, as in *spar, star, scar,* are virtually unaspirated. If we assume that the change from wide-open glottis to the voicing position occurs normally at a rate of about 1000 mm^2 per second,

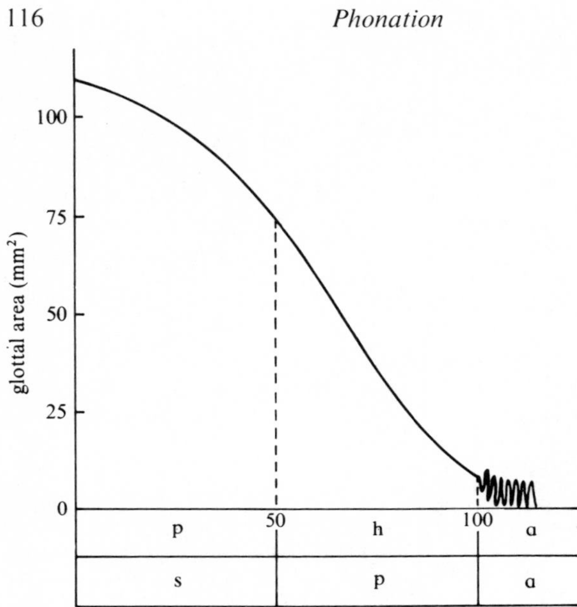

Figure 26. Initial [p^h] and [sp] in English

or 1 mm^2 in every millisecond, then we can picture the relation between area of glottal opening, and oral articulation, as in figure 26.

The quite plausible inference behind this is that, in English, initial voiceless consonants, or voiceless consonant-clusters, always begin with the glottis widely open. The time-lag between this wide open state of the glottis, and fully vibrating vocal cords for the following vowel is always roughly the same; alternatively, approximately the same quantity of air is always driven through the glottis in any English voiceless syllable onset. This would account not only for the facts referred to above, but also for the fact that in English, initial [p, t, k] plus [l, r, w] or [j] involves a fully or partially voiceless second term in the initial cluster, that is, [pl̥, tw̥, kj̊], and so on.

SEVEN

Articulation 1: Stricture Types

Articulation is one of the two basic components of vocal sound production. After initiation has set in train a flow of air, articulation acts upon the air-stream to 'shape' it, as it were, into a sound of specific type and quality.

For instance, pulmonic pressure-initiation generates an undifferentiated egressive flow of air up and out of the vocal tract. A close approximation of the articulating organs forms a narrow channel through which the air-stream forces its way, becoming turbulent in the process: articulation has thus 'shaped' the undifferentiated air-stream into a sound of specific type, a fricative. Moreover, the specific kind of fricative depends on the location of the articulatory channel: compare, for instance, [f, s, ʃ]. In the corresponding voiced fricatives [v, z, ʒ], phonatory activity in the larynx generates the sound of 'voice', but it is the articulatory process that once again takes the pulsating voiced air-stream and shapes it into the specific fricatives [v, z, ʒ]. Again, in vowel sounds like [i, ɑ, u] (roughly as in *tea, tar, too*), phonation imposes the pulsations of voice upon the air-stream, but it is articulation that finally shapes the voiced air-stream into the specific sounds of [i, ɑ, u]: the oral resonance frequencies are manipulated by placing the articulatory organs into different positions.

Glottal closure (glottal stop) has sometimes been regarded as a type of phonation. It is, however, the 'final shaping' function of articulation that explains why we regard glottal stop [ʔ] as a form of articulation, not of phonation. This is particularly clear in languages in which [ʔ] takes its place alongside other stops, such as [p, t, k]. Here the glottal closure of [ʔ] is the final shaping activity, which converts the undifferentiated pulmonic egressive air-stream into a specific sound, just as do the other articulators for [p, t], and so on.[1]

Articulations, like phonations, can be described in terms of their stricture-types and their locations. The vocal tract from the glottis upwards may be imagined as a horizontally straightened-out, bifurcated (nose/mouth), four-dimensional tube, the parameters of articulation corresponding more or less to these four dimensions—the *vertical, transverse* and *longitudinal* space dimensions, and *time*.

The articulatory parameters corresponding to these four dimensions are as follows. The vertical dimension is represented by the parameter of stricture-type in the narrowest sense, comprising different degrees of closeness of approximation (in a quasi-vertical direction) between articulating organs (articulators), forming articulatory channels of varying cross-sectional area. The transverse dimension is represented by the parameter of *oral airpath,* the air-stream passing through the mouth either along the centre line (for 'central' articulations), or along one or both sides (for 'lateral' articulations). The longitudinal dimension is represented by the parameter of *location*—the fact that the nasal cavity is parallel to the oral cavity does not destroy the generally 'longitudinal' nature of the location parameter.

The fourth articulatory dimension, time, enters into the picture in a number of ways. All sounds have a certain duration in time, and the temporal sequence of speech on several strands (for example, the temporal succession and overlaps of articulatory postures and movements, and the temporal relationships between articulation, phonation and initiation) are matters to be discussed later, especially in Chapter 11. In a first approach to the study of articulation, however, time is minimally invoked as a minor parameter of stricture-types, separating off those sound-types that involve an essentially and obligatorily *momentary* articulatory posture (such as *flaps* and *semivowels*) from those that are essentially *prolongable,* even though they may sometimes occur quite short in speech.

It is clear that articulatory stricture-types, like those of phonation, can be of different degrees of openness. It is obvious that the articulatory channel for a vowel like [e] (roughly as in English *say*) is much more open than the channel for [z]. There is, indeed, a continuum of possible degrees of openness running from the complete, tight, closure of a stop, like [p] or [b], to the maximal openness of a vowel like [a]. A basic problem of phonetics is, and always has been, to find natural, non-arbitrary criteria for the segmentation of this continuum. To do this we shall proceed, as we did with phonation, to experiment in our own vocal tracts.

It is obvious that complete articulatory closure is possible, as in [p, t, k, b, d, g], for example, so, for the moment we shall ignore this. We begin, then, by producing a prolonged and vigorous voiced fricative, for example [v], preferably in front of a mirror. Let the vocal effort, (the initiator power and resultant sound-intensity) be about that of fairly loud conversation. Note, in parenthesis, that all basic phonetic experiments must be done with firm, definite, articulation and with a reasonably powerful initiation. There is little to be learned from indecisive fumbling articulation and feeble kitten-like mewings. In saying this prolonged and vigorous [v] we note that it is markedly fricative in sound: the hiss of turbulent air-flow can be clearly heard above, and mingling with, the sound of voice.[2] Observe that, in a strongly fricative [v], it is the inner part of the lower lip that is in close contact with the edges of the upper teeth, and that the opening between the lips is quite small. Now, while saying [v], slowly and carefully slide the lower lip downwards, so that the labial opening gradually gets bigger and bigger. It will be observed that, very soon, the 'hiss and buzz' sound of the voiced fricative has ceased, and only the 'smooth' non-fricative sound of voice remains. As a rule, the cessation of turbulence occurs well before one reaches the point where the outer (as opposed to the inner) lip is in contact with the edges of the upper teeth. There is, as it happens, a special phonetic symbol for this 'non-turbulent [v]': it is a letter 'v' of rounded shape [ʋ]. Repeat the experiment several times, carefully and slowly sliding back and forth between fricative [v] and non-fricative [ʋ]: [v-ʋ-v-ʋ-v-ʋ].

The type of non-fricative articulation with which we have just been experimenting, with an articulatory channel just a very little wider than that of a fricative, is called an *approximant*, a term invented, I believe, by Ladefoged, although used by him in a slightly different sense.[3] On this see further on page 122. So far we have seen that a voiced approximant has non-turbulent air-flow through a channel slightly larger than that of a fricative. We must now experiment with the devoicing of both fricatives and approximants.

Produce a vigorous, fully-voiced highly-fricative [v]. Now, while maintaining as nearly as possible the same vocal effort (employing approximately the same initiator power), devoice it. As the glottis 'valve' is opened up one can feel the voiceless air-stream surging through at a higher volume-velocity, with a highly turbulent flow through the articulatory orifice and a rather loud fricative hiss. Repeat the sequence [v-f-v-f] several times.

Now go back again to voiced fricative [v], and this time open up the articulation a little, just to the point where the air-flow ceases to be turbulent, so that you are saying the approximant [ʋ]. You will probably feel as you do so that you have cut down in 'vocal effort' a little. In fact, if one were to use the same initiator power on the more open approximant [ʋ], the approximant sound would appear very much louder, and it is probably the monitoring effect of auditory feedback that leads us to cut back the initiator power as we pass from fricative [v] to approximant [ʋ]. Now, with a good, non-turbulent approximant going, suddenly devoice, while maintaining roughly the same vocal effort. As the glottal valve opens one feels the surge of the much increased velocity of the voiceless air-stream, and the flow through the labio-dental orifice at once becomes turbulent. The symbol for this voiceless labio-dental approximant is [ʋ̥]. Now switch back and forth between the voiced and voiceless approximant two or three times: [ʋ–ʋ̥–ʋ–ʋ̥]. Note these important facts: in the *voiced* approximant, the flow through the articulatory channel is laminar—there is no fricative-like hiss; in the *voiceless* approximant, the flow through the articulatory channel is turbulent—there is a hiss like that of the corresponding fricative, although somewhat weaker.

One can carry out a similar experiment with vowels. Say a long, rather strong and tense [i] vowel (like the vowel in English *see,* or, better, French *si*). Notice that there is no turbulence. Now devoice it: that is, rigidly maintain the tongue-articulation for [i] but open the glottal valve, producing voiceless [i̥]. Note that the flow through the tongue-palate articulatory channel is now turbulent. The vowel [i], then, is an approximant. Now say a long, voiced [i] again, noting that it is non-fricative, and try to maintain (or even increase) the initiator power, while slowly and deliberately closing up the articulatory channel till the flow becomes turbulent. In this way you can convert the voiced dorso-palatal approximant (or 'vowel') [i] into the voiced dorso-palatal fricative [ᴊ].

It will now be abundantly clear that we can distinguish two kinds of articulatory stricture-types involving small oral channels: *fricative* and *approximant.* And clearly one difference between them is that (at roughly the same initiator power within each pair) fricatives have turbulent flow through the channel, whether they are voiceless or voiced, whereas approximants have turbulent flow only when voiceless. We give a more precise and formal characterization of fricatives and approximants below.

Meanwhile we must carry our experiments one step further. First go back to the voiced labio-dental fricative [v]: note the very small articulatory channel. Now slowly and carefully open up the channel very little, just to the point where turbulence ceases. This is the voiced labio-dental approximant [ʋ]. Hold the articulatory posture for [ʋ] and switch off voice: the result is the turbulent voiceless approximant [ʋ̥]. Now hold that approximant position: breathe in, and again start up the somewhat turbulent voiceless approximant [ʋ̥], but this time, slowly and carefully open the articulatory channel still further. In a moment the flow through the articulatory channel ceases altogether to be turbulent: all you can hear is the faint sound of 'audible breath', that is, turbulent flow through the glottis. This, then, is a third stage in the process of opening up the articulatory channel, one in which flow through the (oral) articulatory stricture itself is quite non-turbulent, even with voiceless phonation. We may call an articulatory stricture of this type *resonant,* since there being no turbulent flow at the articulatory stricture, the sound is entirely generated at the glottis, and the articulatory stricture merely has the function of shaping the resonance chamber of the mouth.

Typical resonants are the more 'open' vowels. Note the difference between a vowel like [i], which is an approximant, and a vowel like [ɛ], which is a resonant. If you say an [i], then, while maintaining exactly the [i]-stricture, devoice it, the resultant voiceless [i̥] quite clearly has turbulent flow through the oral (dorso-palatal) articulation channel. If you now say [ɛ] and then devoice it, the resultant voiceless [ɛ̥] has no oral turbulence at all, merely the turbulent flow of air through the glottis, generating the hushing sound of breath that is modulated by the oral resonance chamber.

We can now summarize the difference between the three 'open' (non-stopped) types of articulation: *fricative, approximant* and *resonant.*

There are several variables involved: the actual sizes of individual vocal tracts, the variable cross-sectional areas of glottal and oral channels, the varied pressures and volume-velocities involved, and so on. Nevertheless, certain proportions hold good, and some degree of approximate quantification is possible. The relative magnitude of figures quoted in the following sections are undoubtedly correct, even if precise values are occasionally uncertain.

In the process of distinguishing between fricative, approximant and resonant articulations, the relationship between the cross-sectional area of the oral articulatory channel, and that of the glottal phonatory channel, is important. It is precisely on account of these dimensional relationships that the different turbulence characteristics of fricative, approximant and resonant are what they are. With normal initiator-power ranges there is oral articulatory turbulence whenever the area of the oral channel is less than that of the simultaneous glottal channel. If the oral channel is larger than the glottal channel then the oral flow is normally non-turbulent (but see below on voiceless resonants).[4]

In *fricative* articulation the articulatory channel is very small and the flow through it is always turbulent, whether the sound is voiceless or voiced, at about the same initiator power. The cross-sectional areas of fricative articulation channels range from about 3 mm^2 in an exceptionally 'tightly' articulated [s] up to around 20 mm^2, which is about the region of changeover to approximant. In the most typical fricatives, with articulatory channel areas of about 6 to 12 mm^2, the oral articulatory channel is always smaller than the glottal phonatory channel. This is obvious in the case of voiceless fricatives, for which the glottal area may be of the order of 100 to 140 mm^2 ; but in all probability it is also smaller than the mean glottal area in voiced phonation, which, in fricatives, probably involves fairly wide opening of a somewhat relaxed glottis. Typical fricatives are the [f, v], [s, z], [ʃ, ʒ] sounds of English and other languages.

In *approximant* articulation the articulatory channel is somewhat larger, and flow through it is turbulent only when voiceless, otherwise it is non-turbulent. The cross-sectional area of the articulatory channel ranges from about 20 mm^2 to around 80 to 100 mm^2. In a typical approximant the articulatory channel is smaller than the glottal area for voicelessness, but larger than the mean glottal area for voice. It is possible that voiced phonation for approximants is always 'tighter', keeping the mean glottal area smaller, than for fricatives. Typical approximants are 'close' vowels, like [i] or [u], 'semi-vowels' like [j], such as the *y* in English *yes*, the voiced labio-dental approximant [ʋ], common in Indian languages, a very common type of English /r/, and the 'liquid' [l]-sound of English and most other languages. It will be found that all of these sounds have the characteristic feature of approximants, that is, they have *non-turbulent* flow when voiced; but the flow becomes *turbulent* when they are made voiceless, at about the same initiator power.

As we pointed out above, the term approximant was first used by Ladefoged in *A Phonetic Study of West African Languages* (1964), where it is defined (p. 25) as 'a sound which belongs to the phonetic class vocoid or central resonant oral (Pike 1943) and simultaneously to the phonological class consonant . . .'. In his later work, *Preliminaries to Linguistic Phonetics* (1971), Ladefoged revised his definition to read (p. 46) 'Approximation of two articulators without producing a turbulent air-stream.' Here he tacitly eliminates the restriction of the term to *central* resonant oral sounds, and indeed he includes a lateral approximant [l] among his examples, and later (p. 53) explicitly mentions such sounds. Our definition of approximant differs from Ladefoged's later definition only in that it implies an *upper* limit to the area of the articulatory channel as well as a lower limit: the approximant has non-turbulent air-flow only when voiceless. This enables us to delimit the category so as to exclude from it wide open front vowels of the type [ε, a], which are included in the *next* class of stricture.

In *resonant* articulation the articulatory channel is still larger, ranging from about 100 mm^2 upwards. In a typical resonant the oral articulatory channel is always larger than the glottal channel, whether for voiced or voiceless phonation. In voiced resonants, for example, more or less 'open' vowels, such as [ε], the trans-glottal jets of voice set the oral resonators ringing, and the function of the open articulatory stricture is merely to shape the oral resonating cavity appropriately. In voiceless resonants, such as [ɛ̥], air-flow through the glottis is turbulent, and in this case it is the turbulent hiss of audible breath that sets the resonators ringing. In voiceless resonants there must always be turbulent flow through the glottis; if there were not, there would simply be silence. Flow through the oral articulatory stricture may or may not be turbulent. However, in a voiceless resonant the oral channel is always larger than the glottal channel, and consequently, even if there is some oral channel turbulence, the glottal turbulence is greater, and its resultant hiss tends to mask the hiss of oral turbulence. For example, in a high-velocity voiceless resonant with a volume-velocity of 1000 cm^3/s, a glottal channel of 90 mm^2, and an oral channel of 150 mm^2, the respective Reynolds Numbers for flow through the channels are, glottal: Re = 8570, oral: Re = 6600. Both of these are well above the critical Re of 1700, so flow in both cases will be turbulent. But since the Re for glottal flow is about 1·3 times that for oral flow, the glottal turbulence will be that much stronger, and the acoustic intensity of the glottal hiss will be nearly twice that of the oral hiss. Typical resonants are the opener vowels of [ɛ] and [a] type.

Figure 27 is a diagrammatic representation of voiceless and voiced fricative, approximant, and resonant articulations. The numerical values inserted in the diagrams, although merely hypothetical are nevertheless realistic.

In figure 27.1a we have a voiceless fricative: the glottis is wide open, so that the pressure is (virtually) equal in both the subglottal (left) and supraglottal (right) parts of the tract. The initiatory pressure is 6·5 cm H_2O, which generates a pressure-flow velocity of 3320 cm/s; since the air is flowing through an articulatory stricture of 10 mm^2 area (as it might be for [s]) the volume-velocity is 3320 × ·1 cm^3/s, that is, 332, or roughly 330 cm^3/s. In order to drive air out at the rate of 330 cm^3/s against a pressure-load of 6·5 cm H_2O, the pulmonic initiator has to develop an initiator power (*IP*) of ·210 watts. The general aerodynamic conditions are represented in this case by a Reynolds Number of 8410. This is about four and a half times the critical Re of 1700; consequently, flow through the articulatory channel will be highly turbulent, generating a loud hiss noise.

Figure 27.1b represents a voiced fricative, in which the pulmonic initiator is generating a subglottal pressure of 9 cm H_2O; the supraglottal pressure is 3 cm H_2O, so the pressure difference is 6 cm H_2O, corresponding to an average pressure-flow velocity of 3191 cm/s through the glottis. Assuming a mean glottal opening of 15 mm^2 this gives a mean volume-velocity of 480 cm^3/s for each burst of air through the glottis. Since the vibrating glottis, producing voice, is

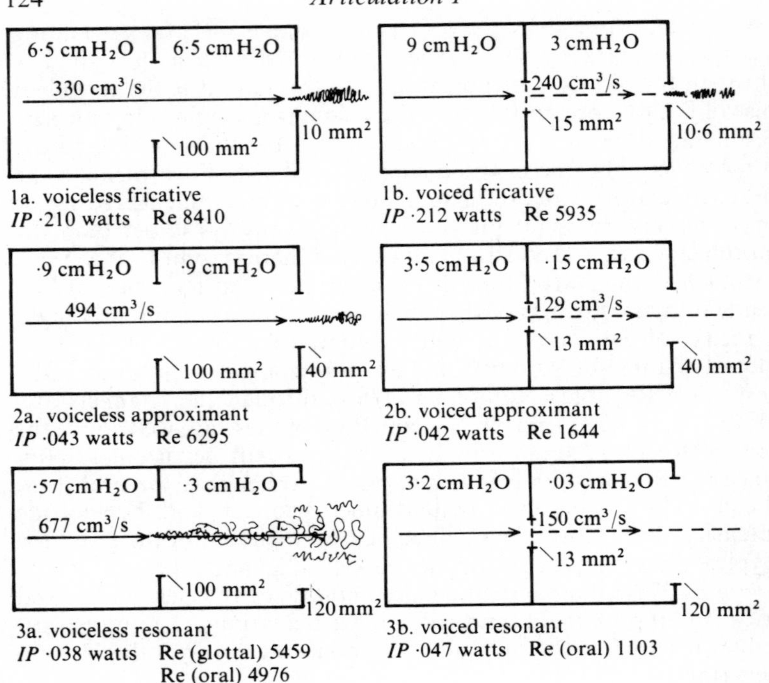

Figure 27. Fricatives, approximants and resonants

(let us say) completely shut half the time, this corresponds to a long-time average flow of 240 cm^3/s, which is the value shown in the figure. The average power output of the initiator is thus that which is necessary to drive air at 240 cm^3/s against a pressure-load of 9 cm H_2O, which is about ·212 watts—that is, about the same power as was used in the corresponding voiceless fricative (figure 27.1a). The pulsating, voice-modulated air continues through the supra-glottal cavity at an average volume-velocity of 240 cm^3/s, through an articulatory channel of 10·6 mm^2 area. For this aerodynamic situation the Re is 5935, so that once again we have strong turbulence and noisy hiss superimposed on (and intensity-modulated by) the buzzing sound of voice.

Figures 27.2a and 2b represent voiceless and voiced approximants. The reader can now follow through for himself the pressure and flow conditions, and so on. In this case it will be seen that the *IP* is much lower (·043 and ·042 watts), chiefly because of the relatively slight articulatory impedance in approximants. The Re for flow through the articulatory stricture in the voiceless approximant (2a) is 6295—turbulent and hence noisy. In the voiced approximant, Re is only 1644, which is sufficiently below Re(crit) for the flow to be non-turbulent.

Figures 27.3a and 3b represent resonants. In the examples shown the *IP* of the voiceless resonant (3a) is ·038 watts; that of the voiced resonant (3b) is ·047 watts—somewhat larger, but of the same order of magnitude. In this particular voiceless resonant there would be turbulent flow both through the glottis (Re 5459) and through the oral articulatory stricture (Re 4976). The noise generated at the glottis would, however, be about 25 per cent louder than that generated in the mouth. In this voiced resonant, Re of flow through the oral stricture is only 1103, and consequently the oral flow is completely non-turbulent and noiseless.

Having thus indicated characteristic values for some of the aerodynamic and other features associated with various stricture-types, we go on to figure 28, which is a chart showing the relationship, on two logarithmic scales, between cross-sectional areas of articulatory (or phonatory) channels in mm^2 on the vertical axis, and volume-velocity, in cm^3/s, on the horizontal axis. The diagonal line on the chart represents the relationships between channel area and volume-velocity for critical Re = 1700. Flow through channels with the area/volume-velocity dimensions to the left of the critical Re line is non-turbulent; through channels with the dimensions to the right of the line it is turbulent.

The zones in which fricatives, approximants and resonants are typically found are marked off, with deliberate fuzzy borders between them, to emphasize the fact that there are no absolute lines of division between the categories. Within each category variation is possible, and we can, if we wish, set up arbitrarily bounded categories of *narrow* and *wide* fricatives, approximants and resonants; and of course, the wider a fricative is the more like an approximant it is; the wider an approximant is the nearer a resonant it is, and so on.

In English, for instance, [s] and [z] are rather narrow fricatives. [θ] and [ð] (as in *thin* and *then*) are wide fricatives, bordering on approximants. On the other hand, the Danish sound often transcribed [ð] is normally an approximant [ð̞], but a fairly narrow one. Thus, the typical form of the English word *gather* and the Danish word *gade*, often transcribed alike as ['gæðə] should more correctly be ['gæðə] and ['gæð̞ə] respectively. In ordinary speech, however, the English wide fricative [ð] may often slip over the border into the approximant category, and (probably much less often) the Danish approximant [ð̞] may sometimes slip over the border into the fricative category.

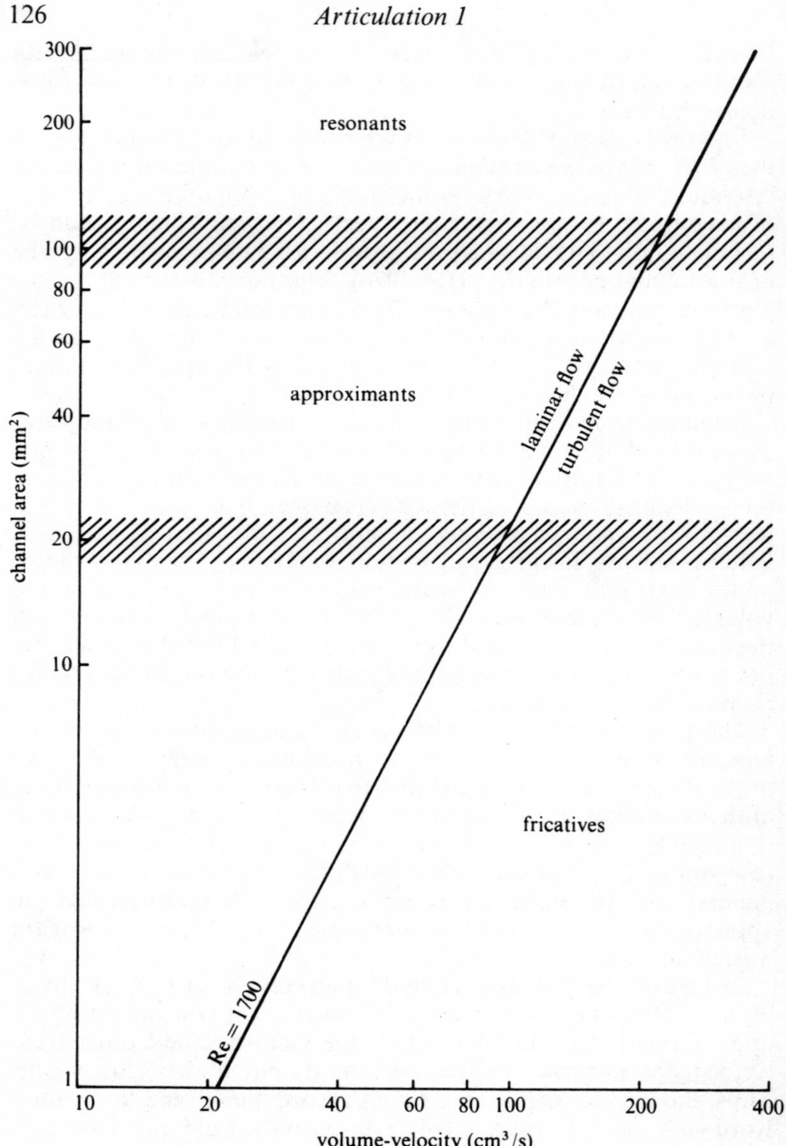

Figure 28. Laminar and turbulent flow in relation to some major stricture types

Some writers make a considerable point of differences in the cross-sectional shape of articulatory strictures, distinguishing between typically *grooved* fricatives (such as English [s]), and typically *slit* fricatives (such as English [θ]). In grooved fricatives there is a narrow, central groove between the articulators, while in slit fricatives the lower articulator has a flatter shape, so that the articulation channel itself is rather wide and flat. As we saw in Chapter 3 the distinction between circular, rectangular and elliptical channel shapes affects the critical Reynolds Number. We allow for this somewhat by stating our generalized critical Reynolds Number for speech as being 1700 ± 200. Nevertheless, the slightly different degrees of ellipsis found in fricative or approximant channels is undoubtedly of very minor importance compared with cross-sectional *area* of the channel, whatever its shape.

We have seen how the continuum of articulatory stricture can be divided into four 'natural' or non-arbitrary segments: *stop, fricative, approximant* and *resonant*. We now have to consider a fifth type of articulation. This is the stricture-type known as *trill,* in which one flexible organ flaps repeatedly against another, as in the tongue-point trilled [r] of Italian and many other languages; or two flexible organs flap against each other as for example, the lips, in a bilabial trill.

In the practical acquisition of trills it is perhaps best to start with the bilabial one. Push the lips forward somewhat, keeping them relaxed so that their inner surfaces are in light contact. Now blow hard, and the result ought to be a voiceless bilabial trill. Switch on voice and make a voiced bilabial trill. Experiment with slightly different degrees of tension of the lips. Note, also, that the lips, like the glottis, can be set in periodic vibration from two different starting points, either closed or open. If closed, they are forced open by the pressure building up behind them, snap shut, are forced open again, and so on. If slightly open, the rising velocity of air-flow through the narrow space between them creates a Bernoulli vacuum and they snap shut, only to be forced open again by the rising air-pressure, and so on.

For those who have not learned to use a tongue-tip trilled [r] in their native language, this is somewhat more difficult to acquire than the labial trill. All one can do is to place the tip of the tongue very lightly on, or very near to, the ridge behind the upper teeth and blow hard. It is better to start this way, aiming at a voiceless trilled [r̥]. Keep on making small adjustments in tongue-position, tongue-tension and volume-velocity of the air-flow till you hit upon the right combination, at which time the tongue will go into periodic vibration. Another type of trill is produced by periodic vibrations of the uvula within a longitudinal furrow in the back of the tongue. Uvular trill [ʀ] can best be learned from 'gargling', at first with a little water, then merely with saliva, and, of course, starting with a strong *voiceless* air-stream.

Trill can be thought of as a kind of loosely formed stop in which the closure is intermittent, and repeated at least two or three times. It may thus be regarded as intermediate between the tight, maintained closure of stop, and the narrow, maintained, open channel of fricative. Trill is itself a maintained posture, providing for an aerodynamically generated, periodic flapping.

All the articulatory stricture-types that we have seen so far have this in common: they can all be maintained for a considerable period of time. Thus, once we have formed the closure for a (pulmonic pressure) voiceless stop we can hold it for several seconds—indeed for as long as we can exist without breathing. For reasons explained in Chapter 5 we can maintain a voiced stop for a much shorter period. The one absolutely obligatory feature of stop articulation is indeed the maintained closure. A stop may have no perceptible approach to the closure (as when we pronounce an initial [p] after a period of merely keeping the lips closed), and it may have no audible or perceptible release. But, to be a stop consonant at all, it *must* have a closure, and this closure must be maintained for a perceptible period of time—not less than 2 or 3 centiseconds, and in many cases, very, very much longer. This point—the essential *prolongability* of stops—is a taxonomically important one.

Fricatives, approximants and *resonants* are all likewise characterized by an articulatory posture that may be maintained for a very long time—up to 20 seconds or so. It is important to make this point very clear. Stop consonants, for instance, are sometimes characterized as 'momentary' as opposed to 'continuant' fricatives; but this is a misleading, if not actually erroneous appellation. Naturally, the *release* of a stop consonant is a momentary event; but so, too, is the release of any consonant; so this is not a particularly relevant or distinctive feature of stops. As we have said, the one and only truly specific and characteristic feature of any stop consonant is the *absolute closure* of the vocal tract, and that this closure is *maintainable* for quite a long period of time.

Contrasting with all these essentially maintainable or prolongable sounds are two types of articulation specifically and uniquely characterized by the fact that they cannot be prolonged. These essentially momentary articulations are known as *flap* and *semi-vowel.*

In *flap,* one articulating organ approaches another, makes momentary contact and then recedes again. Thus, for instance, in the flapped, or 'one-tap' 'r' [ɾ] that speakers of British RP may use in the middle of a word like *merry* ['mɛɾɩ], and many Americans substitute for [t] in the middle of a word like *city* ['sɩɾi], the tongue tip flicks upwards to make a momentary brief contact with the ridge behind the teeth (the alveolar ridge).

There are, in fact, two quite distinct types of flap. In one type the flapping articulator shoots out from its position of rest to flick lightly against the other (stationary) articulator, returning again to its original position. This type of flap, which might be more expressively termed a 'flick', is the kind we have already described, symbolized by [ɾ].

In the other type of flap, the flapping articulator performs a rapid movement from a starting position to a quite different finishing position, momentarily striking, or 'flapping', against the stationary articulator on the way. An example of such a flap is the 'retroflex flap' of numerous Indian and African languages, written [ɽ] and exemplified in, for example, Hindi ['ghoɽɑ] *horse*. In articulating [ɽ], the tip of the tongue is lifted up and somewhat back. From this retroflex position somewhere behind the anterior arch of the hard palate, it shoots forward and downwards, the underside of the tongue-rim momentarily striking the palate on the way, and ending by flopping down onto the floor of the mouth. Another variety of this type of 'transient flap', in which a moving articulator momentarily strikes a static articulator in passing, is the 'labio-dental flap' of the West African language, Margi. In this sound, which appears to be really a sequence of labio-dental stop and flap, the lower lip starts somewhat bent back behind the upper teeth. It then shoots forward, striking against the edges of the upper teeth in passing, to end up in the normal, rest position. For a full description see Ladefoged (1964, p. 18). These two different types of flap may be suggested diagrammatically as in figures 29a and b.

Although we may correctly say that flaps are characterized by their *momentariness*, nevertheless, the 'hit' registered by a 'flick',

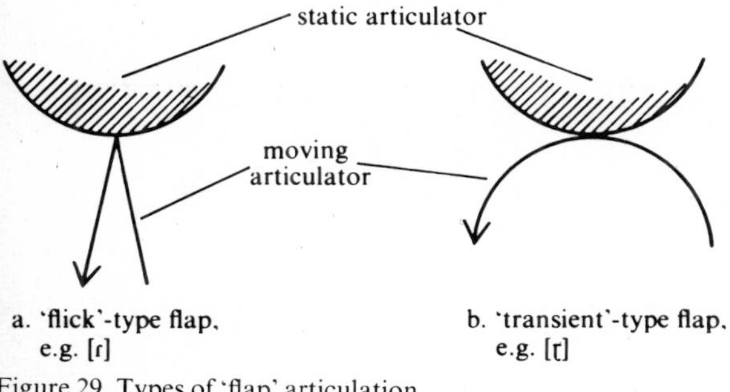

Figure 29. Types of 'flap' articulation

or by a passing 'transient flap', has a measurable duration, of the order of 1 to 3 centiseconds. This, however, is short compared with the duration of most stops—usually from 5 to 6 centiseconds upwards. But, as we have already said, the truly distinctive feature is that *a stop can be prolonged; a flap cannot be prolonged.* The flap gesture is essentially a dynamic, flicking, or 'hit and run' motion. Both stops and flicks, may be ballistic movements, that is, the articulator is sent on its flight, like a projectile, by a single muscular twitch, and then twitched back again at the end of its trajectory. The difference would then lie in the fact that the flick starts its flight further from the static articulator than does the stop. Consequently, the flick completes its trajectory, whereas the stop is arrested in mid-flight by contact with the static articulator. According to this theory, a flick would start its trajectory further from the static articulator, as in figure 30. The broken line in figure 30b shows the path that the stop articulator would have followed if the static articulator had not interrupted its flight. Of course, it is obvious that stops that have a closure maintained for more than a very few hundredths of a second are not ballistic.[5]

Flaps ('flicks' and 'transients') also differ significantly from *trills.* A flap as we have said is a single ballistic flick or hit-and-run *gesture.* A trill, as we pointed out above, is a maintained and prolongable *posture:* the vibrations that occur in a trill are aerodynamically imposed on the posture. Any idea that a trill is 'a rapid series of flaps', or that a flap is just an 'ultra-short trill' is quite wrong. The frequency of alveolar and uvular trills [r] and [ʀ] is of the order of 30 cycles per second. This is much higher than the maximum rate at which one can produce a series of [ɾ]-flaps (about five or six per second). Once again it is clear that the flap is an essentially and obligatorily *momentary gesture:* a trill is an essentially *prolongable posture,* the maximum durations being roughly five to ten seconds for voiced [r, ʀ], three to five seconds for voiceless [r̥, ʀ̥]. These,

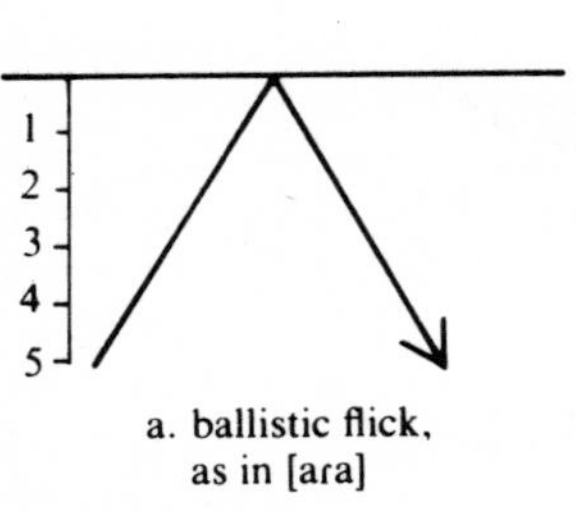

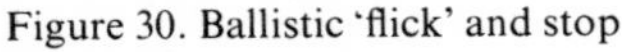
a. ballistic flick,
as in [aɾa]

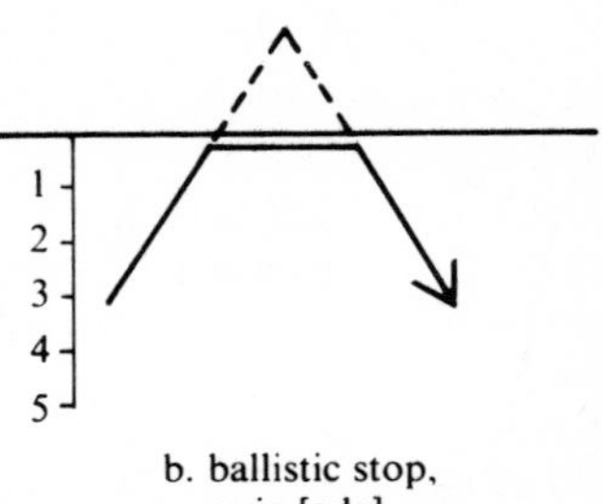

b. ballistic stop,
as in [ada]

Figure 30. Ballistic 'flick' and stop

of course, are for pulmonic pressure trills. A glottalic pressure trill [r'] is also possible, but owing to the small amount of air that can be utilized with glottalic initiation it cannot be made to last for more than about 1/5 second.

Semivowel is likewise an essentially momentary type of articulation, a dynamic gesture of approach to, and/or departure from, a vocalic approximant or resonant position. Most commonly, what are called semivowels are obligatorily momentary movements towards and/or away from an [i]- or [e]-type stricture (symbolized by [j]), or an [u]- or [o]-type stricture (symbolized by [w]).

Experiment by saying a sequence of three very long vowels of the type [æ::::i::::æ::::] in which [æ::] is a (prolonged) vowel as in English *bad,* and [i::] is a (prolonged) vowel as in English *see.* Now try to keep the flanking [æ::]-vowels long, but shorten the [i::] more and more. When it becomes nothing but a rapid 'flick'-like gesture towards [i] and then back again it is the semivowel [j].

Carry out an analogous experiment with [æ::::u::::æ::::], where [u::] is a (prolonged) vowel as in English *too,* reducing the duration of [u::] virtually to zero, when it becomes the semivowel [w]. Semivowels written [j] and [w] can be formed by moving rapidly to and from opener vowels than [i] and [u], for example, [e] and [ɛ], [o] [ɔ], as in [ae̯a], [aɛ̯a] (where [e̯] [ɛ̯] mean ultra-brief, non-syllabic, [e] and [ɛ]) = [aja], and [ao̯a], [aɔ̯a] = [awa].

Although semivowels normally have higher, or closer tongue positions, that is, a narrower articulatory channel, than contiguous vowels, it is theoretically possible to have semivowels that are more *open* than contiguous vowels. Thus, having experimented with [æ:iæ:] becoming [æ:jæ:], and so on, one can reverse the relationships, and say [i::æ::i::], reducing the [æ] finally to a momentary [æ̯] semivowel: [i::æ̯i:]. In practice, such open semivowels are rare in languages, although there is a variety of 'defective r', not uncommon in England, which is essentially a [ə] semivowel, [ə̯] (where [ə] represents a vowel much like that at the end of the English word *sofa*). Thus, *Mary* may be pronounced [mɛ:ə̯ɩ].

We have completed our survey of the 'vertical' dimension (degree of openness of articulatory channel), and the 'time' dimension (prolongable/momentary) of articulation. We must now briefly consider the 'transverse' dimension: the location of the *oral air-path* in the side-to-side dimension, that is, the distinction between *central* and *lateral* articulation.

The best way to become aware of this distinction is to silently form an [s]-articulation, then breathe in (that is, start up a pulmonic ingressive air-stream). Note the sensation of cold air passing into the mouth over the central part of the tongue. Now silently form an

[l]-articulation—imagine you are saying an [l] as in English *lee*. Now holding the [l]-articulation breathe in, and note the sensation of cold air passing into the mouth down the side(s) of the tongue: [s] has a typically *central*, [l] a typically *lateral* articulation channel.

It is, of course, possible to make central or lateral channels at any point in the mouth. Thus one can make a narrow central channel (as for [β] or [w]) between the lips; or, one can keep the central part of the lips tightly shut, and open a little channel at one or both sides, to form a bilabial lateral. Such sounds are extremely rare in any language.[6] Generally we are concerned only with lateral articulation channels formed between the tongue and the sides of the mouth—sounds, that is, of the [l]-type.

A typical [l] of English and other well-known languages is a voiced apico-alveolar ('tongue-tip-gums') approximant. The point and rim of the tongue is firmly placed on the roof of the mouth just behind the upper teeth. The sides of the tongue are somewhat drawn in (laterally contracted) so that articulation channels are formed between the tongue-sides and the molar teeth. In some cases the [l] is unilateral, that is, it has a channel only at one side, but this distinction makes virtually no difference to the resultant sound, and no language is known which makes distinctive linguistic use of the opposition between unilateral and bilateral articulation.

That normal English [l] is an *approximant* can be demonstrated by devoicing. Say a prolonged [lː] (preferably, like the [l] in *leaf* rather than the [l] in *feel*—on this distinction see Chapter 10). Now, devoice it: [llll̥l̥l̥], where [l̥] is the symbol for voiceless [l]. Notice that so long as the [l] is voiced the flow through the lateral channel(s) is non-turbulent. When the [l] is devoiced, the hissing sound generated by turbulent flow eddying round the molar teeth can be heard. In most types of English a voiceless, or partially voiceless [l̥] occurs in such words as *please* or *claw* ([pl̥iːz] [kl̥ɔː]). Since this kind of [l] has turbulent flow when voiceless, but no turbulence when voiced, it fulfils exactly the criterion for approximants.

It is possible to produce a *fricative* lateral. To do this, start from the voiceless [l̥], then try to 'strengthen' the hiss-noise by squeezing the sides of the tongue more strongly against the molar teeth, narrowing the lateral linguo-molar channel(s), at the same time slightly increasing the air-flow. This should now be the voiceless alveolar lateral fricative [ɬ]. Now, keeping the strong hiss going, voice this [ɬ]. Provided the lateral channels are still narrow enough, and the air-flow strong enough, the flow should remain turbulent when the sound is voiced, being, in fact, the voiced alveolar lateral fricative [ɮ]. Voiceless lateral fricatives are not particularly uncommon: they occur, for instance, in Welsh, Icelandic, Burmese, Tibetan, and other well-known languages. Voiced lateral fricatives are somewhat rarer: they occur, for example, in Adyghe and Kabardian in the north-west Caucasus, in Zulu, and a few other African languages.

If the lateral contraction of the tongue is great enough the lateral channel(s) may be so wide that flow is non-turbulent for both voiceless and voiced laterals. Such 'resonant laterals' are rare, but occasionally occur: for example, [l]-sounds at the end of syllables in Javanese seem sometimes to be resonants rather than the normal approximants.

Stops cannot be central or lateral in precisely the same way as the more open articulations can, since during the essential and most characteristic phase of a stop there is, naturally, complete vertical and transverse closure. However, the *approach* to a stop, or the *departure* from it (the release) may be either central or lateral. Thus in an English word like *head* [hɛd], towards the end of the resonant [ɛ], the tip of the tongue rises to make contact with the gums behind the upper teeth. The shape of the tongue is such that, as it rises up towards and into the concave roof of the mouth, the tongue-sides make contact first, the central part closing with the gums last of all; if you say *head* several times, slowly and silently, you will feel this. However, in the word *held* [hɛld], the initial contact is central, and it is only after the central contact of the [l] is made that the tongue swells out laterally to complete the closure for the [d]. (Say this, too, slowly and silently.) Thus the final approach to [d] in *head* is the closing up of a central channel, but the final approach to [d] in *held* is the closing up of a lateral channel, or channels.

Similarly, in a pair of English words like *muddy* and *muddle* (['mʌdɩ] ['mʌdl]) we find an analogous contrast between the centrally released [d] of *muddy* and the laterally released [d] of *muddle*.[7]

The contrast between a stop released into a central fricative (such as [ts] or [dz]) and a stop released into a lateral fricative (such as [tl]) is not uncommon in languages. Such 'sequential phonemes' will be dealt with below in Chapter 11.

The most normal trills, [r] and [ʀ], involve loose and periodic contact between articulators in the centre of the mouth. Consequently they cannot be lateral. If the tongue-tip, for instance, makes a firm central contact in order to leave open lateral articulation channels, it cannot simultaneously be vibrating against the roof of the mouth. However, a certain kind of 'lateral trill' can be produced. Set up a unilateral channel by firmly clamping the tongue to the roof of the mouth, except for a channel along one side. Now produce a powerful voiceless pulmonic egressive air-stream—that is, blow hard through this unilateral channel. With a little manoeuvring, you may get the upper lip, on the side where the lateral channel is, vibrating against the upper teeth. This kind of 'unilateral, supra-labio-dental trill' is not known to occur in any language.[8]

To conclude this chapter, we summarize the possible articulation types and their combination with the two oral air-paths in the diagrams of figures 31 and 32. Figure 31 shows, diagrammatically, the gestures involved when one (moving) articulator approaches a static articulator, and then departs from it, with an intermediate maintenance of the posture or not according to whether the sound is prolongable or momentary. The conventions are fairly self-explanatory, but note that the broken line represents voiced air-stream, the solid line voiceless air-stream.

In figure 31 note that *fricative* has turbulent air-flow when voiceless or voiced, *approximant* has turbulent flow when voiceless, non-turbulent when voiced, and *resonant* has non-turbulent flow for both phonation types.

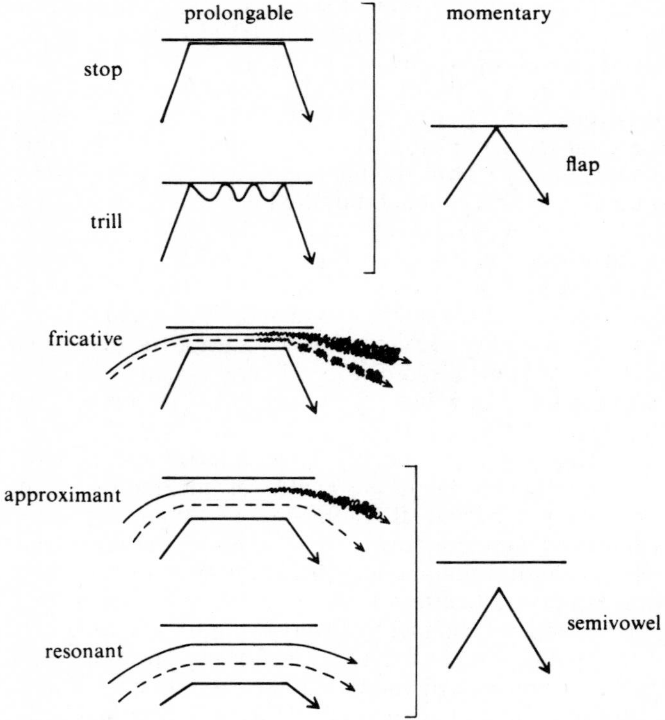

Figure 31. Stricture types

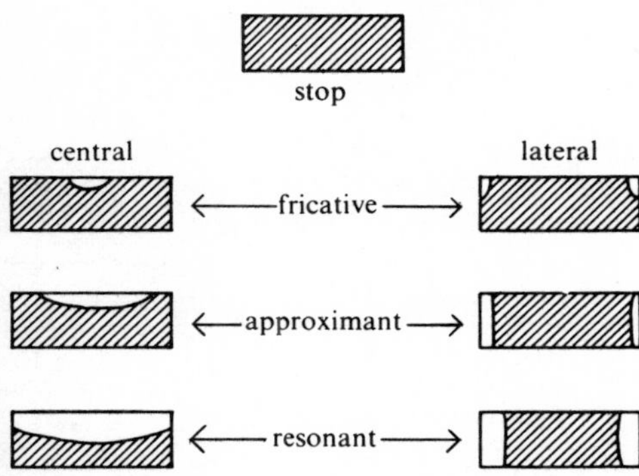

Figure 32. Diagrammatic frontal view of stricture types

In figure 32 we present a stylized frontal view of the mouth cavity, diagrammatically indicating the difference between central and lateral channels of various types. Note that the areas of the articulatory channels shown here are, in fact, actual size for typical sounds of the types named.

In Chapters 3, 5, 6, and 7, we have presented basic information on such aspects of aerodynamic phonetics as Reynolds Number, pressure, velocity, volume-velocity and the relation of these to cross-sectional area of vocal tract channels, and also to initiator power. In figure 33 we now summarize much of that information in a chart, which can be used as a kind of 'Phonetic Ready Reckoner' enabling one to get a quick approximation to many aerodynamic phonetic quantitative relations.

Thus, knowing the volume-velocity and the up-stream excess pressure of a given sound we can quickly get from the chart a rough idea of the cross-sectional area of the channel, the particle velocity of air-flow, the initiator power and the Reynolds Number for that aerodynamic condition. Indeed, knowing values for any two of the parameters included in figure 33 (overleaf), we can immediately find approximate values for the other four.

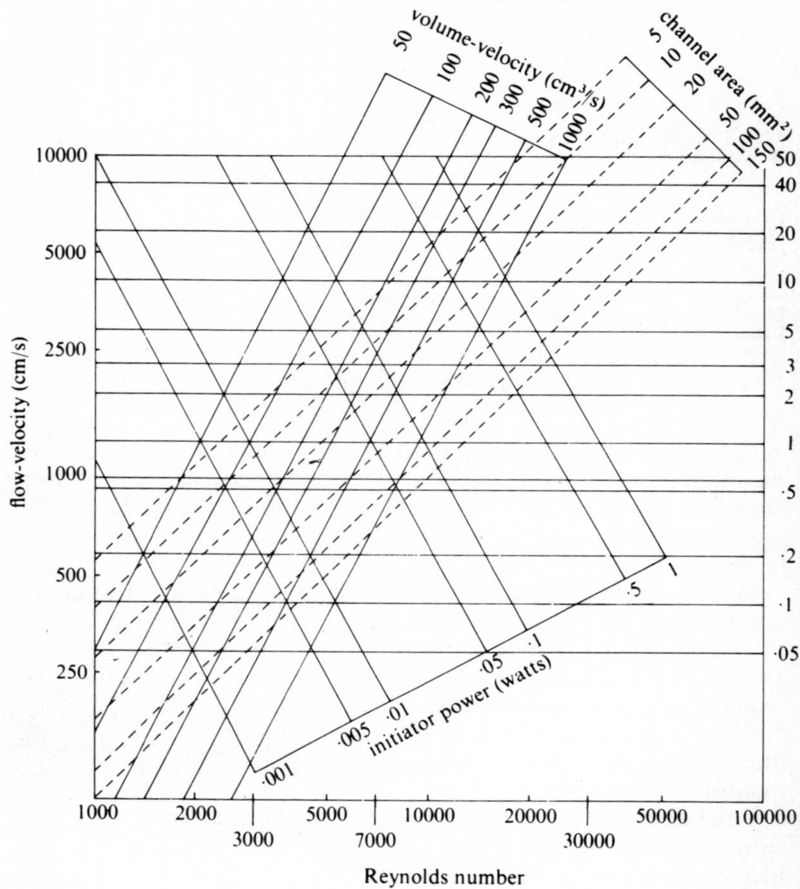

Figure 33. Combined chart of six phonetic parameters

EIGHT

Articulation 2: Location

In Chapter 7 we discussed the 'vertical', 'transverse' and 'time' dimensions of articulation. Now we must turn our attention to the quasi-longitudinal dimension, the location within the vocal tract at which articulations can occur.

The simplest way to approach this problem is to regard the vocal tract as divided into three major areas: *nasal, oral* and *pharyngeo-laryngeal*. There is a clear-cut, natural division between the nasal area and the others, constituted by what medical people sometimes call the 'nasal port', and phoneticians, after Pike (1943), 'the velic opening'—that is, the orifice between the nasal cavity and the pharynx, which is controlled by the valvular soft palate, or velum.

The oral and pharyngeo-laryngeal cavities are, in effect, outer (or 'horizontal') and inner (or 'vertical') parts of a single 'bent tube', which runs from the lips to the glottis. Although these two articulatory areas form an unbroken continuum it is convenient to treat them as separate.[1] The division between them is an imaginary plane cutting the oro-pharyngeal tube at the extreme back of the mouth in such a way that the entire roof of the mouth and the entire tongue back to the tip of the epiglottis are in the oral area. Figure 34 is a diagrammatic saggital section of the head and neck indicating the three areas of articulatory location.

The *nasal area* consists of the nasal cavity, which, as we pointed out in Chapter 2, is for the most part a complex but immobile cavity, coated with mucous membrane, which may swell pathologically, as when we have a cold, but which is not capable of muscular movement. Some muscular activity, and hence some variety of articulation, is possible only at the two extremities of the nasal cavity. We will return to these two articulatory zones—*nareal* and *velic*—in a moment.

Traditionally, all sounds produced with the velum lowered (nasal port open), so that air can flow from the pharynx into the nose or vice versa, are termed *nasal* or *nasalized.* The distinction between them is this: in nasal consonants there is a complete closure some-

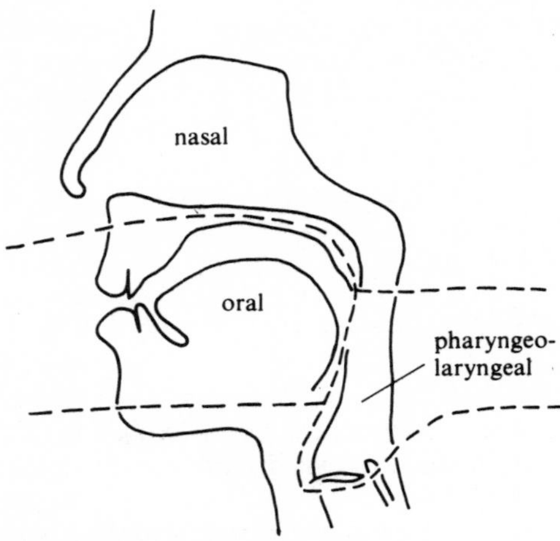

Figure 34. The major articulatory areas

where in the mouth, so that the air flows out (or in) solely through the nose. In nasalized sounds the mouth is not completely closed, and the air, in consequence, can flow simultaneously through both mouth and nose. Typical examples of nasal sounds are the nasal consonants [m, n, ŋ] (as in *long*) of English and other languages. Typical examples of nasalized sounds are the nasalized vowels of French [œ̃, õ, ɛ̃, ɑ̃] (as in *un bon vin blanc*). Both nasal and nasalized sounds are often said to be characterized by 'nasal resonance', and this is correct, acoustically speaking, in that when the nasal cavity is coupled into the vocal tract by opening the nasal port it adds a resonance chamber, and this results in the addition of some fairly high frequency formants, shifts of formant frequencies, and so on. However, it is incorrect to regard nasal consonants as 'resonants' in the strict technical sense defined in the last chapter: they are, in fact, approximants, as we shall show below.

Nareal articulation is produced at the nostrils, or *nares*. If you produce a long [mːː] sound, then, while keeping a powerful pulmonic egressive air-stream going, devoice it, you will produce 'voiceless m' [m̥]. Now, at any but a very low volume-velocity it will be evident that [m̥] is characterized by turbulent flow through the nostrils—*nareal turbulence*. The nasal [m], then, is produced with no turbulence when voiced, but with nareal turbulence when voiceless; it could thus be correctly described as a *nareal approximant*. A further narrowing of the nostrils will convert a nareal approximant into a nareal fricative. Experiment by setting up the articulation for [m], and starting up a pulmonic egressive voiceless air-stream. Notice the hiss generated by turbulent flow through the nostrils. Now, while this sound is going on, contract the nostrils so as to make the nareal channel narrower. Immediately the intensity of the hiss increases. Now add voice, keeping the hiss of turbulence going at the same time. This is a voiced nareal fricative, which we may represent as [m˔]. Although 'voiceless nasals' (that is, voiceless nareal approximants, or fricatives) are not uncommon in the languages of the world, for example, in Burmese and Tibetan, voiced nareal fricatives are so far unknown, although there is no reason why they should not exist.

In spite of the fact that such sounds as ordinary [m] [n] are, to be precise, 'nareal approximants', in this book we shall follow traditional practice in calling them simply 'nasals'.

Velic articulation takes place at the 'nasal port', that is, between the upper or rear side of the soft palate and the back of the pharynx. When the velic orifice is closed, air can flow out of and into the vocal tract only through the mouth. Thus, a 'velic stop' articulation is a passive accompaniment to all purely oral articulations. In such cases, velic closure need never be mentioned in descriptions. Every stop articulation, such as [p, b, t, d], in reality involves two stops: an oral stop, and a velic stop. When a stop is flanked by oral sounds both before and after (which is most commonly the case) the velic orifice remains closed throughout. It is only when the stop is flanked by a nasal, or nasals, that we have active velic participation in the stop. Thus, in a common English pronunciation of such words as *mutton, sudden* [ˈmʌtn̩], [ˈsʌdn̩] (where [n̩] = 'syllabic [n]') the oral closure is retained from the stop right on through the nasal; the release of the stop is made by suddenly opening the velic orifice and allowing the high-pressure air in the mouth and pharynx to escape into the nose. Such 'velic stop' release of a stop is often called 'nasal plosion', and will be referred to again under 'sequence phenomena' in Chapter 11. It is possible to narrow the velic orifice to a greater or lesser degree, producing velic fricative and approximant articulations. A pulmonic suction, strong, voiceless, velic fricative is a variety of 'catarrhal snort'. In 'nasalized sounds', for example, nasalized vowels such as [ɛ̃, ɑ̃], so much air escapes through the mouth that, no matter how narrow the velic channel may be, there is no velic turbulence. However, one language is known, namely Chinantec of Oaxaca, Mexico, in which two degrees of nasalization of vowels occur. In this language there are oral vowels (for example, [ha] *so, such*), lightly nasalized vowels (for example, [hã] (*he*) *spreads open*), and heavily nasalized vowels (for example, [hã̃] *foam, froth*). It seems probable that a comparable distinction between lightly nasal and heavily nasal consonants occurs in the Indonesian language, Achinese. It is conceivable that the lightly nasalized vowels have an approximant-like velic orifice, while the heavily nasalized vowels have a resonant-like velic orifice.

The *oral area* consists of the entire cavity of the mouth, bounded at the front by the lips, and merging at the rear with the pharyngeal cavity; for taxonomic purposes, however, we include in the oral area only those articulations that involve the under side of the soft palate, right back to the uvula, and the tongue, back to about the point reached by the tip of the epiglottis at its furthest extension up the back of the tongue. Articulation between epiglottis (or extreme back of tongue) and back wall of pharynx are thus arbitrarily, but usefully, excluded from the oral area.

Articulations in the oral area are produced by juxtapositions of articulators attached to the lower jaw, such as the lower lip and the tongue, with other articulators attached to the upper jaw (upper lip, palate, and so on). We may call these, respectively, *lower* and *upper articulators*.[2]

The lower articulators consist of the *lower lip*, the *lower teeth*, and the whole of the *tongue* from its forward attachment down behind the lower teeth, up over the tip, and along its whole dorsal surface back to the tip of the epiglottis. The upper articulators consist of the *upper lip* and the entire 'roof of the mouth' from the teeth back to the uvula, which is the extreme rear end of the soft palate.

Before exploring his mouth tactilely the reader should identify those parts of it which he can see in a mirror, as in figure 35. Identify the lips, the upper and lower teeth, the tongue, the rear end of the soft palate including the uvula, the back wall of the pharynx, the faucal pillars, and (if you can get your tongue deeply enough furrowed) the tip of the epiglottis.

We can now go on to look in more detail at the articulatory zones in the mouth, and we will begin with the upper articulators.

The *upper lip* is obvious enough, but note that when it is at rest part of it is lying against the upper teeth, and part is free: there is thus an *inner* and an *outer* part of the upper lip (and this is true also of the lower lip).

Behind the upper lip lie the *upper teeth*. With the tip of the tongue one can feel the rather sharp edges of the upper teeth, forming a semi-circle at the front of the mouth—the upper teeth *rim*, with the outer surface of the teeth lying in front of the rim, the inner surface sloping upwards and backwards behind the rim. Still using the tip of the tongue one can feel a hard ridge immediately behind the upper teeth, the *alveolar ridge*. Sliding the tongue slowly backwards one can feel the alveolar ridge running back a little way

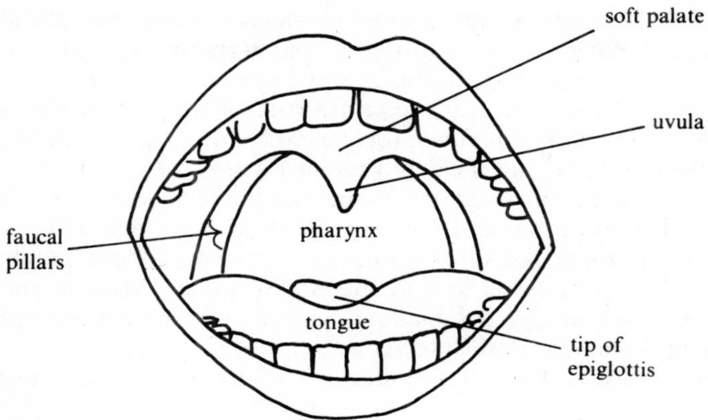

Figure 35. Some features of the oral cavity

almost horizontally, and then curving upwards to merge with the palate. Most people have a fairly distinct alveolar ridge, which can be identified by its general convexity, which, after its surface begins to turn upwards, merges with the concavity of the palate. The alveolar ridge may be said to end at that point, not very clearly defined, where convexity is replaced by concavity.[3]

Continuing exploration with the tongue and, when that can reach no further back, a finger, one can locate the rear end of the hard palate—the point where the roof of the mouth ceases to be hard and becomes soft and yielding. This is the beginning of the soft palate or velum.

We see, then, that the upper articulatory continuum can be divided up in a partly natural, and partly arbitrary way into a number of sections, which we may call, in a hierarchical arrangement, divisions, regions, zones, and finally subzones. There are two *divisions: labial,* the upper lip, and *tectal,* the whole roof of the mouth. The labial division has no further subdivisions except the ultimate subdivision into outer (*exolabial*) and inner (*endolabial*) subzones.

The tectal division falls naturally into two *regions: dentalveolar* (upper teeth and alveolar ridge back to where convexity gives place to concavity) and *domal* (the whole concave dome of the hard and soft palate behind the alveolar ridge).

The terms *tectum* (related to our 'tectal') and *domal* have both been used before, although in somewhat different senses. Kemp Malone (1923) used the term 'tectum' to refer to the whole roof of the mouth excluding a little more than what we call the dentalveolar region, while Hockett (1955) uses *dome* and *domal* with reference only to the hard palate. Since we sometimes have to make generalized statements about large articulatory regions, particularly in phonological discussions, it seems useful to employ these terms in a hierarchical way, using *tectal* for the entire roof of the mouth (from upper teeth to uvula), and *domal* for the entire 'domed' part of the roof of the mouth behind the dentalveolar region.

Both regions (dentalveolar and domal) of the tectal division can be subdivided into zones and subzones. In descriptive phonetics as a rule only the zonal and subzonal descriptive terms are commonly used. It is, however, useful to have the more general divisional and regional terms available for making certain kinds of generalized phonetic and phonological statements.

The following is, then, a summary of upper oral articulatory locations:

LABIAL Division (also zone)
outer (exo-) subzone
inner (endo-) subzone

TECTAL Division
Dentalveolar Region
Dental zone: rim and backs of upper teeth
Alveolar zone: whole alveolar ridge
alveolar subzone (proper): front half of alveolar ridge
postalveolar subzone: rear half of alveolar ridge

Domal Region
Palatal zone: the entire hard palate
prepalatal subzone: the front half of the hard palate (the prepalatal arch immediately behind the alveolar ridge)
palatal subzone (proper): the rear half of the hard palate
Velar zone: the whole soft palate, including the uvula
velar subzone (proper): the front half of the soft palate
postvelar or uvular subzone: the rear half of the soft palate, including the uvula

Figure 36 shows these divisions, regions, zones and subzones in relation to a slightly flattened representation of a saggital section through the upper oral articulators.

The lower articulators include the *lower lip,* which, like the upper lip, has an inner and an outer part (a distinction which it is sometimes desirable to make), the lower teeth, which play relatively little part in speech, and the tongue. At this point it is necessary to look more closely at the tongue. The tongue is highly mobile and of variable shape, and also has few clear-cut natural divisions. Never-

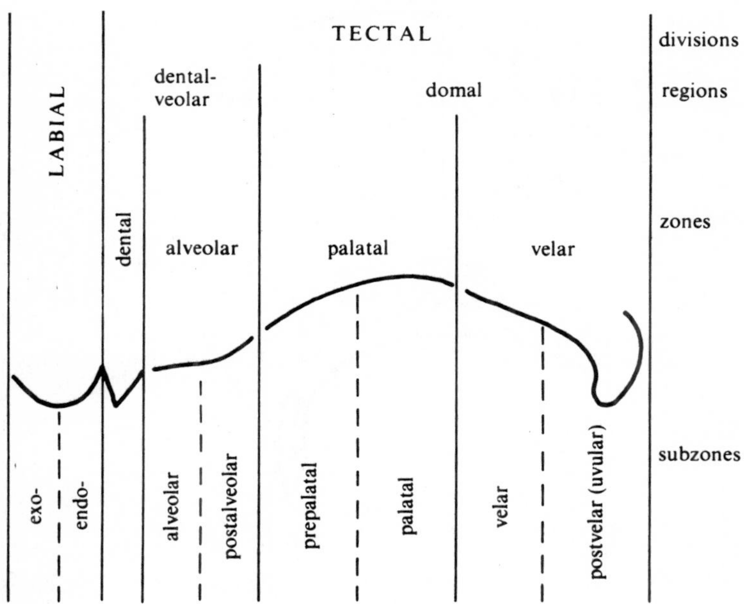

Figure 36. Upper articulatory locations

theless, for phonetic purposes we can divide it fairly unambiguously into four or five zones. Figure 37 shows the tongue as seen from above and from the side, and illustrates these zones.

The forward edge of the tongue is its *rim,* and the central point of this edge is the tip or *apex*. On the upper surface of the tongue running back about 10 to 15 mm along the central line is the *blade* or *lamina*—the part that lies opposite the teeth and alveolar ridge when the tongue is at rest. This use of the term 'blade', it should be made quite clear, is the traditional one, going back at least to Henry Sweet. Recently some writers, notably Peterson and Shoup (1966) have used the term 'blade' in some such sense as 'front half of the tongue' (to judge from the illustration on p. 19 of their paper). This does not seem to be a taxonomically useful innovation, however, and we do not adopt it. The rest of the upper surface of the tongue, back to the tip of the epiglottis is the *dorsum.* Most often it is not necessary to subdivide the dorsum, since in the description of oral articulations it can normally be taken for granted that the part of the dorsum involved is that which normally lies below the particular upper articulatory zone in question. If necessary, however, one can roughly divide the dorsum behind the blade into two equal

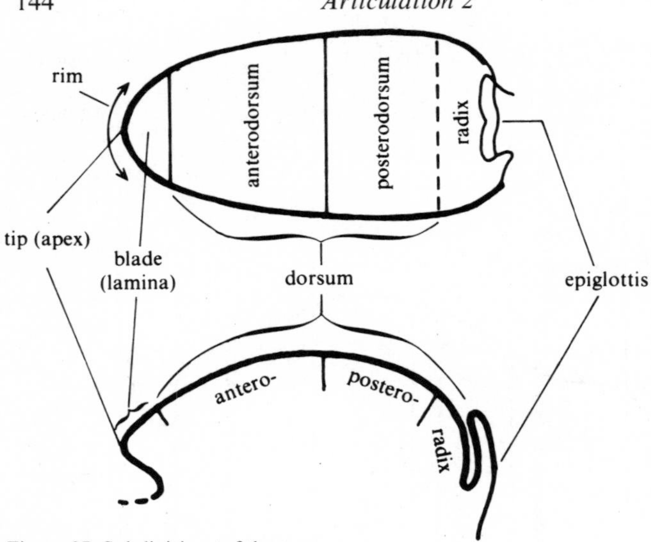

Figure 37. Subdivisions of the tongue

parts—front (*antero-*) and back (*postero-*), the last third of the back part being the root or *radix,* which continues on down in front of the epiglottis. Returning to the front end of the tongue, the under surface, from the apex back about 10 to 15 mm is the underblade, or *sublamina.*

The reader should examine his tongue in a mirror. Note its position of rest, look at its shape when protruded, when placed in position for vowels such as [i] and [ɛ], or for [k], and get as clear an idea as possible of the location of apex, lamina, sublamina, dorsum, anterodorsum, posterodorsum, and radix. It should be noted that in the specification of oral articulations we describe, in fact, only the organic contacts or approximations along the central, saggital line. This is reasonable, since most articulations are more or less symmetrical about this line, and even if they are not, the assymetry is of little phonetic consequence.

Lower articulators are traditionally named by truncated latinate forms such as *labio-, linguo-, apico-* prefixed to the upper articulatory terms. Figure 38 represents the lower articulatory zones and shows the prefixal terms used to designate them.

In formal analytical designation of oral articulations we conjoin a prefix signifying a lower articulator to a term signifying an upper articulator. Thus contact, or approximation, between lower lip and upper teeth is designated by *labio-dental,* or, where greater exactitude is required, by *endolabio-dental* (for the typical English [f, v]),

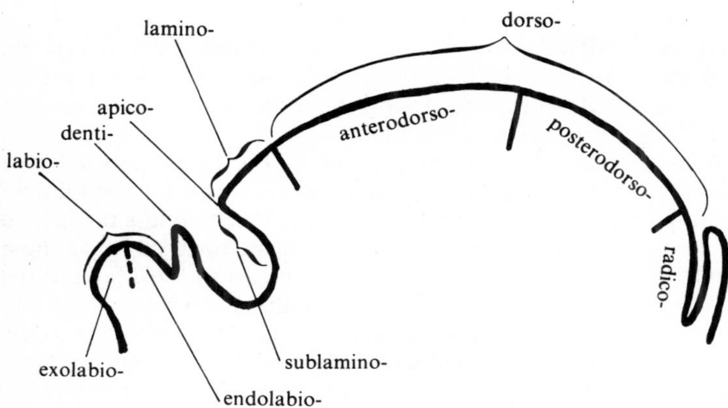

Figure 38. Lower articulatory locations

and *exolabio-dental* (for typical North Indian [ʋ]). Approximation between tongue surface and hard palate, as for [i] is *dorso-palatal* . . . and so on. It must be observed that not all writers adhere rigorously to the convention that is strictly followed in this book, namely that a latinate prefix and a second descriptive term means 'lower articulator plus upper articulator'. One sometimes finds, for instance, 'dentilabial' used for what we would call 'labio-dental' (in this book, *labio-dental* = 'lower lip and upper teeth' while *denti-labial* = 'lower teeth and upper lip'). Or, again, writers who do not scrupulously follow the convention that 'prefix = lower articulator' sometimes use the term 'labio-velar' to refer to a sound with simultaneous labial and velar (more fully, labio-labial and dorso-velar) articulation, which is more correctly designated 'labial / velar' (see Chapter 10 on Co-articulation). It is obvious that 'labio-velar' articulation, with lower lip touching soft palate, is anatomically impossible and it might therefore be argued that the term is acceptably unambiguous. Nevertheless, no purpose is served by motiveless departure from the rigorous convention, so one might as well avoid this dubious usage.

As we have said above, in formal analytical designations one must use the fullest possible term. In practice, however, it is very often possible to use abbreviated terms: thus *bilabial* to mean *labio-labial*: or even *labial* to mean this and also *labio-dental*. In particular, it is not uncommon to omit the prefix designating the lower articulator whenever this can be done without ambiguity. In the following listing of oral articulations we will give some of the abbreviated forms.

The reader should form all the articulations described here, both silently, and with a pulmonic egressive air-stream.

Labio-labial
Also called *bilabial,* or even simply *labial,* this term covers all articulations formed by juxtaposition of lower and upper lip, thus [p, b, m, ɸ, β, w], and so on. Using the more precise terms we can explore all anthropophonic possibilities.

Exolabio-exolabial: juxtaposition of the more external part of lower and upper lip. This is the most normal articulation for the bilabial nasal [m], stops [p, b], and fricatives [ɸ, β]. Voiced bilabial fricative [β], varying to approximant, is the intervocalic form of /b/ in most varieties of Spanish; [β] also occurs, in contrast to both [v] and [w] in the west African language Ewe, which also has voiceless [ɸ] and [f]. A voiceless bilabial (exolabio-exolabial) [ɸ] occurs in a few Caucasian languages, for example, Ingush and Tabasaran, and is a variant of /h/ occurring before /u/ in Japanese. Most commonly, the 'rounding' of rounded front vowels is made in this way (see below).

Exolabio-endolabial: the lower lip pushes upwards against the inner part of the upper lip, which is thus somewhat lifted and pushed forward. Stop, nasal and fricative articulations, at least, can be formed this way, but are not known to occur regularly in any language.

Endolabio-exolabial: the lower lip is somewhat 'pouted' or pushed forwards so that its inner part makes contact with the outer part of the upper lip. Stops, nasal and fricative are possible, but not known to occur.

Endolabio-endolabial: both lower and upper lip are pushed forward somewhat, so that their inner parts are juxtaposed. This labial gesture, plus further contraction of the lateral fibres of the orbicularis oris muscle, producing a fuller, 'rounder' pouting effect, is the usual 'rounding' of rounded back vowels (see below) and is the labial component of the bilabial/velar approximant [w]. It is also a common form of *labialization* (see Chapter 10), or secondary labial articulation accompanying other articulations.

The 'pure', flat, *endolabio-endolabial* articulation—flat, 'unrounded', juxtaposition of the inner lips, both upper and lower—is the labial component of certain so-called 'labialized' sounds in some Caucasian languages. Thus, 'labialized' /tʷ/ /dʷ/ and /tʷ'/ in Abkhaz are strictly bilabial/dental stops, with simultaneous *apico-dental* (tongue-tip on backs of upper-teeth) and *endolabio-endolabial* stops. In the articulation of the glottalic egressive /tʷ'/ = [t͡p'] there is sometimes a slight endolabio-endolabial trill on release of the stop. In another Caucasian language, Lak, there is a 'labialized' /kʷ'/, which is, in fact, a simultaneous dorso-velar stop and endolabio-endolabial stop. Finally, endolabio-endolabial articulation is normally used for the bilabial trill, voiceless of voiced, sometimes used to express extreme cold, or, in some countries, to urge on horses. It should be noted that there is a phonemic (linguistically relevant) opposition of endolabio-endolabial versus exolabio-exolabial stops in Irish (see le Muire & ÓHuallacháin, 1960).

Labio-dentalveolar

There are articulations between the lower lip and the teeth and/or alveolar ridge. The lower lip can make contact with the teeth edges and back, and possibly the alveolar ridge, but no further back than that. The anthropophonic possibilities are *endolabio-dental, exolabio-dental,* and *exolabio-alveolar.*

Endolabio-dental: the lower lip is lifted slightly so that its inner surface makes contact with the edges, and perhaps a little of the fronts of the upper teeth. The upper lip may be simultaneously lifted a little out of the way. This is the articulation of the [f] and [v] sounds of English and many languages. It is difficult, although not impossible, to form a complete, air-tight, closure between the inner lower lip and the fronts of the upper teeth. It is probable, therefore, that the labio-dental stops reported for certain languages are exolabio-dental, with the lower lip bent backwards so that its outer part contacts the backs of the upper teeth. A labio-dental (presumably endolabio-dental) nasal is said to occur in some languages, for example, English and Italian, and there is a special phonetic symbol for it [ɱ]. In English it is said to occur before [f] or [v] in such words as *triumph* and *triumvirate.* It is doubtful, however, if any English speakers really pronounce this as a genuine nasal, which, as we saw above, involves a complete oral closure. It is most commonly, perhaps always, an open, fricative-type articulation, more correctly described as an endolabio-dental nasalized voiced fricative [ṽ]. Of course, so much air is diverted through the nasal cavity that the labio-dental air-flow is non-turbulent; nevertheless, the articulatory stricture is of fricative type. A slightly modified type of endolabio-dental articulation occurs as a secondary *labio-dentalized* component of some modified articulations (see Chapter 10).

Exolabio-dental: strictly speaking perhaps two types—outer half of lower lip against edges of upper teeth, and outer half of lower lip against backs of upper teeth. The best known example is the approximant [ʋ] of North Indian languages, such as Hindi. An exolabio-dental stop can be produced by bending the lower lip backwards over the lower teeth and forming a complete closure between the outer part of the lower lip and the backs of the upper teeth. Probably this is the type of labio-dental stop reported by Guthrie (1948) as occurring in Tonga, and by Ladefoged (1971) as an allophone, or positional variant of [pf] in Shubi. The labio-dental flap of Margi (West Africa), described in Ladefoged 1964, is another example of an exolabio-dental articulation.

Exolabio-alveolar: by starting from an exolabio-dental stop (with lower lip against backs of upper teeth) and sliding the lower lip a little further back one can produce exolabio-alveolar stop, nasal, fricative approximant. These are not known to occur in any language.

Figure 39 shows saggital sections of various labio-labial and labio-dental articulations.

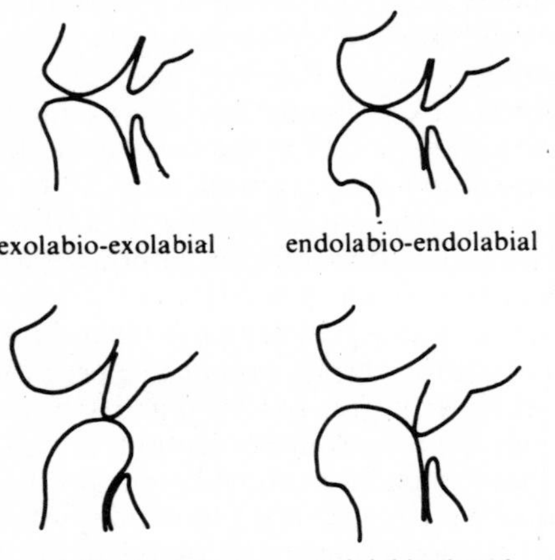

Figure 39. Types of labio-labial and labio-dental articulation

Denti-

Denti-labial: lower teeth against (any part of) upper lip. A kind of [f, v] can be produced this way, and this type of fricative is probably substituted for more normal labio-dental [f, v] by persons with a projecting lower jaw.

Denti-dental or *bidental:* lower teeth closed against upper teeth, lips kept out of the way, and tongue flat. By blowing through the teeth in this way denti-dental voiceless and voiced approximants can be produced (probably not fricatives, since the bidental articulatory channels are cumulatively large enough that flow through them is turbulent only when voiceless). A voiceless bidental approximant occurs in a variety of Shapsugh, a Western dialect of Adyghe (North Western Caucasus). Here, the bidental approximant corresponds to the voiceless velar, or palatalized velar fricative of other dialects, in such words as [xɨ] *six* ['daxə] *pretty*.

We come now to articulations in which various parts of the tongue articulate against the upper lip and various parts of the tectal division. The reader should now make certain that he can identify, kinaesthetically, the various tectal zones, particularly in the dentalveolar region and the immediately posterior palatal zone. Place the tip of the tongue against the edges of the upper teeth. Now, keeping contact with the roof of the mouth, slide the tongue very slowly backwards. Feel, first, the backs of the upper teeth, then, immediately behind them, a rather flat part of the alveolar ridge. Sliding the tongue-tip slowly further back one can now feel it going round the corner, so to speak, at the back of the alveolar ridge, and heading upwards into the vault of the hard palate. Now, take the tongue-tip back to the upper teeth. Feel the edges and backs of the teeth again: both constitute the *dental* zone. Now let the tongue-tip slide back, just clear of the backs of the teeth but no more. This is the *alveolar* subzone. Now, slide a very little further back and stop the tongue-tip on the very edge of the alveolar ridge—that is, on the most convex part of the ridge, where it is swinging upwards into the palate. This is the *postalveolar* subzone. Now, continue a very little beyond until it is just clear that the tongue is no longer on a 'ridge'. This is the start of the *prepalatal* subzone. By this time you will probably feel that the tongue is turned to point upward to such an extent that it is no longer the *apex,* but rather the underblade—the *sublamina*—which is in contact with the palate. Palates vary a good deal in height, and tongues in length and mobility. Nevertheless, you should be able to run the apex and underblade of your tongue pretty well up to the highest point of the palate. This should be about the end of the prepalatal subzone and the start of the palatal subzone, which continues back to the point where the hard palate ends. Some people can take their tongue all the way back to the soft palate. Others will have to locate the division between the (hard) *palatal* zone and the (soft) *velar* zone by means of a finger, or, possibly, the dorsal surface of the tongue.

The *dental, alveolar, postalveolar* and *prepalatal* upper articulatory (sub)zones should be fairly clear. It remains to experiment a little with the forward zones of the tongue: *apico-, lamino-,* and *sublamino-*.

With the mouth nearly closed, place the apex (and rim) of the tongue against the backs of the lower teeth. Now, keeping the apex down in that position, let the blade of the tongue make contact successively with the backs of the upper teeth (dental), the flat part of the ridge immediately behind the teeth (alveolar) and the extreme, convex, back part of the ridge (postalveolar): these are *lamino-dental, lamino-alveolar,* and *lamino-postalveolar* articulations.

Silently alternate *apico-* and *lamino-* articulations at each of these (sub)zones. Repeat these alternating contacts with weak pulmonic pressure initiation: in other words, produce a series of quiet t-sounds with apico-/lamino-dental, apico-/lamino-alveolar and apico-/lamino-postalveolar articulation. You may notice that it is easy to make a clean, sharp, break of contact between the apex and the upper articulator, but the break of contact between the blade and the upper articulator tends to be a little less clear cut, a little more 'sloppy'. This is a way in which one can sometimes detect *lamino-* articulations when one hears them.

Now, experiment with forming fricative-type channels between the apex and lamino (blade) and the various dentalveolar (sub)zones. If you are a native speaker of English, silently articulate your [θ] (as in *thin*), [s] (as in *sin*), and [ʃ] (as in *shin*), and try to analyze their articulation. The probability is that [θ] will feel somewhat *apico-*, with the apex of the tongue a little behind the teeth (hence *apico-dental,* although perhaps a little retracted); [s] and [ʃ] on the other hand may feel neither completely *apico-* (with the tongue-tip fully raised) nor completely *lamino-* (with the tongue-tip down behind the lower teeth). They are rather often neither clear-cut apico nor lamino but 'apico-lamino', but there are individual variations, and one must experiment and find out for oneself.

Finally, one must experiment a little with sublamino-articulation. Place the apex of the tongue on the extreme back of the alveolar ridge, in the apico-postalveolar position. Now, slide still further back till you can clearly feel the underside of the tongue in contact with the prepalatal zone. Make a stop in that position, and then relax the tongue and make a fricative. Withdraw the tongue still further back into the mouth and make a voiced approximant or resonant in that position. All these are sublamino-prepalatal articulations. Since they involve the point of the tongue being lifted up and curled back, as it were, they are often called *retroflex* articulations—although this term tends to be quite loosely used, on the one hand for certain apico-postalveolar articulations, and on the other for vowel (voiced) articulations in which the tongue point is somewhat lifted and drawn back into the body of the tongue without actually being retroflexed: an example is a typical Mid-Western American /r/ consonant or vowel as in *bird.* This is often loosely termed 'retroflex'. In reality it is most frequently an 'apex-retracted, advanced velar approximant', which may be described as an 'apico-postalveolarized, advanced velar approximant'.

Apico-

We can now continue to survey oral articulations: apico- articula-

tions are formed by the point of the tongue in conjunction with upper articulators from lips to postalveolar, and possibly prepalatal.
Apico-labial: point of tongue on upper lip. Both endo- and exo-labial contacts are possible. A glottalic egressive apico-labial stop is sometimes used for the ejection of a small foreign body from the tip of the tongue. A 'linguo-labial'—presumably apico-labial—stop is said to occur in Umotina, a South American language (Ladefoged 1971).
Apico-dental: point of tongue against rims or backs of upper teeth, often simply called 'dental'. Apico-dental stops [t̪, d̪], nasal [n̪], and lateral [l̪] are common in the world's languages, including some northern dialects of English—although English more commonly has apico-alveolars. The stops, nasal and lateral require a firm and complete closure against the backs of the upper teeth. There is usually also some lamino-alveolar contact at the same time. The important point, however, is that the apex (rim) of the tongue is in contact with the teeth: this makes the articulation apico-dental, no matter what the blade of the tongue may be doing.

Apico-dental fricatives and approximants usually have the rim of the tongue close to and just behind the rim of the upper teeth. The English apico-dental fricatives [θ, ð] are sometimes called 'inter-dental', implying that the rim of the tongue is placed between the upper and lower teeth. This is certainly not the most normal articulation of these English sounds. The English [θ, ð] are wide-channel fricatives, near the borderline of approximants, and, from the aerodynamic point of view, they are less 'dental' than the 'alveolar' [s, z] and postalveolar [ʃ, ʒ]. We shall take up this aspect of the aerodynamics of these sounds again.
Apico-alveolar: apex of tongue on the relatively flat part of the alveolar ridge immediately behind the upper teeth, often simply called alveolar. This is the articulation of the commonest variety of English [t, d, n, l]. A slightly 'whistling' form of [s, z] can be articulated this way, though English [s] and [z] are more commonly lamino-.
Apico-postalveolar: apex of tongue on or near the curved rear end of the alveolar ridge, often simply called postalveolar. A typical apico-postalveolar is the (British) English approximant [ɹ]—the *r* in *red,* for example. The English [t, d] sounds that come before the apico-postalveolar approximant [ɹ] in words like *try, dry,* are sometimes said to be apico-postalveolar stops. It is probable, however, that they more often have a 'sliding' apico-alveolar to postalveolar articulation—that is to say, the tongue point goes up and makes momentary contact in the alveolar zone but immediately slides back to the postalveolar zone.

The stops that are usually transcribed [ʈ, ɖ] and called 'retroflex' are typically sublamino-prepalatal. However, in Hindi and some other North Indian languages the so-called 'retroflex' stops are sometimes no further back than apico-postalveolar.

Apico-postalveolar fricatives are of [ʃ, ʒ] type. Note that in English such fricatives are most commonly lamino-postalveolar. Apico-postalveolar [ʃ, ʒ] occur in Russian, and [ʃ] often in German. The reader should deliberately make an apico-postalveolar [ʃ], voice it to [ʒ] and then very slightly retract the tongue-point, widening the articulatory channel just to the point where turbulence ceases. This is apico-postalveolar approximant [ɹ]. An apico-postalveolar trill is also possible.

Apico-prepalatal articulation is possible, but it is doubtful if it normally occurs in any language. Once the prepalatal upper articulatory zone is reached it is hardly possible to avoid using either the underblade (sublamino-) or blade (lamino-) or dorsum (dorso-) as the lower articulator.

Lamino-

Lamino- articulations are formed by the blade of tongue in contact with upper lip, teeth, alveolar ridge, to possibly, as far back as the prepalatal arch, although by the time this zone is reached the part of the tongue-surface used as lower articulator tends to be farther back than the blade (anterodorso-).

Lamino-labial: it is possible to keep the point of the tongue on or about the rims of the lower teeth, and to articulate with the blade against the (inner) upper lip. Not recorded in languages.

Lamino-dental: point of tongue just below rims of lower teeth, blade against backs of upper teeth. Varieties of [t̻, d̻, θ, ð] can be produced thus, and lamino-dental [t̻], contrasting with apico-alveolar [t] and retroflex [ʈ], occurs in several Australian languages (O'Grady et al., 1966). A lamino-dental [ð] is said to occur in the South Arabian languages Mehri and Harsusi (Johnstone 1970).

Lamino-alveolar: point of tongue on backs or rims of lower teeth, blade articulating against alveolar ridge. Stops [t, d] can be formed this way, and not uncommonly are in some varieties of English, for example, Cockney, which has (affricated—see Chapter 11) lamino-alveolar [tˢ, dᶻ]. It is quite easy to make a clear-cut sudden breakaway of the tongue-point from the alveolar ridge (in apico-alveolar stops), but when the point is lowered and the contact is made with the blade (lamino-alveolar) it is more difficult to break away cleanly. The blade withdraws from the alveolar ridge more slowly, passing through a perceptible moment of approximation when there is an [s]-like central channel between the blade and the alveolar ridge—hence the

tendency for lamino-alveolar stops to be affricated [tˢ, dᶻ]. Lamino-alveolar fricatives are typical English [s] and [z].
Lamino-postalveolar: blade of tongue against the extreme back—the convex ridge—of the alveolar ridge. Typical lamino-postalveolars are the English lamino-postalveolar fricatives [ʃ] and [ʒ]. Stops can, of course, be formed here too: in English the stop which precedes [ʃ, ʒ] in [tʃ, dʒ] as in *church* and *judge* is often lamino-postalveolar.
Lamino-prepalatal: blade of tongue against the prepalatal arch, behind the postalveolar zone. To achieve this articulation the point of the tongue must be somewhat retracted from the teeth. It is certainly a possible articulation, but it is probable that in languages which have a non-apical, linguo-prepalatal articulation (such as Polish) the channel is formed a little further back on the tongue than the laminal zone.

Sublamino-

Sublamino- articulations are formed with the tongue point raised and pointed upwards—almost backwards, hence the term 'retroflex'—so that the underblade articulates against the postalveolar or prepalatal zones.
Sublamino-postalveolar: underblade against extreme back of alveolar ridge. North Indian [ʈ, ɖ] sounds and possibly the [ʂ] of some languages are commonly articulated here.
Sublamino-prepalatal: underblade against prepalatal arch—the most retroflex of 'retroflex' [ʈ, ɖ] type sounds. The retroflex [ʈ, ɖ, ɳ] of Tamil and other Dravidian languages are often of this type.
At this point it will be well to break off for a moment to consider in more detail the aerodynamics and acoustics of dentalveolar fricatives. It is clear that sounds, especially fricatives, articulated in this region are subject to differentiation along at least three parameters: upper articulatory zone, lower articulatory zone, and channel area.

To take the last first, some writers (for example, Pike 1943), as we mentioned in Chapter 7, have used the terms *groove(d)* and *flat* or *slit* to characterize different transverse shapes of the articulatory channel. According to this terminology [θ] is flat and [s], for example, is grooved. However, as we said there, it is probable that the crucial characteristic here is not the transverse shape of the channel, but its cross-sectional area. Thus [θ], irrespective of the *shape* of its channel, has a channel area that is three or four times that of [s], and this means that for a given volume-velocity the velocity of air-flow through the [s] channel is three or four times that of flow through the [θ] channel, and it is this velocity difference which is crucial.

Some of those who make the grooved/flat distinction describe (English) [ʃ] as flat. It is just possible that, on the average, the channel area of [ʃ] is somewhat larger than that of [s], although there is not much evidence for this. What is certainly true, however, is that, aerodynamically speaking, the channels for [s] and [ʃ] are closely similar, and very significantly smaller than that of [θ].

Taking the phonetic symbols [θ, s, ʃ] to mean broadly 'some kind of wide dental or alveolar fricative [θ], some kind of narrow alveolar fricative [s], and postalveolar fricative [ʃ]', we can characterize the basic aerodynamic and acoustic differences between them as follows:

In [θ] there is a wide articulatory channel (at or near the boundary between fricative and approximant) a little behind the upper teeth ([θ]-type sounds can be either apico-dental or apico-alveolar). Flow through this wide channel is turbulent, but the velocity is low, hence the resultant hiss of channel-turbulence is of low intensity. Since the velocity of the air-stream flowing out past the teeth is low, little or no eddying wake-turbulence is generated there.

In [s] there is a narrow articulatory channel between the tongue and alveolar ridge. Flow through this narrow channel is at a relatively high velocity, and consequently channel-turbulence is fairly intense, and a high-velocity jet is projected against the teeth (both upper and lower) generating strong wake-turbulence downstream from the teeth. The channel-turbulence is responsible for a moderately low-frequency component of the sound, while the dental wake-turbulence is responsible for a component of higher frequency. This can be demonstrated by reversing air-flow through the [s] channel: this eliminates the dental wake-turbulence, since the high-velocity jet is now directed into the interior of the mouth. The resultant lowered frequency of the resultant hiss can be clearly observed.

In [ʃ] the aerodynamic conditions are superficially much as for [s]: narrow channel, strong channel-turbulence and high-velocity jet projected against the teeth. However, there are crucial differences. In the first place, the channel is now linguo-postalveolar, that is, it is located some distance (of the order of 5 mm) further back. Consequently, the jet has further to travel before hitting the teeth and thus has dissipated some of its energy, lost some velocity and broadened its front by the time it reaches them. As a result, dental wake-turbulence is less intense than in [s] and of somewhat lower frequency. Secondly, because the tongue has been retracted, the [ʃ]-jet blows across a little cavity between the lower teeth and the apex and/or underblade of the tongue, and the resonance generated in this cavity is an acoustic component of most [ʃ]-type sounds. It is easy to demonstrate the effect of this cavity by articulating first a normal [ʃ], then a [ʃ] with the cavity behind the lower teeth abolished—filled in, for example, by chewed-up bread, or (for those whose kinaesthetic control is good) by deliberately articulating an anomalous [ʃ] with a regular lamino-postalveolar channel, but with the point and rim of the tongue in contact with the rim of the lower teeth. It is at once apparent that this anomalous [ʃ], with no post-dental cavity, is more [s]-like in its sound. This kind of anomalous [ʃ] articulation appears to be the articulation of those fricatives in North-West Caucasian languages (especially Adyghe and Kabardian) which are described as 'between [s] and [ʃ]' or 'hissing-hushing' (Russian 'svistjašči-šipjaščie') sounds.

The aerodynamic differences we have been discussing are obvious inferences from information about channel areas, and stricture locations, known from direct photography and radiography, and some, as we have shown, are subject to simple experimental verification. Further verification of the role of the teeth in sounds of the [θ, s, ʃ] type was provided by an experiment, carried out with the co-operation of the University of Michigan Dental School, in which

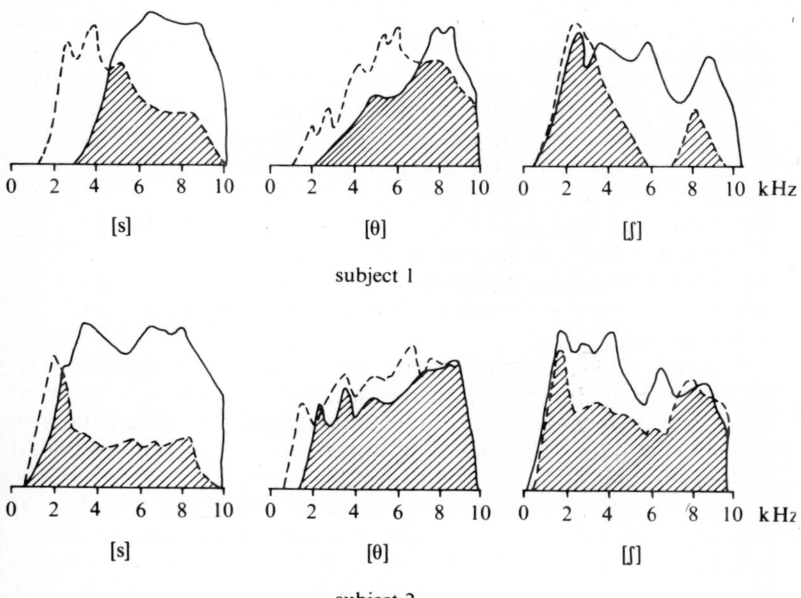

solid line = with all teeth broken line = with no teeth
shaded area = area of overlap of normal and toothless spectrum

Figure 40. Acoustic spectra of some fricatives pronounced with and without teeth

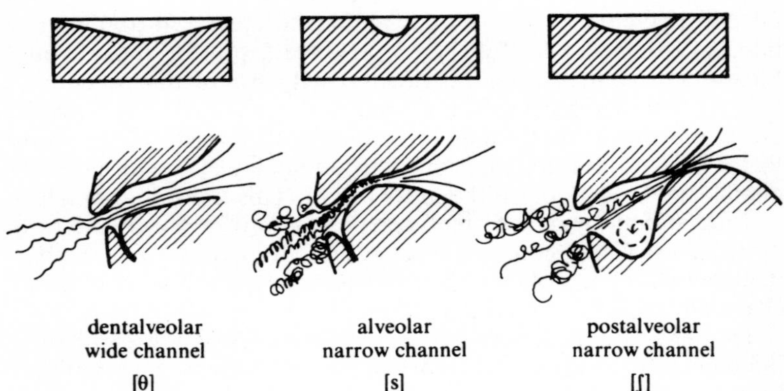

Figure 41. Characteristics of three types of dentalveolar fricatives

two persons with no natural teeth but with full sets of dentures were asked to pronounce these sounds under four conditions: (i) with all teeth, (ii) with uppers only, (iii) with lowers only, (iv) with no teeth. The resultant sounds were recorded, and their acoustic spectra were determined. It is quite clear from these spectra (see figure 40) that the presence of teeth is least important for [θ], most important for [s].

A rough measure of the amount of acoustic change produced by removal of teeth can be obtained by superimposing the spectral envelopes of the normal and toothless sounds and expressing the area in common as a percentage of the area covered by the normal spectrum. The figures are: [s] and [ʃ] both about 44 per cent, [θ] 83 per cent. Thus, the acoustic change wrought on [s] and [ʃ] by removal of teeth is about twice as great as that wrought on [θ]. In other words, the teeth are twice as important for 'alveolar' [s] as for 'dental' [θ].

Figure 41 indicates diagrammatically the main differences between [θ], [s], and [ʃ]. In this figure the upper diagram is a formalized transverse or frontal section indicating roughly the shape and size of the articulatory channel. The lower diagram is a mid-saggital section through the dentalveolar region.

We have now discussed fricatives produced in the dentalveolar region in terms of two parameters—channel area and upper articulatory location. It remains to consider the third parameter, namely lower articulator—especially the opposition apico-/lamino-.

With any normal kind of wide channel dental or alveolar articulation [θ], the apico-/lamino- distinction makes virtually no difference. As long as a wide channel is formed at or just behind the teeth, the sound is generated by low-velocity turbulent flow through that channel, irrespective of which particular lower articulatory zone is involved. The same is true of a narrow dental articulation—a kind of [s] with the tongue thrust as far forward as possible forming a narrow channel just behind the teeth. Whether that narrow dental channel is formed by the apex, or by a forward thrust of the blade (with the apex kept down behind the lower teeth) seems to make no difference.

The situation is different, however, with alveolar [s] and postalveolar [ʃ]. Here, the apico- / lamino- distinction is aerodynamically, and more particularly, perhaps, acoustically important. In the case of [s] the change from lamino- to apico- is liable to have one or both of two effects. In the first place, the lifting of the apex to form the apico-alveolar channel tends to open up, partially, that post(lower)-dental cavity which is characteristic of [ʃ]. Hence any apical [s] may sound a trifle [ʃ]-like. Secondly, for reasons which are obscure, a *strongly apico*-alveolar [s] may acquire a slightly whistled effect. Indeed, one quite common form of whistle is generated at a channel varying from apico-dental to apico-postalveolar.

At the postalveolar subzone the distinction is even more marked. Here the difference is acoustic rather than aerodynamic. Selection of *lamino*- or *apico*- articulation tends to determine the shape of the tongue behind the location of the articulation itself: and this dorsal tongue-shape (more or less convex or concave) affects the size, and hence the resonance properties, of the oral chamber behind the articulation.

If the apex is kept low down and the blade brought close to the postalveolar (or, *a fortiori,* the prepalatal) subzone, the whole body of the tongue behind that point is normally convex, the dorsal surface to some degree forming a smooth convex dome, swelling upwards towards the hard palate. The shape of the oral resonator thus formed behind the articulation is such as to impart some degree of 'clear', 'palatal' or '[i]-like' quality to lamino-postalveolar (or lamino-prepalatal) [ʃ], which consequently appears to be somewhat 'palatalized'.

If, on the other hand, the apex is raised to form an articulation at the postalveolar (or *a fortiori,* the prepalatal) subzone, then the body of the tongue immediately behind the apex will be less convex than in a lamino-postalveolar articulation. It is, in fact, often concave ('sulcalized') immediately behind the articulation, with further back a convexly domed, upward swelling of the dorsum towards the soft palate. The shape of the oral resonator thus formed behind the articulation is such as to impart some degree of 'dark', 'velar' or '[o]-like' quality to apico-postalveolar [ʃ], which, consequently, appears to be somewhat 'velarized'. The effect of lingual concavity,

lamino-postalveolar [ʃ] **apico-postalveolar [ɹ]**

Figure 42. Lamino- and apico-postalveolar articulations

which automatically tends to result from raising of the tip, is, of course, even stronger with 'retroflex' or sublamino-postalveolar and sublamino-prepalatal [s].

Figure 42 is based on tracings of X-rays of the author showing lamino-postalveolar and apico-postalveolar articulations in English: the lamino-postalveolar fricative [ʃ], and the apico-postalveolar approximant [ɹ].

We are now in a position to review various articulations in the dentalveolar region. For the present purpose we shall lump together 'wide' fricatives (such as [θ, ð]) and approximants (such as [ɹ] and its voiceless counterpart [ɹ̥]) as both being 'wide' by contrast with the 'narrow' fricatives ([s, ʃ]).

The significant distinctions that we have seen are summed up in table 16. As we have seen, the apico-/lamino- distinction is very important for postalveolars and narrow alveolars, but negligible for dentals and wide alveolars. This leaves us with nine articulatory types, for which it would be useful to have distinctive symbols. Unfortunately the International Phonetic Association supplies us with only two pairs of symbols for stops: [t, d], [ʈ, ɖ] in, or approximately in, this region, only three pairs of basic symbols for fricatives: [θ, ð, s, z, ʃ, ʒ], or four if we count [ʂ, ʐ] and five if we count [ɕ, ʑ]. Strictly speaking [ʈ, ɖ, ʂ, ʐ] stand for 'retroflex'—that is, most typically sublamino-prepalatal articulations; we may, however, press them into use here. The symbols [ɕ, ʑ] stand for what the IPA calls 'alveolo-palatal' fricatives: this is the unsystematic IPA terminology for what may be regarded as palatals with an alveolar modification, that is, dorso-prepalatal fricatives, such as the Polish ś and ź. We might as well retain them for that usage, which is outside our present region of interest.

Table 16

	dental		*alveolar*		*postalveolar*	
	wide	narrow	wide	narrow	wide	narrow
apico-				4	6	8
	1	2	3			
lamino-				5	7	9

Table 17

stops	*dental*		*alveolar*		*postalveolar*	
apico-	t̪	d̪	t	d	ʈ	ɖ
lamino-	ˢt̪	ˢd̪	ˢt	ˢd	ˢʈ	ˢɖ

For approximants in this region the IPA supplies only [ɹ], with, of course, [ɹ̥] for its devoiced counterpart.

Tables 17 and 18 suggest possible symbols for articulations in the dentalveolar region. In the stop table, for want of anything better I indicate lamino- articulation where necessary by a small s placed above and to the left—this recalls the fact that [s] is often regarded as primarily lamino-alveolar and also that lamino-dentalveolar stops often have some [s]-like affrication. In the fricative/approximant table I indicate apical articulation where necessary by ̺ under the symbol.

Table 18

fricative/	*dental*				*alveolar*				*postalveolar*			
approximants	wide		narrow		wide		narrow		wide		narrow	
apico-							s̺	z̺	ɹ̥̺	ɹ̺	ʂ	ʐ
	θ	ð	s̪	z̪	θ-	ð-						
lamino-							s	z	ˢɹ̥	ˢɹ	ʃ	ʒ

Dorso-domal

After this long digression, we can pass on from the various linguo-dentalveolar articulations to dorso-domal articulation.

Dorso-prepalatal: the surface of the tongue, from just behind the blade backwards a centimetre or two, approximates to the forward arch of the hard palate. Stop, fricatives, approximants, a nasal and lateral can all be articulated here. There are special symbols only for the fricatives [ɕ, ʑ] (Polish ś, ź). For the rest, we use the symbols for the palatal consonants [c, ɟ, ɲ, ʎ], with a (+) after them, if necessary, to show that they are advanced. The (+) is not necessary when [c] and [ɟ] are combined with [ɕ] and [ʑ] to indicate prepalatal affricates. We thus distinguish between, for example, Serbo-Croat ч and ћ—apico-postalveolar and dorso-prepalatal affricates—as [tʂ, dʐ] and [cɕ, ɟʑ].

Dorso-palatal: dorsal surface of the tongue, from about one third to one half of the distance from apex to tip of epiglottis, articulates against the high vault of the hard palate. Stops [c] [ɟ], nasal [ɲ], fricatives [ç, ʝ], lateral [ʎ], approximants [j] [i, ɩ, e] and resonants æ, a]. The best way to learn to make dorso-palatal articulations start from an [i] vowel. Keep a strong air-stream going and up the channel from [i] slightly: the result should be the voiced palatal fricative [ʝ]. Devoice this to [ç]. Now close up still further with the articulators in the [i]-position till you form a dorso-palatal stop [c].

Dorso-velar: dorsal surface of the tongue, about two thirds of the distance from apex to tip of epiglottis, articulating against the soft palate. Typically English [k, g], as in *car, gone,* are dorso-velar. So, too, is the nasal [ŋ] as in *long*. Form a [k]-closure, build up a little pulmonic pressure behind it. Now, keeping the whole tongue in precisely the same position, open up a small central channel, out of which the pent-up air should flow, turbulently. This is a voiceless dorso-velar fricative [x]. Now voice it to [ɣ]. It is possible to produce laterals here too, though they are rare. A series of velar lateral fricatives and affricates occurs in the Caucasian language, Artchi (Mikailov 1967). Approximants include the vowels [u] and [ɯ], and the semi-vowel [w], which is strictly bilabial / dorsovelar, since it also has an endolabio-endolabial articulation.

Dorso-uvular: dorsal or radical surface of tongue against extreme end of soft palate, including the uvula. Stops [q, ɢ], nasal [ɴ], fricatives [χ, ʁ], trill [ʀ], approximant (vowels) [ʌ, ɔ]. Dorso-uvular stops or fricatives, can be acquired from [k] or [x], by holding the dorso-velar articulation, then sliding the tongue backwards (while simultaneously slightly opening the mouth) as far as it can go and still be in contact with the roof of the mouth.

Voiceless uvular stop [q] occurs in classical Arabic (ق) and many other languages, but the voiced correlate [ɢ] is very much rarer. It is one form of Persian ق, and is a regular sound of Burushaski, where it contrasts with voiceless [q] and [q^h].

The dorso-uvular trill involves the formation of a furrow at the back of the mouth within which the uvula passively vibrates in an egressive air-stream. It can be learned by 'gargling', first with some water, then only with saliva, then, as nearly as possible, dry.

This rapid survey has covered the whole area, and it will be well to summarize some of the material we have considered.

Articulations in the oral area involve the approximation of a lower and an upper articulator. We can, therefore, represent any oral articulation as a point, or area, of intersection on a two-dimensional chart in which the horizontal axis represents the upper articulatory divisions, regions, zones, and subzones, and the vertical axis the lower articulatory zones.

Figure 43 is such a chart, with an indication of its relationship to the actual contours of the upper and lower articulatory areas. The shaded area indicates, roughly, the extent of anatomically possible articulation. Of course, the upper and lower articulatory surface are continua, or quasi-continua. In dividing the chart into squar we have, as it were, digitalized the information it conveys.

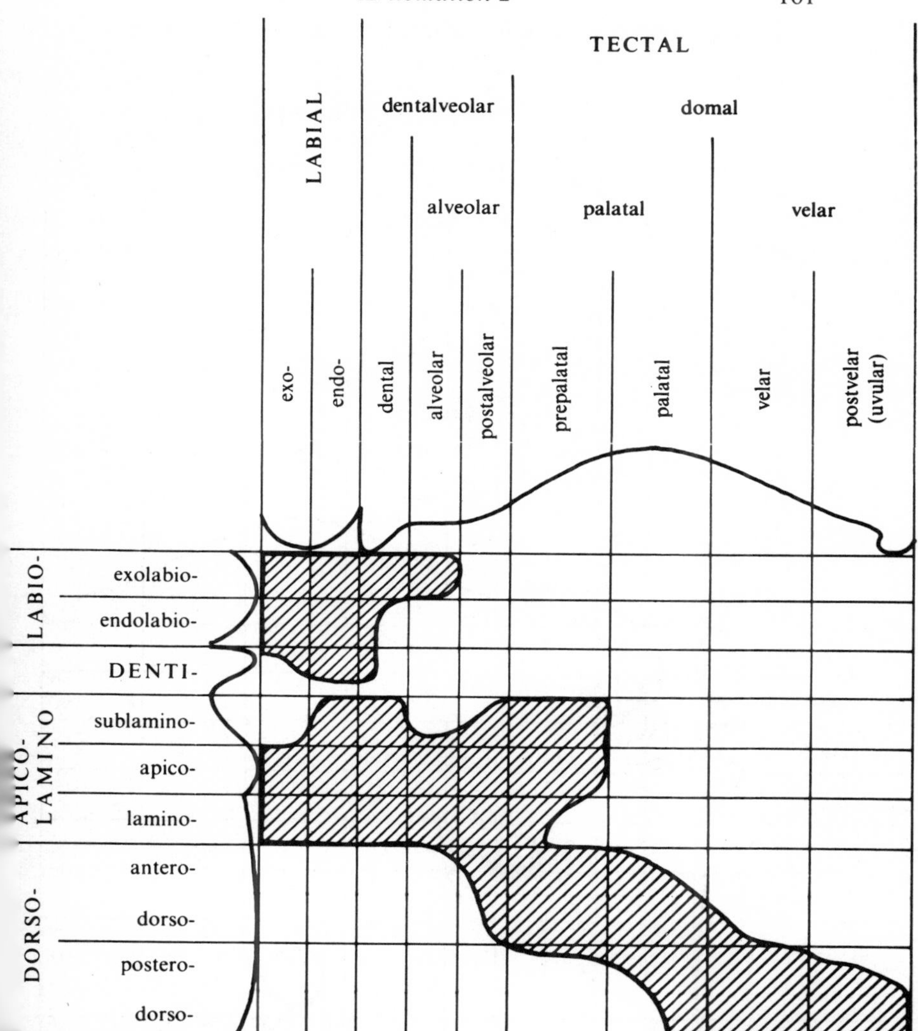

gure 43. Anatomically possible oral articulation

Figure 44 presents a similar chart for English consonants.

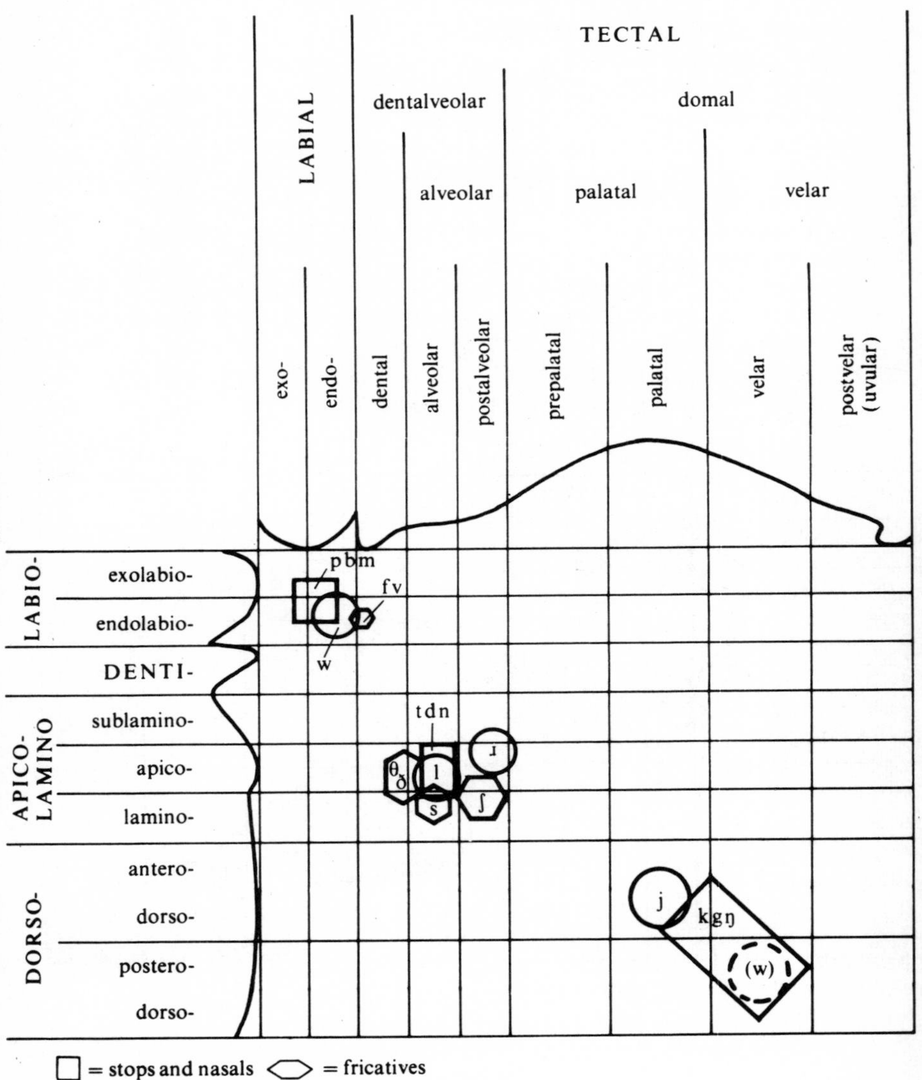

Figure 44. The oral articulations of English consonants

To complete our initial survey of articulatory locations we must now consider the pharyngo-laryngeal area.

Pharyngeal: Articulation in the Pharynx

Faucal or transverse pharyngeal: in faucal or transverse pharyngeal articulation the part of the pharynx immediately behind the mouth is laterally compressed, so that the faucal pillars move towards each other. At the same time the larynx may be somewhat raised. This appears to be the most common articulation of the pharyngeal approximants [ħ] and [ʕ]. It is largely a sphincteric semi-closure of the oro-pharynx, and it can be learned by tickling the back of the throat, provoking retching.

Linguo-pharyngeal: in this articulation the root of the tongue, carrying with it the epiglottis, moves backwards to narrow the pharynx in a front-back dimension. This may be the articulation of Danish 'pharyngeal r', and of the pharyngeal component of various types of pharyngealized articulation.

Laryngeal: Articulation in the Larynx

There are two zones, *ventricular* and *glottal.*

Ventricular: the ventricular bands are brought together (see Chapter 6 on phonation), plus some generalized constriction of the upper larynx and pharynx. A ventricular stop can thus be produced, almost certainly involving simultaneous glottal stop. This ventricular or strong glottal stop may be represented by [ʕʔ]. It occurs in some Caucasian languages, where it contrasts with plain glottal stop [ʔ]. Ventricular, or glottal plus ventricular stop has also been described as a 'pharyngealized glottal stop', for example, by Gaprindashvili (1966, p. 191, 'laringalńyj faringalizovannyi smyčno-vzryvnoj'). Another ventricular sound is the *breathy-voiced* (or *whispery voiced*) *ventricular fricative trill* [ɦʕ] which occurs in some of the Abkhazo-Adyghe languages of the north-west Caucasus, notably in Abaza and in Arabic loan-words in Adyghe and Kabardian. According to Rogava (1941) this sound formerly occurred as a regular phoneme in all the Abkhazo-Adyghe languages, but has been lost in Adyghe and Kabardian, except where it has been retained as representing Arabic *'ain* [ʕ]. The most common type of Arabic *'ain* seems to be an *upper pharyngeal* or *faucal* approximant. The Adyghe sound is produced much deeper in the throat, with occasionally 'bleat-like' ventricular trill plus ventricular turbulence. On the other hand, Adyghe [ħ] (regarded as the voiceless counterpart of the *glottal plus ventricular* 'bleat' [ɦʕ]) is articulated in the upper pharynx, as are both [ħ] and [ʕ] in Arabic. It is interesting to note that Ibn Sīnā (370 AH (980 AD)—428 AH (1037 AD)), the great mediaeval (Persian) Arab scholar, also known as 'Avicenna', in his treatise on Arabic phonetics described [ʕ] as formed 'deeper in the throat, in the place where the air involved in vomiting is located' than [ħ], which is formed 'at the place where the air for clearing the throat is located'. (Semaan 1963.) It is possible that Ibn Sīnā was describing a mediaeval Arabic sound more like the modern Abkhazo-Adyghe one, which is no longer used, at least in the better-known varieties of Arabic.

Glottal: the vocal cords are brought together to form glottal stop [ʔ], and glottal fricative, voiceless [h] and voiced [ɦ]. Voiced [ɦ] is simply what has earlier been described as the 'phonation type' whispery voice. When, however, either [h] or [ɦ] function consonantally (as a syllable-margin unit) in the phonology of language, particularly if it takes its place as one of a series of fricative, then we usually regard the glottal component as articulatory rather than phonatory and call it a 'glottal fricative'.

NINE

Vowels

It will have been observed that up to the present those sounds of the type represented by [i, e, u] and the like, which are commonly called 'vowels', have received no more than passing and incidental reference. We must now look at them in more detail.

Most of the older works on phonetics present the distinction between vowel and consonant as absolutely basic. Nevertheless, as Pike (1943) points out, it is notoriously difficult to set up clear-cut criteria to differentiate between them; and, moreover, much of the time the distinction is based not on a consistently articulatory criterion, such as we are using in this book, but rather on the function of a particular sound-type in relation to the syllable, vowels being syllabic central units, consonants being syllabic marginal units. It was for this reason that Pike introduced the term 'vocoid' for a particular, arbitrarily delimited, articulatory class. The principal area of difficulty discovered by Pike concerned the distinction between 'semi-vowels' such as [w] and [j] and 'vowels' such as [u] and [i]. In terms of a system of articulatory description that distinguishes only location and stricture-type, but not the temporal distinction that we use in Chapter 7, it is obvious that [w] and [u] on the one hand, or [j] and [i] on the other, are, or may be, articulatorily identical pairs. Consequently, it is clear that the older phonetician's differentiation of them into 'vowel' and 'consonant' was based not on any difference of articulation but on their different functional distribution within particular languages. Pike proposed to keep the term 'vowel' for this kind of *functional* class, but to use the term 'vocoid' for a purely *articulatorily* defined class. We have resolved, or at least side-stepped, this particular problem in Chapter 7 by introducing 'time' as an articulatory parameter. We accept the fact that both the 'vowel' [i] and the 'semi-vowel' [j] involve an identical type of articulatory stricture—that of an *approximant;* but they can be taxonomically separated from each other by taking note of the fact that [i] always has a noticeable duration, whereas [j] is essentially a rapid *glide* away from (or to) an approximant-type stricture.

The approximant-type stricture for a semi-vowel is typically momentary, and the glide is typically more rapid than that from one vowel to another. This disposes of a major source of confusion as between vowel and consonant. There seems, therefore, to be no compelling reason to use the term 'vocoid' at all, and we shall, in consequence, use the commoner term 'vowel' in this chapter and throughout.

The term 'vowel', then, as generally understood, refers to a class of maintainable sounds with non-fricative central, oral, dorsọ-domal, or linguo-pharyngeal articulation. This clearly includes all central (not lateral) approximants and resonants, except for apico-, lamino- and sublamino- articulations. Although approximant articulations in the apico-alveolar or apico-postalveolar zone are not usually regarded as primary articulations of vowels, they may occur as secondary modifications of vowel articulations (for example, 'retroflexed vowels').

It would seem obvious that the articulatory description of vowels should follow exactly the same principles as the articulatory description of other sounds. Thus, in articulating [i] we have the dorsum of the tongue raised up, forming a fairly narrow articulatory channel between tongue and hard palate. A few moments experiment will clearly demonstrate that [i] satisfies the criterion for an approximant: non-turbulent flow when voiced, turbulent flow when voiceless. The vowel [i] is thus a dorso-palatal approximant. And, if one proceeds from [i] through [e] as in French *été* or German *See* or, roughly, English *say,* to [ɛ] as in French *tête* or, roughly, English *bet,* to [a] as in French *patte* or [æ] as in English *pat*—if one proceeds through such a series of sounds one finds that all are dorso-palatal, with increasingly large articulatory channel areas. The first one, [i], is clearly a narrow approximant; [e] is a wide approximant; [ɛ] is a resonant, but a moderately narrow one; while [a] is a wider resonant.

Again, if one articulates [u] it is easy to see that this too is an approximant, with dorso-velar (perhaps a little advanced towards dorso-palatal) articulation, plus endolabio-endolabial 'rounding' of the lips; [ɔ] is a dorso-uvular approximant, and so on.

Nevertheless, it has long been common practice to classify vowels in a way that departs radically from the way in which we classify consonants. We classify consonants in terms of location and stricture type: for the dorso-domal oral region this means in terms of zones of approximation between tongue-dorsum and roof of mouth, and degrees of closeness of the articulatory contact, in a direction essentially perpendicular (or, in geometrically more accurate terms, 'normal') to the upper articulatory surface. For vowels, we tend to consider the shape and position of the tongue: the location within the mouth of the 'hump' or 'dome' of the tongue, and the height to which it is raised. In addition, we take note of the accompanying position of the lips—whether they are spread, neutral, or rounded. In other words, in describing consonants, we refer to the location of the closest approximation between articulators; for vowels, on the other hand, we refer to the 'absolute' height of the tongue, and the location of this 'highest point' of the tongue, irrespective of whether this is also the location of closest approximation. That is to say, for vowels we superimpose, as it were, a grid upon the oral cavity with quasi-absolute vertical and horizontal dimensions. Figure 45 attempts to characterize this difference of approach.

It seems quite irrational to make this switch in classificatory principles, and, later, we will consider some of the implications of the more 'rational' classification of vowels in consonantal terms. Meanwhile we must look at the system of vowel classification which has become the accepted, or 'traditional', one since the publication of Alexander Melville Bell's *Visible Speech,* in 1867.

This 'traditional' system of vowel classification, which works quite well in practice, is based on the three parameters of *vertical tongue*

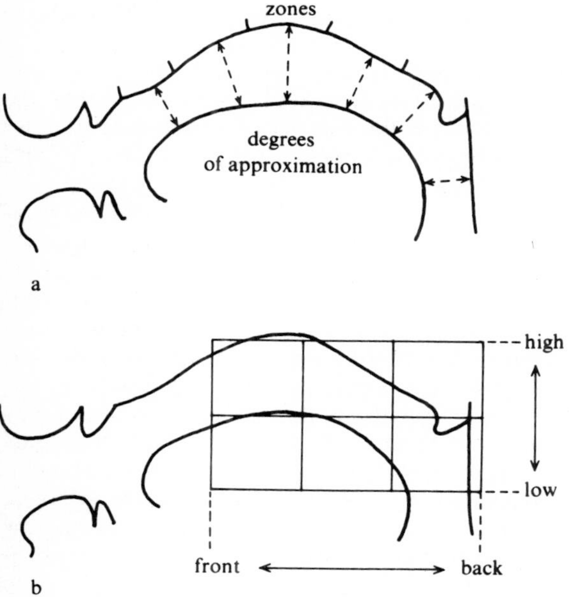

Figure 45. Two ways of classifying oral articulation (a) that commonly used for consonants, (b) that traditionally used for vowels

position (high–low), *horizontal tongue position* (front–back), and *lip position* (unrounded–rounded). The first two of these define the location of the 'tongue-hump', particularly of its summit, or highest point, within the mouth.

It is sometimes claimed that vowels can only be learned by an undefined direct process of 'imitation' of their auditory effect, rather than with the help of conscious attention to organic postures and kinaesthetic feedback. Presumably the justification for this view is that most vowels have more open, less clearly localized, strictures than do typical consonants, and that they thus provide less easily identifiable kinaesthetic sensations. This is only partly true: the most typically 'consonantal' sounds, such as stops and fricatives, do indeed involve fairly easily localizable tactile sensations, whereas with vowels such sensations are less evident. Nevertheless, such sensations are not entirely absent, as introspective vowel articulation shows: varying degrees of contact between the sides of the tongue and the upper molar and canine teeth can be felt with vowels of the [ɛ, e, i] type, roughly as in English *bet, bait, beat,* particularly when they are articulated silently. In experiments with vowels, as with consonants, silent articulation, by abolishing the masking effect of the auditory sensation, enables one to concentrate on the kinaesthetic sensations.

The most noticeable kinaesthetic sensations in the silent articulation of vowels, however, are not the tactile ones, but rather the proprioceptive sensations from the intrinsic and extrinsic muscles of the tongue: these provide an impression of the general shape and location of the tongue.

In a useful discussion of the nature of vowel quality and a brief history of vowel classification, Ladefoged (1967, Chap. 2) suggests that the nineteenth-century English phoneticians were really operating with auditory sensations when they tried to describe vowels in articulatory terms. 'They set out', he says, 'to describe the positions of the vocal organs during the production of different sounds; but their success in this enterprise was only partial. They did, however, succeed in providing categories with which to describe their auditory impressions.' It seems to me, however, that it would be more accurate to say that they were providing categories to describe proprioceptive impressions received from their tongue muscles. Melville Bell (1867) hints at this here and there in his description of how he came to invent his Visible Speech notation and vowel classification. An example occurs on p. 17 where, in talking of filling gaps in the vowel scale that he was developing, he says: '. . . experiment proved that the missing sounds could all be produced by organic arrangements corresponding with the theoretical classification.' He goes on to say: 'In fact, any desired sound, known or unknown, could be produced at pleasure by first adjusting the organs tentatively for its neighbor-sounds, and then allowing these to coalesce, as it were, into an intermediate.' This last is a clear description of the well-known applied phonetics technique of silently trying to merge the proprioceptive sensations of two imagined vowel-sounds so as to produce an intermediate muscular adjustment. Sweet (1877, pp. 17–18) is quite explicit on this matter: 'Whispering the vowels will be found a great help in analysing their formation. After a time the student will be able to recognize each vowel solely by the muscular sensations associated with its formation: he will be able to say to himself, "Now my tongue is in the position for (i)", "Now I have changed (i) into (ih)", etc., while not uttering the slightest sound, confident that if voiced or whispered breath is allowed to pass through the mouth the required sound will be produced.'

Bell and Sweet in describing vowels as 'high–low' 'front–back', and so on, were almost certainly not attaching articulatory labels to auditory sensations but were directly labelling estimates of the general shape and location of the tongue based on proprioceptive feedback. Indeed, we can probably attribute the 'break-through' in vowel classification, which occurred with Bell and Sweet, to the fact that these scholars substituted careful introspective experimental observation of proprioceptive sensations for the earlier writers' reliance on gross visual impressions and auditory sensations.

It is certainly true that one of the most powerful techniques that can be used in learning to produce and to identify and classify vowels is *silent* experimentation, such as Sweet recommended. Readers who are not already fully competent in vowel classification will find it useful not only to carry out the few experiments sketched here, but also to continue with intensive silent practice until the proprioceptive sensations can be reliably felt and accurate motor control is established.

Of the three parameters of vowel classification 'lip position' is the most obvious and easiest to control. By silently alternating a vowel of the [i] type (roughly as in English *see*) with a vowel of [u] type (roughly as in English *too*) one can easily feel the difference between an unrounded and a rounded vowel. Speakers of many varieties of English may notice that in uttering a word like *too* there is not a fixed degree of lip-rounding: at the start of the word the lips are spread, but they become more and more closely rounded as the utterance goes on, finishing up quite narrowly rounded at the end of the vowel. It is important to learn to say a long [u:] vowel with no change in lip position throughout.

Having silently alternated [i] and [u] several times one should try to dissociate the lip position from the specific vowels [i] and [u]. To do this, one spreads the lips as if for [i], then in a slow controlled way one progressively rounds them as if for a closely rounded [u], and one repeats this several times, while noting the muscular sensations.

By way of consolidating one's power of controlling lip-rounding as an independent parameter one should, silently and aloud, add lip-rounding to familiar unrounded vowels, and remove lip-rounding from familiar rounded vowels. Thus starting from an [i]-type vowel, with widely spread lips, one should concentrate on holding that imaginary [i], while slowly and deliberately rounding the lips. Once the lips have been strongly rounded, while keeping the tongue posture for [i], one should maintain this posture, generate voice, and hear the resultant sound, which should be [y], roughly the French vowel of *lune* [lyn]. If one performs this experiment again with whisper throughout, it should be possible to hear the pitch of the whisper going down about an octave in the passage from [i] to [y]. This, of course, represents the downward shift of the second formant; the addition of lip-rounding, by changing the oral resonating chamber from being wide mouthed to being narrow mouthed, always has the effect of lowering the frequency (perceived as pitch) of all vowel formants.

The next experiment should be the removal of lip-rounding from an [u]-type vowel. In this case one silently maintains the tongue posture for [u], while slowly and deliberately opening and spreading the lips.

One can experiment further with adding lip-rounding to all kinds of unrounded vowels and removing it from rounded vowels.

Turning to what we have called 'vertical tongue position' we experiment with a series of silent vowels of the types [i, e, ɛ, æ], roughly as in English *beet, bait, bet,* and *bat*. It is obvious both from watching in a mirror and from the kinaesthetic sensations that [e] is, in some sense, more 'open' than [i], [ɛ] is more open than [e], and [æ] is most open of all. It will probably be noticed that this increasing openness is achieved partly by increased lowering of the jaw, and partly by increased lowering of the tongue. One can eliminate each of these two variables in turn. To eliminate jaw movement, place the end of a pencil between the teeth and bite on it. While thus holding the jaw in a fixed position, run through the series [i, e, ɛ, æ] aloud and silently. It will be clear from this that tongue movement alone is sufficient to produce the different vowel qualities. On the other hand, one can fixate the tongue in relation to the lower jaw in the tongue position adopted for [i], and then produce the same series of sounds by lowering the jaw while keeping the tongue static.

What these experiments show is that the difference between [i, e, ε, æ] depends on the distance between the surface of the tongue and the roof of the mouth, however that is achieved. In 'real life' it may always be achieved by a combination of tongue and jaw movements. For the purpose of developing phonetic skill, however, it is best to concentrate on the proprioceptive sensations derived from the movements and postures of the tongue.

Analogous experiments can be carried out with a second series of vowels: [u, o, ɔ, ɑ], very roughly as in English *too, toe, law, lah.*

The third parameter to experiment with is 'horizontal tongue position'. One can begin to experience this parameter by saying [æ] as in *cat* and [ɑ] as in *far*. Silently alternating these one can feel that for [æ] the tongue is somewhat thrust forward in the mouth, while for [ɑ] it is pulled back. The different proprioceptive sensations are clearer if one deliberately strains to pull the tongue as far back as possible in saying [ɑ].

The 'horizontal', front–back movement can also be observed with the 'high' or 'close' vowels [i] or [u]. However, a particular difficulty will be observed in this case. If one silently alternates between [i] and [u] it becomes apparent that the proprioceptive sensation of lip-rounding tends to mask the sensation of tongue retraction. To become clearly aware of the front–back tongue movement it is necessary to eliminate the accompanying change of lip position. One should start, therefore, by adding close lip-rounding to [i], forming [y], then silently alternate [y–u–y–u]. The horizontal shift of tongue position can now be more clearly felt. One should also remove lip-rounding from [u], producing [ɯ] and silently alternate [ɯ–i–ɯ–i]. Once again, in the absence of the masking effect of changing lip position, one can feel the back–front shift of tongue position. Further silent (and, ultimately, whispered or voiced) experiments should be made with the other pairs of front and back vowels: for example, say [e], round it to [ø] then slide back to [o]. Unround [o] to [ɤ], slide forward to [e], and so on.

It is interesting to note that the masking effect of lip-rounding probably hindered the older phoneticians in their attempts to devise a system for classifying vowel sounds, and Bell's important discovery that lip-rounding was a separately controllable parameter thus contributed to the 'break-through' mentioned above. The older phoneticians had classified vowels as linguals, that is [i, e, æ], and labials, [u, o, ɔ]. Bell tells us (1867, p. 16) that, while he was experimenting with certain vowels 'the discovery that these sounds were each susceptible of labial modification . . . revealed the principle that the so-called Labial Vowels were all, in reality, compound formations, in which a definite lingual quality was involved. The analysis of the English vowels *oo, o,* and *aw,* by removal of labial modification, cleared away the whole remaining mystery.'

The three basic parameters of vowel articulation, as we have seen, are vertical tongue position (high–low), horizontal tongue position (front–back) and lip position (unrounded–rounded). There are some additional details to be added concerning these parameters.

The high–low parameter refers to the degree of convex 'bunching up' of the tongue. A high, or close vowel has the surface of the tongue bunched up, usually in a smooth convex curve from front to back. As the tongue position is lowered the curvature normally becomes less, although the main part of the dorsal surface of the tongue always remains convex in the longitudinal dimension. In the modification known as 'retroflexion' the blade and very front part of the dorsum may be concave. Variations in degree of convexity occur in the transverse dimension: some vowels may involve the formation of a longitudinal trough, or furrow, along the tongue.

The front–back parameter refers to the general location of the bunched-up part of the tongue, as being relatively further forward or further back in the mouth. For vowels in which the tongue-hump is about midway between front and back, the term 'central' is used. In high, back vowels (such as [u]) the whole tongue may be drawn back, the apex being retracted, so that the whole of the tongue above its root may adopt a more or less spherical shape; or the apex of the tongue may remain well forward, just behind the lower teeth, so that there is a more or less gentle slope up to the tongue summit at the back of the mouth. This variation of shape does not seem to make much difference in the resultant sound.

There are two remarks to be made about lip-rounding. In the first place, there is, generally, a close correlation between tongue height and the degree of rounding. The higher the vowel the smaller the labial aperture and vice versa. Thus, the rounding of [u] is closer than that of [ɔ], and the rounding of [y] is closer than that of [œ] (the rounded counterpart of [ɛ]). So natural and quasi-universal does this correlation seem, that we take it as normal, indicating departures from this norm by the special terms 'over-rounding' and 'under-rounding'. The second special point to note about lip-rounding is that the form of it generally varies according to whether it is applied to a back vowel or a front vowel. In the rounding of back vowels, the corners of the lips are somewhat pushed inwards towards the centre line, and the lips are 'pouted', so that the articulation is somewhat of the type we described in the last chapter as endolabio-endolabial. At the same time, the forward projection of the lips tends to pull the cheeks slightly inwards. In the rounding of front vowels, most commonly, though not universally, the corners of the lips are compressed vertically: the lips are not pouted, and the articulation is rather exolabio-exolabial. This distinction was termed 'inner' versus 'outer' rounding by Henry Sweet, and it is acoustically and perceptually understandable. Pouting the lips lengthens the resonance cavity in front of the tongue articulation, and accentuates the lowering of the formant frequencies, which is a major acoustic characteristic of rounding. To avoid over-lowering, particularly of the second formant, and hence to preserve more clearly their front quality, front vowels are usually rounded without pouting—that is, exolabially.

Traditional vowel classification, as we have said, is based on the position of the lips, and of the tongue. As far as the latter is concerned it is the location of the bunched-up part, or hump, that is regarded as important, and the location of the highest point, the summit of the tongue-hump, is taken as an indication of this. Figure 46 shows tongue positions of high and low, front and back vowels, the highest part of the tongue being marked by a dot.

The account of vowels that we have given so far is a rough description of the principles according to which we classify vowel sounds, but it lacks the precision required in giving a clear and unambiguous characterization of the vowels of a particular language, let alone the specific vowels uttered by a particular speaker at a particular time. A description such as 'high front' would fit a great many obviously different sounds, such as the French vowel of *si,* the English vowel of *see,* the first vowel of English (RP) *pity,* the second vowel of the same word, and so on.

Consequently, at least since the work of Bell (1867), phoneticians have sought to establish some kind of 'standard vowel scale'—a set of 'cardinal vowels' (a term apparently introduced by Bell) by reference to which any vowel could be described with some precision. The most satisfactory system of Cardinal Vowels currently in

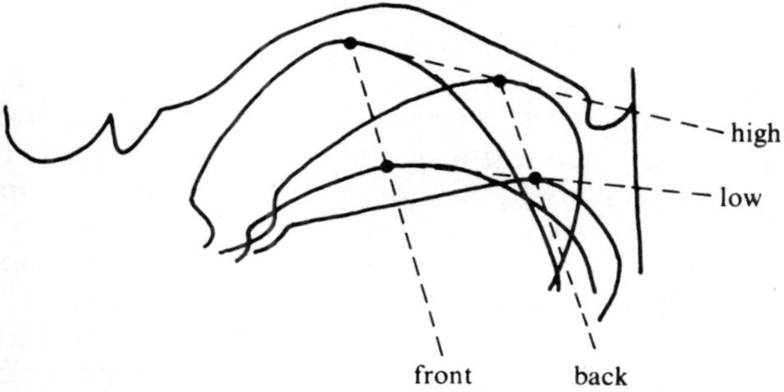

Figure 46. The 'highest point of the tongue' in traditional vowel classification

use is the one invented by Daniel Jones about the time of the first World War, and adopted by the International Phonetic Association. This system is described in many of Daniel Jones' books, for example, Jones (1917) and (1962), and by Abercrombie (1967, pp. 151 ff.), and is also evaluated in Ladefoged (1967). A record of the Cardinal Vowels spoken by Daniel Jones is published by HMV (Eng. 252–3, 254–5).

In Jones' system there are eight basic, or primary cardinal vowels. They are not the vowels of any particular language, and for this reason they are sometimes said to be 'arbitrarily selected'. This is misleading, however, since they are not at all arbitrary in relation to the theory upon which they are based, namely the theory of a 'vowel limit' within the mouth, with a periphery outside of which no vowel sound can be produced. Every anthropophonically possible vowel sound thus has its tongue position (as marked by the highest point of the tongue) either on the periphery, or within the 'vowel space' which it encloses.

The theoretical vowel limit is arrived at in this way. Owing to the general convexity of the tongue and concavity of the roof of the mouth it is not possible, barring quite exceptional contortions, to bring the highest point of the tongue-hump more than a certain distance forward or downward in the mouth; moreover, if the tongue is raised up closer than a certain distance from the roof of the mouth, then, at normal operational volume velocities, flow through the channel so formed will be turbulent, and the sound will become a fricative, and hence no longer a vowel. We have already pointed out that some of the higher, or closer, vowels like [i] and [u] are approximants: it is therefore easy to convert them into fricatives.

The vowel limit, then, is constituted by these anatomico-phonetic constraints, and its shape is somewhat as indicated in figure 46. The highest point of the tongue for any vowel must lie either on the periphery of this limited area, or within it.

The eight Cardinal Vowels, which are intended as standard reference points for the description of all other vowels, supposedly have their highest tongue points on the periphery of the vowel space. Two of them are more or less precisely fixed points: these are Cardinal Vowel no. 1 [i], and Cardinal Vowel no. 5 [ɑ]. So far we have been using the symbols [i] and [ɑ] in a fairly loose way to indicate vowels somewhat like the English vowels in *see* and *car*. From now on, we shall use vowel symbols in this book to refer strictly and specifically to Cardinal Vowels, unless otherwise stated.

Cardinal Vowel 1 [i] is the highest and most frontal vowel possible. The domed tongue is thrust forward and upwards as far as possible without generating a palatal and/or prepalatal fricative. In auditory quality it is the 'sharpest' possible [i]-type sound. This, then, is a more or less anatomically fixed point.

Cardinal Vowel 5 [ɑ] is the lowest and furthest back vowel possible. The jaw is dropped so that the upper and lower teeth are about 1½ to 2 cm apart, and the tongue kept as flat as possible in the mouth, consistent with still being convex, and drawn back so far that any further retraction would generate a radico-pharyngeal fricative sound. The auditory quality of this sound is a very 'deep' [ɑ], somewhat reminiscent of [ɔ], although quite unrounded and, of course, more open.

The intervening Cardinal Vowels 2, 3, 4, are vowels on the periphery of the vowel space, and at approximately equal distances apart, between [i] and [ɑ]. Their symbols are [e, ɛ, a], and the first five Cardinal Vowels thus form a scale of apparently equidistant vowel sounds going from the highest and most frontal [i] possible, to the lowest and most back [ɑ] possible—thus, [i–e–ɛ–a–ɑ]. The reader should make an effort to produce approximately this series of sounds: voiced, whispered, and silent. Note, once again, that [i] is as high and as front, and [ɑ] as low and as back as is anthropophonically possible. Having got these points fixed, try again and again to fit three vowels, each made with the tongue arched and pushed forward as far as possible, in between them, at what appear to be equal intervals: [i–e–ɛ–a–ɑ]. Cardinal Vowels 6–8 continue this series of equidistant sounds upwards from [ɑ], tongue straining (tiringly) backward all the time, to a high, fully rounded, fully back [u]: [ɑ–ɔ–o–u].

We have intentionally omitted to say in what sense the intermediate Cardinal Vowels are 'equidistant' from each other. Daniel Jones described these vowels as 'acoustically' (that is, auditorily) equidistant, but he also treated them as if they were organically equidistant. In fact, they *feel* equidistant from each other in terms of both auditory and proprioceptive sensations, and in learning them one must attend to both aspects, frequently attempting to produce them both aloud and silently.

The eight Cardinal Vowels are thus presumed to have tongue positions on the periphery of the vowel space (the vowel limit) as indicated in figure 46. They can therefore be shown by dots on a figure representing the vowel limit. The figure most commonly used is a simplified and regularized representation of the vowel limit, as in figure 47. Black circles represent unrounded vowels; white circles represent rounded vowels. The terminology used by Daniel Jones, and the IPA, is given above and to the left of the figure, namely: *front, central* and *back* for horizontal tongue position, and *close, half-close, half-open, open,* for vertical tongue position. On the right,

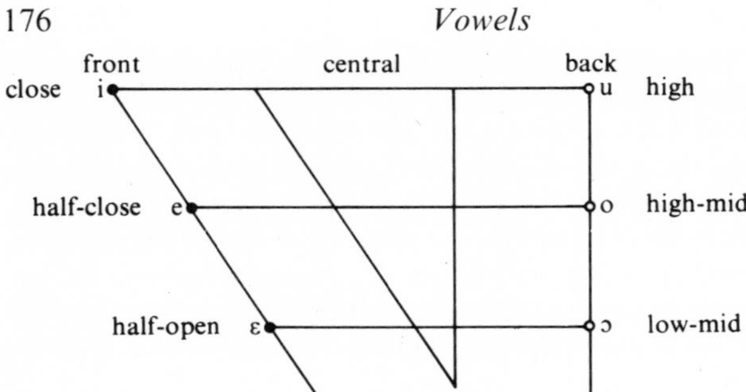

Figure 47. Stylized representation of the 'vowel limit' and the eight primary cardinal vowels

in parentheses, are given alternative terms for vertical tongue positions: *high, high–mid, low–mid, low.*

Although it is difficult to acquire absolute precision in the production and identification of the Cardinal Vowels without instruction from a competent teacher, anyone who wants to understand how the system works should spend a good deal of time studying them: he should try to produce voiced, whispered and, above all, *silent* vowels that conform as closely as possible to the descriptions given here. The following notes are for the guidance of English speaking readers. No. 1 [i] is closer and more frontal than the [i] of almost any variety of English. A great effort must be made to force the tongue as far forwards and upwards as one can without actually producing a palatal fricative. Considerable contact can be felt between the sides of the tongue and the upper teeth to as far forward as the first premolars or canines. The lips are well spread.

Unlike the nearest vowel in most types of English, no. 2 [e] is a pure vowel, not a diphthong. (By a diphthong we mean a vowel that starts at one position and glides to another, within a single syllable. Typical diphthongs are the [aɩ] and [aɷ] of English *high* and *how.*) In many types of English the vowel of *say* is a diphthong, starting somewhere between CV2 and CV3 and gliding upward. Check your pronunciation of *say* in a mirror and by kinaesthetic introspection. CV2 [e] has a rigid, unchanging, tongue position, like the non-diphthongal [e] vowel of some types of Scottish and Irish English.

CV3 [ɛ] is more open than the vowel of *set* in RP, although something very close to it occurs in mid-west America and northern England. It is much like the Parisian French vowel of *bête.*

CV4 [a] is pretty much the Parisian French vowel of *patte.* It is like a variety of the vowel of English *cat* often heard in the north of England, and from Standard English speakers in Scotland. In Scots dialects the vowel of *cat* is usually much further back than CV4, often approaching CV5. In RP and in most types of American English, the *cat* vowel is much closer than CV4 and may (specially in mid-west America) be a diphthong near CV3, of the type [ɛə]. One way to learn CV4 is to produce a very open [ɑ]-type or [a]-type vowel—as in RP *cart,* American *cot*—and then push the tongue well forward, so that it feels exactly as if it belongs to the front series with [i, e, ɛ], but is as low as possible.

CV5 is as low and as far back as you can go without producing some kind of pharyngeal fricative. An [ɑ] of about this quality may be heard in Cockney English, in words like *cart, park* [kɑːt] [pɑːk]: the corresponding RP vowel is considerably further forward, as is often the American vowel of *father* or *cot,* often transcribed [fɑːðəɹ] [kɑt]. In fact, in mid-west America, for example, in Detroit and Chicago, the vowel of *cot* is often nearly as far forward as CV4.

In the whole back series [ɑ–ɔ–o–u], care must be taken to make these vowels fully back: in all of them there should be a feeling of strain in and around the root of the tongue as one pulls it as far back as possible. The back vowels of most real languages tend to be less retracted than the Cardinal Vowels.

CV6 is not unlike RP [ɔ] in *law:* most, particularly mid-western American [ɔ] vowels are much more open than CV6, so that *law* is nearly [lɒː], with a rounded back vowel almost as open as [ɑ]. The Parisian French [ɔ], as in *note* has about the right tongue height, but is very centralized, that is, far from being fully back. CV6 has open, endolabio-endolabial rounding.

CV7 [o] is, like all the CVs, a pure vowel, not a diphthong. The nearest vowel for most English speakers is that of *go,* but note that in most types of English this is a diphthong, often starting with a strongly centralized, only slightly rounded vowel of a height between CV6 and CV7, gliding upwards and backwards—this may be represented by [ɵɷ] or [əɷ]. The French [o] of *mot* is near CV7, but in modern Parisian it is slightly centralized. CV7 has somewhat closer endolabio-endolabial rounding.

CV8 [u] is, again, a pure vowel. The nearest English vowel, as in *too,* is often somewhat diphthongized, and nearly always somewhat centralized. The French vowel [u] of *tout* is also further forward than CV8. It helps many people to get a really backward CV8 to think about [o] while saying [u]. CV8 has strong endolabio-endolabial rounding.

The eight Cardinal Vowels already dealt with are often referred to as the *primary* Cardinal Vowels. In addition there are *secondary*

Cardinal Vowels. Eight of these are directly derived from the primary Cardinal Vowels by reversal of the lip positions: that is to say, their tongue positions are identical with those of the Cardinal Vowels, but where the primary CV is unrounded the secondary is rounded, and vice-versa. The symbols for the first eight secondary CVs are: [y, ø, œ, ɶ, ɒ, ʌ, ɤ, ɯ].

Their relations to the primary CVs are:

[y] = CV1 [i] rounded, like, but closer and fronter than, French *u* German ü.

[ø] = CV2 [e] rounded, like, but closer and fronter than, French *eu* in *jeu,* German *ö* in *schön.*

[œ] = CV3 [ɛ] rounded, like, but closer and fronter than, French *eu* in *leur,* German *ö* in *Götter.*

[ɶ] = CV4 [a] rounded (very slight rounding).

[ɒ] = CV5 [ɑ] rounded (very slight rounding) English RP *o* as in *hot.*

[ʌ] = CV6 [ɔ] unrounded, like *u* in *but* in some Scots dialects. Most other English 'but'-vowels are very much more central.

[ɤ] = CV7 [o] unrounded. An advanced form of this is the vowel of *good* in many varieties of American English.

[ɯ] = CV8 [u] unrounded.

There are six more vowels which are sometimes regarded as additional Cardinal Vowels. These are, in unrounded and rounded pairs:

[ɨ] and [ʉ], which are close central vowels, half way between [i] and [ɯ] and between [y] and [u] respectively.

[ɘ] and [ɵ] are half-close central vowels, half way between [e] and [ɤ] and between [ø] and [o] respectively.

[ɜ] and [ɞ] are half-open central vowels, half way between [ɛ] and [ɔ] respectively: [ɜ] is a common variety of English RP vowel in *bird.* [ɞ] is only a little more central than the French vowel of *note.*

The IPA alphabet provides another six symbols for vowels that are not regarded as cardinal. These are [ɩ, ʏ, æ, ə, ɐ] and [ɷ]. Their descriptions are as follows:

[ɩ] raised retracted half-close front unrounded—the vowel of English (RP) *sit.*

[ʏ] the same vowel rounded, as in German *hübsch.*

[æ] lowered half-open front unrounded, about half way between [ɛ] and [æ]—the RP vowel of *sat.*

[ə] is a mid-central unrounded vowel; the symbol [ə] and the general type of obscure central vowel it represents are often known as *schwa* (the German form of the name of the 'obscure' [ə]-like Hebrew vowel). The symbol is often used for a fairly wide range of reduced or 'obscure' central vowels, such as the English unaccented vowel in the first syllables of *again,* and *potato.*

[ɐ] is used to represent a more open central vowel than [ə] or [ɜ], usually somewhat below half open, often occurring finally in RP, as in *better* ['bɛtɐ].

[ɷ] is a raised advanced half-close back rounded vowel, as in English RP *good.*

The diagrams in figure 48 show all the unrounded and rounded Cardinal Vowels (primary and secondary), represented by dots, and the six additional vowels, represented only by their symbols.

Once the Cardinal Vowels have been thoroughly mastered, one can describe any vowel chiefly by reference to the Cardinal Vowels. Thus the English (RP) vowel of *sit* is retracted and raised from CV2, the English (RP) vowel of *cot* is slightly raised from CV5 rounded, [ɒ], and so on, and one can indicate the basic tongue position of any vowel by placing a dot at the appropriate point on the diagram. Of course, one must add a description of lip position,

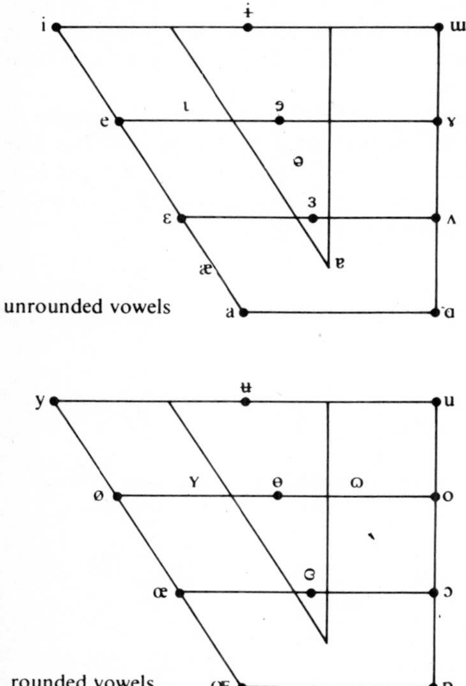

Figure 48. Primary and secondary cardinal vowels, and the additional vowels ɩ æ ə ɐ ʏ and ɷ

and, where necessary, of certain secondary modifications such as retroflexion, or pharyngealization, which are not indicated by the diagram.

In practice phoneticians place vowels on the CV diagram in one or more of the following ways:

(a) Start by producing a really good imitation of the vowel under investigation, then silently, and with kinaesthetic (proprioceptive) introspection, discover in what direction the tongue must be moved in order to convert it to a cardinal vowel. Thus, if a slight raising and fronting of the tongue brings one to CV3 [ɛ], one knows that the vowel is a retracted and lowered [ɛ].

(b) Start by producing what seems to be the nearest CV, then shift the tongue around in known directions until one hits on exactly the vowel required; this can then again be identified by proprioceptive introspection of the extent and direction of movements from the CV.

(c) Say the vowel under investigation several times, aloud, and also say what seems to be the nearest CVs aloud, then judge by ear how the new vowel is related to CVs. This is probably the least efficient way of 'placing' vowels.

In figures 49, 50 and 51 are samples of some of the vowels of English, French and Russian plotted on CV diagrams. The dots with lines represent diphthongs, the line indicating the direction of the diphthongal glide.

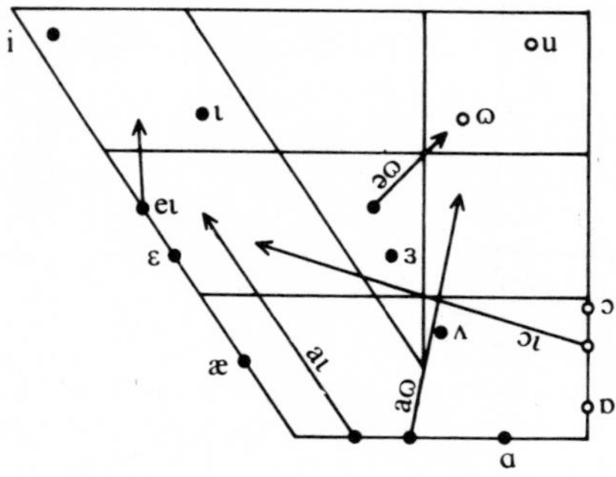

i as in	[bit] *beat*	ɒ as in	[pɒt] *pot*
ɪ	[bɪt] *bit*	ɔɪ	[bɔɪd] *Boyd*
eɪ	[beɪt] *bait*	ɔ	[pɔt] *port*
ɛ	[bɛt] *bet*	ʊ	[pʊt] *put*
æ	[bæt] *bat*	u	[but] *boot*
aɪ	[baɪt] *bite*	ʌ	[bʌt] *but*
aʊ	[baʊt] *bout*	ɜ	[bɜt] *Bert*
ɑ	[bɑt] *Bart*	əʊ	[bəʊt] *boat*

Figure 49. Some English vowels in a variety of RP

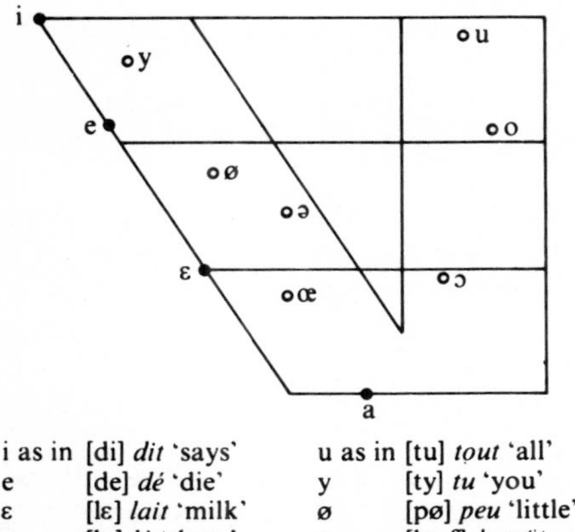

i as in	[di] *dit* 'says'	u as in	[tu] *tout* 'all'
e	[de] *dé* 'die'	y	[ty] *tu* 'you'
ε	[lε] *lait* 'milk'	ø	[pø] *peu* 'little'
a	[la] *là* 'there'	œ	[bœf] *bœuf* 'ox'
ɔ	[nɔt] *note* 'note'	ə	[lə] *le* 'the'
o	[do] *dos* 'back'		

Figure 50. French oral (non-nasalized) vowels

In figure 49, English (RP), note that several vowel symbols here, for example, [ʌ], are used for vowels that are quite far from the CV they would normally represent.

Most vowels can be described in terms of the Cardinal Vowel system, but there are some possible modifications of vowel articulation that must be noted. These are all referred to elsewhere in this book as *secondary* articulations or other modifications. They include *nasalization, retroflexion, pharyngealization,* and *tenseness.*

Nasalized vowels are simply vowels that are articulated with the soft palate lowered, so that the pulmonic, egressive air-stream passes simultaneously out of both the mouth and the nose. Nasalization is symbolized by the diacritic tilde placed over the vowel symbol: õ. Nasalized vowels are common in the languages of the world, the best known examples probably being in French. Modern Parisian French has nasalized [ε̃] [ɑ̃] [õ]; conservative speakers may have a fourth nasalized vowel, [œ̃]. All four may be observed in *Un bon vin blanc* [œ̃ bõ vε̃ blɑ̃], as illustrated in Chapter 8.

Retroflexed vowels are often said to be articulated with the point and blade in the 'retroflex' position, that is, the point raised to roughly the position for a wide approximant with an apico-postalveolar, or sublamino-prepalatal articulation. The reader should experiment with combining this type of apical pronunciation with various vowels. It will be found that some vowels lend themselves to retroflexion more easily than others. Thus the open [ɑ], in such a word as mid-west American or south-west English *far* may be pronounced with a distinct upward turn of the tongue point. With closer vowels, however, retroflexion is more a matter of the tongue point being raised and drawn back into the body of the tongue, without there being any actual retroflex 'pointing' of the tongue. On this see also Chapter 10.

Pharyngealized vowels involve a compression of the pharynx simultaneously with the primary vowel articulation. This is usually effected by a backward thrust of the root of the tongue, tending to narrow the pharynx in a front-to-back dimension. Such vowels occur in several Caucasian languages of Dagestan, notably in the Tsez languages Tsez and Khwarshi, and in several of the Lezgian languages.

Pharyngealization adds a slightly 'squeezed' quality to the auditory impression of vowels in these languages and tends to impart a somewhat 'fronted' (advanced) quality to back vowels, both in terms of auditory impression and formant-shifts in spectrograms. See further in Chapter 10.

Tenseness. Many writers have used a category of tenseness, contrasting tense versus lax, in their systems of vowel classification. The nature of this parameter of vowel classification is discussed in Chapter 10.

We pointed out at the beginning of this chapter that the traditional way of classifying vowels is a departure from the methods used in classifying consonants. Vowels are classified in terms of location of the highest point of the tongue in quasi-absolute vertical and horizontal dimensions. Consonants are classified in terms of the location of the articulatory stricture, and the degree of narrowness of this stricture—and by 'location of the articulatory stricture' we mean the articulatory zone in which the complete closure or the narrowest channel occurs.

A striking difference between the two systems of classification is seen in connection with 'tongue-height' versus 'cross-sectional area of articulatory channel'. These two do not necessarily coincide. In the series [i-e-ɛ-a] it is clear that they do coincide. The progression from 'close' through 'half-open' to 'open' is also a progression from 'narrow approximant' [i] through 'wide approximant' [e] to 'narrow resonant' [ɛ] and 'wide resonant' [a]. And all these strictures are made more or less under the palatal zone, though the tongue-hump moves back as we go from [i] to [a]. But there is no such coincidence between 'close vowel' and 'narrow approximant' at some other locations. Remembering that a narrow approximant has only a slightly wider channel than a fricative we can slide the tongue back over the roof of the mouth, and we can also bring the root of the tongue close to the back wall of the pharynx, and at every zone or subzone

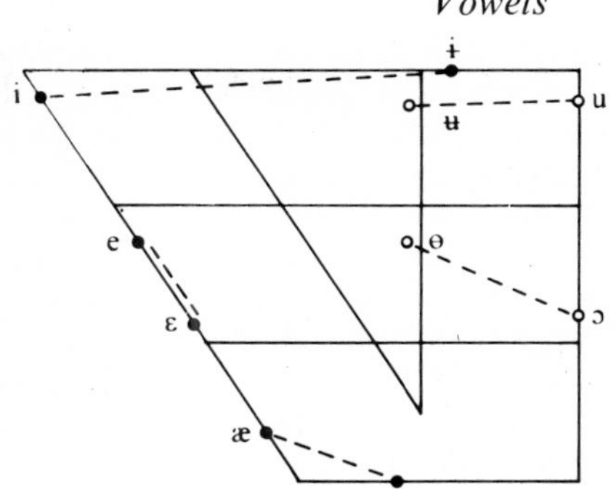

i as in	[p̧iɫ] *пил* 'drank'	ɔ as in	[tɔt] *тот* 'that'
ɨ	[pɨɫ] *пыл* 'glow'	ɵ	['ţɵtə] *тётя* 'aunt'
e	['d̦eţɩ] *дети* 'children'	u	[tut] *тут* 'here'
ɛ	['d̦ɛtkɔ] *детка* 'child'	ʉ	[ţʉļ] *тюль* 'tulle'
æ	[şæţ] *сядь* 'sit down'		
a	[sat] *сад* 'garden'		

Figure 51. Russian stressed vowels (allophones of one and the same phoneme are joined by broken line)

we can produce a fricative, then widen its channel a little into that of an approximant.

In this way, we form a dorso- (front) velar fricative [ɣ +]; open it up a little and we have the dorso- (front) velar approximant [ɯ], which is CV8 unrounded; add lip-rounding and we have [u]. Sliding the articulation channel further back we have a dorso- (back) velar fricative [ɣ −]: open it up a little and we have the dorso- (back) velar approximant [ɤ], CV7 unrounded; add lip-rounding and we have [o]. From a dorso-uvular fricative [ʁ], we can open up to dorso-uvular approximant [ʌ], and round it to [ɔ]. And finally, from a radico-pharyngeal fricative, we can open up to a radico-pharyngeal approximant [ɑ].

It thus becomes clear that vowels can be integrated perfectly well into the general classificatory scheme along with consonants, but with a curious result. Whereas in terms of the traditional system [i] and [u] are 'close' vowels, while [o], [ɔ], [ɑ] are 'half-close', 'half-open' and 'open' respectively, in terms of this integrated description *all* the high and back peripheral vowels, that is, not only [i] and [u] but also [o], [ɔ] and [ɑ] are 'close', in the sense that every one of them is a narrow approximant.

One can demonstrate this by whispering a series of Cardinal Vowels, each on relaxation pressure, and noting, for each, how long it takes for the breath to run out. Provided the 'back' vowels are all truly back vowels—with the tongue drawn as far back as possible without generating fricatives—the result ought to be that the duration of [i, u, o, ɔ, ɑ] is about the same; [e], on the other hand, is somewhat shorter than this, [ɛ] is still shorter, and [a] is shortest of all. The results of one such experiment were as follows: [i, u, o, ɔ, ɑ] all about 11–13 seconds, [e] 9 seconds, [ɛ] 7 seconds, [a] 5 seconds. Now, of course, duration under these circumstances is inversely proportional to volume-velocity, and volume-velocity is directly proportional to articulatory channel area.[1] It is clear, then, that [i, u, o, ɔ, ɑ] all have a narrow articulatory channel, the cross-sectional area of the channel progressively widening as one passes through [e] and [ɛ] to [a].[2]

It seems possible, then, and more in accord with the articulatory parameters involved, to represent the vowel space of the mouth and the relative positions of the Cardinal Vowels not in the usual CV quadrilateral, but rather as a segment of a circle, as in figure 52. Whereas in the traditional system vowels can be described in terms of co-ordinates of vertical and horizontal tongue position, in the apparently more rational system presented here they can be described in terms of polar co-ordinates, or in terms of the normal articulatory location and stricture-type terms.

Figure 52 is, like the standard CV figure, oversimplified, but in some respects it appears to be much nearer 'reality', and it certainly seems to be an advantage to be able to use the same terminology for description of both vowels and consonants. Moreover, this display elucidates the aerodynamics of vowels better than the CV system does.

However, when we attempt to use the polar co-ordinate system as a basis for vowel description, some curious difficulties arise. In the first place, though obviously more 'rational' than the traditional system, it is much more difficult to use in practice. It seems to be easier to slide the tongue as a whole vertically or horizontally, rather than along the radii of the polar co-ordinate system; assessment of the relationship of vowels to Cardinal Vowels is thus easier using the traditional figure.

In the second place, the traditional quadrilateral is more appropriate than the polar co-ordinate system for the display of various types of vowel systems that match up with the quadrilateral much better. For example, many languages have a more or less 'triangular' vowel-system of the /i–a–u/ type. This fits the Cardinal Vowel diagram, which indicates clearly how [i] [a] and [u] are 'extreme' vowels, thus providing an explanation for the naturalness of such vowel systems. The 'extreme' nature of [i] [a] and [u], however, is less apparent on the polar co-ordinate system, as figure 53 shows.

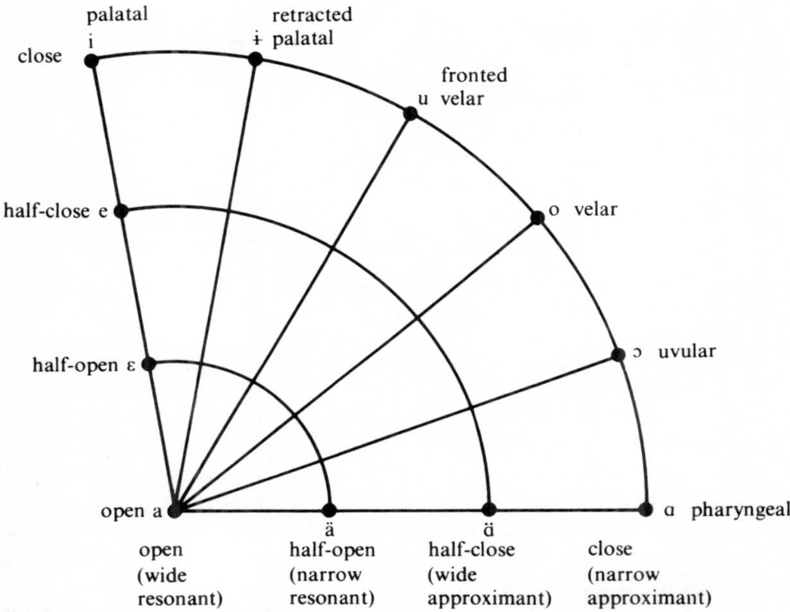

Figure 52. A 'polar co-ordinate' vowel diagram

Again, there are some languages in the world (for example, north-west Caucasian and some languages of New Guinea) with a 'vertical' vowel system: a set of oppositions, that is, only between a 'high' phoneme (represented by a series of more or less close vowels), a 'mid' phoneme, and a 'low' phoneme. One can indicate this kind of vowel system in a manner that has a 'rational' appearance on the traditional vowel diagram, since it matches categories of the 'vertical'

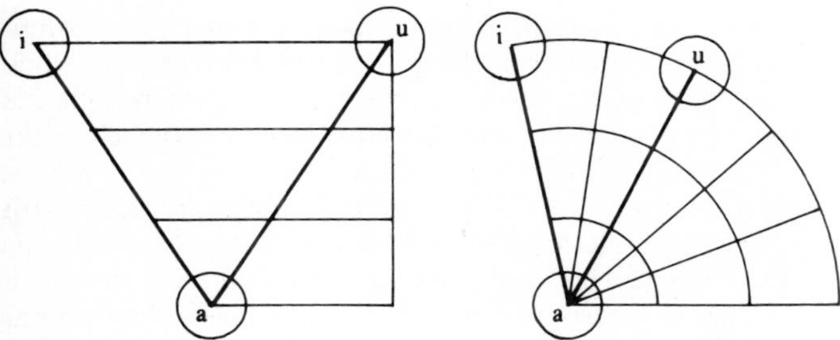

Figure 53. A 'triangular' vowel system on the traditional and the polar co-ordinate diagrams

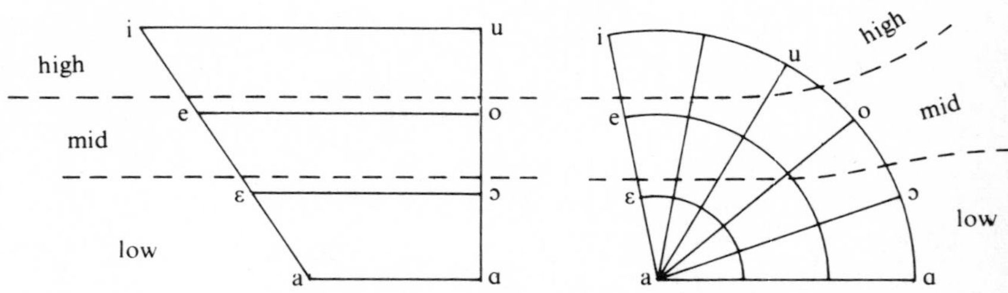

Figure 54. A 'vertical' vowel system on the traditional and the polar co-ordinate diagrams

parameter. On the polar co-ordinate diagram it simply cuts across the categories in an irrational-looking way, as shown in figure 54.

There appear to be two reasons for these anomalies, an acoustic one and a physiological one. If we plot the Cardinal Vowels on an acoustic formant chart, showing the values of F_1 reading downwards on the vertical axis and the values for F_2 reading right to left on the horizontal axis, we get an arrangement not very dissimilar from the shape of the Cardinal Vowel chart, as in figure 55. It is clear from this chart that, in terms of values of F_1 and F_2, [i] [a] and [u] are, acoustically, the most extreme or most differentiated vowels, and the CV chart displays this feature more clearly than the polar co-ordinate chart.

The physiological (and psychological) fact is one that has been repeatedly mentioned throughout this chapter, namely, that judgements about the articulatory postures of vowels are chiefly based on *proprioceptive* information from the intrinsic and extrinsic muscles of the tongue. Now, to a large extent, the muscles involved in the production of close vowel positions are the same—whether these vowels are front or back—namely, the geniohyoid and the posterior fibres of the genioglossus, which bunch the tongue up by pulling the hyoid bone and the tongue-root forwards; the longitudinals, which aid in tongue-bunching; and the styloglossus, which helps in raising the tongue. Likewise, the muscles that retract the tongue are to a considerable extent the same (to a greater or lesser degree—the glossopharyngeus and hyoglossus) whether these vowels are close or open. It is not surprising, therefore, that both close vowels (as opposed to open vowels), and back vowels (as opposed to front vowels) 'feel' like natural classes, whereas the series [i–ɨ–u–o–ɔ–ɑ], which certainly forms a 'natural' class of peripheral 'narrow approximant' vowels, does not in fact 'feel' proprioceptively like a natural class.

It seems, then, that for several reasons we must continue to treat

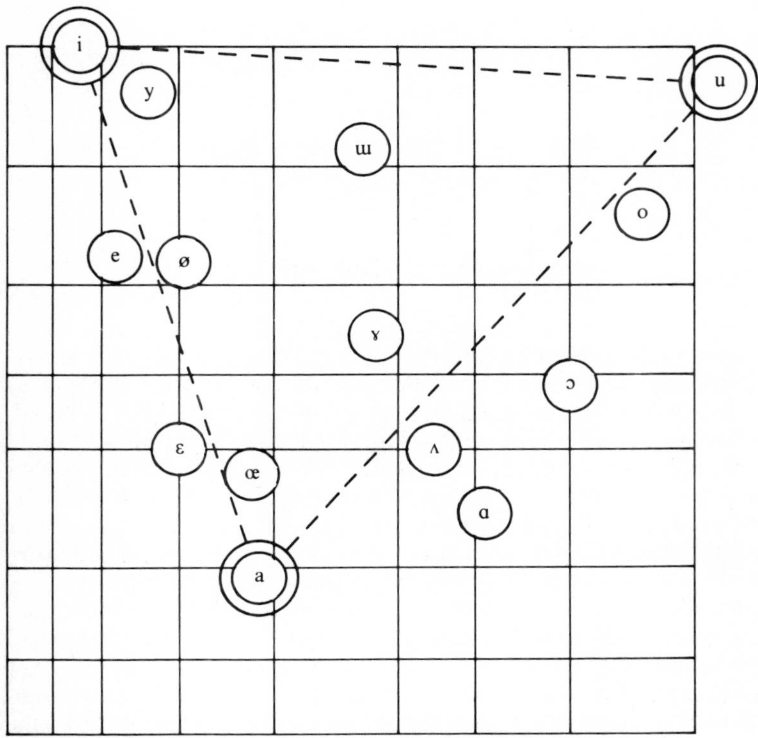

Figure 55. Cardinal vowels (including the 'extreme vowels' [i, a, u] on an acoustic formant chart)

vowels differently from consonants for purposes of practical classification. It is equally clear, however, that from a purely theoretical point of view vowels can be well fitted into the normal taxonomic parameters of location and stricture type if we wish to treat them this way.

TEN

Co-articulation and Modified Articulation

In preceding chapters we have generally implied that articulations can be unambiguously described in terms of a single, particular, articulatory location; only in the case of vowels did we explicitly refer to simultaneous articulation at two distinct zones, in 'rounded' vowels, which combine a labial and a lingual articulation.

In this chapter we shall deal with two types of deviation from the implied articulatory norms of the preceding chapters—namely, two kinds of *co-articulation* (*co-ordinate co-articulation* and *secondary co-articulation*), and after that with two types of articulatory *modification,* namely *duration* and *tenseness*.

By *co-articulation* we mean simultaneous articulation in more than one articulatory area (for example, oral and nasal) or in more than one articulatory zone (for example, labial and velar). It is necessary to distinguish two kinds of co-articulation: *co-ordinate* and *secondary*. In *co-ordinate* co-articulation, the two articulations are of the same stricture-type, or the same *strictural rank*. In *primary* and *secondary* co-articulation, the secondary articulation is of lower strictural rank than the primary articulation. By strictural rank we mean, simply, relative degree of openness of stricture. Thus, basically, the rank order of stricture types is *stop–trill–fricative–approximant–resonant*. Traditionally, however, certain departures are made from this basic ordering. In the first place, as we saw at the beginning of Chapter 8, all sounds with simultaneous oral stop plus nasal approximant articulation ([m, n], and so on). are simply called 'nasals'—not 'nasalized oral stops', as they would be if we rigorously followed strictural ranking, in which the relatively open nasal part of the articulation would be secondary to the complete oral closure. Secondly, any combination of non-occlusive oral articulation with nasal (approximant) articulation is termed 'nasalized', even when the oral articulation is of lower strictural rank than the nasal one, as in the case of a wide resonant (such as [a]) accompanied by nasal approximant articulation [ã]. We call this a 'nasalized vowel' rather than an 'oralized nasal approximant'. Thirdly, any pharyngeal articulation accompanying a vowel is treated as secondary. Thus an open [ɛ] vowel accompanied by a pharyngeal approximant articulation is called a 'pharyngealized vowel' rather than an 'oralized pharyngeal approximant'. The reason for these last two departures from the strict principle of rank is, of course, that vowels cover a wide range of stricture types, going from narrow approximant (for example, [i]) to wide resonant (for example, [a]). It would be inconvenient if, following strict procedure, we had to say that [ĩ] was a 'nasalized vowel' but on the other hand that [ɛ̃] was an 'oralized nasal approximant'. Finally, where we have a non-lateral co-articulation with a lateral, the lateral is regarded as primary. Thus a dorsovelar approximant accompanying an apico-alveolar, lateral approximant is regarded as secondary: we refer to this sound as a 'velarized apico-alveolar, lateral approximant', and symbolize it [ɫ].

In naming and transcribing the two types of co-articulation we adopt the following conventions. Co-ordinate articulations are named by location labels separated by a hyphen, and, where no special symbol is available, by two letters linked by a ligature: thus, *labial-velar stop* [p͜k], *postalveolar-velar fricative* [ʃ͜x], and so on. Note that special symbols are available for the *labial-velar* and *labial-palatal approximants* [w] and [ɥ], which occur, for instance, in French *Louis* [lwi] and *lui* [lɥi].

Secondary articulations are named by placing an adjective in *-ized* before the locational term, and are transcribed with the help of diacritic marks added to the symbol for the primary articulation: thus, *labialized lamino-alveolar fricative* [sʷ], *velarized apico-alveolar stop* [ᵵ], and so on.[1]

There is often some advantage in being able to distinguish between co-ordinate and secondary articulations, for example between bilabial-dorso-velar (or, simply, labial-velar) [p͜k] and labialized dorsovelar [kʷ]; but there are undoubtedly some cases where it is difficult to decide whether we have to do with co-ordinate or secondary articulation. In dealing with the phonology of a particular language it is sometimes desirable to lump together the two types of co-articulation (co-ordinate and secondary) as merely different realizations of one and the same phonological category. Thus in a phonological description of Abkhaz (north-west Caucasus) we might use the same term 'labialized' to refer both to the truly labialized [kʷ] [gʷ] and to the endolabial-dental [p͜t] [d͜b], regarding them *both* as embodying realizations of the phonological category of labialization, even though only the first, [kʷ], strictly involves *secondary* labialization, the second being a *co-ordinate* labial-dental stop articulation (Catford 1972).

In theory, co-ordinate articulation can be of any strictural type, though a few of the theoretical possibilities do not seem to occur in any language—for example, *apico-alveolar-dorso-uvular trill* [r͜ʀ] is anthropophonically possible, but apparently does not occur. Co-ordinate stops, particularly bilabial-velar [p͜k] [b͜g] and bilabial-alveolar [p͜t] and [b͜d] are common in West African languages, more sporadic in Caucasian languages (Abkhaz [p͜t] [d͜b] have been mentioned, and [p͜k] as a realization of 'labialized [k]' occurs in Lak).

Co-ordinate *oral-glottal* stops are common in British dialects, notably Cockney, East Anglian, Northumberland, Central and south-west Scots and Ulster: for example, 'paper'—Cockney ['pɐɩʔpɐ], Nhb ['piɛʔpɒ], Ulster [pʰeːʔpəɹ]; 'baker'—Cockney ['bɐɩʔkɐ], Nhb ['biɛʔkɒ], and so on. In such cases, the glottal closure, of course, excludes the possibility of pressure build-up behind the oral stop, which may thus be barely audible, except as a distinctive 'on-glide' and 'off-glide' to and from the glottal stop. In the case of [ʔ͜t] the oral closure may be reduced to a mere flick of the tongue, for example, in Northumbrian 'water' ['waʔ͜tɒ] or ['waʔ͜ɾɒ]. In such a case one might more properly speak of an 'apico-alveolarized glottal stop' rather than an 'apico-alveolar-glottal stop'. In many dialects, of course, for example, Cockney and central and south-west Scots, there is no oral articulation whatsoever in a word such as *water*—the [t] being replaced here by a simple glottal stop. It should be noted that oral-glottal stops are quite distinct from glottalic stops. In the former the glottal closure has a purely articulatory function, whereas in glottalic stops its function is initiatory and there is an upward (or downward) displacement of the larynx that generates a positive (or negative) pressure behind the oral closure, which is completely absent in co-ordinate oral glottal stops. Those who, like Pike, regard all glottal strictures as of lower rank than oral stricture may wish to call [ʔ͜p, ʔ͜t, ʔ͜k] 'glottalized' oral stops; but in this case the term 'glottalized' must certainly not be used as well to refer to the completely different glottalic pressure stops [p', t', k']. Co-ordinate nasals, particularly [m͡ŋ], are not uncommon in African languages.

Co-ordinate fricative articulation is undoubtedly rarer than co-ordinate stop articulation, and it is often somewhat difficult to discern whether there actually is turbulent (fricative) air-flow at each of the two stricture locations. Voiceless and voiced bilabial-palatal fricatives occur in Abkhaz, [ɸ͜ç] [β͜ʝ], where the voiced one minimally contrasts as fricative with same articulatory location, with the bilabial-palatal approximant [ɥ]. Since we have this special symbol [ɥ] for a bilabial-palatal approximant we can use the symbols [ɥ˔] and [ɥ̊˔] for voiced and voiceless bilabial-palatal fricatives, the diacritic (˔) indicating a closer, or narrower, articulation channel, together with the diacritic for voicelessness. Although one may, perhaps, regard Abkhaz [ɥ˔] and [ɥ̊˔] as co-ordinate fricative articulations, my impression from hearing two or three speakers of each dialect, is that in the Abzhui (literary) dialect of Abkhaz the labial articulation dominates somewhat—generating stronger turbulence—whereas in the Bzyb dialect the palatal articulation is somewhat dominant.

We have already noted the occurrence of bilabial-palatal approximant [ɥ] in French and Abkhaz. Another, and much more common, co-ordinate approximant is the bilabial-velar one, [w], also occurring in French, Abkhaz, and many other languages. Ladefoged reports a dental-palatal co-ordinate approximant in the West African language Kamba (Ladefoged 1967, p. 39), but does not mention it in the later version of this work (1971).

Among the principal secondary articulations are the following:
Bilabialized or, simply, *labialized,* symbolized by [^{w}], for example, [k^{w}], a secondary articulation found in many languages in Africa, the Americas, the Caucasus, and elsewhere.
Labiodentalized, symbolized by [x^{f}] or [x^{v}], for example, [s^{v}]. Labiodentalized alveolar or postalveolar fricatives occur in several African and Caucasian languages, and perhaps elsewhere. In West Africa, Kom and Kutep are reported to have labiodentalized sounds (Ladefoged 1964, 1971) and in the Caucasus, the Fij dialect of Lezgin (Meilanova 1964), Tabasaran, some Eastern varieties of Aghul, and Abkhaz all have labiodentalized fricatives and affricates. In Sechuana there is a special type of labiodentalization described in Jones and Plaatje (1916). The Abkhaz and Tabasaran labiodentalization is of somewhat similar type.
Apico-dentalized, apico-alveolarized, lamino-alveolarized, and *lamino-postalveolarized* are all possible secondary articulations, although not known to occur in any language—unless the apicodental component of the Kamba dental-palatal approximant is really of lower rank than the palatal articulation.
Apico-postalveolarized articulation possibly occurs in the south Swedish (Skåne) variant of [ʃ], which appears to be apico-postalveolarized velar fricative [$x^{ʃ}$]—unless the articulation is actually co-ordinate. Something varying from *apico-postalveolarized* to *sub-lamino-prepalatalized* is the secondary articulation often described as 'retroflex'. Such retroflexed vowels occur in south-west English dialects and in the Californian language Serrano (see Hill 1969). A raising of the apex of the tongue, which thus 'points at' the post-alveolar zone, although rather far from it, is characteristic of a common variety of American /r/ consonant or vowel (as in *bird*). This 'apico-postalveolarized, advanced velar approximant' is what

Uldall (1958) has described as 'molar "r"'. A somewhat similar but more forward sound is the Burushaski sound transcribed by Lorimer (1935) as [y.], as in the words [ay.a] 'my-father', [bʌ'y.um] 'mare'. According to my own observations of the Nagir dialect of Burushaski, this is an apico-postalveolarized, dorso-palatal approximant. *Palatalized,* symbolized by [̡], involves some degree of convex raising of the anterodorsum of the tongue towards the hard palate. As mentioned in 8.74 above, some degree of palatalization is the almost inevitable accompaniment of lamino-postalveolar articulation: thus, English [ʃ] and [ʒ], which are typically lamino-postalveolar, are slightly palatalized, whereas Russian [ʃ] and [ʒ], which are apico-postalveolar are not. Russian, and several other Slavic languages, opposes a whole series of palatalized consonants to non-palatalized ones. Thus, in addition to [p b m f v t d n l r s z] Russian has [ᶈ ᶀ ᶆ ᶂ ᶌ ƫ ᶁ ᶇ ᶅ ᶉ ᶊ ᶎ]. In the bilabial and labiodental series, where the secondary palatalization is formed by a quite separate organ from the primary articulation, consonants such as [ᶈ, ᶀ] simply consist of simultaneous (not successive) articulation of [p, b] and [j]. In the palatalized consonants of the dentalveolar zone some modification of the primary articulation occurs. Thus, while Russian [t] and [d] as in [tot] 'that' and [da] 'yes' are normally apicodental, the [ƫ] and [ᶁ] of ['ƫöƫə] 'aunt' and ['ᶁæᶁə] 'uncle' are normally lamino-alveolar or even lamino-postalveolar; moreover, they are often somewhat affricated, sounding rather like palatalized lamino-(post)alveolar [tᶊ, dᶎ]. Somewhat unusual are the palatalized uvular stops and fricatives of Ubykh, Abkhaz, and Abazin of the north-west Caucasus. In sounds of this type the primary articulation is between the posterodorsum of the tongue and the uvula or back velum, but the front part of the dorsal surface of the tongue is simultaneously raised towards the hard palate.
Velarized sounds involve a secondary raising of the back of the tongue towards the soft palate. Symbol [~]. All the non-palatalized consonants of Russian tend to be velarized, some more noticeably than others. Thus, Russian apico-postalveolar [ʃ] and [ʒ] have the part of the tongue immediately behind the apex and blade slightly hollowed, and the back slightly raised, giving a somewhat velarized effect. Russian /l/ as opposed to /ᶅ/ is strongly velarized [ɫ], and the same is true of eastern Polish *l*, although in Standard Polish the tongue-tip contact of the *l* is lost altogether, leaving in place of a velarized apico-alveolar lateral—simply a central velar approximant [ɯ̆], that is, a kind of unrounded [w].

In RP, a slightly palatalized [l] (often called 'clear l') occurs before vowels in the same syllable, and before [j], as in *look* or *million* [lʊk] ['mɪljən], whereas a slightly velarized [ɫ] (often called 'dark l') occurs elsewhere, for example, in *cool* or *bottle* [kuːɫ] [ˈbɒtɫ]. In other varieties of English the distribution of l-sounds is different. Thus, in most types of Scottish English /l/ is slightly velarized in all positions, and in some types of Irish English it is slightly palatalized in all positions.

Arabic has a series of strongly modified consonants, usually called 'emphatics', among which are [ʈ, ɗ, s, ʐ] and [ɫ]. Examples are [ʈiːn] 'mud' contrasting with [tiːn] 'figs', and [seːf] 'summer' contrasting with [seːf] 'sword'. These Arabic sounds are often described as velarized, and it may well be that in some dialects they are velarized. More often than not, however, the whole back part of the tongue is pulled backwards, (rather than raised toward the soft palate), so that they may be more properly called *uvularized* or *pharyngealized.* *Uvularized* sounds are similar to velarized sounds, except that the secondary tongue-raising is lower and further back. As we have mentioned, the Arabic so-called velarized consonants may perhaps be more properly described as uvularized. There is no special symbol for uvularization, the diacritic [~] being used for this purpose. *Pharyngealized* sounds involve some degree of contraction of the pharynx either by a retraction of the root of the tongue, or by lateral compression of the faucal pillars and some raising of the larynx, or a combination of these. There is no generally accepted diacritic for pharyngealization, the velarization diacritic being used for this modification as well thus [ʈ] = pharyngealized [t]. Pharyngealized consonants are said to occur in Kurdish (Zinder 1960), and in Ubykh (Vogt 1963), and, as we said above, the Arabic 'emphatics' are sometimes pharyngealized. Pharyngealized [χ̴] and [χ̴ʷ] occur in the Bzyb dialect of Abkhaz, in contrast with both plain uvulars and plain pharyngeals. Pharyngealized vowels occur in several Caucasian languages. In Tsakhur for example, pharyngealized [i, e, a, o, u, ɨ] all occur, in contrast with non-pharyngealized vowels of the same types.

Laryngealized is a term which is used to describe a feature more properly regarded as a variety of phonation than as a secondary articulation. According to Ladefoged (1964, 1971) laryngealization consists of *creaky voice* (see Chapter 5), and in the West African language, Margi, laryngealized stops and vowels contrast with non-laryngealized ones.

Some attention has been given in passing to differences in the nature of co-articulation according to the relative locations of the articulations involved. It may be desirable to formalize this here. According to the locational relations between pairs of articulators, we can refer to any two articulations as being *heterorganic, homorganic,* or *contiguous,* and these different relations have important effects on articulatory processes, both in *sequences* (to be discussed in the next chapter) and in *co-articulations*.

Two articulations are *heterorganic* when they involve quite distinct articulators, that is to say, articulators that can be freely moved, independently of each other. Thus, all *labio-* articulations are heterorganic with respect to all *linguo-* articulations (with the exception of the rare linguo-labial articulation, which is contiguous to labiolabial). In addition, among *linguo-* articulations, *posterodorso-* is heterorganic with respect to apico- and lamino- since, to a very large extent, activities of the back of the tongue are independent of activities of the apex and blade. On the other hand, *anterodorso-*articulation is contiguous, not heterorganic, with respect to both posterodorso- and lamino / apico-.

Two articulations are *homorganic* if they involve exactly the same articulators: thus, labiodental and labiodental, or apico-alveolar and apico-alveolar. Naturally, no question of homorganic co-articulation can possibly arise: this category is relevant only to articulatory sequences. In connection with co-articulation, it is only the categories *heterorganic* and *contiguous* that are relevant.

Two articulations are *contiguous* if they involve adjacent articulatory zones or sub-zones, with the proviso that the entire dentalveolar region is regarded as contiguous with the entire palatal zone. In other words, contiguous articulations are those that involve articulators so close to each other that they cannot be moved completely independently of each other.

We have already noted the effect in Russian of palatalization on apico / lamino-dentalveolar articulation: this is a case of the kind of accommodation that occurs in co-articulation by contiguous articulators. Palatalization has analogous effects on contiguous articulations behind it. Thus a palatalized [p̡] is merely a perfectly normal labiolabial stop, with a simultaneous (heterorganic) dorso-palatal stricture of, roughly, approximant type; but palatalized [k] is a dorso-velar stop, which usually has the anterior edge of the area of contact between tongue and roof of mouth shifted forward somewhat by the raising of the contiguous anterior part of the dorsum towards the hard palate.

It is thus clear that co-articulation in contiguous zones may involve a longitudinal *extension* of the articulation. Thus an apico-dental [t] has the rim of the tongue pressed against the backs of the upper teeth. An apico-dental lamino-alveolar [t̪͜t], a co-ordinate, contiguous stop articulation, has contact from the backs of the upper teeth over the alveolar ridge and from the apex (rim) of the tongue back over its blade. As a matter of fact, it may well be that most so-called apico-dental articulations are, indeed, of this extended type, and most of the time we may take this for granted. It is useful, however, to be able to deal with such longitudinally extended articulations explicitly when required, and the concept of contiguous co-articulation allows us to do this.[2] Other examples of longitudinally extended articulation are the palatalized uvulars [qʲ] and [χʲ] of Abkhaz and Abaza, and the uvular-pharyngeal [χ̝] of the Bzyb dialect of Abkhaz. In the former pair, [qʲ] involves a dorsotectal contact extending over virtually the entire length of the soft palate, and [χʲ] a grooved posterior channel within which the uvula vibrates somewhat, and a moderately narrow approximant-like channel extending forward to the division between hard and soft palate. In [χ̝] there is a fricative-like channel extending from the rear velar zone, over the uvula and down into the radico-pharyngeal zone. In Bzyb, incidentally, 'extended' uvular-pharyngeal [χ̝] contrasts with both [χ] and [ħ], as in [aˈχ̝ə] 'head', [aˈχə] 'lead' (n.), [aˈħawə] 'air'.

Apart from the difficulty mentioned above, of deciding on strictly phonetic grounds in some cases whether we are dealing with co-ordinate or secondary articulation, it is sometimes desirable, on phonological or comparative-descriptive or comparative-historical grounds, to regard secondary and co-ordinate articulations as 'weaker' and 'stronger' degrees of one and the same phenomenon. Thus, as we point out above there may be grounds for describing such sounds as the endolabio-endolabial-dental [p̲t̲, b̲d̲] of Abkhaz, or the analogous [p̲k̲ʷ] of Lak, as 'strongly labialized [t, d] and [k]', respectively. Chomsky and Halle (1968), discuss the interpretation of labial-velars (which, following an unfortunate tradition, they call 'labio-velars'—pp. 308–11) as *strongly labialized* (*rounded*) *velars,* or as *strongly velarized labials,* and they add 'We know of no languages that exhibit parallel variations in degree of narrowing concomitant with palatalization or pharyngealization. . . .' As a matter of fact, 'strong palatalization' is a fairly well-known synchronic or diachronic phenomenon in several branches of Indo-European, notably Slavic, Greek and Romance. Examples are Cypriot Greek [pcos] for Athenian [pjos] 'who', or Latin 'sapiat' represented by Rhäto-Romance [sapca] Provençal [saptʃa], French [saʃ].

Co-articulation is one particular type of simultaneous (as opposed to successive) modification of articulations. Two other types of articulatory modification which we must discuss here are *duration* and *tenseness.*

Duration

As we said in Chapter 7, certain kinds of articulatory stricture are essentially momentary: these are *flap* (both what we call 'flicks' and 'flaps' proper) and *semi-vowel*. There can be no question of the prolongation of either of these types of articulation, since 'momentariness' is part of the definition of each. It is true that there are languages in which flap and trill, for example, [ɾ] and [r], are opposed to each other as the 'short' and 'long' members, respectively of a phonological correlation of duration or 'quantity' as it is often called; but, as we showed above, from a rigorous phonetic point of view a trill is not a lengthened flap.

Duration, or 'quantity', then, is a type of modification of articulation, just as 'stress' is a type of modification of initiation, and 'tone', or 'intonation' is a type of modification of phonation. A sound is said to be 'long' if its characteristic articulatory posture is maintained for a relatively long time, or (since few sounds involve absolutely 'steady-state' articulation) if its characteristic sound is maintained for a relatively long time.[3] There are certain absolute limits to duration. The lower limit is given by the distinction between momentary and maintainable sounds. A stop or approximant, for instance, must have a minimal duration to distinguish it from flap or semivowel, but what this minimum is it is hard to say with precision. One would assume it to be near the value of the JND, or 'just noticeable difference', in duration, but this has been established only within the rather wide limits of from 10 to 40 milliseconds. (On this see Lehiste (1970) Chap. 2.) The upper limit of duration is fixed by physiological or aerodynamic considerations. One can obviously hold a voiceless stop articulation for as long as one can hold one's breath. The maximum duration of a fricative depends on the length of time for which one can keep a turbulent air-stream flowing through the articulatory channel, and this, in turn, depends on lung capacity and volume-velocity of flow: at 200 cm^3/s using two litres of tidal air one can clearly keep a fricative going for 10 seconds. With the glottalic initiator, and a very narrow articulatory channel one can keep a glottalic pressure fricative going for about 2 seconds, but no more. As we saw in Chapter 6, there are severe aerodynamic limitations on the duration of voiced stops. These can be maintained as such (that is, as *voiced* stops) only as long as a pressure-drop of about 2 cm H_2O across the glottis can be maintained. Without a special effort being made to enlarge the supraglottal cavities the pressure difference is likely to be abolished after an interval of only one centisecond or less.

The absolute limits of duration of vowels are much like those of fricatives. It has, however, been noted by a number of investigators that the actual duration of vowel-sounds in speech is related to their degree of openness. In general, other things being equal, the more open a vowel is, the longer it is. This is easily explained by the fact that the change of articulatory position from that of a consonant to that of an open vowel and back again involves a longer movement and hence requires more time than the movement to and from a less open vowel. In addition, there is some indication that the duration of vowels is determined in part by the articulatory location of surrounding, particularly following, consonants. Fischer-Jørgensen (1964) concludes, from a careful study of this phenomenon, that the conditioning factor is the length of movement required to pass conditioning factor is the length of movement required to pass from the vowel position to the consonant position: thus all vowels, in her study (of Danish vowels), are shorter before [b] than before [d] or [g]. The presumed reason for this is that since [b] is not homorganic or contiguous with the lingual vowel articulation, no lengthy time is required to pass from the vowel to the consonant. Similar observations, referred to in Lehiste (1970), have been made for other languages. In a number of languages, of which English is one, it has been found that, by and large, vowels are longer when followed by voiced consonants than when followed by voiceless consonants. For example, in such English word-pairs as *cat/cad, cease/seize* the voiceless consonant is always longer than the voiced consonant, while the vowel preceding the voiceless consonant is shorter than that preceding the voiced one. There are good aerodynamic reasons for the voiced consonant being shorter than the voiceless consonant (see Chapter 5), so this is no mystery. Apparently in English there is a kind of 'duration quantum' available for the syllable, so that if the final consonant is short the vowel must necessarily be long, and vice versa, as indicated in table 19. No other convincing explanation of this phenomenon has been suggested.

Table 19

	duration quantum		
k	æ	t	*cat*
k	æ	d	*cad*

Quite apart from these more or less intrinsic duration differences, we must note that articulatory duration is much under conscious control: within the limits sketched above one can vary duration as desired. Consequently, many languages make phonological use of duration differences: the phonological use of duration is known as 'quantity'. Among the better-known languages that utilize phonological opposition of long and short vowels are Czech, Serbo-Croatian, Hungarian, and Thai. In many other languages there are said to be oppositions between short and long vowels, but on examination it turns out that the duration difference is always accompanied by a very considerable difference in quality, so that it is questionable if one should regard the durational difference as the primary distinction. This is true of many varieties of English. In RP, for example, the vowels of *ship* and *sheep* /i/ /iː/, *pull* and *pool* /u/ /uː/, and *cot* and *caught* /ɔ/ /ɔː/ are often regarded as short-long correlates. However, even if, other things being equal, the first vowel of each pair is always shorter than the second (and this is questionable), the most noticeable effect is a difference of vowel quantity. Even in languages like Czech and Serbo-Croat, where there is a very clear-cut length-difference, this is accompanied by a considerable quality-difference. Thus, as Lehiste (1970) shows by spectrographic data in Czech long /iː/ and long /uː/ are very different in quality from their short correlates /i/ and /u/, though the other pairs of long-short vowels in Czech are much less different from each other. In Serbo-Croat, on the other hand, long and short /iː/ /i/ and /uː/ /u/ resemble each other very closely, the greatest qualitative differences being found between long and short /eː/ /e/, /oː/ /o/ and /aː/ /a/. (In this and the next chapter, following a well-known convention, we use / / for phonemic and [ ] for more purely phonetic transcriptions.)

From these examples it is clear that the relationship between duration and quality is not an anthropophonic universal but a language-specific, and therefore learned phenomenon. In languages with a short-long vowel distinction, there is considerable variation in the ratio of short vowel to corresponding long vowel, going from about 30 per cent to 60 per cent. Moreover, there seems to be some variation in the average absolute duration of short and long vowels. In Czech, for instance, average durations are: short *c.* 80 ms, long *c.* 160 ms; in Serbo-Croat, short *c.* 140 ms, long *c.* 210 ms. Finally, in connection with vowel-quantity, we should note that there are some languages in which there is a phonological opposition of more than two vowel durations. The best-known example is Estonian, where there is an opposition of short, long and extra-long vowels (and also consonants). Lehiste (1970) cites average durations of 118·8 ms, 204·4 ms, and 240·4 ms, respectively, for vowels of three different quantities. Incidentally, these values are for the first vowel in Estonian dissyllabic words. In such words the second vowel becomes progressively shorter as the duration of the first increases, thus enhancing the perceptual effect of increasing duration. Numerous attempts have been made to explain away the undoubtedly existing three degrees of phonologically relevant duration in Estonian as involving something other than quantity, for example, a doubling or trebling of phonemes. It is said that triple quantity exists also in the Samoyedic language, Nenets (Tereščenko 1966) and in the Amerindian languages Hopi and Mixe. According to Lehiste, who deals at length with these matters, there may be even more than three degrees of length in Lappish.

Consonant duration is also utilized phonologically in some languages, although, more often than not, long consonants, particularly when they are intervocalic and stretch across a syllable boundary, are regarded as sequences of two successive occurrences of the same consonant—'geminate' sequences to use the special term referred to in Chapter 11.

Tenseness

To conclude this chapter we must consider one more type of general modification, namely the parameter whose opposing poles are labelled vaguely as *fortis / lenis, strong / weak, intensive / non-intensive* with reference to consonants, and *tense / lax* with reference to both consonants and vowels. We include a discussion of this parameter under 'articulatory modifications' because it is widely believed that its principal manifestation is the degree of 'tenseness', whatever that may mean, of the articulators, although some of the phenomena commonly treated under this heading are, in fact, phonatory or initiatory.

Largely owing to the loose use of such terms as 'tense' and 'lax' as virtual synonyms for 'voiceless' and 'voiced' or 'aspirated' and 'unaspirated' the whole discussion of this subject is difficult and confused. In what follows we will first consider some applications of the 'tense / lax' terminology to consonants, going on later to vowels.

One source of the tense / lax discussion was the observation that in English such pairs as /p–b/, /t–d/, /f–v/, /s–z/ are quite clearly phonologically distinct, but it is not always easy to lay one's finger on the precise physiological or acoustic feature that maintains this distinction. Traditionally, such pairs have been described as 'voiceless' versus 'voiced'. It has long been known, certainly since Sweet (1877), that in certain phonetic contexts the so-called 'voiced' stops and fricatives of English exhibit little or no actual vocal-fold vibration. Thus, initial and final /b/ in *babe* or initial and final /v/ in *verve* are clearly much less voiced than the medial /b/ in *baby*, or the medial /v/ in *heavy*. Indeed, some observers have claimed that such sounds can be totally voiceless in these positions. What, then, is the feature which keeps them quite obviously distinct? It is clear that for pairs like initial /p–b/, /t–d/ the presence or absence of aspiration may be adduced as a primary distinguishing feature. It is not easy, however, to maintain that English voiceless and voiced fricatives are kept distinct by aspiration: here /f/ is sometimes noticeably aspirated, but /s/ and /ʃ/ are much more rarely aspirated. Moreover, it seemed reasonable to many writers to regard the stop following the /s/ in such words as *spar, star, scar* as /p, t, k/ rather than /b, d, g/, yet here there is no aspiration. A simple solution to the problem was to label English sounds such as /p, t, f, s/ as tense, and /b, d, v, z/ as lax. 'Laxness' would thus be an invariant feature of all occurrences of /b, d/, whether they were fully voiced, partially voiced, or completely voiceless, and 'tenseness' could be an invariant feature of /p, t/, whether they were strongly aspirated, only slightly aspirated, or not at all aspirated.

Jakobson, Fant and Halle ('Preliminaries' 1952), who applied the tense/lax distinction to English stops and fricatives, defined tenseness in consonants as 'manifested primarily by the length of their sounding period, and in stops, in addition, by the greater strength of the explosion'. They further characterize tense phonemes as 'articulated with greater distinctness and pressure than the corresponding lax phonemes'. Jakobson and Halle (1964) further characterize 'fortis' (that is, tense) consonants as opposed to 'lenis' (lax) 'by a higher air pressure behind the point of articulation and by a longer duration' adding further, that tense consonants 'show primarily a longer time interval spent in a position away from neutral'. These writers are careful to point out that tenseness is independent of aspiration; although it happens that in English the tense /p, t, k/ are normally aspirated, nevertheless, as they point out (Preliminaries, 2·434) there are some languages of the Caucasus in which lax stops have a redundant feature of aspiration. Again, Chomsky and Halle (1968) explicitly point out that aspiration and tenseness are independent of each other. If lengthening, or gemination, is indeed a symptom of tenseness (which is dubious) then the independence of aspiration and tenseness is demonstrated by the fact that in those Caucasian languages (of Southern Dagestan) that oppose short and geminate (tense) stops it is the *shorts* which are aspirated, while in Cypriot and Dodekanesan Greek, which has a comparable opposition, it is the *geminates* that are aspirated.

Consonantal tenseness has seemed to many to consist chiefly in longer duration, more energetic articulation, and heightened air-pressure behind the articulation. Attempts have been made to verify these articulatory features with respect to English and a few other languages.

As far as duration is concerned, as was pointed out, above, the English voiceless stops and fricatives are generally longer, other things being equal, than the corresponding voiced phonemes. In particular, it is well known that the final voiceless stops in such words as *bat* and *back* are longer than the final so-called 'voiced' stops of *bad* and *bag*, and that the vowel in the latter pair is longer than in the former. Thus, there appears to be a kind of compensatory factor in evidence, a certain fixed 'quantum' of duration being available for the monosyllable, the vowel being lengthened when the consonant is shortened. This may be compared with the compensatory progressive shortening of the vowel of an unstressed syllable in Estonian, as the duration of the vowel in the preceding stressed syllable increases, mentioned above. But neither of these length phenomena seems to have anything to do with tenseness.

The other suggested characteristics of tenseness—more 'energetic' articulation and 'heightened air-pressure'—have both been investigated. Harris et al. (1965) on the basis of EMG measures (measures of the action potential voltages of muscles used to close the lips) found a slight average tendency for the EMG measures to be higher for the supposed tense sounds for some subjects only. Most other EMG studies of English stops have been quite inconclusive. There is virtually no evidence that the articulation of the fortis stops is more 'energetic' (in terms of muscle action potential voltages) than that of the lenis stops.

Another measure of 'energy of articulation' is the actual measured pressure exerted by the articulators against each other during articulation. For English stops this measure has again been inconclusive, one research team (McGlone and Proffit 1967) even finding considerably higher contact-pressure exerted in /d/ than in /t/, while others, for example, Lubker and Parris (1970), found no consistent articulatory pressure difference. Interestingly enough, in a later study by Harris with other collaborators (Harris et al. 1968), it was found that there was considerable EMG voltage difference between /p/s in normal and in emphatically stressed syllables. If 'more energetic articulation' is utilized at all in English stops it seems to be used to mark emphatic stress rather than a particular category of consonant.

Another easily measured variable is the air-pressure behind the articulation. Here we have much more clear-cut data. It has frequently been found that the intra-oral pressure in /p, t, k/ and /f, θ, s, ʃ/ is higher than that in /b, d, g/ and /v, ð, z, ʒ/. When the latter group are actually voiced, then it is obvious that the intra-oral pressure must be kept low, in order to maintain trans-glottal flow (cf. Chapter 5), whereas in the voiceless correlates there is no such constraint. The fact that intra-oral pressures in /p, t, k/ are higher than in /b, d, g/ is absolutely no evidence of greater tenseness in the former than the latter.

Malecot (1970) sums up the fortis/lenis discussion with respect primarily to English in a valuable review of the evidence. He picks out air-pressure as the most reliable indicator of the distinction, and suggests that 'the lenis-fortis feature of consonants is primarily a synesthetic interpretation of magnitudes of intrabuccal air-pressure and is conveyed variously in different contexts by the durations of the consonant closure and of the preceding vowel'.

Studies of the tense/lax consonant distinction in some other western European languages, such as French, Danish, and Swedish, give some slight, but mostly inconclusive, evidence that the so-called tense (usually voiceless) stops and fricatives tend to have slightly higher articulatory pressure and intra-oral air-pressure.

Certain languages are particularly well known as possessing some kind of tense/lax distinction that appears to be quite independent of voicing: these languages include most of the eastern Caucasian languages spoken in Dagestan, Korean, and Javanese.

Trubetzkoy (1931) describes the 'Intensitätsgegensatz' of east Caucasian languages, and characterizes the 'strong' members of the opposition as involving greater muscular tension, a firmer closure in stops, and a narrower articulation channel in fricatives. These are all impressions gained by direct observation, but the last one at least—the narrower channel—is also borne out by palatograms of 'weak' and 'strong' or 'lax' and 'tense' fricatives in Dargi dialects in Gaprindashvili (1966). In addition, Trubetzkoy mentions that, in general, the weak consonants are aspirated, the strong ones not, and that the strong consonants are usually longer than the weak ones.

These points are confirmed by my own observations on such east Caucasian languages as Lak, Kubatchi, Tabasaran and Tsakhur. Avar on the other hand exhibits some unusual features. In this language strong velar and uvular stops are strongly affricated. The contrast is very clear in such a pair as /k'al/ 'mouth' and /kk'al/ 'ravine'. The first has a simple explosively released ejective [k']; in the second the [k'] is released into an ejective [x'], which has a duration of several centiseconds, thus [k'al] and [kxx'al]. In affricates the contrast is one of a shorter versus a longer, and stronger, and unaspirated, fricative part, thus /č/ vs /čč/ = [tʃʰ] vs [tʃʃ].

In Korean, it is well known that there is a triple series of stops /p, ph, *p/, /t, th, *t/, /k, kh, *k/ in which /*p, *t, *k/ are strong and relatively unaspirated. The Korean phonetician Kim, in two publications (1965, 1970), has thrown considerable light on these sounds. His conclusion, based on instrumental evidence, is that both /ph/ and /*p/ (and likewise /th/ and /*t/, /kh/ and /*k/) are tense, in opposition to /p, t, k/, which are lax. The tense pairs differ from each other only in their degree of aspiration. Together, however, they differ from the lax /p, t, k/ by being longer, having higher intra-oral air-pressure, higher air-flow rate and amplitude in the following vowel, and a higher EMG voltage recorded from lip muscles.

The third case cited is Javanese. In Javanese stops and affricates there is no voicing difference, except after nasals. Thus, such sounds commonly written as /pb, td, kg/ are all voiceless (and slightly aspirated). There *is* a difference between them, however, and the /p, t, k/ series have been described as 'intensives', which is why we are referring to them here. The observed differences are (1) that /b, d, g/ are pronounced with the larynx lowered, and this lowered larynx position persists into the following vowel, and (2) the vowel following /b, d, g/ is phonated with relaxed vocal folds, and some escape of air through a constant whisper-like chink—that is, the vowel following /b, d, g/ is 'whispery voiced', whereas the vowel following /p, t, k/ has much more tense phonation. Our observations of these Javanese sounds made in the Phonetics Laboratory at the University of Michigan showed that the *acoustic intensity* of vowels following /b, d, g/ was about the same as, or even slightly less than, that of vowels following /p, t, k/, while the volume-velocity of air-flow following /b, d, g/ was 4 to 6 times greater than that following /p, t, k/. These results strongly indicate that we do, indeed, have here a difference in vocal fold tension : in other words, a difference in phonatory (but not articulatory) tenseness.

It thus seems that a case, although not a very strong one, can be made for the existence of a parameter, or rather of several possible parameters, of tenseness with respect to consonants, quite independent of such other parameters as phonation and aspiration. It is necessary, however, to note that the realization of tenseness may vary from one language to another, and the terms tense/lax, strong/weak, fortis/lenis, and so on, should never be loosely and carelessly used without precise phonetic specification.

Although, as we have indicated, there are languages for which a precisely defined parameter of consonantal tenseness may be postulated, English is not one of them. There seems to be no justification at all for the use of the terms tense versus lax as major phonetic categories in the description of English /p, t/ versus /b, d/ and so on. Recent investigations, using various 'glotto-graphic' techniques (see Chapter 12), indicate, as Sweet pointed out nearly a century ago that the so-called 'lax' phonemes, such as /b, d, g, v, ð, z/, always involve some degree of narrowing of the glottis, even if not to the point of actual production of voice. It is probable that the differences of intra-oral pressure—the *only* generally observed 'tenseness' characteristic—as between, for example, /b, d, g/ and /p, t, k/, can be adequately accounted for by differences in glottal adjustment. So we are, after all, entitled to describe the difference between /b, d, g/ and /p, t, k/ in terms of phonation : the former being actually or potentially *voiced*—that is, always involving some degree of glottal constriction not present in /p, t, k/.

We must now turn our attention to the parameter of tenseness with respect to vowels. The tense/lax distinction in vowels was formerly called primary/wide (Bell 1867), and narrow/wide (Sweet 1877). Sweet points out that 'in forming narrow sounds, there is a feeling of tenseness in that part of the tongue where the sound is formed, the surface of the tongue being made more convex than in its natural "wide" shape, in which it is relaxed and flattened. This convexity of the tongue naturally narrows the passage—whence the name'. Figure 56 indicates what Sweet undoubtedly meant by this distinction.

The reader should experiment, particularly if he is a native speaker of English, by silently articulating [i-ɩ-i-ɩ-i-ɩ] (the vowels of *seat* and *sit*) a number of times. While doing this it is possible to feel a slight tensing and upward bulging of the centre of the tongue during [i] and some degree of relaxation and flattening during [ɩ]. Further silent experiments with such pairs as the [e] of French *été* and the [ɛ⊥] of English (RP) *bet,* or the [ɛ] of French *bête,* and the [æ] of English (RP) *bat,* may convince the reader that there is a consistent difference of tongue surface convexity and tenseness between the members of these pairs. But the sensation is a somewhat elusive one, and it becomes even more so with respect to central and back vowels, with the exception of the high back pair [u/ɷ] (as in RP *pool/pull*). It was partly because of the general dubiety of the narrow/wide or tense/lax distinction that it was discarded by Henry Sweet's distinguished successor Daniel Jones. Moreover, it has long been the custom to assess tongue-positions for phonetic purposes in terms of the position and shape of the *saggital* or *longitudinal center line* of the tongue. Now, it is perfectly clear that, with respect to the center line, the effect of greater convexity (= narrowness ; in Sweet's sense, or tenseness) is identical with the effect of a general raising of the body of the tongue—namely, the center line of the tongue is brought closer to the roof of the mouth (see figure 56, opposite).

Consequently, when Jones developed the system of Cardinal Vowels (see Chapter 9) the only parameters included in the system were vertical tongue-position, horizontal tongue-position and lip-position. In terms of the Cardinal Vowel System [ɩ] can be regarded either as a retracted and slightly raised [e], or a retracted and considerably lowered [i], but *not* as a lax variant of [i].

cross section : solid line = tense or 'narrow' vowel
broken line = lax or 'wide' vowel

saggital section : solid line = centre line of 'bunched-up' tongue for tense (narrow) vowel

broken line = centre line of relaxed tongue for lax (wide) vowel

Figure 56. Tongue-shapes for narrow/wide (Sweet) or tense/lax vowels

The tense/lax distinction with reference to vowels has, however, remained popular with some writers, sometimes redefined. Thus, Heffner (1960), referring to an article of Meyer (1910), claims that lax vowels have a more open glottis, a higher rate of air-flow and consequently a lower subglottal pressure than tense vowels. Jacobson and Halle (1964) apparently accept this dubious finding of Meyer's. They add that 'the heightened subglottal air pressure in the production of tense vowels is indissolubly paired with a longer duration'. It is difficult to see why this should be so, and it is certainly not the case in English, where duration is independent of the so-called tense-lax distinction. The English lax vowel [ɩ], for instance, under certain conditions of intonation can be extremely long : for example, 'he did !' [hi ⁓ dɩ:::d], with a rising–falling–rising tone on 'did', expressing astonished enquiry.

Jakobson, Fant and Halle (1952) maintain that in tense phonemes (including vowels) 'the muscular strain affects the tongue, the walls of the vocal tract and the glottis. The higher tension is associated with a greater deformation of the vocal tract from its neutral position'. No evidence is adduced to support this theory of 'muscular strain' in the walls of the vocal tract and the glottis, and, indeed, it is very doubtful if it exists. Chiba and Kajiyama (1958) in their classic work on the vowel explicitly state that 'the flaccidity of the walls of the vocal organs produce no great effect upon the vowel quality'. Jakobson, Fant and Halle as well as Jakobson and Halle (1964) and Chomsky and Halle (1968) make the point that tense vowels involve a greater deviation from the neutral or rest position of the vocal tract. There are several problems about this view. In the first place, it implies that there is a definite, universal, neutral or rest position, which is far from being certain. It is very suggestive, in this respect, to note that the 'hesitation sound' used by speakers varies. If there were a 'universal neutral position' one might expect everyone to say [əː . . . əː] (the 'er . . . er' of English). However, Scots say [eː . . . eː]. If we do accept the postulated neutral position it is still difficult to apply the criterion of 'greater deviation' from this position. Chomsky and Halle (1968) say that in the neutral position the tongue is raised 'to about the level that it occupies in the articulation of the English vowel [ɛ] in the word *bed*'. They mention merely the 'level' of the vowel [ɛ], but not the horizontal location of the highest point of the convex tongue, so we cannot be sure if they mean that this neutral position is, indeed, that of English *e* (=[ɛ˔]), that is, a front vowel, somewhat closer than CV3, or merely a vowel of this tongue-height, perhaps a *central* vowel of the indicated tongue-height, which would make it about the vowel of English (RP) 'bird'[ɜ]. There is, indeed, quite widespread, often tacit belief that the 'neutral position' must be of the [ə] or [ɜ] type. In either case, difficulties arise in the application of the 'greater deviation' criterion of tenseness, as figure 57 indicates.

Using figure 57a as the representation, on a Cardinal Vowel diagram, of the neutral point at [ɛ˔] we find that the directions of deviations from this point agree rather well with some generally accepted lax/tense pairs. Thus lax [ɷ] and tense [u] are precisely on a line of deviation, lax [ɩ] and tense [i] are decidedly off the line, but at least [i] is closer than [ɩ], and this difference is very roughly in accord with the direction of deviation. However, figure 57a completely reverses the relationship of French [ɛ] and English (RP) [æ], taken by Bell, Sweet, and others to be tense and lax, respectively: here lax [æ] is seen to deviate further from the neutral position than tense [ɛ].

Figure 57b, which many phoneticians would regard as locating the neutral position more plausibly at a vowel of [ə] or [ɜ] type, is not much more satisfactory.

Jakobson, Fant and Halle posit for the acoustic phase of tense vowels a greater deviation of formants from those of the 'neutral

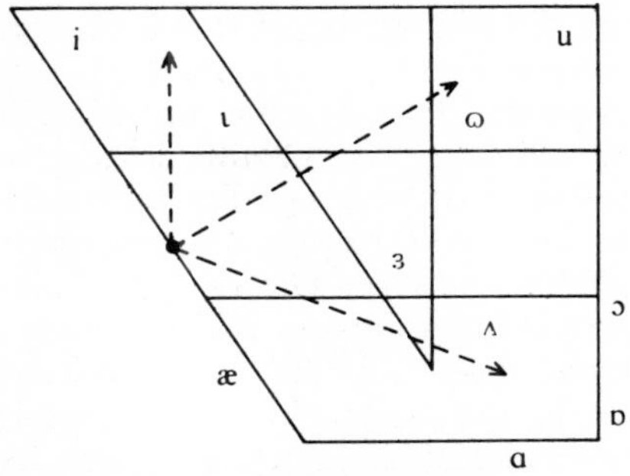

a. neutral point at English [ɛ˔] as in *bed*

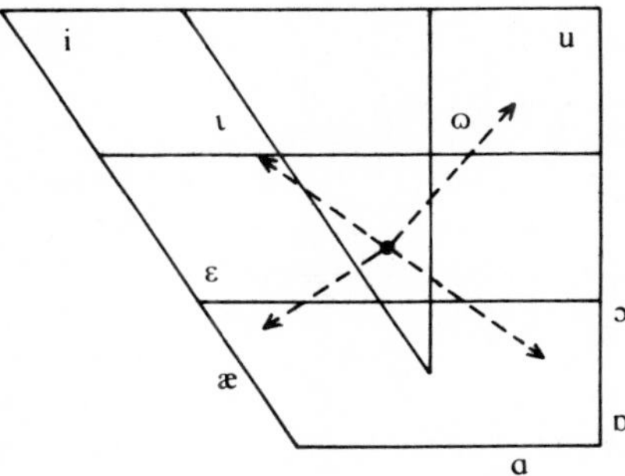

b. neutral point at English [ɜ] as in *bird*

deviations from the 'neutral point' in the direction of 'more tense' indicated by broken line

Figure 57. 'Tenseness' of vowels as amount of deviation from 'neutral' position

vowel', no doubt corresponding to the alleged physiological deviation from the neutral position. They present a table of paired French vowels, allegedly tense and lax. Of the four pairs shown, two agree more or less with the deviation directions of figure 57b, but two are at variance with them.

From all this, it emerges that with respect to vowels the tense / lax parameter is extremely dubious, and that Daniel Jones was probably right to discard it. There may be differences of tension of various muscles involved in positioning the tongue for vowels, but we are far from knowing enough about these differences to be able to utilize them as a phonetic parameter. In any case, the effective result of such differences can usually be described in terms of tongue-height and / or horizontal position. There is certainly too little evidence to justify some of the assignments of vowels to the tense or lax categories referred to in the last few paragraphs.

To sum up, then, we can say that there is some justification for the retention of a parameter of tense/lax for the description of consonants. For vowels, the existence of such a parameter is dubious, and the use of tense/lax terminology in the phonetic description of vowels is seldom if ever necessary, and should be avoided. This does not mean that the tense/lax terminology is entirely useless in *phonological* description. Here, tense and lax may, perhaps, be usefully employed as labels to designate phonetically arbitrary classes of vowels that happen to be phonologically distinct. But it should then be made quite clear that the selection of terms may be phonetically vacuous.

ELEVEN

Sequences and Segmentation

With the last chapter's discussion of co-articulation, and certain articulatory modifications, we have come almost to the end of our survey of the major phonetic, or anthropophonic, descriptive parameters. Some residual matters remain for discussion, however, which, although important, do not fit neatly into any of the previous chapters. These residual matters are concerned with (1) articulatory *sequence* phenomena, and (2) the *segmentation* of speech.

During an utterance, the various productive components of speech—the initiatory, phonatory and articulatory movements—ebb and flow, as it were, overlapping and interpenetrating one another. Upon the slightest observation and reflection, this is obvious. Nevertheless, we are to a large extent conscious of speech as a sequence of discrete events: this is because there are, throughout the flux of utterance, major change-points which mark divisions between what we perceive as phonic segments, and which often correspond to divisions between minimal phonological units, or phonemes.

For example, if we say such a word as *sap* we are immediately conscious of a sequence of three phonic events, [s], [æ] and [p]—even the most naïve and uninstructed person is, or can easily become, aware of this. The three apparently discrete segments that we hear in *sap* are delimited by major change-points in the phonatory-articulatory flux. At the same time, they correspond to three of the minimal interchangeable phonological units, or phonemes, of the language. If, now, we say not *sap* but *chap* the situation changes slightly. We may get the immediate impression once again of there being three segments [tʃ], [æ] and [p]: more careful attention, however, suggests a segmentation into *four* discrete segments [t], [ʃ], [æ] and [p]. This observation requires no special phonetic training, being obvious enough to anyone who introspects about his articulation.[1] In particular, it quickly becomes obvious that, whereas before the vowel [æ] in *sap* there is a single consonantal segment, before the vowel [æ] in *chap* there is a *sequence* of segments.

Among articulatory sequences there are certain types which have traditional names: most of these are sequences which occur in some language or other as unit phonemes, or otherwise demand some special recognition in the phonology of the language. All these named sequence-types are absolutely, or nearly, *homorganic;* that is to say, the same, or nearly the same articulators are used in both segments in the sequence. Table 20 indicates some possible homorganic sequence-types, illustrated in each case by sounds with *apico-* or *lamino-alveolar* articulation (although, in fact, most of them can occur at a wide range of locations). Those few types which have a traditional name are in numbered boxes.

Table 20

	stop	*trill*	*fric.*	*lateral*	*nasal*
stop	[1] dd	dr	[2] dz	[3] dl	[4] dn
trill	rd	[1] rr	rz	rl	rn
fricative	zd	zr	[1] zz	zl	zn
lateral	ld	lr	lz	[1] ll	ln
nasal	[5] nd	nr	nz	nl	[1] nn

Type 1, [dd, rr, zz, ll, nn]. These all illustrate what are known as *geminates* or geminate sequences, that is, sequences of two identical articulations. Such a sequence as, say, [zz], involves continuity of articulation—a prolongation of the articulatory posture—and might thus be termed a 'long' consonant, rather than a geminate sequence of two segments. The term 'geminate' is most commonly used when, in spite of the continuity of articulation the bi-segmental nature of the sequence is made clear by the presence of a syllable division within the period of maintained articulation. Thus, an utterance like [azz-a], with a syllable-division (minor diminution and re-establishment of initiator power) *after* the lengthened [z]-articulation would normally be regarded as containing a long [z] and be transcribed [azː-a]. On the other hand, an utterance like [az-za], with syllable division (initiator power diminution) right in the middle of the lengthened [z]-articulation would be regarded as containing a geminated sequence, and be transcribed [azza]. Phonetically geminate sequences occur in English, for example, the sequence [kk] in *bookcase* or [dd] in *good dog.* The term 'geminate' is, however, applied only to those cases where the sequence occurs within one and the same morpheme. Italian is one of the best known languages in which geminates, in this sense, are very common, as in *quello* [kwɛllo], *notte* [nɔtte]. The term 'geminate' has also been commonly used for the 'strong' or 'tense' consonants occurring in east Caucasian languages, mentioned in Chapter 10 above. It is true that when these strong and long consonants occur between vowels they may be divided between two syllables, and hence be geminate in the sense discussed here. When they occur initially, however, and hence entirely within one and the same syllable, the geminates are merely *long*, and, in most east Caucasian languages, unaspirated, as opposed to the short and aspirated 'non-geminates'. Thus, Avar / sali / 'sand', / ssak' / 'cork', or / ʃuri / 'movement', / ʃʃuri / 'whisper' might be transcribed in more phonetic detail as [sʰali], [sːak']; [ʃʰuri], [ʃːuri].

At this point we should mention the 'geminate semivowels', [-ww-] and [-jj-], which occur in Arabic in such forms as [ʔawwal] 'first', [ɫɑjjɩb] 'good'. We defined 'semivowels' (Chapter 7) as essentially momentary and 'non-prolongable'. It would seem then that the 'geminate semivowel' is a contradiction in terms. However, the most prominent feature of these geminate semivowels is their rapid on- and off-glide, and it is this which preserves their semi-vocalic character.

Type 2 [dz] and likewise [ts, tʃ, dʒ, pɸ, bβ, kx, gɣ] are known as *affricates*. An affricate is a stop released with close transition into a homorganic fricative. Generally speaking, we reserve the term 'affricate' just for those sequences of stop and homorganic fricative that occur within one and the same syllable, and that are regarded, for a variety of reasons, not necessarily phonetic, as representing unit phonemes in a given language. Thus, although the final [ts] in German *Spatz* [ʃpats] and English *cats* [kæts] may be phonetically identical, we generally call the former an 'affricate', but the latter merely a sequence of stop plus fricative. This distinction is phonetically arbitrary, being based rather on grammatical considerations: in any word-final sequence of consonant plus [s] in English, the two consonants belong to separate morphemes (the final [s] normally being exponent of the genitive case, or plural morpheme with nouns, and of the third-person-singular-present morpheme with verbs). In German, on the other hand, such a sequence may occur in the expression of one and the same morpheme.

Type 3 [dl] represents a *stop with lateral plosion*. This type of sequence occurs for instance, in many varieties of English in such words as *middle* ['mɩdɫ] or *little* ['lɩtɫ]. In each of these, the complete oral closure of the stop is released, not in the centre (so that the stop opens up into a vowel, as in [da], or into a central fricative as in [dz]) but at the side(s) so that the stop opens up into a homorganic lateral. In these English examples the lateral has a more than minimal duration, and may involve a slight renewed initiator-power pulse, and is thus called 'syllabic'. Where, however, (a) the lateral part of such a sequence is (lateral) fricative and (b) the conditions are otherwise such as would lead us to apply the term 'affricate' (that is, stop plus lateral within one and the same syllable and functioning as a unit phoneme), we often refer to such sequences as *lateral affricates*. Lateral affricates of the type (pulmonic) [tɬ] and (glottalic) [tɬ'] are quite common, particularly in Amerindian and Caucasian languages. Voiced [dl] or [dɮ] is much rarer. A glottalic velar lateral affricate [kʟ'], that is, a glottalic velar stop released into a scrapy, rather rattly velar (molar) lateral in which the velar central contact is maintained, occurs in Zulu, in Artchi, and apparently in at least one dialect of Avar.[2] An apparently pulmonic laterally released velar stop is reported for some New Guinea languages (Wurm 1964).

Type 4, [dn] (and likewise [bm], [gŋ], [pm̥], etc.) represents a *stop with nasal plosion*. This type of sequence occurs, for instance, in many varieties of English in such words as *sudden* ['sʌdn̩] and *button* ['bʌtn̩].[3] In these English examples the nasal has a more than minimal duration, and may involve a renewed initiator-power pulse, and is thus called syllabic.

Non-syllabic nasal release of stops, phonemically contrasting with oral release, is found in Wolof, and in some south Australian languages. See page 214, below.

Type 5, [nd] (and likewise [mb], [ŋg], [mp], etc.), represents a *pre-nasalized stop*. As in the case of affricates, the specific term 'pre-nasalized stop' is generally used only in that specific case where the sequence *nasal* plus *homorganic stop* occurs within one and the same syllable, and is regarded as forming a single unit phoneme in the language in question. Such pre-nasalized stops are not uncommon in Malayo-Polynesian languages.

There are no special names for any of the other possible sequences shown in the table. There is absolutely no reason on purely phonetic grounds why such sequences as, say, fricative plus homorganic stop [st], [xk], or lateral plus homorganic stop [ld],[l̥t] should not be accorded special names such as 'pre-affricated', 'pre-lateralized' or 'pre-lateral-affricated'. The fact is, however, that there is no tradition of such nomenclature, even though at least one case of a 'pre-affricated stop' functioning apparently as a single phonological unit is known. This is the case of Old Church Slavonic [ʃt] as in [noʃtĭ] 'night', which is commonly assumed to have represented a unit phoneme. There is a not dissimilar phoneme in modern Russian, which might be described as a 'pre + post-affricated' [ʃtʃ], often reduced to [ʆʆ], as in *ещё*, pronounced [jɩʃtʃo] or [jɩʆʆo].

We have pointed out that sound-types such as 'affricate' and 'lateral affricate' and 'nasal plosion' are simply articulatory sequences, rather than special articulatory types. This does not mean, however, that the successive sounds have no influence upon each other. In all cases of *close transition* between articulations there is a strong tendency to mutual influence between successive articulations. Indeed, this is precisely what characterizes close transition as opposed to *open transition,* on which more below.

A more detailed consideration of the difference between the normal, fully orally released stop, as in [ta, da], and stops with affrication, as in [tsa, dza], or lateral plosion [tla, dla], or nasal plosion [tna, dna], leads to the following remarks. In cases of 'normal' stop-release (or 'plosion') the articulators, during the stop itself and at the moment of release, are in what might be called a state of 'neutrality', or relatively uniform muscular tension over the whole contact-area of the stop. When the lower articulator moves smartly away from the upper, the contact is broken as nearly as possible simultaneously over the whole contact-area of the stop: or, to be more precise, the order in which different parts of the contact are broken, and the rapidity with which this occurs is determined by purely passive anatomical considerations. In the case of affricates, however, there is an active restriction of the release to a narrow central channel.

Thus, when the lips are smartly separated for [pa] the first breaking of contact normally occurs more or less at the centre, then spreads with extreme rapidity to the corners of the mouth. This order of events, however, is not due to any active 'planning', as it were, but merely to passive anatomical characteristics of the lips. In the case of the affricate [pɸa], however, even before the break-away, there is some tensing of labial muscles towards the corners of the mouth, so that, when the break-away occurs, the opening is at first restricted to a narrow central channel, spreading only later, in a planned, or 'programmed', way to the outer corners of the lips. There is an analogous difference between a dental or alveolar stop [ta], and the corresponding affricate [tsa]. Just before, and during, the release of [ta] the apex and blade of the tongue are in a locally somewhat relaxed state, or, if there is some local muscular tension it is more or less uniform over the entire area of articulatory contact. Consequently, when the break-away occurs it is nearly simultaneous over the whole contact-area, the rate and direction of contact-breaking depending solely on local anatomical conditions—surface irregularities, and so on. In [tsa], on the other hand, there is some local tensing of surface tongue muscles towards the sides of the contact-area even before the break-away, and consequently when this occurs, a channel opens up first in the centre, and then spreads to the sides at a rate determined by the 'planned' relative timing of contraction and relaxation of the local surface tongue muscles, and of the more distant intrinsic and extrinsic tongue muscles that control the actual pulling away of the tongue.

There is a similar distinction between the neutral break-away of a stop and the actively controlled break-away of a lateral affricate, such as [tla], or a stop with lateral plosion. In this case, just before and during the break-away there is a slight tensing of local surface muscles in the *centre*-line, so that when the break-away occurs it starts at the side(s) and spreads inwards. The time-lag between the first, lateral break-away and the final full opening depends, again, on relative timing of contraction and relaxation of local and more distant tongue muscles. In the case of lateral plosion in English, for example in words like *little, middle,* where an alveolar stop is released into a relatively prolonged syllabic [l], it is clear that final break-away is long delayed. In some languages, however, the lateral phase of a lateral affricate is so minimal that the whole sequence might well be regarded as a lateral stop, rather than a lateral affricate. This is the case with the so-called 'weak' or 'plain' lateral affricates, pulmonic [tɬ] and glottalic [tɬ'] of Akhwakh, a Caucasian language of the Andi group of West Dagestan. In Akhwakh, 'weak' [tɬ] and [tɬ'] contrast with 'strong' [tɬɬ] and [tɬɬ'] in such minimally, or near minimally contrasting pairs as: [tɬutɬu] 'blow (imper.)!' [tɬɬut'] 'wedge'; [tɬ'ini] 'malt', [tɬɬ'ini] 'sleeps'.

In such words, the 'strong' lateral affricate has a relatively long and noisy fricative phase, lasting on the average 160 ms [tɬɬ], 84 ms [tɬɬ'] in isolated words. The weak lateral affricate, however, has a fricative phase of on the average 70 ms [tɬ], 43 ms [tɬ'], that is, no longer than the aspiration of many an aspirated stop. We might, therefore, characterize Akhwakh [tɬ] and [tɬ'] as 'lateral stops' as opposed to the 'lateral affricates' [tɬɬ] and [tɬɬ']. Similar laterally released stops apparently occur in the Bhalesi dialect of Bhadarwahi, in Jammu-Kashmir (Varma 1948).

In the transition from stop to homorganic nasal, in 'nasal plosion', there is probably nothing quite parallel to the kinds of differences in muscle activity discussed above. There is, however, something analogous to the special case of 'lateral stop' (as opposed to 'stop with prolonged lateral release'). In the case of nasal plosion in English, in such words as *button* and *sudden,* there is continuous apico-alveolar articulatory contact, the sudden velic opening (sudden lowering of the soft palate) in the middle of it being followed by a prolonged nasal sound, forming a new syllable. It is, however, reported that in Wolof, a Niger-Congo language of Senegal, stops with non-syllabic short nasal release, represented by [p$^{\text{m̥}}$], [t$^{\text{n̥}}$], [kŋ̊] occur finally, in contrast with stops with oral release [p^{h}, t^{h}, k^{h}], as in the words:

[lapᵐ] 'to drown' as opposed to [lapʰ] 'be thin'.

[gɔkŋ̊] 'horse's bridle rope' as opposed to [gɔkʰ] 'white chalk' (Coustenoble 1929).

In addition, several south Australian languages, for example, Aranda, Arapana, and Wailpi, have a series of nasally released stops contrasting with orally released stops and, in Wailpi, also with laterally released stops (O'Grady et al. 1966, Wurm 1972).

So far, we have discussed, or at least referred to, five different types of sound-sequence for which there are traditional terms, namely *geminate, affricate, lateral affricate* (or lateral plosion), *nasal plosion* and *pre-nasalized stop*. It will be noted that all of these are sequences which would normally be termed 'consonantal'. However, sequences of vowels or vowel-like sounds are also common, and one type of vowel sequence has the traditional name *diphthong*.

Diphthong

In the chain of speech, in principle, any vowel may be followed by any other. When two identical vowels succeed one another we might well refer to this as 'geminate' vowel sequence, although, in fact, this term is not normally used. In such a case the two vowels may fuse into a single long or ultra-long vowel, or they may be separated by a momentary diminution of initiator power, or by the insertion between them of a glottal stop—although in this last case we no longer have, strictly speaking, a geminate vowel sequence, but rather a sequence of vowel plus consonant [ʔ] plus vowel. The reader may experiment with such English sequences as [iːiː] in *bee-eater,* [ɑːɑː] in *spa-artist,* [ɔːɔː] in *law-order,* and [uːuː] in *new ooze,* under various conditions of stress and intonation, comparing each of these with single vowels, as in *beater, spartan, Lauder, news.*

A *diphthong* may be defined as a sequence of two perceptually different vowel sounds within one and the same syllable. Provided none of them involves a renewed burst of initiator power any of the following represent diphthongs: [ei, ɛi, ɛɩ, ɛe, æe, ɑɔ, ɑo, aω, əu, ωu, ie, eɛ, øy, ɯɤ], and in each case the first symbol, for example, the [e] in [ei] or the [ɯ] in [ɯɤ], represents the starting point or *first element* of the diphthong, while the second symbol, for example, the [i] in [ei] or the [y] in [øy], represents the finishing point or *second element* of the diphthong.

In point of fact, a diphthong may, indeed, consist of two distinct, discrete 'elements', with a relatively rapid transition between them. On the other hand, it may be more correctly characterized as a continuous, gliding movement from a starting point to a finishing point. There are thus two extreme types of diphthong, a 'sequential' type, which may be represented diagrammatically by __/‾‾, and a 'gliding' type, represented by , with, of course, a continuum of possible gradations between these extremes. In many types of English the 'narrower' diphthongs, such as the [eɩ] of *day* or the [əɷ] of *go,* are more often than not of the gliding type, while the 'wider' diphthongs, such as the [aɩ] of *buy* or the [ɔɩ] of *boy,* are of the more distinctly segmented sequential type.

A second, and more traditional, division of diphthongs is into *falling* and *rising*. It is important to note that these terms, contrary to expectations, do *not* refer to the direction of the transitional or gliding diphthongal movement. What they do refer to is the relation of the diphthong to the 'stress curve', or initiator-power pulse with which it is associated. A falling diphthong is one with what may be called 'decrescendo stress', symbolized by > . A rising diphthong, on the contrary, has 'crescendo stress' < . The more weakly stressed element of a diphthong, is often indicated by placing a diacritic over the symbol representing it. Examples of the two types of diphthong would thus be :

falling (>) [aĕ] [oɛ̆] [ɩə̆] [œy̆], etc.
rising (<) [ŏɛ] [ɩ̆a] [y̆ɛ] [ɯ̆ɑ], etc.

In such cases, the diphthongal element marked by the diacritic is said to be the 'non-syllabic' element, the other being the 'syllabic' element. There is no hard and fast line of division between the non-syllabic element of a diphthong and a semivowel: it is solely a question of degree. The shorter the duration of the 'non-syllabic' element and the more sudden the transition to or from it, the more like a consonantal semivowel it is. Thus, in principle, the difference between the English *pie* and the French *paille* lies in the rapidity of transition and the duration of the second element: English *pie* 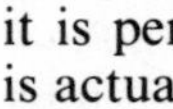 or 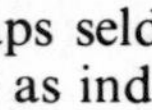 [paɩ̆], and French *paille* 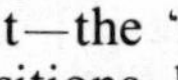 [pa:j].

The traditional representation of diphthongs is often misleading. Thus, the English diphthongs in *tie* and *cow* are often transcribed as [taɩ], and [kaɷ] (or their equivalent), in which the second elements are represented as being the vowels of *sit* and *put.* These symbols adequately indicate the direction of the diphthongal movement; but it is perhaps seldom that the final point—the 'second element'—is actually as indicated here. In final positions, before pause, as in *tie* and *cow* we often have diphthongs ending about [e] or even [ɛ], and centralized [ö], thus [taĕ] or [taɛ̆] and [kaö]. The reader should practise making falling and rising diphthongs of all kinds. The course of a diphthong can be well represented on a Cardinal diagram, and it is useful to draw a number of 'vector' lines on such a diagram and to try to produce the diphthongs they represent, as in figure 59. It is obvious that, in terms of the direction of the diphthongal movement, diphthongs can be classified as *closing* (for

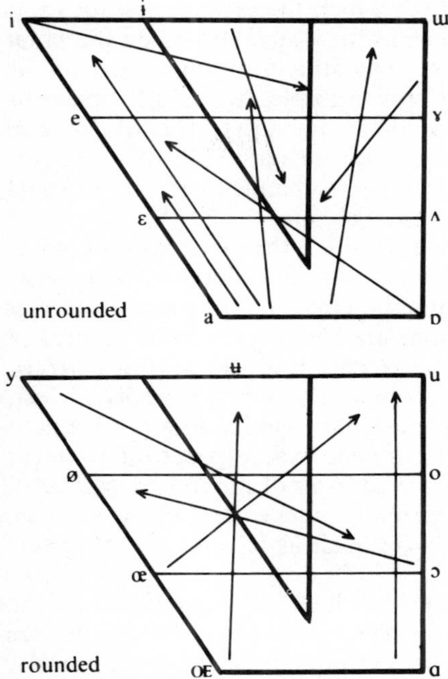

Figure 59. The representation of diphthongs on a cardinal vowel chart

example, [aɪ̆, əɪ̆, ɑʊ̆]) or *opening* (for example, [ɪɛ, ʊɑ])—not to be confused with 'rising' and 'falling'; *fronting* (for example, [ɔɪ, uy]), *backing* (for example, [ɛʊ̆, ɪŭ]) and *centring* (for example, [ɪə, ɛə, ʊə, ɔə]). The only one of these terms commonly used is the last one. We often refer collectively to the English (RP) diphthongs in *beer* [bɪə], *bear* [bɛə], *boor* [bʊə], *bore* [bɔə] as 'the English centring diphthongs'.

Consonantal Sequences

We have referred in passing to *open* and *close transition*. These terms refer, primarily, to two different ways of passing from one consonantal segment to another. The different types of transition can best be studied in the light of the three possible types of consonantal sequence in terms of the articulatory relationships between them: these are *homorganic, heterorganic* and *contiguous*. These have already been referred to in relation to co-articulation (Chapter 10), but are even more important in relation to sequences and sequence phenomena.

A *homorganic* sequence is one in which the articulatory location of both members is identical, such as [tt, ss, ŋŋ]. Provided the same articulators are used the sequence is still homorganic even if it involves a change of phonation, for example, [td, zs, ʒʃ, bp], or a change of stricture-type, for example, from stop to fricative or vice versa [ts, zd, ɸm], or a change of oral air-path (central to lateral or vice versa), for example, [tl, ld, lz], or a change from oral to nasal or vice versa, for example, [bm, nd, ŋk].

A *heterorganic* sequence is one in which the articulators used in the two segments are quite different. 'Quite different' means that the articulators can be freely manipulated independently of each other. Thus, all labial articulations are heterorganic with respect to all lingual articulations (with the exception of the very rare apico-labial articulation, to which this obviously does not apply). Thus, sequences such as [pk, fx, gv] are heterorganic. Again all apico- and lamino- articulations are heterorganic with respect to all postero-dorsal articulations, since the extreme front of the tongue (the apex and blade) can be manoeuvred virtually independent of the extreme back of the tongue. Thus sequences such as [tk, sx, qʃ] are heterorganic.

A *contiguous* sequence is one in which adjacent parts of the same articulator are used, with the consequence that the articulators used in the two segments cannot be manipulated independently. Thus, labial articulation is contiguous with respect to labiodental; dental, alveolar, postalveolar and palatal are contiguous to each other; palatal and velar or uvular are contiguous to each other. The following are examples of contiguous sequences: [pf, θs, ʃt, kj, lɹ].

In English (RP), with 18 consonantal segments that can occur in syllable- (or word-) *final* position [m, n, ŋ, p, b, t, d, k, g, f, v, θ, ð, s, z, ʃ, ʒ, l] and 21 that can occur *initially* [m, n, p, b, t, d, k, g, f, v, θ, ð, s, z, ʃ, ʒ, h, w, ɹ, j, l] there are 378 possible two-segment sequences. Of these, 63 are homorganic, 96 are contiguous, and the remaining 219 are heterorganic. Table 21 displays, with one simplification, all these English consonantal sequence types. The simplification, to render the table less unwieldy, is that only a single (voiceless) representative is given of each voiced-voiceless pair of phonemes, thus [st] for instance can be taken to represent also [zt, sd, zd]. The types surrounded by a solid line are homorganic sequences, while those surrounded by a broken line are contiguous sequences, all the rest being heterorganic. Note that the sequences [mw, pw, fw] (implying also [bw] and [vw]) are marked as contiguous. Insofar as [w] also has a velar component in its articulation it might be regarded as heterorganic with respect to labials. However, in sequences con-

Table 21

Finals (11)	Initials (14): m	p	w	f	θ	n	t	s	l	ʃ	ɹ	j	k	h
m	mm	mp	mw	mf	mθ	mn	mt	ms	ml	mʃ	mɹ	mj	mk	mh
p	pm	pp	pw	pf	pθ	pn	pt	ps	pl	pʃ	pɹ	pj	pk	ph
f	fm	fp	fw	ff	fθ	fn	ft	fs	fl	fʃ	fɹ	fj	fk	fh
θ	θm	θp	θw	θf	θθ	θn	θt	θs	θl	θʃ	θɹ	θj	θk	θh
n	nm	np	nw	nf	nθ	nn	nt	ns	nl	nʃ	nɹ	nj	nk	nh
t	tm	tp	tw	tf	tθ	tn	tt	ts	tl	tʃ	tɹ	tj	tk	th
s	sm	sp	sw	sf	sθ	sn	st	ss	sl	sʃ	sɹ	sj	sk	sh
l	lm	lp	lw	lf	lθ	ln	lt	ls	ll	lʃ	lɹ	lj	lk	lh
ʃ	ʃm	ʃp	ʃw	ʃf	ʃθ	ʃn	ʃt	ʃs	ʃl	ʃʃ	ʃɹ	ʃj	ʃk	ʃh
k	km	kp	kw	kf	kθ	kn	kt	ks	kl	kʃ	kɹ	kj	kk	kh
ŋ	ŋm	ŋp	ŋw	ŋf	ŋθ	ŋn	ŋt	ŋs	ŋl	ŋʃ	ŋɹ	ŋj	ŋk	ŋh

taining labial or labio-dental plus [w] the *rounding* of the lips present in [w] gets partly anticipated in the preceding [p], [b], [f] or [v], and this kind of 'accommodation' (see below) is characteristic of contiguous sequences. Note, further, that sequences [s] and [t]/[d], [n], [l] are treated as homorganic. On the whole this is reasonable, though for some speakers with very markedly lamino- [s]/[z] and markedly *apico-* [t]/[d], [n], [l] such sequences would be, more properly, contiguous.

Examples of these various English sequence types are the following:

Homorganic

identical	[pp] as in *top part*, [ʃʃ] *fish shop*
with phonation change	[dt] *bad time*, [θð] *both these*
with stricture change	[zd] *these days*, [ts] *that sack*
with airpath change	[ŋg] *anger*, [dl] *bad leg*
with voice and stricture change	[sl] *this lot*, [ds] *dead centre*

Contiguous

same phonation	[pf] as in *top four*, [θs] *both sexes*
with phonation change	[fw] *tough woman*, [sr] *this range*
with stricture change	[tʃ] *that shop*, [ðl] *breathe less*
with voice and stricture change	[bf] *ebb furiously*, [ʒt] *rouge tops*

Heterorganic

[mt] *them too,* [pt] *stop two,* [ft] *muff two,* [tp] *cutpurse,* [tk] *Atkins,* [ʃf] *push four,* [ʃk] *push cups,* [kp] *back part,* [nk] *ten kings,* and so on

Having considered the various types of consonant sequence in terms of the similarity relationships between the segments involved, we can now go on to discuss the difference between *open* and *close* transition.

In *open* transition, there is always a momentary, minimal, break of articulatory continuity between the successive segments. In *close* transition there is no such break. The characteristics of the two types of transition can best be summed up by a table such as the following, which shows these characteristics in relation to the three sequence types that have just been discussed.

sequence type	*open transition*	*close transition*
Homorganic	articulatory non-continuity	articulatory *continuity*
Heterorganic	no overlap	articulatory *overlap*
Contiguous	no accommodation	articulatory *accommodation*

All these types of transition can be illustrated from English, which makes phonological (linguistically significant) use of the distinction between close and open transition: compare, for instance, the sequence [kp] in *take the back part* [kp]—close transition, and *take the back apart* [k · p]—open transition. For a description of English phonology that shows how the opposition between close and open transition fits into the total picture see Catford (1966).

In *homorganic close transition* there is absolute continuity of the articulatory stricture. In examples such as *top part* [pp], *that time* [tt], *these zeros* [zz], *this sort* [ss], *glove fair* [vf] the articulators retain the identical position throughout, whether there is a change in phonation-type or not.

In *homorganic open transition,* on the other hand, the transition is marked by a momentary relaxation of the articulatory stricture followed by a renewed tensing into the former position. Indicating the open transition by a raised dot [·] we may illustrate with the following examples, which are in minimal, or near-minimal contrast with the examples of close transition just given: *top apart* [p · p], *that attire* [t · t], *this assortment* [s · s], *these azaleas* [z · z], *brief affair* [f · f], *love affair* [v · f].

The similarities and differences between the two types of transition can be demonstrated first with the last example. In *glove fair* (presumably a special sale of gloves), it is clear that the (inner part of the)

lower lip remains steadily and unmovingly in contact with the upper teeth throughout the sequence [vf]—the only change being the switch-over from voiced to voiceless phonation in the middle of the articulation. In *love affair,* on the other hand, the sequence [v · f] is characterized by a momentary relaxation of the articulatory stricture right in the middle. The lower lip moves very slightly downwards, so that the labio-dental fricative [v]-stricture momentarily opens up into a slightly wider channel, resembling that of the labio-dental approximant [ʋ]. The pronunciation of *love affair* may thus be fairly accurately represented as ['lʌvʋ'fɛɐ] as opposed to *glove fair* ['glʌv'fɛɐ].

Other good pairs for careful comparison are [zz]/[z · z] *these zeros/these azaleas,* [pp]/[p · p] *top part/top apart.* In *these zeros* ['ði · z'ziəɹəɷz] there is a continuously maintained apico-lamino-alveolar fricative articulation throughout [zz]. In *these azaleas,* however, there is a momentary relaxation of this articulation, with a momentary widening of the channel to that of an apico-lamino-alveolar approximant. There is no special symbol for this, but we can indicate it by using the 'widening diacritic', as in [z̦]. *These azaleas* is thus pronounced ['ði · zz̦'zɛ˕ɩljəz] as opposed to *these zeros* ['ði · z'zɩəɹəɷz]. In the sequence [pp] in *top part* the bilabial stop articulation is maintained without break throughout. In *top apart,* on the other hand, the bilabial articulation in [p · p] is momentarily relaxed, so that the lips very briefly break away from each other in the centre forming a momentary channel of bilabial fricative or approximant type. We might thus accurately transcribe *top apart* as ['tʰɒpɸ'pα̈ · tʰ] as opposed to *top part* [tʰɒppα̈ · tʰ].

We must carefully note the difference between the minimal articulatory opening that occurs in simple open transition, with the much wider opening that occurs when a full vowel (and not merely a vowel-less transition) occurs between the consonants. Thus we can compare the open transition [ʋ] of *love affair* ['lʌvʋ'fɛɐ] with the full vowel of *lover fair* (as in 'Was her lover fair?') ['lʌvɐ · 'fɛɐ]. Measurements made on a high-speed ciné film of *take the cop part, take the cop apart, take the copper part,* and *take the cop up, Art,* gave the following results: For [pp] in *cop part,* no movement of lips; for [p · p] in *cop apart* a momentary opening up of a central articulatory channel, with a total duration of 60 ms and reaching a maximum labial channel area of only 20 mm^2, which is just on the borderline between the typical channel areas of fricatives and approximants (Chapter 7, figure 2). For the other two, *copper part* [pɐ · p] and *cop up, Art* [pʌp] the durations were of 160 and 150 ms, and the labial channel areas of the order of 250 and 220 mm^2 respectively.

In *heterorganic close transition* there is no articulatory continuity, but there is articulatory *overlap.* That is to say, the articulatory stricture for the second consonant is formed before the stricture for the first is released. English examples are [kp] in *back part,* [tp] in *cutpurse,* [tk] in *Atkins,* [zf] in *these fairs,* and so on.

In all such cases, the second articulation is formed well before the first is released, as indicated by this diagram for *back part:*

In the Phonetics Laboratory at the University of Michigan, using the technique known as 'continuous palatography', with electrodes inserted in a false palate, so that whenever and wherever the tongue makes or breaks contact with the roof of the mouth can be recorded, we have measured the articulatory overlap occurring in such English utterances as: *cutpurse* [tp], *Atkins* [tk], *actor, acting* [kt], *pulp, help* [lp], *apply* [pl], *clay* [kl].

In such examples, the duration of the overlap is from 29 per cent to 45 per cent (with a mean of 33·75 per cent) of the combined duration of the two consonants. In other words, in the [kt] of a word like *actor,* the velar stop articulation of [k] and the alveolar stop articulation of [t] co-occur during about half of the duration of each of them, and this amount of overlap seems to be normal in English heterorganic close transitions.

In *heterorganic open transition,* illustrated by *back apart* [k·p], as opposed to *back part* [kp], *these affairs* [z·f] as opposed to *these fairs* [zf], *Parade St.* [p·ɹ] as opposed to *Praed St.* [pɹ], *palatial* [p·l] as opposed to *play* [pl], and so on, there is no articulatory overlap. The articulators are probably in the process of coming together for the second consonant during the release of the first, but actual overlap is avoided so that there is a quite momentary vowel-like, approximant-like, or fricative-like gap between the two articulations. One noticeable difference between such close and open transitions is that in such pairs as [pl] and [p·l], [pɹ] and [p·ɹ], the overlapping [l] or [ɹ] in *close* transition starts off voiceless, because the aspiration of the [pʰ] is carried on into it. In *open* transition, the aspiration may have, so to speak, 'blown itself out' before the [l] or [ɹ] articulation is fully formed. Thus, while *play* and *Praed* may be rather accurately represented as [pl̥lɛ˔ɪ̆], [pɹ̥ɹɛ˔ɪ̆d], *palatial* and *Parade* with open transition [p · l] and [p · ɹ] might be represented as [pʰˈlɛ˔ɪ̆ʃᵊɫ], [pʰˈɹɛ˔ɪ̆d].

As indicated here, it is not uncommon for open transition between voiceless consonants to be itself fully, or partially voiceless, and this, together with extreme shortness, and absolutely minimal channel opening, differentiates mere open transition between consonants from the occurrence of a vowel between the consonants. Thus, compare [kp] in *back part,* [k·p] in *back apart,* and [k + vowel + p] in *backer part* or *back up, Art*:

back part ['bæk˺'pʰɑ̈·tʰ] (in which [˺] indicates the inaudible release of the overlapping k)
back apart ['bækh 'pʰɑ̈·tʰ] or ['bækx 'pʰɑ̈·tʰ]
backer part ['bækʻɐ·'pʰɑ̈·tʰ]
back up, Art ['bækʻʌp 'ɑ̈·tʰ]

In *contiguous close transition* the characteristic phenomenon is one of articulatory *accommodation.* The successive contiguous articulations are, so to speak, knit closely together by one or other of two types of accommodation, either shift or gliding.

Accommodation of *shift* type occurs, for example, in the close transition [kj] in *back yard,* here the velar articulation of [k] is accommodated, by a forward shift, to the contiguous palatal articulation of [j], so that the sequence is pronounced [k̡j], with palatalized [k̡] substituted for velar [k]. Another example of the shift type of accommodation may be seen in the contiguous sequence [tθ], as in *eight things,* or *eighth.* Here, the apico-alveolar stop [t] may be shifted forwards to accommodate to the contiguous apico-dental fricative [θ], so that the sequence is pronounced [t̪θ], with dental [t̪] substituted for alveolar [t].

Accommodation of *gliding* type more commonly occurs in, for instance, the initial [tɹ] of *train.* Here, the apex of the tongue goes up to touch the forepart of the alveolar ridge as if for the apico-alveolar stop [t]. It never actually stops there, however, but immediately on touching the alveolar ridge it begins to slide, or glide backwards, stroking the alveolar ridge as it does so, to the apico-postalveolar position of [ɹ]. The representation [tɹ] is thus something analogous to the representation of a gliding diphthong, indicating starting point and finishing point, between which there is continuous articulatory movement. Incidentally, since the [ɹ] in such cases of close transition from contiguous [t] is partially voiceless, in a detailed transcription we must represent *train* as [tɹ̥ɹɛ˔ɩn]. Another example of gliding close transition between contiguous articulations is furnished by [sʃ] in *this shop* (contrasted with *fish shop* [ʃʃ]), as in *This shop's a fish shop*). Some English phoneticians have represented the [s] of *this shop* as [ʃ], implying a complete shift of articulation, as though a full *lamino-postalveolar* articulation—identical to that of the second consonant—were substituted for the *apicolamino-alveolar* articulation of [s]. It is doubtful if this commonly occurs. What certainly occurs in my own pronunciation is *gliding accommodation* of [s] to the following [ʃ]. This gliding accommodation manifests itself in two ways: (1) the apex and blade of the tongue go up to the forepart of the alveolar ridge as though to form an [s], but they begin immediately to slide back towards the postalveolar position for [ʃ], and (2) the lips, which are unrounded for [s], but require open rounding for [ʃ], are unrounded at the beginning of [s], but become progressively more rounded while the tongue is sliding backwards towards [ʃ], so that when [ʃ] is reached they are in the requisite rounded position.

If *this shop*, with [sʃ] is compared with *fish shop*, with [ʃʃ] the distinction is clear. In [ʃʃ] the tongue goes directly to the [ʃ]-position and stays there immoveable throughout the whole homorganic sequence, and the lip rounding for [ʃ] starts to come on during the preceding vowel, and stays there immoveable during the whole homorganic sequence. By contrast, the gliding accommodation of tongue and lip articulation in the contiguous sequence [sʃ] can be clearly observed.

In *contiguous open transition* there is no accommodation at all. The articulations merely follow one another with a minimal opening up of articulators between them.

In *back a yard* with [k·j] as opposed to *backyard* with [k̟j], there is a normal dorso-velar closure for the [k], a minimal opening during which the tongue shifts forward, followed by the dorso-palatal articulation of [j].

In *eight Athenians* with [t·θ] as opposed to *eight things* with [t̪θ], there is a normal English [t] with apico-alveolar articulation, followed by a momentary opening (to something like an alveolar approximant [z̹]), followed in turn by a new dental fricative articulation: the two utterances may be transcribed:

eight things	tθ	[ˈɛ˕ɪ̆t̪ ˈθɪŋz]
eight Athenians	t·θ	[ˈɛ˕ɪ̆tz̹ ˈθi·nɪənz]

In *terrain*, with [t·ɹ] as opposed to *train* with [tɹ] there is, again, a normal static apico-alveolar [t] articulation. The tongue tip momentarily *detaches* from the alveolar ridge then goes up again after the shortest possible interval to make contact with the extreme back of the alveolar ridge for the post-alveolar approximant [ɹ].

Finally, in *this a shop* (as in *Call this a shop*!), with [s·ʃ] as opposed to [sʃ] in *this shop*, there is, once again, a clear 're-articulation'. The apicolamino-alveolar [s] is formed, then the tongue relaxes and 'backs off' a very little from the alveolar ridge (perhaps merely to an approximant channel position) and then comes back to form the lamino-postalveolar channel for [ʃ].

We have seen that in cases of close transition between contiguous articulations accommodation takes place. This articulatory accommodation is a particular case of the more general phenomenon known as *assimilation,* the process by which one or both of two successive segments become more like the other. In our contiguous examples we were concerned only with close transition, and only with certain types of accommodation of articulatory location (shifting and gliding), and to some extent accommodation of stricture-type—for example, the anticipatory lateral articulatory tensing that may occur in a central affricate sequence, as described above. Other types of assimilation may occur, particularly of phonation type. We have, in fact, seen how something of this sort occurs in the heterorganic, overlapping, sequences [pl, kl] in English, where immediately after the release of the stop closure, the [l] is momentarily voiceless. The assimilation in this case operates, as it were, forwards—from left to right in terms of normal transcription. The preceding segment affects the succeeding one: this is called 'progressive' assimilation. Assimilation of voicing operating in the opposite direction ('regressive') is common in French, in such sequences as *bec de gaz* pronounced [bɛgdəgaz], with voiced [g] in *bec* under the influence of the following [d]. This particular assimilation may take place right across an open transition, since consonantal transitions in French are indifferently of close or open type.

Some, particularly British phoneticians make a sharp distinction between assimilation and *similitude.* The latter term, first used by Daniel Jones in the third edition of his *Outline of English Phonetics* in 1932, is applied to what we may call 'permanent' accommodations, since they involve sequences of segments that are permanently adjacent in a language: thus the partial devoicing of [l] in English *play* would be called a *similitude* because [p] and [l] in this word are in a kind of permanent association. On the other hand, the articulatory perturbation of [s] in *this shop* would be called a 'juxtapositional assimilation' because here the peculiar effect upon the articulation of [s] is observable only in the particular case when this [s] is followed by a [ʃ]. The whole question of assimilation is discussed at length in Abercrombie (1967, pp. 133–9) and, with numerous examples, in Grammont (1933, pp. 185–228), so need not be further considered here.

Before we leave the subject of consonantal sequences we should perhaps mention once again that, from a general phonetic (anthropophonic) point of view, there is no difference between an affricate and a close-transition sequence of stop plus homorganic or contiguous fricative. Much has sometimes been made of the fact that affricates are a 'special type' of stop, with a kind of 'slow release' of the stop stricture. There is, however, no essential articulatory difference between the English sequence [t + ʃ] in *that shop*, and the so-called affricate in [tʃɒp]. In close transition the same articulatory accommodation occurs in both, and the only difference is that a syllable-division (diminution of initiator power) occurs between the segments in *that shop* but before them in *chop;* for a minimal contrast compare *courtship* and *core-chip*.

What has been said above about consonantal sequences is largely applicable to sequences involving both consonants and vowels. Such sequences may be homorganic, as would be, for instance [içi] [ɯkɯ] [uwu], or heterorganic, for example, [ipa] [apa] or, as is very often the case, contiguous, for example, [eke] [ata]. Heterorganic sequences of consonant and vowel exhibit articulatory overlaps similar to those of heterorganic consonant sequences, and contiguous sequences of consonant and vowel exhibit articulatory accommodations similar to those occurring between contiguous consonants. There is, apparently, some variation from one language to another with respect to the direction of such accommodations. For example, Gairdner (1925), still one of the leading authorities on Arabic phonetics, indicates that when the Arabic uvular stop [q] is in contact with a palatal (front) vowel, such as [i] [e], the vowel is modified either by being somewhat centralized or by developing an [ə]- or [ɯ]-like glide between the [q] and the vowel, the [q] remaining uvular. On the other hand, Zhghent'i (1956) presents X-ray tracings showing how the Georgian uvular [q'] has its articulation shifted forwards somewhat before [i]. In general, it has long been known to phoneticians that the precise location of the articulation of consonants is affected by the articulations of the vowels that precede and follow them, and upon which they may be regarded as superimposed. Recent studies of Öhman (1967) and Perkell (1969) provide some useful instrumental confirmation of this well-known fact.

Segmentation

So far in this chapter we have referred rather frequently to 'sequences of segments', without having said much about the actual problem of segmentation of the chain of speech. Throughout this book, we have presented the speech process as a complex event consisting of more or less constantly varying states, or 'values', of a number of parameters or ranges of conditions of co-occurring components of the speech event. At the beginning of this chapter we mentioned, in passing, that there are moments of rapid change, which define for us, or tend to define for us, the limits of successive segments. We must now examine the identification of segments in more detail. These 'moments of rapid change' are changes occurring in any one, or more, of the co-occurrent component parameters, and we must look at these. The production of such a word as *stand* [stʰææ̃ndd̥ʰ]

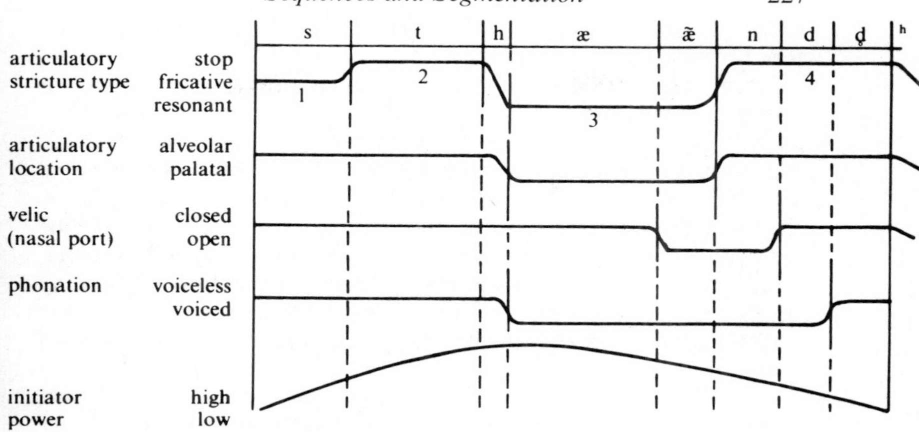

Figure 60. The segmentation of the word *stand*

may be diagrammatically illustrated as in figure 60. Here, changing values are indicated for a number of parameters.

If we follow the line representing values along the parameter of *oral articulatory stricture type* we have the value 'fricative' for a time, then there is a sudden shift to *stop,* followed by a sudden switch to *resonant,* and later back to *stop* (since the oral stricture of [n] is, of course, of stop type). As a result of the changes mentioned here, the parameter of stricture-type throughout this utterance is divided into four (numbered) parts, or four *spans,* as we shall call them, of relatively steady state, separated by three fairly rapid *transitions* from one state to the next.

For the parameter of *articulatory location* only two states are designated, namely *alveolar* (short for apicolamino-alveolar) and *palatal* (short for dorso-palatal). Each of these, of course, is a short-hand description of a tongue posture. It will be observed that in this case there are only three spans, the first stretching across two spans of stricture-type.

The parameter of state of the velic or nasal port has two values, *closed* and *open* and it can be seen that there is one short span of *open,* the start of which does not correspond to the start of any other span.

The phonation parameter again breaks down into three spans, a *voiceless* one, a *voiced* one starting almost immediately after the release of the [t], which, being preceded by [s], has minimal aspiration, and ending with a renewed short span of *voicelessness.* These spans are not quite co-extensive with any other spans.

Finally, there is a single pulse of the pulmonic initiator, a single rising–falling curve of initiator power, constituting a single span of initiatory activity.

Each change in the state of any one parameter is, of course, a change in the whole sound-productive event. Consequently, each such change defines the limits not only of one componential or parametric span, but also of a whole segment. On this basis, then, in *stand* we recognize eight segments, [s, t, ʰ, æ, æ̃, n, d, d̥], or nine, if we count the releasing [ʰ] at the end of the utterance. It is perfectly possible to perceive all these segments, auditorily or kinaesthetically, if one tries. Without giving special attention to what is going on, however, one may observe only five segments, [s, t, æ, n, d], these segments corresponding to so many minimal linear phonological units, or phonemes, of English.

From a purely phonetic point of view, then, we may define a segment as a stretch of speech marked off by divisions between componential spans—that is, as a period of relatively steady state in all components, bounded by moments of rapid change in the state of at least one of the components. This definition is quite useful, but it fails to explain why we readily perceive essentially momentary articulations (such as flaps and semivowels) as segments. In general, we have no difficulty in perceiving, for example, [ɾ] in British RP *berry* ['bɛɾɩ], American *Betty* ['bɛɾɩ], or [w] in *away* [ə'weɩ] as a segment, even though in each case there is no, or virtually no 'steady state' but merely a rapid glide to and from ('on-glide' and 'off-glide') an articulatory position. There are no doubt two reasons for our easy perception of [ɾ, w], and so on, as glides. The first, and rather obvious one, is that they operate as unit-phonemes in English phonology. The second, and phonetically more interesting reason, is that we are accustomed to perceive as segments all articulatory postures (or quasi-postures) flanked by an approaching transition (on-glide) and a departing transition (off-glide): and this still holds good even when the intervening quasi steady-state is reduced to zero.

In the recordings made in instrumental phonetics some types of segments are more difficult to delimit than others: this is particularly the case with semivowels like [w] and [j]. In an acoustic spectrogram, for instance, such sounds may appear as a very noticeable gliding shift of formants from a preceding location to an extreme position, then back again, with virtually no steady-state at all—merely a reversal of direction of formant-shift at the extreme point. In such a case, all we can do is to make an arbitrary decision: for instance, the duration of the semivowel is to be measured from the half-way point in the on-glide to the half-way point in the off-glide.

We have been discussing here the theoretical, perceptual, and instrumental segmentation of speech. Any linguistic phonetician must be aware of these problems when he is analysing utterances in real languages. But, in addition to this, the ability to take one's own utterances and to perform, as it were, a practical segmentation on their production is a useful phonetic skill. This skill is often called *isolation*—the ability to say a word or sentence, and then to pick out of it a single segment, and to utter that in a manner as nearly as possible identical to the form it had in the original utterance. In this way, the isolated segment becomes more readily available for introspective analysis.

The technique is to say a word containing the required segment again and again, in as natural a way as possible, and taking care to pronounce it in as nearly as possible the same way each time. At each repetition, one 'drops off' a little of the word, at first articulating it silently, then merely imagining it. Thus one might isolate first the initial, then the final [s] in *sauce* [sɔːs] for the purpose of comparing them. To do this, one says [sɔːs] a number of times, then, taking care to keep the pronunciation as nearly identical as possible, [sɔː], then [s(ɔː)] with merely imaginary [ɔː], ending up with an isolated initial [s-]; again, by dropping off the initial parts, saying [sɔːs] [ɔːs.] [(ɔː)s] one arrives at an isolated final [-s]. One can then compare them, noting the increasing air-flow in initial [s-] and the abrupt release of the stricture as the jaw drops for the 'imaginary' following [ɔː], and, on the other hand, the decreasing air-flow in final [-s] and the absence of an abrupt release of the stricture.

The reader should practise isolating and introspectively analysing all manner of sounds: for example, the [k] of *call* and the [k̡] of *key*, the stressed vowel of the first syllable of *city* and the unstressed vowel of its second syllable, the initial and final [l]-sounds of *lull*, and so forth. Not only is this a powerful technique for introspective analysis, it is also a valuable technique for use in learning and teaching the sounds of foreign languages. The language teacher must, when necessary, be able to pronounce any sound of the language he is teaching in isolation, but as nearly identically as can be to the way he pronounces it in context.

TWELVE

Instrumental Phonetics

Although this book is not a laboratory phonetics manual, it nevertheless seems desirable to review some of the techniques available for the study of speech in the laboratory. The reader will undoubtedly be reading works that make use of the findings of instrumental phonetics, and he may himself wish to take some of his linguistic phonetic problems into the laboratory. For this latter purpose, the present chapter may be useful as a kind of check-list of laboratory techniques.

The techniques and the instruments used in laboratory research in phonetics can be classified in several different ways. Among these are the following: function in relation to *research strategy,* in relation to *phases of the speech process,* and in relation to particular *linguistic problems.*

In relation to research strategy, instrumentation and techniques can be placed under five headings: (1) speech recording/playback, (2) data recording, storage, and retrieval, (3) data processing and analysis, (4) data display, and (5) simulation.

Speech Recording/Playback

Nearly all phonetic research involves recording and listening to speech, and conventional tape recorders have many functions. They enable the investigator to keep a record of experiments and they record data in a convenient form for later processing. The beginner in phonetic research must, however, be cautioned against excessive use of tape recordings. It must never be forgotten that tape recordings in themselves are practically useless for scientific linguistic purposes: to be useful they must be transcribed and, where the purpose of the research is a phonetic one, transcribed by a competent phonetician. Even so, it must be remembered that transcriptions made solely from tape recordings alone are always to some degree suspect. There is no substitute for face-to-face transcription from the informant in the field. On tape, some data are always irretrievably lost, most obviously, of course, visual data. It is often extremely difficult, for instance, to tell whether a certain vowel is, say, a front rounded [ø] or a back unrounded [ɤ], unless one can see the informant. Phoneticians rely heavily on visual cues in making transcriptions. Beginners in phonetics sometimes imagine they can escape the task of field analysis and transcription, or perhaps conceal their incompetence, by making tape recordings in the field and taking them back to the laboratory for instrumental analysis. They are deluding themselves. There is no instrument in existence which can identify and analyse exotic sounds as well as a competent phonetician face to face with the informant. Moreover, it must be remembered that transcription from tape takes time. Depending on the difficulty of the material, the speed of utterance, and the degree of accurate detail that is sought, the process of transcribing takes from about ten to forty times the duration of the actual recorded material: that is, every hour's worth of tape takes from ten to forty hours to transcribe. A great amount of valuable data lies locked up in the tape libraries of the world because no one has had the time or energy to transcribe it.

Having sounded these strong cautions against the excessive and over-optimistic use of tape recordings we must nevertheless repeat that tapes are a virtually indispensable part of almost any phonetic research.

In addition to a high-quality fixed tape recorder, in a sound-insulated studio, a good portable tape recorder is obviously an essential piece of equipment for phonetic research. If one is making expeditions to remote places, clearly a battery-operated machine is essential.

Multi-track tape recorders are valuable for the recording and storage of several simultaneous signals, for example, recorded dialogue, plus comments or descriptions of the situation, on a second track; for the superimposition of clicks or other sounds at pre-determined points; for certain listening experiments, and so on.

A tape-loop repeater system is a valuable aid to the detailed transcription of tapes. It is even more valuable if fitted with a reversible loop for listening to recordings played backwards. This is often a considerable help in transcription, particularly for the identification of such things as the starting and finishing points of diphthongs, and intonations.

Some form of speech-stretcher that permits playback at reduced speed with minimal distortion is a useful aid to listening. 'Stretched' speech can also be used as an accompaniment to slow-motion films of movements of the organs of speech, for teaching purposes.

Finally, taped-card recorders, such as the Bell and Howell 'Language Master' provide easily accessible storage of recorded utterances: each card has a short stretch of tape on it, on which a few seconds of speech can be recorded while a transcription and other data can be recorded on the card. The cards, with their recorded speech and transcriptions, can be filed and stored.

Data Recording, Storage, and Retrieval

In addition to its obvious speech-recording function magnetic tape-recorders can, of course, record any signals within their frequency range, and can thus often be used for general data recording and storage.

Other data recording techniques include *photography* (particularly immediately available Polaroid) and *cine-photography*, and various types of graphic recorder. These latter all involve a device which drives a strip of paper past a recording point at variable speeds, and include those in which the recording point is a pen (as in the Sanborne), or a jet of ink (which gives a faster response), as in the Oscillomink, or a beam of light (faster still) as in the Visicorder.

All recording devices provide also for storage and retrieval of data. Graphic recorders have the advantage over magnetic tape in that the data are simultaneously restored and also are immediately available for inspection and measurement. Other data-storage devices include punch-cards and punched tape, both of which require special punching and retrieval equipment.

Data Processing and Analysis

This includes the simple, but time-consuming process of *tape-splicing,* often useful in preparing various types of listening experiment. Various acoustic analysis devices such as the sound-spectrograph and fundamental frequency recorders (both referred to below) are used for the processing of data stored on tape. Almost infinitely sophisticated possibilities of processing data are now provided by computers: suitable programmes enable us not merely to store the data of natural speech, but to analyse it in many ways and to incorporate any desired modification. On this see O'Malley and Kloker (1972).

Data Display

Real-time display of speech data is useful in teaching, and also in monitoring ongoing experiments. Display instruments include such things as the following: the Cathode-ray oscilloscope, in which an electron beam is projected onto a fluorescent screen (as in a TV set). Where the beam strikes the screen a spot of light appears. A fluctuating electrical voltage deflects the spot vertically, and the electron beam itself can be made to sweep with great rapidity from one side to the other. The vertical deflections then appear as the vertical component of a wave-form visible on the screen. The fluctuating voltage, which causes the vertical deflections, may itself be the output of any of a number of devices, such as an air-pressure transducer, or a fundamental frequency analyser, and the oscilloscope screen presents an immediate, real-time picture of the particular time-varying pattern. This display can, of course, be photographed for permanent storage.

Other types of real-time display are those provided by, for instance, a continuous spectrograph, which gives a continuous and continually varying presentation of the distribution of acoustic energy over the frequency range; see the brief description of the sound-spectrograph below.

Yet another type of real-time display is one that presents an enlarged diagram of the roof of the mouth, with small light-bulbs on it lighting up to show the location of contacts between tongue and palate in one form of continuous palatography.

Simulation

Finally, simulation is a technique which has several uses. The most common types of simulation are those which involve the *synthesis* of speech. In theory, simulated or synthetic speech can break into the phases of speech at several points. For example, Ladefoged (1964a) has proposed a simulation technique for investigating vocal-tract muscle-action by constructing a replica of the tract, made of materials with mechanical properties similar to those of skin, muscle, bone and cartilage. By studying the forces that have to be applied to the replica to simulate speech-producing movements one could learn a great deal about the organic phase of speech.

Various types of simulation of the organic and aerodynamic phases have been tried. Humboldt, for instance, produced a speaking automaton, and more recently, Sir Richard Paget synthesized speech with bellows and plasticine models of the mouth. However, most simulation of speech at the present day cuts into the speech process at the acoustic phase, sometimes, indeed, using an acoustic vocal-tract model, but more often than not speech synthesis takes up the simulation at a purely acoustic level, with some form of acoustic parametric synthesizer.

Simulated speech can often be used with value in experiments on the perception of speech where it is desirable to introduce precisely controlled variations such as cannot well be introduced into natural speech. It is, however, now possible, using computer techniques, to take recorded natural speech and to introduce controlled modifications into it for experimental purposes.

Another aspect of simulation is that concerned with speech recognition. This is a simulation of the perceptual phase of speech. Most attempts at automatic speech recognition have utilized only the acoustic phase of speech. This has, as yet, not been very successful, and it is certainly worth considering whether automatic speech recognition would not be more successful if it utilized other forms of data as well. The human listener to speech, under normal daylight conditions, certainly uses visual as well as auditory clues, and probably identifies heard speech to a large extent on the basis of a kind of empathic immediate awareness of the motor processes of speech production, based on quite scanty auditory clues. This kind of 'empathic' awareness cannot be duplicated in a machine; but it would certainly be possible to develop a machine that would pick up aerodynamic and other kinds of articulatory information as additional clues to speech recognition. A start was made in the development of an aerodynamic sensing device as part of such a system some years ago at the University of Michigan Center for Research on Language and Language Behaviour (see below, and Catford et al. 1968).

Perhaps a more useful way of organizing our discussion of instrumental techniques for a book on general phonetics is in terms of the various phases of the speech process. In this section, then, we will systematically look at the kinds of experimental technique available for the study of each of the several phases of speech production.

It should be said that since all the various phases of the speech process are causally related we can, and sometimes must, obtain information about one phase by inference from a preceding or following one. For instance, we can investigate the action of whole muscles chiefly by investigating the neuro-electrical activity in individual motor units (see below) that results in whole muscle contractions, or by observing the movements of whole organs that result from muscle contraction. Certain aspects of the organic phase of speech can be most easily investigated by inference from the aerodynamic or acoustic phases. Finally, the perceptual phases of speech, which cannot easily be investigated directly, can often be studied inferentially through investigation of the acoustic phase, or of relations between this phase and the hearer's response.

Neuromuscular Phase

It will be remembered that this phase involves the transmission of nerve impulses along efferent, or motor nerves from the speaker's brain to the muscles. Each motor nerve cell has associated with it a number of muscle fibres, from about 100 in the smallest muscles up to nearly 2000 in large limb muscles. A single nerve cell, plus the group of muscle fibres associated with it, is called a 'motor unit'. When a muscle cell is at rest there is a difference of electrical potential between the interior and the exterior of the cell. When a nerve impulse reaches the junction between the motor nerve and the muscle a chemical reaction occurs, as a result of which the properties of the muscle cell's outer membrane changes: the cell releases its electrical charge and the muscle fibre contracts. This process is called the *firing of a motor unit*, and the change in electrical potential that occurs is called an *action potential.*

It is possible to register the minute electrical changes, the action potentials, which mark the firing of a motor unit, by means of an electrode placed close to the motor unit. This will record the potentials being conducted through the surrounding tissue, with reference to a second electrode placed further away from the source of the potentials.

The process of recording the action potentials associated with the firing of motor units is known as *electromyography*. The electrodes used in EMG can either be placed on the surface of the skin immediately over the muscle to be investigated (surface electrode), or else inserted, in the form of a needle, into the muscle itself (needle electrode). Needle electrodes have the advantage, at least when dealing with deep-seated muscles, that they pick up stronger signals, and are more likely to register the action potentials resulting from the firing of a single motor unit, or a small group. The action potentials picked up by EMG must be amplified, and can be averaged, or processed in other ways, by computer. The best general description of the EMG technique applied to speech is that of Fromkin (1965).

Other possible techniques for studying the neuromuscular phase of speech include the electrical stimulation of nerves or of cortical projection areas, which can be carried out in the course of brain operations. The selective blocking of motor nerves by anaesthesia is another technique, which has been little used.

Organic Phase

The single technique of EMG, which we have briefly described, can be used with only minor variations for the investigation of the activity of any of the sixty or seventy muscles whose contractions are most important in the production of speech. The successive or simultaneous contraction of these muscles sets in motion the six or seven distinct movable organs of speech. These, unlike the motor units, are accessible to different types of investigation according to where they are located. For the discussion of techniques of investigating the organic phase we therefore proceed topographically, starting with the lungs and moving upwards.

Movements of the thoracic cavity can be studied by X-ray cinephotography (cineradiography). More commonly, however, we study thoracic movements and changes of lung volume in other ways. These include *pneumography,* a technique (or several techniques) whereby changes in the circumference of the chest are recorded by placing some form of belt or belts around the chest, registering variations in the tension or stretch of these by any suitable recording device. A more elaborate technique is *plethysmography*. This involves placing the subject in a tank, with his head protruding through an opening which is hermetically sealed at the neck, somewhat after the manner of an 'iron lung'. As the subject's chest expands and contracts air is driven out of and into the tank. The volume of air thus displaced can be measured by a spirometer (see below, and cf. Draper, Ladefoged and Whitteridge 1960); or, the volume-velocity of air-flow out of or into the tank can be measured by some form of air-flow transducer, as in the experiments by Catford and Beresford, referred to in Chapter 5. This latter technique gives an approximate indication of the rate of lung-volume change, which corresponds to initiator velocity in sounds with pulmonic initiation.

More often than not, we investigate movements of the thoracic cage and changes in lung volume indirectly, by inference from aerodynamic measurements.

The gross movements of the larynx, and the activity of organs within the larynx can be investigated in a number of ways. Vertical larynx displacements, which are relevant to glottalic initiation, to pressure regulation in voiced phonation, and to the fundamental frequency of voice, can be recorded by cinephotography, or by an instrument called a *cricothyrometer,* which, through a telescopic arm, tracks vertical movements of the larynx; see Vanderslice (1967).

Various aspects of the activity of the larynx cartilages can be studied by *transverse cineradiography*: this can be used to show the relative tilt of the thyroid and cricoid cartilages, movements of the arytenoid cartilages, of the epiglottis, and so on. *Frontal tomography* can indicate the degree of approximation of the vocal folds and their cross-sectional shape; see, for example, the studies of Hollien and others (1960).

Other methods of observing the state of the glottis and the activities of the vocal folds are *laryngoscopy* and *glottography*. Laryngoscopy involves direct inspection, or photography of the glottis from above. The older method of doing this is by placing a sloping mirror against the soft palate, using it simultaneously to reflect light down to the glottis and to reflect the glottal image back to the eye, or camera lens. A more modern technique involves the insertion of optical fibres through the nose and into the pharynx. These, like the old laryngoscopy mirror, can be used both to carry light down to the glottis and the image of the glottis up to the experimenter's eye, or camera. They have the advantage over the old laryngoscope mirror that they scarcely interfere with normal speech. In either case, stroboscopy can be used to create the illusion of rest for the still photography of various phases of the cycle of glottal movement in voicing, or else high-speed cinephotography can be used to record details of this cycle. Incidentally, the recording of vocal-fold movements in voicing is the only type of phonetic research which necessitates ultra-high-speed cinephotography, of the order of 1000 frames per second or more. For all other uses, a speed of about 100 frames per second is fast enough.

The second group of techniques for investigating states of the glottis is known as glottography. Here there are two kinds of technique. The first of these, *electroglottography*, is a means of recording movements of the vocal folds by recording the varying impedance offered to a weak high-frequency current passed across the glottis from one side to the other. The second technique is known as *photoelectric glottography*, or 'transillumination of the glottis'. Techniques vary in detail, but all involve passing light upwards or downwards through the glottis and converting the variations of light intensity resulting from variations of the glottal area, into a varying voltage. For details see Ohala (1966).

Information about vocal-fold activities can also be obtained indirectly by aerodynamic and acoustic techniques. Thus, variations in the recorded volume-velocity of air-flow through the glottis, for a constant acoustic intensity, may indicate the degree to which the glottal closure is absolute during the closed phase of the glottal cycle.

The next part of the vocal tract to be considered is that which lies immediately above the larynx, namely the pharynx. The pharynx is accessible, of course, to radiography and, in a certain degree, to direct photography. Direct photography through the mouth can reveal folding of the back wall of the pharynx, approximation of the faucal pillars, and so on.

The position and movement of the soft palate or velum can be observed by (cine)radiography, or by *nasal endoscopy*—that is, by direct inspection of the position of the upper surface of the velum by means of an endoscope inserted into the nose. For most phonetic purposes, however, the most convenient method of observing the position of the soft palate is indirectly—by recording air-flow out of the nose.

Movements of the lower jaw are, of course, accessible to cinephotography as well as radiography, and can also be tracked by means of mechanical or optical recordings of jaw movements.

The tongue is one of the most versatile organs involved in the production of speech, and correspondingly presents some problems in the study of its movements and postures. With suitable illumination and the selection of a suitable angle, some information on tongue postures and on the oral articulatory channels formed by contact between tongue and roof of mouth can be obtained by direct photography.

Very valuable information on the areas of contact between the tongue and the roof of the mouth can be obtained by *palatography*. In its older form, palatography involved the construction of a thin, well-fitting, false palate. The false palate, usually dark coloured, is dusted with a white powder such as French chalk and then carefully inserted into the mouth. The subject then utters a sound or word, and carefully removes the false palate. Now, wherever the tongue has touched the roof of the mouth the chalk has been removed, and this 'wipe off' pattern can be drawn or photographed. Nowadays it is perhaps more unusual to employ *direct palatography* in which no false palate is used, but the roof of the mouth itself is sprayed with a dark powder. A sound or word is uttered, and then the open mouth is placed over a mirror and a photograph is taken, showing the area of 'wipe off'. Provided a suitable camera is available (a Polaroid camera is particularly useful) a palatography instrument—a *palatoscope*—can be constructed very cheaply.

Palatography is maximally informative only if a cast is made of the subject's palate, and an outline saggital section prepared. When the palatographic wipe-off is keyed to a palate section of this type, then palatography is one of the most informative of instrumental phonetic techniques. It can be even more valuable if each *palatogram,* as palatographic records are called, is accompanied by a *linguagram,* or photograph of the tongue, showing the parts of the tongue which have been coloured in the process of 'wiping-off' the dark powder from the roof of the mouth.

Continuous palatography is a technique for making continuous records of contacts between the tongue and the roof of the mouth. In this case, a false palate is used, with a number of electrodes embedded in it, plus a single electrode elsewhere, for example on the subject's arm. As the subject speaks, his tongue successively makes contact with varying palate electrodes. The output of each palate electrode may be displayed on a single channel of a multi-channel recording device, so that a continuous record of the varying tongue-palate contacts can be made. Or else they can be displayed on some form of screen or diagram representing the roof of the mouth. On this see Kydd and Belt (1964), Kozhevnikov and Chistovitch (1965), Fujimura et al. (1972).

Tongue positions of steady-state articulations can be recorded by still radiography. For 'natural' speech recording, cineradiography is necessary (at speeds of at least 50 to 100 frames per second). Since the tongue is less opaque to X-rays than the teeth and other surrounding bony structures, special means are usually necessary to make such films maximally useful. Coating the tongue surface with barium is only partly successful. The technique adopted by Houde (1968) is a useful one. This involves placing X-ray opaque markers at selected points on the tongue surface. Not only do these show up on X-ray films, but they can be used as reference points for measurements.

X-ray cinephotography of the tongue (or, indeed, of other organs) requires a variable-speed (down to single-frame) movie projector for subsequent study of data. Frame-by-frame tracing and measurement is laborious, and a technique for automation of this is required. A light-pen device, feeding data into a computer, would be a possible technique.

Another development is simultaneous playback of a slow-motion X-ray movie and a stretched magnetic tape recording of the utterance.

The lips are easily accessible to direct still and cinephotography, as well as to various types of mechanical or pneumatic recording.

Aerodynamic Phase

As we have seen earlier in this book, the postures and movements of the organs in the vocal tract do not of themselves generate sounds: they merely create the necessary aerodynamic conditions for this. Varying shapes of the oral cavity in vowels, for example, are, of course, responsible for differentiating different sounds. But the organic activity here does not *generate* sounds: it merely modulates sounds that are generated (aerodynamically) elsewhere, for example, by periodic release of high-velocity air-jets through the glottis (for voiced vowels), by continuous turbulent air-flow through the glottis (for whispered vowels), and so on. It is the air-flow itself, initiated and regulated by organic activities, that generates sounds. Consequently, the aerodynamic phase is an important link between the organic and acoustic phases of the speech process.

The *volume* of air used in speech can be measured by *spirometry*, that is, by the use of a spirometer. A commonly used kind of spirometer (Krogh type), involves an empty metal box into which air is led by a wide-bore tube from a mouthpiece. The box has a movable lid, the sides of which are rendered airtight by a water-seal, and counterbalanced so that extremely little force is required to move it. As air flows into the box, the lid is displaced, and a record of its displacement is made mechanically or electrically on a moving drum. By means of spirometry, one can measure the actual volume of air utilized by a speaker in any utterance. By fully emptying the lungs, and adding together this amount, the amount used in the actual utterance, and a further 1500 cm^3 as an estimate of the residual air still left in the lungs, one can roughly estimate the total lung and vocal-tract volume of the subject at the time of the utterance. This figure is necessary for certain calculations concerning volume and pressure (see Chapter 3).

The *pressure* of air in the oral and pharyngeal cavities can be measured by inserting a tube into the mouth and/or the pharynx—the latter through the nose—connected to a *pressure-transducer* (of which several different kinds are available), which converts, or 'transduces', the variations of air pressure into variations of voltage, which in turn can be made to operate some form of graphic recording device.

Subglottal pressure can be measured directly by means of a tracheotomy tube—that is, a small tube inserted into the trachea through a hole made just below the larynx. Naturally, this can only be done by a qualified medical practitioner. Indirect measurements of subglottal pressure can be made by inserting a catheter, terminating in a small, partly inflated balloon, into the oesophagus. The balloon is placed just below the larynx. Pressure variations in the trachea are transmitted through to the oesophagus at this point where they are picked up by the oesophageal balloon, and can be measured by means of a pressure transducer. This indirect measure of intratracheal pressure is a valuable one, but requires careful interpretation. On this see Ladefoged (1967) pp. 8–10.

The *volume-velocity*, that is, the volume discharged per unit time, of air out of or into the vocal tract can easily be computed from continuous spirometry. It can, on the other hand, be measured directly by *kymography*. This old-established technique formerly used rubber diaphragms and tracings made on smoked paper wrapped round a clockwork driven drum. Nowadays electrical or electronic equipment is used. In either case, it involves the collection in a face-mask of the air flowing out of (or into) the mouth and/or nose. The air-flow is conducted to some form of *flow-transducer*. This may be one of several different types, for example, an 'open-ended' pressure-transducer system, which measures the drop in pressure that occurs as the air flows through a gauze or other obstruction, the pressure-drop being proportional to the volume-velocity; or it may be a hot-wire anemometer placed inside a tube and thus measuring the particle-velocity of flow through a channel of constant and known cross-sectional area, which is proportional to the volume-velocity; or, again, it may be a device in which the air flows through a tube with elastic, collapsible, walls: light passing through the same tube falls onto a photo-electric cell, the quantity of light reaching the cell being proportional, in turn, to the volume-velocity of the air-flow. Whatever type of flow-transducer is used, its electrical output, in the form of a varying voltage, is used to operate an oscilloscope or a graphic recorder of some type.

These techniques record volume-velocity of air-flow out of or into the mouth. During steady-state articulation, this can be taken to represent the volume-velocity of subglottal air-flow as well. However, at times when oral articulatory movements are rapidly changing the volume of the mouth, these oral volume changes accelerate or decelerate the oral air-flow, which is then no longer the same as subglottal flow. This point must always be kept in mind in interpreting records of volume-velocities. Subglottal and transglottal volume-velocities at such times can be estimated only by making allowance for the volume-velocity increments or decrements caused by articulatory movements, and this effect can be very considerable.

One problem that arises in connection with the recording of volume-velocity is this: the use of a mask over the face makes it difficult to obtain high-quality acoustic recordings simultaneously with the flow-recordings; and yet, this is often desirable. This problem is overcome by a device designed by N. S. McKinney and the author, at the University of Michigan, and hence known as the 'Catford-McKinney Box'. This consists of a wooden box of one cubic foot volume, lined with sound-absorbent material and containing a high-quality microphone. In one side of the box there is a hole with a flexible rubber mouthpiece, or part-mask, surrounding it. In the opposite side of the box there is a hole leading to a flow-transducer. The subject places his mouth in the mouthpiece and speaks. The volume-velocity of the air-flow out of his mouth is picked up by the flow-transducer (with some smoothing out of the relatively high-frequency flow fluctuations of voice, but otherwise unaffected by the air-stream's passage through the box), while a high-quality tape recording can be made via the microphone in the box. As an additional refinement, the side of the box opposite the speaker has a perspex window, and there is a light inside the box. It is thus possible to make a high-speed motion picture of lip movements simultaneously with the air-flow and acoustic recordings—a unique facility.

The measurement of *velocity* (or 'particle-velocity' as opposed to 'volume-velocity') can be carried out by means of a *hot-wire-anemo-*

meter. In this device, an electric current is passed through a very fine, slightly heated wire. This 'hot-wire' is placed in the air-stream, and as air flows past it the wire is cooled, the degree to which it is cooled depending on the velocity of the air. The cooling of the wire changes its resistance to the electric current, and this change, which is proportional to the flow-velocity, can be electrically or electronically recorded.

The sum of the particle-velocities recorded by a number of hot-wire anemometers placed in a plane at right angles to flow is a measure of the volume-velocity of the total flow. A grid, or network, of hot-wire anemometers placed in front of the mouth has thus sometimes been used as an alternative to a mask, for obtaining information on volume-velocity. Since such a grid also provides a map, as it were, of the particle velocities at different points, distributed over the flow-front, it provides an additional dimension to the study of air-flow out of the mouth. Another, and simpler technique for recording information about the shape of the flow-front of air flowing out of the mouth involves speaking in front of a copper screen, which is frosted over after being dipped in liquid nitrogen, the frost melting where the air-flow hits the screen. On both these methods of recording air-flow data just outside the mouth see Catford et al. (1966 and 1968).

Another aspect of air-flow that may be investigated is the *type of flow*—the determination of whether the flow is laminar or turbulent. The hot-wire anemometer can be used for this purpose: its response is rapid enough to show up the velocity fluctuations characteristic of turbulence. Alternatively, the presence of turbulent flow can be inferred from acoustic records, which indicate the presence of aperiodic hiss-sounds generated by turbulent flow. Either of these procedures can be used to determine the critical velocity for various types of sound.

A fuller understanding of the nature of air-flow in speech depends on *flow-visualization*, that is, on techniques of rendering visible the actual course of stream-lines in vocal tract air-flow. This can hardly be done for flow inside the vocal tract, except by simulation techniques. The flow of smoke, or of dye-streaks in water, can be studied in transparent models of the vocal tract, provided that the dimensions of the model and the flow-velocities of the fluid are so manipulated that the relations involved can be expressed in an appropriate Reynolds Number, that is, about 1700 ± 200 for critical velocity in flow visualization experiments simulating fricatives (cf. Chapter 3). We have already mentioned techniques for studying velocities distributed over the flow-front outside the mouth. Some indication of the course of stream-lines outside the mouth can be obtained by the

Schlieren technique, a method for enabling flow to be photographed using the deflection of parallel light-rays by density-gradient, provided by speaking after inhaling helium. The density of the helium flowing out of the mouth is different from that of the surrounding air, and the resultant deflection of the light-rays enables the flow to be photographed.

The effect of the aerodynamic phase of speech is the generation of sound-waves—the *acoustic* phase of speech. Various aspects of this phase can be investigated instrumentally, including *amplitude* or *speech-power*, fundamental *frequency* of voice, the *wave-form* of speech, and the *acoustic spectrum*. Any well-equipped phonetics laboratory will have apparatus for the performance of all or most of these tasks, the most generally useful piece of equipment being the *sound-spectrograph*. In the usual model of sound-spectrograph, a few seconds of recorded speech are played back repeatedly at high speed. The playback output is passed through an acoustic filter that is slowly moving up the frequency scale; if there is any acoustic energy in the signal at any particular frequency a mark is made at a corresponding level on paper wrapped around a revolving drum. In the resultant trace the horizontal scale represents time; the vertical scale shows the component frequencies present at the times indicated, and the lightness or darkness of the mark indicates the amplitudes of these components. The whole trace, called a spectrogram, shows the acoustic spectrum, varying through time. Such records are extremely valuable for many purposes, particularly for the determination of vowel qualities. They are, however, not the most economical of records, particularly with respect to time, since every three or four seconds of speech takes several minutes to process. Nor are spectrograms the most useful records for some purposes, such as the determination of the divisions between segments, and the measurement of segment duration. For the latter purpose, it is often better, and certainly much quicker, to use records of acoustic intensity or speech power, presented in real time on a strip-chart.

All these aspects of the acoustic phase of speech can now be efficiently investigated by means of a computer. Programmes are available that enable us to store information on recorded speech, and then perform spectral and other types of acoustic analysis upon it.

We must now consider the types of linguistic-phonetic problems that we may wish to submit to instrumental investigation, and here we must begin by repeating a warning given at the beginning of this chapter. The laboratory should not be used as a cloak for phonetic incompetence. If the investigator cannot himself identify the exotic sounds produced by an informant it is unlikely that instruments will help him very much, for all instrumental recordings require interpretation, and correctness of interpretation depends heavily on the investigator's general phonetic knowledge. Ideally, the phonetician should be able to replicate in his own vocal tract any speech sound that he is investigating: the most reliable interpretations of instrumental records are those which are supported by the investigator's introspective analysis of the kinaesthetic sensations that accompany his replication of the sounds in question. Laboratory workers who cannot use this kind of personal kinaesthetic control of their instrumental findings sometimes misinterpret their data in a ludicrous way.

What, then, does instrumentation supply? Principally, detailed and quantified specification. Every competent phonetician can tell unerringly that one sound is longer than another, that one is aspirated, another unaspirated, that one syllable is uttered on a level pitch, another on a falling pitch, that a sound is palatalized, pharyngealized, and so on. His instruments can show him the precise duration of the sounds, the precise duration of the voicing-lag in aspirated sounds, the precise frequency, and pattern of frequency change, the precise location of dorso-palatal articulation, the precise degree of pharyngeal compression, and so forth. Only very rarely do instruments provide answers to basic questions of classification and description of sounds.

Bearing all this in mind, we may briefly consider what instrumental techniques are likely to be most useful in supplementing our direct observations on the various aspects of speech.

In the investigation of initiation-types, recordings of air-flow may be useful in supporting or confirming assessments of 'direction' of initiation. But any such determination must be made with caution. As we indicated in Chapter 5, the real distinction between the 'direction' of initiation is not so much whether egressive or ingressive *flow* is involved, as whether the initiatory pulse is one generating pressure or suction. Thus, intra-oral or intra-pharyngeal *pressure* recordings may be even more important than *air-flow* recordings in such determinations, as also may be cricothyrometer recordings of vertical movements of the larynx, or pneumographic or plethysmographic recordings of chest movements.

'Stress' in the sense of initiator power (cf. Chapter 5) is, of course, an initiatory function; some indication of initiator-power can be obtained by simultaneous recording of subglottal pressure and air-flow out of the mouth. It must again be remembered, however, that it is not the air-flow itself, but the rate of *initiator* movement which is the relevant quantity. Great care must therefore be taken to discount the component of total air-flow rate that is due to articulatory movements. In English the situation is further complicated by the fact that what is often called 'primary stress' is, chiefly, a dynamic *tone*. To make 'pure' comparative measures of initiator power in English one must manoeuvre the items to be compared into positions in utterances where they will have identical intonations: for example, to compare the initiator-power patterns of, say, *ímport* (noun) and *impórt* (verb) one must place them in some such frame as '*I* said . . .' where, as a result of the contrastive emphatic tone on '*I*' the rest of the utterance is on a low monotone.

The relation of initiator power to amplitude or acoustic intensity is a complex and indirect one. Both the mode of operation of the vocal folds (the phonation type) and the quality of vowel sounds, for instance, affect the acoustic intensity, more open vowels in general having a higher acoustic intensity than closer vowels. One can use a measure of acoustic intensity as a measure of initiator power only when items being compared are as nearly as possible identical in phonation and articulation.

The study of *phonation* lends itself to many different types of investigation. The simple determination of whether a given sound in an utterance is voiced or voiceless can often be made by means of a simple recording of the acoustic envelope of the sound picked up by a microphone, a throat microphone being perhaps best for voicing detection. Very often an acoustic-intensity trace gives good indications of the presence or absence of voice, particularly if its print-out is logarithmic, since this accentuates the low-intensity sound of voicing in voiced stops, and so on. Acoustic-intensity traces are also useful for determining the presence of aspiration and the duration of the voicing-lag in aspirated sounds. Combined recording of acoustic intensity and volume-velocity of air-flow also helps in the identification of 'tense' and 'lax' or 'whispery-voiced' phonation-types, and so on. More detailed study of glottal activity in speech requires special techniques such as laryngoscopy, glottography, or the electromyographic study of the action of laryngeal muscles.

Pitch variations—tone and intonation—are functions of phonation, and they, of course, can be studied by means of a fundamental frequency analyser. In addition, a cricothyrometer, recording vertical movements of the larynx incidentally gives indirect readings of pitch variation.

For the investigation of details of *articulation* many methods are available. To determine the duration of successive segments, acoustic intensity traces are very useful, and at points where they fail to give a clear indication of segment boundaries, spectrograms often help, though the spectrograph is not itself an efficient tool for the segmentation of long utterances.

It is clear that many aspects of articulation can be investigated by the techniques of electromyography, photography, radiography and palatography. Indirect information about articulatory postures and movements can be obtained from aerodynamic and acoustic records. Variations in volume-velocity of air-flow throw light on the nature of articulatory strictures: the cross-sectional area of an articulatory channel can be calculated, as we showed in Chapter 3, from intra-oral air pressure and volume-velocity. Among acoustic analysis instruments, the sound-spectrograph is particularly valuable for the analysis of vowel sounds.

Instrumental phonetics has a history going back about a century. The compendious work of one of the great pioneers of instrumental phonetics, the Abbé Rousselot (1901), is still well worth studying for the wealth of information it contains, but it is also an object lesson in the necessity for the instrumental phonetician to be a competent practical phonetician as well, which Rousselot could hardly be, since there was in his day little or no opportunity for practical phonetic training in France. Among other things, Rousselot describes as 'sons inspiratoires' a Russian [l] and [n] which show a momentary negative volume-velocity immediately on release of the articulatory strictures. It is quite clear that these were really velarized [ɴ] and [ɫ], and that the flow reversal resulted from the sudden enlargement of the oral cavity from nearly closed mouth for [ɴ] and [ɫ] to wide-open mouth for [a]. If Rousselot had been a competent practical phonetician he would have replicated these sounds in his own vocal tract and would immediately have perceived that the negative volume-velocity was a purely local, articulatory effect.

Some of the best instrumental work of recent years has been carried out by very competent phoneticians at the University of California, Los Angeles, and the reader is referred in particular to numerous works of Ladefoged, for example (1967), and the Working Papers in Phonetics of the UCLA phonetics laboratory (1964–71). A useful summary of non-acoustic techniques of instrumental phonetics is provided by Keller (1971). Finally, anyone who plans to set up his own phonetics laboratory should see the suggested list of equipment for a Basic Linguistic Phonetics Laboratory in Ladefoged (1971a).

Notes and References

Chapter 1. Introduction

1 Here and throughout, we follow the common practice of enclosing phonetic symbols within square brackets.

Chapter 3. The Aerodynamic Phase

1 To be meticulously accurate, 1 ml = 1·000028 cm^3. The reason for this discrepancy is that the standard kilogram (the mass of a platinum-iridium cylinder kept at Sèvres, near Paris) was originally intended to be the mass of a cubic decimetre of water at its maximum density, but was found to be 28 parts per million too large! Thereupon, the cylinder was taken as an arbitrary standard of mass while the volume of water that had exactly the same mass was defined as one *litre*. As a result of the error in the mass of the standard kilogram, the volume of one litre is thus not 1000 cm^3 but actually 1000·028 cm^3.

2 These estimates are based partly on various published estimates or measures of vocal tract volume, partly deduced from data on the intra-oral pressures generated in the production of *glottalic egressive* stops, partly from X-rays of my own pharynx and mouth and from measurement of the volume of water I am able to hold in the mouth, with the lips closed and a tongue-back uvular closure—about 80–100 cm^3. The estimate of 50 ml (= 50 cm^3) for total supra-glottal volume, given in Rothenberg (1968, p. 91), is undoubtedly much too low.

Chapter 5. Initiation

1 It is worth outlining here the history of the terminology of initiation. Up to the 1930s, initiation types other than *pulmonic pressure* were not very well understood, and in phonetics textbooks they tended to be relegated to footnotes or obscure paragraphs dealing with 'exotic' sounds. One often had the absurd situation that such a book would begin with a statement to the effect that all sounds are produced by air expelled from the lungs, followed by a footnote further on, recanting and saying, in effect, 'well, actually, some aren't'. In 1937 D. M. Beach in his *Phonetics of the Hottentot Language*, seeking a more rational classification of 'clicks' (by which he evidently meant, simply, suction sounds) introduced the terms *pulmonic, glottalic* and *velaric*. Catford, in 1939, in an article on 'The Classification of Stop Consonants' attempted to clean up the situa-

tion in general phonetics by regarding these initiatory considerations as basic to the description of speech in general, and proposed that the terms *pulmonic, glottalic* and *velaric,* and *pressure* and *suction,* be applied not only to clicks but to stops, and indeed to other types of sound. By 1941, Catford had completed the generalization of this type of classification to all sounds and began referring to the categories as *pulsion-types* (since they referred to the basic *pressure-pulse* movements of speech production). In 1943, Pike, in his *Phonetics*, adopted the general concept of the Beach-Catford pulsion types, and though he introduced the term *initiator* he used the expression 'air-stream mechanism' for initiation. Pike's was the most comprehensive and clearest account of initiation types to that date, although he did not, in fact, adopt the 'pulmonic', 'glottalic' terminology, but preferred to speak of sounds using 'lung air' 'pharynx air' 'mouth air'. He did, however, introduce the terms *egressive* and *ingressive,* which for long seemed to me an improvement on pressure and suction—although I now realize that they have led to misunderstandings. Moreover, Pike, unfortunately as it seems to me, perpetuated the common and misleading American usage of 'glottalized' in the sense of 'glottalic'.

In the present book I make use of Pike's term *initiator,* from which *initiation,* although not used by Pike, is an obvious derivate, parallel to *phonation* and *articulation*. I use Pike's *egressive* and *ingressive* to refer, strictly, to air-flow out of or into the vocal tract, and have reverted to my own earlier *pressure* and *suction* as clearer and more explicit labels for the actual initiation types.

2 My criticism of the term 'glottalized' for what is more correctly termed 'glottalic' is primarily directed to the use of this as a strictly *phonetic* term. There is sometimes justification for the looser, or wider, use of the term 'glottalized' in phonological description, where it may occasionally be expedient to lump together in one phonological category a number of anthropophonically different types of sounds, some of which are, in fact, *glottalic* while others are normal pulmonic sounds, with a glottal modification—that is, are *glottalized.*

3 By 'checked' sounds, Jakobson, Fant and Halle clearly mean 'ejectives', that is, glottalic pressure sounds; their examples from Navaho, Circassian, and Kabardian prove this. Their description, however, is incorrect. 'An abrupt decay' they say 'is the opposite of a smooth one. In spectrograms, checked phonemes are marked by a sharper termination . . .'. Under their figure 1, a spectrogram of the Circassian word [p'a] 'place', they say, 'In the checked consonants the closure is abrupt and is followed by a period of silence'. In point of fact 'checked consonants' (i.e. ejectives) have no more abrupt closure than others. What they have identified as 'abrupt closure' is, in fact, the *opening* of the oral (labial) closure, which, of course, is followed by a period of silence until the release of the glottal closure occurs. In their spectrogram, the interval between oral release and glottal release is unusually long; they give no time scale, but it appears to be well over 100 ms (compare this with the average intervals between glottal and oral release given on p. 69). Nevertheless, the characteristic features of a glottalic egressive stop are as described there. There is no specially

'abrupt closure' in these sounds. Aoki (1970) having apparently followed Jakobson et al. in (wrongly) defining 'glottalized stops' in terms of 'abrupt closure' (p. 68), later refers to 'the interval between the initial release of outer closure and the subsequent one of inner closure' (p. 71). This shows a correct understanding of these sounds, in spite of the earlier misleading definition.

4 That larynx-lowering is an accompaniment to pulmonic pressure voiced stops has been known to practical phoneticians for about a century—e.g., Ellis (1877), Jespersen (1889)—and indeed it is kinaesthetically obvious to anyone who experiments in his own vocal tract with the production of long, voiced stops. This feature of voiced stops has been 'rediscovered' several times by instrumentalists.

5 We made these films in 1966 with the assistance of Jean-Denis Gendron of the Phonetics Laboratory, Université Laval, at the Hotel Dieu hospital in Quebec.

6 It should be borne in mind in considering these matters that small upward and downward movements of the larynx will generate large supraglottal pressures, but very small subglottal pressures. This, of course, is because pressure is inversely proportional to volume. Given a supraglottal volume of, say, 100 cm^3 and a subglottal volume of, say, 3000 cm^3, then it is obvious that an upward larynx movement displacing 5 cm^3 both above and below it represents a supraglottal volume decrease of 5 per cent, but a subglottal volume increase of only ·17 per cent. Consequently, the supraglottal pressure will be raised 5 per cent, and the subglottal pressure lowered ·17 per cent. Assuming starting pressures are atmospheric (say 1050 cm H_2O), the resultant excess pressures will be supraglottal +52·5 cm H_2O, subglottal −1·8 cm H_2O.

7 In these experiments, the subject was placed in a body plethysmograph, so that movements of the chest wall were recorded as indicating pulmonic-initiator movements, and the subglottal air-pressure was inferred from pressure measurements made from a small balloon in the oesophagus.

Chapter 6. Phonation

1 To be precise, one should probably say that the phonatory posture for whispery voice is assumed during the stop; whether or not whispery voice is actually generated during the stop no doubt depends on the subglottal pressure and other factors.

Chapter 7. Articulation I: Stricture-types

1 When, for instance, glottal stop is a weak and barely audible 'hard attack' to an initial vowel we may be tempted to call its function 'phonatory' rather than 'articulatory'—all the more so in a language which does not include glottal stop as a regular, distinctive sound. Nevertheless, if it is the 'last halt' so to speak on the air-stream's journey through the vocal tract, the last, indeed *only* 'shaping' of a specific sound, then, from the strict phonetic-functional point of view, we must call glottal stop an *articulation*. A glottal stop, like any articulation, may of course be a

component of a *multiple articulation*, that is, it may be accompanied by some other articulation in the mouth. For instance, [ʔ] like any other articulation may be modified by a specific auxiliary secondary shaping of the oral cavity. Thus, glottal stop may be 'labialized' as in the [ʔʷ] of the Adyghe languages of the north-west Caucasus. In these languages, [ʔʷ] is a specific modified articulation contrasting with [ʔ] in just the same way as [kʷ] and [gʷ], for example, contrast with [k] and [g]. Again, the glottal stop that is simultaneous with oral closure in the [ʔp, ʔt, ʔk] of many dialects of English (for example, Cockney ['pʰɐɩˀpɐ], Northumberland ['pɩɛʔpɒ], Belfast [pʰeːʔpəɹ] for *paper*) clearly has an articulatory and not an initiatory function. It is part of a 'co-articulation', or multiple articulation, quite unlike the glottal closure of an 'ejective' (glottalic pressure) [p' t' k']. In the ejective, the glottal closure, accompanied by an upward thrust of the larynx, is part of the initiatory mechanism.

The problem of whether we are dealing with phonation or articulation also arises in relation to [h]-type sounds. The question is whether in, for example, [hɔ·l] *hall*, [h] is to be described as a *glottal fricative* (articulation) or a *voicelessness* (phonation), accompanying a vowel [ɔ̥ɔ·l] (where the subscript circle is the symbol of voicelessness). The first point to note is that [ɔ̥], or *voiceless vowel*, to be audible at all must involve turbulent air-flow at some point. If this turbulent flow actually occurs in the mouth rather than the glottis, then, clearly, we have to do with an ordinary oral articulation, and the glottal voicelessness is merely phonatory. Any voiceless vowel with an articulatory stricture narrower than the glottal stricture (certainly [i]- and [u]-type vowels, and possibly [e]- and [o]-types) will be an (oral) approximant and will have turbulent flow through the oral channel. Any vowel with an oral channel more open than the glottal channel will not generate turbulent flow at that point. What one hears in voiceless open vowels of the [ɛ̥]- [ḁ]-type is glottal turbulence modulated by the oral-shaping for the vowel.

From a strictly phonetic point of view, then, in sounds like [i̥ u̥] we have *oral approximant articulation* with voiceless phonation (voiceless vowels). In sounds like [ɛ̥ ḁ] we have *glottal fricative articulation,* with some, vowel-like oral modulation. This appears to be the most rigorous and consistent method of resolving the problem on purely phonetic grounds. The question whether it is expedient in relation to some particular language to describe any sounds, such as [i̥, u̥, e̥, ḁ], as 'glottal fricatives', 'oral approximants', or 'voiceless vowels', is a problem rather for phonology.

2 This intimate 'mingling' of the turbulence-generated 'hiss' of the oral articulation with the periodic 'tone' of voiced phonation is no illusion, but a physical reality. In voice, as we know, air bursts upwards through the vibrating glottis in a rapid sequence of separate high-velocity jets. By the time the voiced air-stream reaches an oral articulatory channel, the radical velocity changes of the pulsating transglottal flow have been somewhat smoothed out. Nevertheless, there still are rapid periodic changes in velocity, and the amount of turbulence generated by flow through the articulatory channel fluctuates in time with these periodic velocity changes. The

'hiss' of a voiced fricative is thus intensity-modulated in time with the frequency of the voice vibrations. One can hear this phenomenon for oneself by forming an extremely small articulation channel (say, an exceedingly 'tight' [s]) and producing *creak* as strongly as one can. It is then possible to actually hear the fricative hiss coming out in minute bursts, in time with the low-frequency vibrations of creak. If one experiments with 'inverse voiced fricatives', that is, sounds of the type [v, z] pronounced with pulmonic suction, on a pulmonic ingressive air-stream, one can see that the croaky 'inverse voice' does not integrate with the oral fricative hiss. The reason is that in pulmonic ingressive [v, z] the hiss is generated by steady ingressive turbulent flow (at an unchanging velocity) through the articulatory channel, while the glottis, being 'downstream', merely puffs its pulsations of inverse voice down into the trachea, without modulating the hiss in any way.

These observations have *inter alia* some relevance to synthetic speech. In electronic speech-synthesis, 'voiced fricatives' may sound unrealistic unless the fricative hiss component is intensity-modulated in time with the fundamental frequency (voice) component.

3 The older term for 'approximant'—the one used in publications of the International Phonetic Association—is 'frictionless continuant'.

4 These relations are no doubt true of voiceless fricatives, approximants, and resonants: it is doubtful if they are absolutely true with respect to their voiced counterparts. However, even if the oral channel is not always smaller than the mean glottal channel (during the open phase of the voicing cycle) in voiced fricatives, nevertheless there is a tendency in that direction. The glottis does appear to be more loosely closed for the voicing of fricatives than it is for the voicing of approximants and resonants: consequently, the glottal area, in its most open phase, is wider for fricatives than for the other stricture-types.

It is obvious that the criterion given here for distinguishing stricture-types—namely, fricatives, always turbulent; approximants, turbulent when voiceless; resonants, never turbulent—is less than perfect, since it assumes a 'standard', but undefined, level of vocal effort, or initiator power for each voiced/voiceless pair. No better criterion, however, exists, and this one certainly works well in practice.

5 A further point about flaps is that they may involve a much smaller area of contact between articulators than the corresponding stop. This distinction is demonstrated in the continuous palatograms presented in Fujimura et al. (1972), showing Japanese [t, d] and flapped [r]. The maximum contact area of [r] is somewhat less than that of [d] and much less than that of [t].

6 A bilabial lateral is said to occur in some dialects of Irish Gaelic, and I have observed a bilabial lateral articulation as a realization of lip-rounding in the production of [u] by a Frenchman; but this was a highly idiosyncratic individual peculiarity.

7 This holds good of most varieties of English but not of Scottish English. Many, perhaps most, Scots do not release the [d] of a word like *muddle* directly into the [l]. Instead of the lateral release they have a central release,

and a very short vowel-like [ə] before forming the central closure and lateral channels for [l]: [mʌdəl].

8 In languages with a strong, rather high pressure, voiceless or, even better, glottalic pressure, lateral a kind of trill may be generated between the inner side of the cheek and the extreme back molar teeth, or even the tongue, behind that. This kind of 'geno-molar' trill (with a frequency somewhat higher than that of most trills, being about 50 or 60 Hz) constitutes the very 'scrapy' or 'rattly' sound of, for instance, strong or 'geminated' glottalic pressure alveolar lateral affricate [tɬɬ'] in Avar and several other Caucasian languages of Dagestan.

Chapter 8. Articulation II: Location

1 The principal reason for distinguishing between the oral and pharyngo-laryngeal areas is that there is a straightforward and consistent method of describing all articulations in the oral area in terms of juxtaposition of lower and upper articulators. This descriptive method breaks down when we get to the pharyngo-laryngeal area and have to deal, *inter alia,* with more generalized sphincteric compression of the pharynx, and so on.

2 Some writers refer to 'active' and 'passive' articulators; but this is an awkward and somewhat ambiguous terminology. For instance, in 'uvular trill' the uvula certainly vibrates in a furrow at the back of the tongue. Is it, however, an 'active' articulator in any interesting sense? Probably not, for although it is certainly mobile, it is merely passively vibrating 'in the breeze', and it is the tongue which has actively assumed the necessary posture. Again, there are undoubtedly bilabial articulations in which both lips make an active contribution to the articulation. For such reasons as these the non-committal terms 'lower' and 'upper' seem preferable designations for articulators than 'active' and 'passive'.

3 A few people have little or no alveolar convexity. For them the important alveolar zone of articulation can be arbitrarily defined as that part of the roof of the mouth which extends about *one quarter* of the way from the rear edge of the teeth to the rear end of the hard palate.

Chapter 9. Vowels

1 More precisely, what actually seems to happen is this: the volume-velocity in whispered vowels is controlled by varying the area of the glottal opening —the aim being to control the orifice sizes so as to generate turbulent flow through the *glottis*, but not through the *oral* channel—consequently, the glottal orifice is kept smaller than the oral orifice. In other words, the glottis 'throttles down' maximally for narrow approximant vowels, and is more and more open the opener the oral channel. It is the narrowed glottis (rather than the narrowed oral orifice) which reduces the volume-velocity, and the more widely opened glottis which increases it. Nevertheless, the volume-velocity of the whisper (and hence its duration at relaxation pressure) is certainly an index to the degree of narrowness of the articulatory channel, even if only indirectly.

Paget (1930) drew attention to an observation that may be the very phenomenon we are talking about here. He says 'L. P. H. Eijkman of the Hague, has shown that in whispering the various vowel sounds, the size of the opening made by the glottis varies directly with the frequency of the lower vowel resonance—the opening being larger for the vowels of high resonance'. If Paget had in mind English vowels, the 'vowels of high (lower) resonance' would include such resonant or wider approximant vowels as [eᶥ, ɛ, æ, ɜ, ʌ, ɑ], as in *say, set, sat, curt, cut, cart.* Paget tries to explain this 'Eijkman phenomenon' unconvincingly, as it appears to me, in acoustic terms. It seems to me that the aerodynamic explanation given here is more plausible.

2 It is perhaps significant that it is precisely with respect to the narrow approximant type vowels [i, ɨ, u, o, ɔ, ɑ] that it is most difficult to locate the centres of two formants, as Ladefoged (1967, p. 101) points out. Ladefoged goes on to say 'It seems unlikely that the clues utilized by the ear in assessing the quality of vowels of this sort will be the pitches of the formants.' He speculates concerning the acoustic cues which might be used to identify these vowels. It is possible, however, that just these 'consonant-like' approximant type vowels are identified less by acoustic clues than by use of the 'motor empathy' phenomenon (see 1.23)—the heard vowels being referred for identification to their proprioceptive sensations on the basis of minimal acoustic clues of the transition type, such as help in the identification of many consonants.

Chapter 10. Co-articulation and Modified Articulation

1 Unfortunately not all writers adhere rigorously to these conventions for the systematic naming of co-articulations. Thus, we often find the term 'labiovelar' used for either *labial-velar* (type [k͡p]) or *labialized velar* (type [kʷ]). In terms of the usual conventions of systematic phonetic terminology 'labiovelar' could only mean the anatomically impossible juxtaposition of lower lip and velum. The fact that this interpretation of 'labiovelar' is, in fact, ruled out by its semantic impossibility does not seem to me to be adequate justification for its rather common unsystematic use. Another example of terminological abuse, which we mention elsewhere, is the use of 'glottalized' to mean 'with glottalic initiation' rather than 'with secondary glottal articulation': this latter has to be its meaning within systematic phonetic terminology.

2 What we describe as *contiguous co-articulation* or *longitudinally extended articulation* appears to be the same as the feature *distributed,* given by Chomsky and Halle (1968), and defined by them in these terms: 'Distributed sounds are produced with a constriction that extends for a considerable distance along the direction of the air-flow'.

3 This remark may need elucidation. We refer to cases such as that of a fricative, in the production of which a moving (lower) articulator may approach a static (upper) articulator and then immediately retreat again. There is no static posture of measurable duration, only a continuously changing articulatory gesture that creates a rapidly narrowing and then

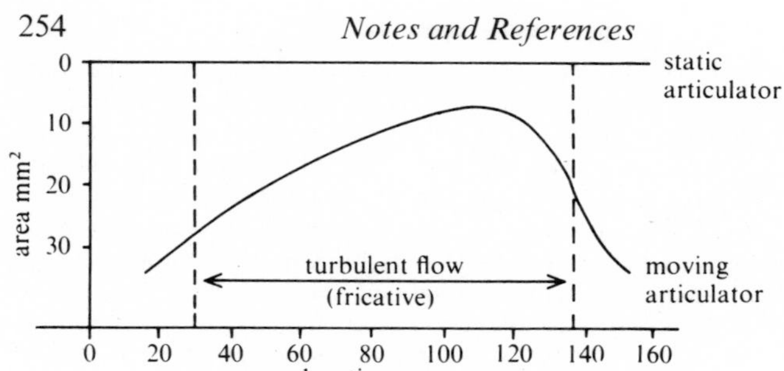

Figure 58. Duration of turbulent flow during the articulatory gesture of a fricative

rapidly widening articulatory channel. Although the gesture is totally non-static, there is a certain period of time during which the channel is narrow enough (say, less than about 20–30 mm^2 cross-sectional area) for turbulent air-flow to occur. Figure 58 suggests the course of events. It represents a typical articulation for a syllable-initial fricative. Recordings of acoustic intensity of such sounds often show a pattern of hiss intensity rather closely relatable to this type of articulatory gesture, with narrowest channel, and hence peak velocity and peak noise intensity, near the end of the fricative. It is clear that by changing one or more of the variables—rate of articulatory movement, channel area at nearest approach, volume-velocity of air-flow—we can alter the duration of the period during which turbulence-generated noise occurs, and hence the duration, or 'quantity', of the fricative.

Chapter 11. Sequences and Segmentation

1 That the English initial and final sound of *church* can easily be perceived as a sequence of [t] plus [ʃ] is evidenced by the fact that children learning to write may represent it as *t* + *sh*. This does not mean that we must therefore assume that [t] plus [ʃ] has to be regarded as a sequence of phonemes in English—children often observe many sub-phonemic features of pronunciation. The phonological status of English [tʃ] (and likewise [dʒ]) has long given rise to discussion, and the question 'one phoneme or two?' with respect to this sound-sequence is not yet settled. For useful discussion of this question see, for example, Martinet (1939), Twaddell (1957).

2 My own observation (of only one Zulu informant) agrees with that of Doke (1926), namely that the Zulu sound in question is a glottalic *velar* lateral affricate. Ladefoged (1971), however, transcribes this as [cʎ'] and defines it as a 'palatal lateral glottalic stop'. This may reflect a difference in dialect, or idiolect, of our informants. In Catford (1943) I described Avar as having a glottalic egressive velar lateral affricate, as in the verb *кьезе* [kɬ'eze] 'to give'. It is possible that this was a variant of the more usual Avar [tɬɬ'] peculiar to the Chokh dialect of my 1943 informant. It may, on the other hand, have been an error. The velar pronunciation is not mentioned in Mikailov's work on Avar dialects, nor was it used by

three Avar informants I have worked with more recently, although it must be noted that none of those three spoke Chokh dialect.

3 Both 'nasal plosion' and 'lateral plosion' are sometimes presented as universal English phenomena: however, not all native speakers pronounce in this way. Among Standard English speakers speaking with a Scots accent one very often hears such words as *little* and *button* pronounced ['lɩtəɫ] and ['bʌtən] with a distinct central oral release of [t] followed by a brief [ə]-type vowel, followed in turn by [ɫ] or [n].

List of Works Consulted

ABERCROMBIE, D. (1964) 'A phonetician's view of verse structure', *Linguistics*, 6

–(1964a) 'Syllable quantity and enclitics in English' in *In Honour of Daniel Jones*, London (Longmans)

–(1967) *Elements of General Phonetics*, Edinburgh (Edinburgh University Press)

ALLEN, J. E. (1963) *Aerodynamics, a Space-Age Survey*, New York (Harper); paperback, Harper Torchbooks (1966)

ALLEN, W. S. (1953) *Phonetics in Ancient India*, London (Oxford University Press)

AOKI, H. (1970) 'A note on glottalized consonants', *Phonetica*, 21, 65–74

BAUDOUIN DE COURTENAY, J. A. (1881) 'Nekotorye otdely "sravnitel'noj grammatiki" slavjanskix jazykov' in *Isbrannye trudy*, Moscow (Nauka), 1963

BEACH, D. M. (1938) *Phonetics of the Hottentot Language*, Cambridge (Heffer)

BELL, A. M. (1867) *Visible Speech, the Science of Universal Alphabetics*, London

BERG, J. van den (1954) 'Sur les théories myoélastique et neuro-chronaxique de la phonation', *Rev. laryng.*, LXXIV, Bordeaux

–(1956) 'Direct and indirect determination of the mean subglottic pressure', *Folia Phoniatrica*, 8, 1–24

–(1958) 'Myoelastic-aerodynamic theory of voice production', *JSH Res.*, 1, 3

–(1962) 'Modern research in experimental phoniatrics', *Folia Phoniatrica*, 14:2/3, 81 ff.

–and TAN, T. S. (1959) 'Results of experiments with human larynxes', *Pract. oto-rhino-laryng.*, 21, 425–50

BROSNAHAN, L. F. (1961) *The Sounds of Language*, Cambridge (Heffer)

CATFORD, J. C. (1939) 'On the classification of stop consonants', *Le Maître Phonétique*, 3rd series 65, 2–5. Reprinted in W. E. Jones and J. Laver, eds. *Phonetics in Linguistics, a book of Readings*, London (Longmans), 1973

–(1943) 'Specimen of *Avar*', *Le Maître Phonétique*, 3rd series 79

–(1947) 'Consonants pronounced with closed glottis', *Le Maître Phonétique*, 3rd series, 87

–(1964) 'Phonation types' in *In Honour of Daniel Jones*, London (Longmans)

–(1966) 'English phonology and the teaching of English pronunciation', *College English*, 27:8, 605–13

–(1972) 'Labialisation in Caucasian languages, with special reference to Abkhaz' in *Proc. Seventh Int. Cong. Phon. Sci.*, The Hague (Mouton)

–LANE, H. L., OSTER, R. and ROSS, S. (1966) 'Patterns of airflow during pronunciation', *Studies in Language and Language Behavior*, Progress Report II, Ann Arbor (CRLLB)

–JOSEPHSON, S. and RAND, T. (1968) 'Study of airflow out of the mouth during speech' in *Studies in Language and Language Behavior*, Progress Report VI, Ann Arbor (CRLLB)

–and PISONI, D. B. (1970) 'Auditory vs. articulatory training in exotic sounds', *MLJ*, LIV, 7, 477–81

CHIBA, T. and KAJIYAMA, M. (1958) *The Vowel: Its Nature and Structure*, Tokyo (Phon. Soc. Japan)

CHOMSKY, N. and HALLE, M. (1968) *The Sound Pattern of English*, New York (Harper and Row)

COUSTENOBLE, Hélène (1929) 'Quelques observations sur la prononciation de la langue Wolof', *Le Maître Phonétique*, 3rd series, jan-mars, 1–3

CURRY, R. (1940) *The Mechanism of the Human Voice*, London (J. A. Churchill)

DENES, P. B. and PINSON, E. N. (1963) *The Speech Chain*, Baltimore (Bell Labs.)

DIETH, Eugen (1950) *Vademecum der Phonetik*, Bern (Francke A.G.)

DOKE, C. M. (1926) *Phonetics of the Zulu Language*, Bantu Studies, vol. 2, Special Number, Johannesburg

DRAPER, M. H., LADEFOGED, P. and WHITTERIDGE, D. (1960) 'Expiratory pressures and airflow during speech', *BMJ*, June 18, vol. i, 1837–43

ELLIS, A. J. (1877) *Pronunciation for Singers*, London (Curwen), undated, but based on lectures of 1871 and preface annotated 'MS finished 29 November 1875'

FANT, G. (1973) *Speech Sounds and Features*, Cambridge, Mass. (MIT Press)

FISCHER-JØRGENSEN, E. (1964) 'Sound duration and place of articulation', *Z. für Phonetik*, 17, heft 2–4, 175–207

–(1967) 'Perceptual dimensions of vowels' in *To Honor Roman Jacobson*, The Hague (Mouton)

FROMKIN, Victoria A. (1965) 'Some phonetic specifications of linguistic units: an electromyographic investigation', *WPPh*, 3, UCLA

FUJIMURA, O., FUJII, L. and KAGAYA, R. (1972) 'Computation processing of palatographic patterns' in *Conference Record: 1972 Conf. on Speech Communication and Processing* (USAF)

GAIRDNER, W. H. T. (1925) *The Phonetics of Arabic*, London (Oxford University Press)

GAPRINDASHVILL, Sh. G. (1966) *Fonetika darginskogo jazyka*, Tbilisi (Metsniereba)

GRAMMONT, M. (1933) *Traité de Phonètique*, Paris (Delagrave)
GRAY, L. H. (1939) *Foundations of Language*, New York (Macmillan)
GUTHRIE, M. (1948) *The Classification of the Bantu Languages*, London (Oxford University Press)
HALLE, M. and STEVENS, K. (1971) 'A note on laryngeal features', *QPR* no. 101, 198–213, Cambridge, Mass. (MIT)
HALLIDAY, M. A. K. (1967) *Intonation and Grammar in British English*, The Hague (Mouton)
HARRIS, Katherine S., GAY, T., LYSAUGHT, Gloria F. and SCHVEY, M. M. (1965) 'Some aspects of the production of oral and nasal labial stops', *Language and Speech*, 8, 3
HARRIS, Katherine S., GAY, T., SHOLES, G. N. and LIEBERMAN, P. (1968) 'Some stress effects on electromyographic measures of consonant articulation', *Haskins Labs SR-13/14*, 137–75
HEFFNER, R.-M. S. (1960) *General Phonetics*, Madison (University of Wisconsin Press)
HILL, K. (1964) 'The musculature of the tongue', *WPPh*, 1 (UCLA)
–(1969) 'Some implications of Serrano phonology', *Fifth Regional Meeting of Chicago Linguistics Society*, 357–65
HIXON, T. (1966) 'Turbulent noise sources for speech', *Folia Phoniatrica*, 18, 3
HOCKETT, C. F. (1955) *A Manual of Phonology*, Indiana University Publications in Anthropology and Linguistics. Memoir 11 (Baltimore, Md.)
HOLLIEN, H. (1960) 'Some laryngeal correlates of vocal pitch', *JSpHRes.*, III, 51
–and CURTIS, J. F. (1960) 'A liminographic study of vocal pitch', *JSpHRes.*, III, 361
–and MOORE, E. P. (1960) 'Measurements of the vocal folds during changes in pitch', *JSHRes.*, III, 157
HOUDE, R. A. (1968) *A Study of Tongue Body Motion during Selected Speech Sounds*. Speech Comm. Research Lab. Inc., SCRL Monograph no. 2, Santa Barbara, Cal.
HUDGINS, C. V. and STETSON, R. H. (1935) 'Voicing of consonants by depression of the larynx', *Arch. néer phon. exper.*, 11, 1–28
HUSSON, R. (1960) *La Voix Chanté*, Paris (Gauthier-Villes)
–(1962) *Le Chant*, Paris (Presses Universitaires de France—'Que sais-je?')
–(1962a) *Physiologie de la phonation*, Paris (Masson)
ISSHIKI, N. (1964) 'Regulatory mechanisms of voice intensity variation', *JSHRes.*, 7, 17–29
JAKOBSON, R., FANT, G. and HALLE, M. (1952) *Preliminaries to Speech Analysis*, Cambridge, Mass. (MIT Press)
JAKOBSON, R. and HALLE, M. (1964) 'Tenseness and laxness' in *In Honour of Daniel Jones*, London (Longmans)
JESPERSEN, O. (1889) *The Articulation of Speech Sounds Represented by Means of Analphabetic Symbols*, Marburg (N. G. Elwert)
JOHNSTONE, T. M. (1970) 'A definite article in the modern S. Arabian languages', *BSOAS*, XXXIII, 2
JONES, D. (1917) *An English Pronouncing Dictionary*, London (Dent)

–(1962) *Outline of English Phonetics*, 9th ed., Cambridge (Heffer)

–and PLAATJE, S. T. (1916) *A Sechuana Phonetic Reader*, London (University of London Press)

JOOS, M. (1948) *Acoustic Phonetics*, Lang. Monograph no. 23, Baltimore

KAPLAN, H. M. (1960) *Anatomy and Physiology of Speech*, New York (McGraw-Hill)

KÁRMÁN, T. von (1954) *Aerodynamics*, New York (McGraw-Hill), paperback 1963

KELLER, Kathryn C. (1971) *Instrumental Articulatory Phonetics*, Norman, Okla. (Summer Inst. of Linguistics)

KIM, Chin-wu (1965) 'On the autonomy of the tensity feature in stop classification', *Word*, 21, 339–56

–(1970) 'A theory of aspiration', *Phonetica*, 21, 107–16

KOZHEVNIKOV, V. A. and CHISTOVICH, L. A. (1965) *Speech: Articulation and Perception*, Moscow-Leningrad; English translation, U.S. Dept. of Commerce, Clearing House for Federal Scientific and Technical Information

KYDD, W. L. and BELT, D. A. (1964) 'Continuous palatography', *JSHDis.*, 29, no. 4

LADEFOGED, P. (1958) 'Syllables and stress', *Miscellanea Phonetics*, 3, 1–14 (Int. Phon. Assoc.)

–(1962) *Elements of Acoustic Phonetics*, Edinburgh (Oliver and Boyd)

–(1963) 'Some physiological parameters in speech', *Language and Speech*, 6, 109–19

–(1964) *A Phonetic Study of West African Languages*, Cambridge (Cambridge University Press)

–(1964a) 'Physiological characterisation of speech', *WPPh*, 1 (UCLA), 1–9

–(1967) *Three Areas of Experimental Phonetics*, London (Oxford University Press)

–(1967a) *Linguistic Phonetics*, the first edition of his 1971 *Preliminaries*, which appeared as *WPPh*, 6 (UCLA)

–(1971) *Preliminaries to Linguistic Phonetics*, Chicago (Chicago University Press)

–(1971a) 'A basic linguistic phonetics laboratory', *WPPh*, 17 (UCLA)

–and MCKINNEY, N. P. (1963) 'Loudness, sound pressure and subglottal pressure in speech', *JASA*, 35, 344

LANE, H. H. (1965) 'The motor theory of speech perception', *Psych. Rev.*, 72, no. 4

LAVER, J. D. M. (1968) 'Phonetics and the brain' in *Work in Progress* no. 2, Dept. of Phonetics, University of Edinburgh

LEHISTE, Ilse, ed. (1967) *Readings in Acoustic Phonetics*, Cambridge, Mass. (MIT Press)

LE MUIRE, an tSiúr Annuntiata, RSM, agus ÓHuallacháin, an tAthair Colman, OFM (1966) *Bunchúrsa Foghraiochta*, Baile Átha Cliath (Dublin) Olfig an tSolathair

LIBERMAN, A. M. (1957) 'Some results of research on speech perception', *JASA*, 29, 117–23

–COOPER, F. S., HARRIS, K. and MCNEILAGE, P. E. (1963) 'A motor theory of speech perception' in Gunnar Fant (ed.), *Proceedings of the Speech Communications Seminar*, Royal Inst. Tech., Stockholm

–COOPER, F. S., SHANKWEILER, D. P. and STUDDERT-KENNEDY, M. (1967) 'Perception of the speech code', *Haskins Labs SR-9* (Jan.-Mar.)

LIEBERMAN, P. (1967) *Intonation, Perception and Language*, Cambridge, Mass. (MIT Press)

–(1968) 'Primate vocalizations and human linguistic ability', *Haskins Labs SR-13/14*

–(1971) 'On the evolution of human language', *Haskins Labs SR-27*

LINDQVIST, J. (1969) 'Laryngeal mechanisms in speech', *STL-QPSR*, 2–3, 26 ff.

LISKER, L. and ABRAHAMSON, A. (1964) 'A cross-language study of voicing in initial stops', *Word*, 20

LORIMER, Lt Col. D. L. R. (1935) *The Burushaski Language*, Oslo (Inst. for Sammenlignende Kulturforskning)

LUBKER, J. F. and PARRIS, Pamela J. (1970) 'Simultaneous measurements of intraoral pressure, force of labial contact and labial electromyographic activity during the production of the stop consonant cognates /p/ and /b/', *JASA*, 47, no. 2 (part 2), Feb.

MCGLONE, R. E. and PROFFITT, W. R. (1967) 'Lingual pressures associated with speaker consistency and syllable variations', *Phonetica*, 17, 178–83

MACNEILAGE, P. E. (1970) 'Motor control of serial ordering of speech', *Psych. Rev.*, 77, no. 3, 182–96

MALECOT, A. (1970) 'The Lenis-Fortis opposition: its physiological parameter', *JASA*, 47, no. 6 (part 2), June

MALMBERG, B. (1963) *Phonetics*, New York (Dover)

MALONE, K. (1923) *The Phonology of Modern Icelandic*, Menasha, Wis. (Collegiate Press)

MARTINET, A. (1939) 'Un ou deux phonèmes', *Acta Linguistica*, I.2, 94

MEJLANOVA, U. A. (1964) *Očerki lezginskoj dialektologii*, Moscow (Nauka)

MEYER, E. A. (1910) 'Untersuchung über Lautbildung' in *Festschrift Wilhelm Vietor*, 166–248

MEYER-EPPLER, W. (1953) 'Zum Erzeugungs Mechanismus der Geraüschlaute', *Z. Phon.*, 7, 196–216

MIKAILOV, K. Sh. (1967) *Arčinskij jazyk*, Makhachkala (Dagestanskij filial AN, SSSR)

MIKAILOV, Sh. I. (1959) *Očerki avarskoj dialektologii*, Moscow (Nauka)

NEGUS, V. E. (1949) *The Comparative Anatomy and Physiology of the Larynx*, London (Heinemann)

O'GRADY, G. N., VOEGELIN, C. F. and VOEGELIN, F. M. (1966) 'Languages of the world: Indo-Pacific fasc. VI', *Anthropological Linguistics*, 8.2, 1–197

OHALA, J. (1966) 'A new photo-electric glottograph', *WPPh*, 4 (UCLA)

–(1970) 'Aspects of the control and production of speech', *WPPh*, 15 (UCLA)

–(1972) 'The regulation of timing in speech' in *Conference Record: 1972 Conf. on Speech Communication and Processing* (USAF)

OHALA, J. and LADEFOGED, P. (1969) 'Subglottal pressure variations and glottal frequency', *JASA* (paper at Nov. 1969 meeting of ASA)
ÖHMAN, S. (1967) 'A numerical model of coarticulation', *JASA*, 41, 310–20
O'MALLEY, M. H. and KLOKER, D. R. (1972) 'Computer aided instruction in speech science', *Today's Speech* (Speech Assoc. of the Eastern States), Spring
PAGET, Sir. R., Bart (1922) *Vowel Resonances*, International Phonetics Association
–(1930) *Human Speech*, London (Kegan, Paul, Trench, Trubner)
PANDIT, P. B. (1957) 'Nasalisation, aspiration and murmur in Gujarati', *Indian Linguistics*, 17, 165–72
PASSY, P. (1907) *The Sounds of the French Language* (trans. by D. L. Savory and D. Jones), Oxford (Clarendon Press)
PERKELL, J. S. (1969) *Physiology of Speech Production*, Cambridge (MIT Press)
PETERSON, G. E. and SHOUP, June E. (1966) 'A physiological theory of phonetics', *JSHRes.*, 9, 5–67
PIKE, Eunice (1967) *Dictation Exercises in Phonetics* (2nd revised ed.), Santa Anna, Calif. (Summer Inst. of Linguistics)
PIKE, K. L. (1943) *Phonetics*, Ann Arbor (University of Michigan Press)
RAHN, H., OTIS, A. B., CHADWICK, L. E. and FENN, W. O. (1946) 'The pressure-volume diagram of the thorax and lung', *Amer. J. Phys.*, 146, no. 6
RIPER, C. van and IRWIN, J. V. (1958) *Voice and Articulation*, Englewood Cliffs, N.J. (Prentice-Hall)
ROGAVA, G. (1941) 'Mžɣeri paringaluri sp'irant'i ʕ adiɣeur enebši', Russ. résumé 'Zvonkij faringalńyj spiranty' v adygejskix jazykax', *Isv. Inst. jazyka istorii materialnogo kul'tura im. N. Ja Marra*, tom. x, 272–77, Tbilisi
ROOS, J. (1936) 'The physiology of playing the flute', *Arch. Néer. Phon. Exper.*, 12, 1–26
ROTHENBERG, M. (1968) *The Breath-Stream Dynamics of Simple-Released Plosive Production*, Basel, Bibliotheca Phonetica no. 6
ROUSSELOT, l'Abbé P.-J. (1901) *Principes de phonétique expérimentale*, Paris (H. Welfer), 1901–8
SEMAAN, K. I. (1963) *Arabic Phonetics: Ibn Sina's Risalah*, Lahore (Sh. Muhammad Ashraf, Kashmiri Bazaar)
SHAPIRO, A. H. (1961) *Shape and Flow*, New York (Anchor); London (Heinemann), 1964
SHEN, Y. and PETERSON, G. C. (1962) 'Isochronism in English', *Studies in Linguistics*, Occasional Papers, 9
SMITH, S. (1947) 'Analysis of vowel sounds by ear', *Arch. Néer. Phon. Exper.*, XX, 78–96
SMITH, T. (1971) 'A phonetic study of the function of the extrinsic tongue muscles', *WPPh* (UCLA)
STETSON, R. H. (1928, 1951) *Motor Phonetics* (2nd ed. 1951), Amsterdam (North Holland Pub. Co.)

Sweet, H. (1877) *A Handbook of Phonetics*, Oxford
–(1902) *A Primer of Phonetics*, Oxford (Clarendon Press)
Tereščenko, N. M. (1966) 'Nenetskij jazyk' in *Jazyki narodov SSSR*, tom. III, Moscow (Nauka)
Trubetzkoy, N. S. (1931) 'Die Konsonantensysteme der ostkaukasischen Sprachen', *Caucasica*, 8, 1–52
Twaddell, W. F. (1957) '/č/?'. Paper to Ling. Soc. Amer., Dec.
Uldall, Elizabeth (1958) 'American "molar" R and "flapped" T', *Revista do Laboratorio de Fonetica Experimental da Faculdade de Letras du Duniversidade de Coimbra*, IV, 3–6
Vanderslice, R. (1967) 'Larynx vs. lungs: cricothyrometer data refuting some recent claims concerning intonation and "archtypality"', *WPPh*, 7 (UCLA)
Varma, S. (1948) *The Bhalesi Dialect*, Royal Asiatic Soc. of Bengal, Monograph Series, IV, Calcutta
Vogt, H. (1963) *Dictionnaire de la langue Oubykh*, Oslo (Universitetsførslaget)
Wurm, S. A. (1964) *Phonological Diversification in Australian New Guinea*, Ling. Circle of Canberra Pubn, series B, no. 2, Canberra
–(1972) *Languages of Australia and Tasmania*, The Hague (Mouton)
Zemlin, W. R. (1964) *Speech and Hearing Science Anatomy and Physiology*, Champaign, Ill. (Stipes Pub. Co.)
Zhghent'i, S. (1956) *Kartuli enis ponet'ik'a*, Tbilisi (Tbilisi State University Press)
Zinder, L. R. (1960) *Obščaja fonetika*, Leningrad (Izdat, leningradskogo universiteta)
Žinkin, N. A. (1968) *Mechanisms of Speech*, The Hague (Mouton)

Index